MW00488810

DISCERNMENT AND TRUTH

discernment of spirits

Poor Clares People
morality in choice

Related titles from Herder & Herder

Rowan A. Greer, *Christian Hope and Christian Life: Raids on the Inarticulate* (Association of Theological Booksellers Book of the Year)

Edward Howells, *John of the Cross and Teresa of Avila: Mystical Knowing and Selfhood*

Bernard McGinn, *The Mystical Thought of Meister Eckhart: The Man from Whom God Hid Nothing*

Bernard McGinn and Patricia Ferris McGinn, *Early Christian Mystics: The Divine Vision of the Spiritual Masters*

J. Warren Smith, *Passion and Paradise: The Theological Anthropology of Gregory of Nyssa* (forthcoming)

Amador Vega, *Ramon Llull and the Secret of Life*

Discernment and Truth

The Spirituality and Theology of Knowledge

Mark A. McIntosh

A Herder & Herder Book
The Crossroad Publishing Company
New York

The Crossroad Publishing Company
481 Eighth Avenue, New York, NY 10001

Copyright © 2004 Mark A. McIntosh

All rights reserved. No part of this book may be reproduced, stored in a retrieval system, or transmitted, in any form or by any means, electronic, mechanical, photocopying, recording, or otherwise, without the written permission of The Crossroad Publishing Company.

Printed in the United States of America

Library of Congress Cataloging-in-Publication Data

McIntosh, Mark Allen, 1960-
    Discernment and truth : the spirituality and theology of
knowledge / Mark McIntosh.
        p. cm.
    Includes bibliographical references and index.
    ISBN 0-8245-2138-2 (alk. paper)
    1. Christian life—Anglican authors. 2. Discernment (Christian theology)
3. Truth—Religious aspects—Christianity. I. Title.
BV4509.5.M345 2004
248.2—dc22

                                                    2004001699

1   2   3   4   5   6   7   8   9   10   08   07   06   05   04

For All My Teachers

Contents

Part II: Case Studies in Discernment

Acknowledgments

I am most grateful to the Louisville Institute, a Lilly Endowment Program for the Study of American Religion, whose generous Christian Faith and Life Sabbatical Grant awarded to me for academic year 2002–2003 made possible the final research and writing of this book—and to Loyola University for granting me the necessary research leave.

I am also grateful to the Center for Theological Inquiry in Princeton, of whose working group on faith and reason (most ably chaired by Paul Griffiths and Reinhard Hütter) I was a member, and which prompted me to the first draft of chapter 5.

I thank Catholic University Press for their kind permission to print chapter 6, a slightly different version of which appears as an essay in their book *Revisiting the Idea of Vocation: Theological Explorations,* edited by my colleague John C. Haughey, S.J.

I also am most grateful to Cambridge University Press for their kind permission to publish chapter 7, a different version of which appears as an essay in their book *Silence and the Word: Negative Theology and Incarnation,* edited by Oliver Davies and Denys Turner.

My most sincere apologies for any errors or omissions in this list.

Preface

How we know what we think we know has often been a puzzle for us human beings. Perhaps most deeply we have wondered about the very *measure* of our knowing, namely, about the *truth* of reality: is there such truth? do we genuinely encounter it in certain ways? or are there really only what we might call "dominant views" of reality, ordering the chaos of neuronal firings according to the biological and cultural constraints of a given time and place? This difficult questioning has gathered pace since early modernity, sometimes issuing in a confrontation between the advocates of objective, empirically verifiable data and the great masters of suspicion and their post-modern descendants. I recall this well-known debate only because I believe that Christian thought and practice has a very particular but overlooked contribution to make.

The reasoning of faith has, of course, seemed extraneous at best and dubious at worst to many of the most influential modern debaters about knowledge and truth. And many great modern theologians have labored with remarkable creativity to make Christian thought more plausible to modern critical perspectives—whether scientific, philosophical, or literary. Their achievements are many, and I hope no one will think me too critical of them if I suggest that these efforts at accommodation might have seemed less needed if Christianity's spiritual life and thought had not become so separated from its theology by the later Middle Ages. For in many traditions of Christian spirituality one finds a remarkably *critical* theory and practice of truth, one perhaps capable of many unexpected applications and developments. These traditions of spiritual discernment exhibit, for example, a concern both with concrete and verifiable data and with the powers and influences shaping observation and thought. They attend carefully to the patterns and communities in which readiness for truthful inquiry is formed—and to the often unacknowledged impulses that animate truth-seeking. In and through all these critical perspectives on truth, these traditions of spiritual discernment are always seeking to be alive and responsible to truth. They are never naive about human limitations (or about human capacities for self-deception), but they also report findings of goodness and beauty in the world sufficiently significant to warrant a deep hopefulness about humanity's encounter with truth.

This book studies these traditions of spiritual discernment in their historical development (with some particularity in three cases), and with a very provisional attempt at theoretical advancement. Different readers will, of course, have different interests in the book. I have two chief hopes: that academic readers will find insight regarding the idea of divine interaction with human knowing, or at least a clarified familiarity with Christian thinking about this possibility; and that readers with more immediately practical interests will find a thickness of description intriguing enough to entice them into theology. If, as I have argued here, truth radiates eternally from the trinitarian life of God, then every event of knowing the truth is inherently spiritual and theological at its depths.

As ever, I am deeply thankful for my colleagues and students at Loyola (especially many hard-working graduate research assistants), for my wife and our children, and for all my teachers—past, present, and I trust, to come—to whom in particular this work is dedicated as a sign of thanks for their illumination and friendship. Among the very many to whom I owe so much, I name in particular some whose teaching began for me in a classroom but extended far beyond: Louis Dupré, Hans Frei, Bernard McGinn, John Macquarrie, Jaroslav Pelikan, J. Robert Wright, and David Tracy.

Christmastide, 2003
Chicago, Illinois

PART ONE

History and Theology
of Spiritual Discernment

ONE

Introduction:
The Pattern of a Discerning Life

Then said the Shepherds one to another,
shall we shew these Pilgrims some wonders?[1]

Discernment, Truth, and God

As Christian and Hopeful come to the final stages of John Bunyan's *Pilgrim's Progress,* they find themselves climbing up into the Delectable Mountains. Weary from their struggles and narrow escapes along the way, here the pilgrims find a momentary glimpse of their longed-for goal, the Celestial City shimmering in the distance. The kindly shepherds who greet the pilgrims conduct them to many vantage points from which to look out over all the paths of their journey and discern at last their true pattern and direction. These "wonders" shown by the shepherds are both disturbing and exhilarating. For now that Christian and Hopeful are within sight of heaven, they realize how often they have been close to losing their way forever.

The four shepherds, Knowledge, Experience, Watchful, and Sincere, give the pilgrims a "perspective glass," a kind of telescope for seeing the actual gates to the heavenly City so they can make out the way ahead. But by now, the pilgrims' hands are shaking so violently from the impact of all they have seen, they cannot hold the glass steady! They catch only a dizzying, momentary vision of "something like the Gate, and also some of the Glory of the place." But it is enough, and Christian and Hopeful set out on their final journey singing:

Thus by the Shepherds, Secrets are reveal'd,
Which from all other men are kept conceal'd:
Come to the Shepherds then, if you would see
Things deep, things hid, and that mysterious be.[2]

3

The deep and hidden things that Knowledge, Experience, Watchful, and Sincere reveal to the pilgrims are the realities of their own lives and the true orientation of their journey. And discerning this orientation turns out to be a holy wonder, a vision that comes from walking in company with others, with knowledge and experience. The "perspective glass" of spiritual discernment is a gift, a sharing in knowledge greater than one's own, and yet a real sharing, sufficient to lead one toward truth more mysterious and wonderful than one might ever have imagined.

This book is about discernment in the broadest sense, about discerning the truth of individual lives and communities, but also about discerning what is true. My initial premise is the basic Christian idea, shared with many other religions, that God is truth, and thus that there is a deep connection between how people come to know truth and how people come to be related to God. The apostle Paul's conviction was that the truth of God radiates through all creation and ought to have been "understood and seen through the things he has made."[3] Because humanity, Paul believed, refused to honor and give thanks to God, the human relationship with God was distorted, and the ability of human persons to see God's ways in the world was drastically impaired—they could no longer recognize God's truth shining forth in creation because they were no longer rightly acquainted with God. "They became futile in their thinking and their senseless minds were darkened" (Romans 1:21). So from the earliest Christian thought there has been a strong connection between humans' relationship with God and the capacity to discern reality truthfully.

Paul believed that God's remedy for this distortion in relationship and perception was let a new and humanly transforming light of the divine truth shine into the world: "For it is the God who said, 'Let light shine out of darkness,' who has shone in our hearts to give us the light of the knowledge of the glory of God in the face of Jesus Christ" (2 Corinthians 4:6). The same divine radiance given at creation breaks out anew, Paul declares, as the Holy Spirit reflects into the hearts of believers the divine light as it radiates now from the face of Christ risen from the dead (Romans 1:4). For Paul, the Spirit brings us into Jesus' own relationship with the Father (Romans 8), and thus not only restores human relationship with God but also establishes *a community within which the continual practice of that restored relationship leads to a renewed perception of all truth.* Paul suggests that one can identify authentic love of truth precisely as that which edifies or builds up the community in relationship with God; knowledge that is false or falsely pursued merely leads to an arrogant "puffing up" of the would-be sage. Furthermore, real knowledge seems to be less a human possession and more like something God knows; the believer comes to share in it by loving God and being known by God: "Anyone who claims to know something does not yet have the necessary knowledge; but anyone who loves God is known by him" (1 Corinthians 8:1-3).

In a later chapter I will examine how Paul links Jesus' death and resurrection with a change in the world's noetic (the structure of knowledge). But even in this preliminary glimpse we see the fundamental integrity of spirituality and theology in Christian thinking about knowledge, about what it means to discern truth. I suggest that over the centuries Christian thinking about knowledge has found an important centering point (and proving ground) in the theory and practice of spiritual discernment. The disciplines by which the believing community seeks to know and do the truth through its relationship with God can shed considerable light on what truth might be and how one comes to know it. In this introductory chapter, I want to sketch a basic typology of discernment, showing something of the organic rhythm of a discerning life. This will, I hope, make it easier to avoid missing the forest among the trees when in later chapters we move through major developments in the history of Christian spiritual discernment, some central themes, and appropriation in theology.

The Dynamic Pattern of Discernment

My study of the history, practice, and theology of discernment has led me to conclude that it might be usefully conceived as involving five aspects or phases. 1. *Discernment as faith:* spiritual discernment as grounded in a loving and trusting relationship with God; 2. *Discernment as distinguishing between good and evil impulses that move people;* 3. *Discernment as discretion, practical wisdom, moderation, and generally good sense about what to do in given practical situations;* 4. *Discernment as sensitivity to and desire to pursue God's will in all things;* and 5. *Discernment as illumination, contemplative wisdom, a noetic relationship with God that irradiates and facilitates knowledge of every kind of truth.* If we were to envision this discerning life as always springing from a contemplative mode, extending forth in a practical mode, and always returning to the contemplative, then we could very roughly plot the location of each of these moments in the rhythm of a discerning life as cycle of descending and ascending understanding. Thus each of the moments enumerated just above could be located like this:

Contemplative Grounding

1. Faith   5. Illumination

2. Impulses   4. Divine Will

3. Discretion

Active Practice

Moments (1) and (5) are the most contemplative and transformative, making possible a vision of truth that is, ultimately, the beatifying vision of God. Moment (2) discerns the "whence" of life, the impulses or spirits that move one; distinguishing between these impulses thus clarifies where one's life is "coming from," that is, what animates and drives it. Moment (3) is the most practical; yet such a disposition toward sound judgment depends on the previous moments in order to achieve the stable grounding in God's peaceful abundance (1) and sufficient clarity about one's own motivations (2) in order to act with discretion (3) in any given situation. Moment (4), the "whither," bespeaks the crucial teleological dimension of the whole discerning life, for if one's life (taken either individually or communally) is not consistently pressing on toward the meaning and truth of all reality in terms of God's intention for the whole, then every act of discernment easily becomes short-circuited, falling captive to smaller, meandering desires. Thus the prudential wisdom of true discretion (3) would degenerate into mere self-serving cunning, or the attentive distinguishing of spirits within one's own heart (2) would lapse into a narcissistic self-preoccupation. Moment (5) brings a discerning life to the consummate state of friendship with God in which human life comes to share in God's own knowing and loving of reality. In a sense, of course, all the previous moments "depend" on this last, because they are all pursued in order to reach it; nevertheless, the wisdom of Christian spiritual practice has always suggested that this consummate moment in the rhythm of a discerning life also depends on the years of training, formation, and of practicing what it is like to know the world in companionship with God.

In the rest of this chapter I want to provide a quick tour of each of these moments or aspects of discernment, and do so by suggesting their common biblical grounding. I should first, however, acknowledge that this synthetic picture of an organic rhythm of integrally related moments is, as far as I can tell, my own view. Almost all standard readings of the history and theology of spiritual discernment deal with a series of discrete functions. I have instead tried to see the links between each of these as well as to uncover their spiritual trajectory, so to speak, backward and forward into God. While such a scheme certainly risks the artificiality of any model, it does offer some advantages for understanding discernment.

At the most basic level, it helps to overcome some neoscholastic distinctions that have perhaps now outlived their usefulness and have tended to obscure the intrinsic relationships between different modes of discernment. So, for example, while scholars have always been aware that discernment as distinguishing between spirits and discernment as discretion are both present in the works of John Cassian, the link between these moments of spiritual discernment had grown obscure; the two modes were isolated and categorized according to an overriding scheme of distinctions between nature and grace.[4]

A second advantage to this model derives from its capacity to reflect in a more natural manner the way that different aspects of discernment come to the fore at different moments in the ongoing journey of Christian life. If we see these dimensions of discernment as aspects of the whole sweep of faithful existence, then we can see them in the round as features of a larger process of growth and not as, say, mechanical laboratory instruments switched on and off as the need arises.

Third, by broadening the scope of discernment we are able to relate it to faith on the one hand and wisdom on the other; we can see links with *phronēsis* and *prudentia;* and we can open up the topic constructively toward a broadly Augustinian illumination theology of knowledge. All this allows us to put discernment into a much larger noetic frame; it permits us to give Christian spiritual teaching on knowledge a voice again within the range of our contemporary conversations about knowledge, consciousness, epistemic virtue, and the approachability of truth.

The discerning dimension of Christian life unfolds through many moments that have a basic order or sequence even as they inevitably overlap and cycle round. As we shall see, writers as diversely magisterial as Catherine of Siena, Ignatius of Loyola, and Jonathan Edwards all suggest that these moments each recur throughout a life that is growing toward God, and recur in deeper and deeper forms—until, like Bunyan's pilgrims, believers take the perspective glass given to them by Knowledge and Experience, and shakily but joyfully catch sight of the gate to the City, welcomed at last into a clearer vision:

> Now while they were thus drawing towards the Gate, behold a company of the Heavenly Host came out to meet them: To whom it was said, by the other two shining Ones, These are the men that have loved our Lord, when they were in the World, and that have left all for his holy Name, and he hath sent us to fetch them, and we have brought them thus far on their desired Journey; that they may go in and look their Redeemer in the face with joy.[5]

In every discerning moment of Christian life, in every act of discerning truth, this welcoming and beckoning to journey's end draws believers onward to that vision of truth which is the very life of heaven and a new earth's everlasting joy.

First Moment: Discernment as Grounded
in Loving Trust in God

Much Christian teaching about discernment is focused on the *objects* to be discerned—whether these are very particular, subtle influences on behavior, or the direction and calling of an entire life. Understandably then, a dominant note of urgency deriving from very real practical needs often sounds in any discussion of discernment. Yet the teachers of discernment are wholly united in calling for a patient and persistent attention to the discerning *subject*. By this they do not mean to give priority to the knowing human subject, as in modern epistemology, but on the contrary to emphasize that human knowing needs to be pried loose from the habits of mind it has fallen into and to be completely transformed and attuned to the realities of faith. Or as Paul famously puts it: "Do not be conformed to this world, but be transformed by the renewing of your minds, so that you may discern what is the will of God—what is good and acceptable and perfect" (Romans 12:2).

So while classic Christian approaches to discernment certainly attend to the noetic framework of the human subject, they do not do so to find there a Cartesian ground of certainty or to be chastened by Kantian convictions regarding the inherent categorical limitations of all human knowing. Instead, Christian discernment begins with the confidence that human knowing can become enraptured by the very truth that creates and sustains it, that this truth is nothing less than the radiant logic of God's trinitarian life, and that this life re-creates humankind to become sharers in that ultimate knowing and loving which is God. Unless the discerning life is constantly nourished by the life of God, no growth in truer perception can occur.

Let me try to show why this transforming of the knower is the great prerequisite of a discerning life. The Gospel according to John provides an early Christian witness to this epistemic need and its fulfillment in Christ. I want to risk a perhaps exaggerated reading of this noetic dimension in John; I do so because this Gospel seems to me the consummate expression of the framework within which an organic, developmental life of discernment could come to fruition. The whole structure of the Gospel is conceived as a dramatic shining into a blind world of the true light, the divine logic, incarnate as Jesus. As this light comes into the world, the world's present blindness is ever more intensively revealed through a series of misinterpreted *signs* that culminate in the raising of Lazarus, and finally in the ultimate sign of Christ's own death and resurrection (the master key to perceiving reality).[6] At the wedding at Cana, and at each of the succeeding signs, Jesus offers the unlimited divine abundance of the Father to hearers who persistently misunderstand his words in a (sometimes willfully) shrunken and literalistic manner. Jesus' interlocutors no longer know how to read "signfully" or analogically, and therefore cannot perceive the true nature and destiny of a reality whose deepest truth is *intrinsically* signful, is most *itself* precisely as loving gift of communion with the Giver.

Nicodemus sarcastically inquires about obstetrics when told that he must be "born from above" (John 3:1ff.); the crowds are grossly offended when Jesus tells them that "unless you eat the flesh of the Son of Man and drink his blood, you have no life in you" (John 6:53). Throughout the Gospel, Jesus is shown offering image after image of being grounded and nourished in his own life with the Father. He interrupts the world's economy of scarcity and necessity with an inestimable economy of abundance and grace: he is the true bread that came down from heaven, the true vine, the resurrection and the life. Believers must come to derive their whole existence no longer from their (literally minded) biological life, which ends, literally, with death, but from the ever-

> "Do not be conformed to this world, but be transformed by the renewing of your minds, so that you may discern what is the will of God—what is good and acceptable and perfect." (Romans 12:2)

greater (analogically minded) infinite life of the Father in the Spirit—that is, life that never ends but always points beyond itself to another. Only then can believers finally come to know reality in truth. This is possible because creation is, in truth, suffused by the radiant ever-more of its Creator and can only be perceived truly by those who are themselves attuned to that ever-sharing "more" of divine life. In this sense creation is intrinsically signful (shining with the hidden logic of divine self-sharing abundance) and can only be understood and known as it is read analogically, that is, read in tandem with the divine reality that give rise to it.

Each of the signs in John's Gospel teaches the reader to die to the scarcity of univocal understanding. The beauty of Jesus' giving in each sign teaches the reader to yearn for resurrection of mind and heart into the flowing abundance of an analogical and sacramental vision of reality. John brings this process to its consummation ("it is finished" at 19:30) at Jesus' death, which fractures the world's mendacious reduction of reality to scarcity and fear. Jesus subverts this reduction by perceiving his death as in fact *more* than death, a going to the Father (14:28) and, even on the cross, by creating new life and community (19:26-27, 34). His resurrection inaugurates the permeation of the world with the divine light that John's Gospel so loves by sending the new signful community of disciples into the world, just as Jesus was sent as the sign of the Father. In this way John's Gospel reads Christ's dying and rising as a grounding in a signful, ever-expanding analogical vision of reality. John holds this iconically before the Gospel's readers and draws them into practicing this new mode of understanding for themselves in their reading of the Gospel. Those who refuse to be drawn in risk stumbling as do the obtuse, literal-minded characters that the Gospel depicts.

I am suggesting here that the relational, trinitarian framework woven through John's Gospel corresponds wholly with John's conception of the world's reality as sacramental, that is, as pointing to and sharing in a reality beyond itself. The sharing trinitarian life of God has created a world whose deep structure and meaning reflects that trinitarian life; the world's truth images the triune reality in that it is most itself, most *disclosive* of itself in all its worldly particularity, precisely insofar as it is translucent to its divine source—just as the persons of the Trinity *are* themselves exactly by a ceaseless and delighted giving way of each to each divine other. There is, in other words, a creaturely analogy to this divine existence constituted by showing forth another; and that deep structure of creaturely signfulness, translucent abundance, cannot be perceived by those whose hearts are gripped within a mentality of deprivation, suspicion, and scarcity.

I have also been suggesting that interwoven with this trinitarian vision of reality is a trinitarian vision of the human knower. John 14–17 reveals Jesus training the disciples, preparing them to participate in this ever-sharing reality he has with the Father and the Spirit, and therefore also training his disciples to read the world truthfully in terms of this self-sharing abundance. The paschal mystery awaits as the final transforming sign before the disciples will be gifted with a new understanding, but even so, Jesus is preparing them: "I have told you this before it occurs, so that when it does occur, you may believe" (14:29). As he opens their hearts to receive the gift that will come with the resurrection, Jesus explains:

> I still have many things to say to you, but you cannot bear them now. When the Spirit of truth comes, he will guide you into all the truth; for he will not speak on his own, but will speak whatever he hears, and he will declare to you the things that are to come. He will glorify me, because he will take what is mine and declare it to you. All that the Father has is mine. For this reason I said that he will take what is mine and declare it to you. (16:12-15)

To receive the "many things" that Jesus would yet share with them, the disciples must have Jesus' dying and rising worked within them. They must come to partake of reality in some sense as Christ does, beyond the dominion of death, and that means they must come to share in the infinite Spirit, in the infinite sharing life that is his life with the Father ("all that the Father has is mine"). In his resurrection glory, Jesus breathes the Holy Spirit upon the disciples at last (20:22), and, for John, this means they now participate in that infinite abundance of self-sharing which is the truth, the logic of reality. Now at last, says Jesus, the Spirit will "take what is mine and declare it to you," because now my sharing life with you (which is the very life of the Father) has broken through all the bonds and fears that have hindered and distorted our communication with one another. It is this new life, this new grounding in belief, that will make true discernment possible.

Much of what I have understood of this possibility has been illuminated for me by a theologian, mystic, and poet of the seventeenth century, Thomas Traherne. Traherne senses the crucial link between, on the one hand, a consciousness transformed by sharing in the trinitarian abundance and, on the other hand, the discerning ability to perceive the world truly.[7] I will work more carefully with Traherne in the final chapter, but for our purposes here, let me show how I think he helps to elucidate the noetic theme we have been considering in John. For Traherne, the infinite goodness which is the trinitarian life has freely chosen to extend the divine joy by creating a universe of creatures who have the capacity to reflect that goodness, and, in the case of intelligent creatures, to share freely in the loving enjoyment of it. They do this not only by virtue of a growing capacity to see the world as God's gift but, more precisely, by coming to rejoice themselves in a receiving-and-giving life. As this happens, they come to see the world aright, to discern truly.

In Traherne's view (which seems to me very near to that of such christocentric Neoplatonists as Maximus and Bonaventure), the paschal mystery cracks open human rejection of the loving divine bounty by pouring out love in so *communicable* a fashion that it cannot help but transfigure the consciousness of everyone who is united to it.

> The Cross is the abyss of wonders, the centre of desires, the school of virtues, the house of wisdom, the throne of love. . . . There we may see the most distant things in Eternity united: all mysteries at once couched together and explained. . . . It is the Well of Life beneath in which we may see the face of Heaven above: and the only mirror, wherein all things appear in their proper colors: that is, sprinkled in the blood of our Lord and Saviour. . . . That Cross is a tree set on fire with an invisible flame, that illuminateth all the world. The flame is Love: the Love in His bosom who died on it. In the light of which we do see how to possess all the things in Heaven and Earth after His similitude.[8]

By condensing the whole mystery of divine self-giving on the cross, Christ restores to human minds a glimmering of the true principles of the whole cosmic order. "All things appear in their proper colors" now because they can be seen in terms of the flowing divine life-sharing incarnate on the cross. John's Gospel envisions this transformation of human consciousness in terms of the risen Christ communicating the Spirit of the Father with the disciples; Traherne echoes the Pentecost theme with his reference to the fire of the divine Love that begins to illuminate the world: "In the light of which we do see how to possess all the things in Heaven and Earth after His similitude."

By coming to partake of the divine Love, the Holy Spirit, humankind begins to perceive the world truly—which for Traherne means to possess all things as the delighted gift of the Father to the Son and the Son to the Father in their Spirit. So all creatures are given to be joys and are only fulfilled and achieve their divine purpose *as* they are enjoyed and shared, given and received. Speaking of the human and angelic capacity to discern God's intention in giving us all good things, Traherne remarks, "You are able to discern, that in all these things He is Love to you; and that Love is a fountain of infinite benefits. . . . It endlessly desireth to delight itself, and its delight is to magnify its beloved" (II.25). As Love, God's greatest delight is to give delight to God's beloved, and this, says Traherne, is the world in Christ. Indeed, Traherne even goes so far as to say (echoing Dionysius the Pseudo-Areopagite) that it is precisely in loving the creatures that God the Word is eternally begotten: "For the Love of the Father is the Wisdom of the Father. And this Person did God by loving us, beget, that He might be the means of all our glory. . . . This Person differs in nothing from the Father, but only in this that He is begotten of Him. He is eternal with the Father" (II.43-44).

It is by coming to partake in all things as this infinite, delighted giving that humanity begins to acquire discernment. It is a profoundly communal vision of reality: shared in love, animated with an intense desire to communicate joy and delight. This transformed vision bestows upon believers a discerning eye to see the world in truth as an event of abounding communion, to see it truly therefore because one sees it as being for joy and one receives and gives the divine joy that pulses as the heart of it. As Traherne puts it in one of his most felicitous and justly famous passages:

> You never enjoy the world aright, till you see how a sand exhibiteth the wisdom and power of God: And prize in everything the service which they do you, by manifesting His glory and goodness to your Soul, far more than the visible beauty on their surface, or the material services they can do your body. Wine by its moisture quencheth my thirst, whether I consider it or no: but to see it flowing from His love who gave it unto man, quencheth the thirst even of the Holy Angels.

To consider it is to drink it spiritually. To rejoice in its diffusion is to be of a public mind. And to take pleasure in all the benefits it doth to all is Heavenly, for so they do in Heaven. To do so, is to be divine and good, and to imitate our Infinite and Eternal Father. (I.27)

The whole visible creation is perceived aright when the communion with God it offers is prized and partaken of, and when this occurs, the discerning mind truly participates in the divine way of knowing and loving everything.

This faith grounds every act of discernment, whatever its type or function, and it is to this contemplative abiding in the divine ground of the universe that all discernment journeys. Such a dwelling in God is the vital principle in all true knowing, says Traherne:

Till your spirit filleth the whole world, and the stars are your jewels; till you are as familiar with the ways of God in all Ages as with your walk and table: till you are intimately acquainted with that shady nothing out of which the world was made: till you love men so as to desire their happiness, with a thirst equal to the zeal of your own; till you delight in God for being good to all: you never enjoy the world aright. (I.30)

And yet, the problem remains that though "the world is a mirror of infinite beauty, yet no man sees it. It is a Temple of Majesty, yet no man regards it. It is a region of Light and Peace, did men not disquiet it" (I.31). Learning to discern the impulses and spirits that disquiet and cloud human perception must come next. Because that aspect and the other remaining "moments" will each feature significantly in later chapters, we can now proceed more briefly than in the outline thus far.

Second Moment: Discernment as Distinguishing between Good and Evil Impulses

Discernment is grounded in God's own desire, the Holy Spirit, working the paschal mystery within the unfolding lives of believers. Discernment can only deepen if it leads believers to greater awareness of the *lesser desires* that sometimes captivate and distort perception—and so render believers' judgment impermeable to the light of the Spirit. At the presentation of the infant Jesus in the Temple, Luke's Gospel interprets his manifestation in the world as the definitive moment of discernment: "Then Simeon blessed them and said to his mother Mary, 'This child is destined for the falling and the rising of many in Israel, and to be a sign that will be opposed so that the inner thoughts of many will be revealed—and a sword will pierce your own soul too'" (Luke 2:34-35). Jesus' destiny, sharper than a two-edged sword, is a word spoken to test the world's perception and response to God. What impulses, what spirits, will foster or diminish people's responses to Jesus? With gathering intensity, Luke portrays Jesus' "exodus" (9:31) up to Jerusalem as provoking a terrible division and parting of the ways among those whom he confronts, revealing and distinguishing between the animating spirits of the prodigals and the self-righteous (15:11ff.), between the lowly and the proud who are scattered in the "thoughts of their hearts" (1:46-55).

In this way Israel's heritage of skill in discerning the spirits is itself tested and purified as it is brought to bear on Jesus himself. The synoptics repeatedly portray Jesus' family and the religious authorities as struggling to discern the true nature of the spirit that animates Jesus (cf. Mark 3:20-27; Matthew 12:24-32; Luke 11:15-23, 12:10). This struggle reaches back into the difficulties of distinguishing true from false prophets (e.g., Deuteronomy 18:21ff.; Jeremiah 28), and back to the puzzle of discriminating between the good and evil impulses at work in the judges and kings (e.g., Judges 9:23; 1 Kings 22:18-23). Genesis traces the origins of this discerning the spirits back to the primeval ambiguities set loose in Eden. Jacques Guillet comments insightfully on this primordial struggle of humankind to *recognize* the inner voices who speak so convincingly: besides the mysterious voice of God who seems to call humanity beyond its expectations, there is another voice that seems to express a person's own human desires, but then again to distort or magnify them. "It is clear that the voice does not come from the man himself, but from a source that is disquieting—more rational and stronger than he, more tenacious, more aware of his plans, better informed than he regarding the tendencies of his own heart, and, apparently, capable of understanding the divine purposes (Gen. 3)."[9]

The difficulty is not only a matter of discriminating between truly benevolent inspirations and malign impulses (often characterized by their uncanny capacity to mimic the good: "even Satan disguises himself as an angel of light" [2 Corinthians 11:14]). For each of those voices sounds within the already obscurely reverberating desires of a person or community, producing there a mysterious range of resonances whose true source and origin are not easily recognized. For this reason the early Christian communities, so open and hungry for the leading of the Spirit of Christ, also recognized their vulnerability to other spirits.

The Johannine community's admonition to "test the spirits to see whether they are from God" (1 John 4:1) would give rise to many traditions of testing or criterial signs to be read in everything from emotions and feelings, the direction and fruit of one's life, the moral implications of a teaching, consonance with the scriptures, and the nurturing or fracturing of communal life. But of course the adequacy of such tests depended on the discerning eye of the individual or community employing them, and therefore on a deep grounding in God's ways, a familiarity and sensitivity to the characteristic features of God's presence.

The Pauline literature in the New Testament gives us some of the earliest Christian thinking about these signs by which to test the spirits. While St. Paul clearly identifies "the discernment of spirits" as among the charisms or gifts of the Holy Spirit for the community (1 Corinthians 12:10), the great variety of signs and tests proposed in Paul suggests that there was a constant need for discernment of spirits in the ordinary life of the church. Love and peaceful communion run through Paul's letters as the fundamental tests of healthy impulses:

> Now the works of the flesh are obvious: fornication, impurity, licentiousness, idolatry, sorcery, enmities, strife, jealousy, anger, quarrels, dissensions, carousing, and things like these. . . . By contrast, the fruit of the Spirit is love, joy, peace, patience, kindness, generosity, faithfulness, gentleness, and self-control. . . . Let us not become conceited, competing against one another, envying one another. (Galatians 5:19-26)

It is easy enough from our present post-Cartesian perspective to narrow the focus of the discrimination of spirits to a highly interiorized preoccupation with states of feeling and subjective experience. And certainly Paul includes in this famous passage categories that might be read in an individualist and affective manner as describing emotions or spiritual temperaments. But as I have tried to suggest by extending the passage to include 5:26, Paul's determining measure of spiritual discernment here seems far more communal in orientation; the contrast is not between impulses that lead either to disquieting or tranquilizing feelings, but between ways of being and acting that divide the community and so direct it toward the poisonous pastimes of mutual recrimination or disaffected libertinism—as compared with ways of life that unite the community and so center it upon the unifying joy of the Holy Spirit.

This would seem to mesh well with the observations of the previous section regarding the interrelation between a grounding in God's joyfully self-sharing abundance and a capacity for truer perception. Paul explicitly makes this link: "this is my prayer, that your love may overflow more and more with knowledge and full insight (*aisthesei*) to help you know what is best" (Philippians 1:9-10). The mutual love that Paul seeks to foster in the community is, in his view, the foundation for a clear-eyed reading of reality and the basis for discerning the relative meaning and worth of the impulses that attract or repel the community. This criterion of humble and other-regarding love reaches its apex in Paul, very naturally, with his reflections on the humble self-sharing of Christ in Philippians 2:5ff. The apostle applies this theological awareness and participation in Christ's self-giving (in incarnation and death) as the test of whether one is truly animated by the Holy Spirit: "No one can say, 'Jesus is Lord' except by the Holy Spirit" (1 Corinthians 12:3). Full confidence in the lordship of the humiliated and crucified one sets the community free to trust no longer in its own authority or position or strength in opposition to others, and this freedom becomes a test of the health of its impulses.

Third Moment: Discernment as Discretion and Practical Wisdom

So far we have noticed a developing christological matrix for discernment. In the first moment, discernment partakes in the infinite self-sharing opened into the world in Christ. In the second moment, Christ's appearing in the world provokes a testing of spirits as measured by the liberating humble love of the crucified. Now as we turn to this most practical dimension of the discerning life, it may seem that the christological framework is less apparent. Are we simply dealing with a basic human virtue, good sense, lauded by Aristotle as *phronēsis* and Cicero as *discretio*? Or could this theme equally well be identified with the Bible's reflections on wisdom?

Discernment as discretion is not simply a matter of having sufficient experience of life that one grasps intuitively the most fitting means to good ends. Rather we are considering here a kind of friendship with the divine orderer of all things sufficient not only to recognize the most fitting means in any given situation but also such that one has the desire and actual capacity to pursue that practical wisdom. Plato and Aristotle found it conceivable but highly peculiar to imagine someone actually knowing the good and the means to it and yet remaining unwilling to pursue it. But Paul understood all too well the possibility that one may know the good and even will it and yet fail to do it (Romans 7:14-25). Discernment as spiritual discretion will require more than moderation and seasoned judgment; it will require an authentic yearning for wisdom: "I, wisdom, live with prudence, and I attain knowledge and discretion. . . . I love those who love me, and those who seek me diligently find me" (Proverbs 8:12, 17).[10] And wisdom knows the spirits that animate both those who seek her and those who flee her, for the secret impulses that govern the indiscreet are anything but innocuous: "all who hate me love death" (Proverbs 8:36). Thus discernment as discrimination of spirits is an abiding prerequisite for discernment as discretion or practical wisdom. Without a profound partaking in God's own self-sharing love and the consequent awareness of the motivations at play in life, neither an individual nor a community would truly be free to find the just balance, the judgment of discretion in any given instance.

The New Testament often links this spiritual balance and maturity with a growing capacity to recognize the works and ways of God in Christ. Under the pressure of the last days, warns Jesus in Mark 13, many will misread the times, worry about what to say, be led astray by false messiahs, and fail to keep watch for the hidden advent of the Lord. The needed readiness, insight, and stability come partly as a gift ("do not worry beforehand about what you are to say; but say whatever is given you at that time" [Mark 13:11]), and also partly as a kind of training or formation in reading the signs properly: "From the fig tree learn its lesson: as soon as its branch becomes tender . . . you know that summer is near. So also, when you see these things taking place, you know that he

Discernment as spiritual discretion will require more than moderation and seasoned judgment; it will require an authentic yearning for wisdom.

is near" (Mark 13:28-29). We might even gather the themes of this form of discretion or prudence under the heading of knowing how to be alert for Christ. It is the wisdom of the bridesmaids who prepare for waiting in ways that the foolish omit (Matthew 25:1-13). It is the mature and compassionate insight of those who recognize and respond to Christ in the hungry, the thirsty, the strangers, the unclothed, the sick, and the imprisoned as compared with the insensitive who are oblivious to Christ in all those who suffer (Matthew 25:31-46).

Reflecting biblically on this dimension of discernment, then, would direct us to the ways in which Jesus shapes the experience of the disciples—training them in his own patterns of life, his own confidence in God, his own perception of God's call to him in and through the needs of others. Jesus' characteristic parabolic manner of teaching exemplifies this patterning of a judgment that is capable of recognizing the deep truth in the ordinary exigencies of life. So we are not talking here about a generic prudence, but a deep capacity to recognize and respond to the divine will in everyday existence. The Letter to the Hebrews talks about the difference between the mature and those who are "dull in understanding," who need to be taught "again the basic elements of the oracles of God" (5:11-12). The mature are those who are well trained in the basic elements, who through the long practice of alertness to Christ know how to discern and bring them to bear in any given context. They have a practical wisdom that might be compared to aesthetic judgment: "those whose faculties (*aisthētēria*) have been trained by practice to distinguish good from evil" (Hebrews 5:14).

This understanding of discernment as *discretio* and *prudentia* will, in later authors, sometimes leave its explicitly christological basis unremarked. But I would want to claim at the very least that its properly Christian form is in fact grounded in Jesus' own openness to the call of the one he called Abba in each situation, and in the *practicing* of that availability by the Christian community. The Letter to the Ephesians highlights this formational focus of the community's wisdom as fully integral to the community's baptismal sharing in Christ. Evoking the baptismal imagery of Christ calling believers from the darkness of sin and death into the light of resurrection life, the letter calls on the Ephesians to live into the maturing judgment of those who have been united to Christ: "Live as children of light—for the fruit of the light is found in all that is good and right and true. Try to find out what is pleasing to the Lord. . . . So do not be foolish, but understand what the will of the Lord is" (5:8-10, 17). In this passage we can see how baptismal sharing in the reality of the risen Christ calls forth an attunement to "what is pleasing to the Lord" and a desire to "understand what the will of the Lord is." The fact that the letter then continues with practical directions for how to understand this "will of the Lord" in very mundane concerns suggests that we are indeed dealing with matters of discretion, with a right choosing of proper means to the good end—and that this discretion is understood as the ordinary daily flowering of the community's baptismal grounding in Christ's own pattern of existence.

Fourth Moment: Discernment as Seeking the Truth of God's Will

If discernment as discretion is grounded, as I have just argued, in Christ's own availability to God in everyday life, then we can rediscover a strong relationship between this idea of practical wisdom and the larger vision of God's design for creation. Because in a very real sense the practical wisdom that discerns what is most apt or fitting in a given concrete situation is already oriented toward the wider horizon of truth against which that particular situation plays out. To revert to the analogy with aesthetic judgment, a seasoned sculptor has the artistry to discern the correct tool and stroke to use at a given spot; yet that skill and mature judgment would be of little use were they not guided and inspired by a vision of beauty and truth that animates the entire work of the sculptor.

The aesthetic analogy resonates here with Ignatius of Loyola's way of conceiving this form of discernment; for him, as we shall see in the next chapters, discernment of the truth of God's will always seeks to serve the greater *glory* of God, so that the radiance of the divine beauty and goodness can become manifest in the world. So the skilled artistry of practical wisdom serves this fourth moment of discernment, which is a seeking and serving of the truth of God. This discernment of the true divine intention in all things seeks to make that truth more visible, more luminous, as the beauty of holiness. We might think of it as a contemplative rediscovery of the right use of all creation and an active capacity to bring all things toward the purposes for which they were intended. Patristic writers such as Origen and Evagrius will call this a form of natural contemplation, a discernment of the true meaning, the inner divine intention or *logos* expressed in and as each creature (a theme explored in more detail in chapters 4 and 5). This form of discernment also requires some personal relationship and communion with the divine speaker of all things, and a desire to bring that authoring and therefore authoritative speaking to ever greater expression in the world.

John's Gospel in fact portrays Jesus in just this way, as the one who discerns the truth of the Father's intentions and brings the divine work to embodied form in the world. "My Father is still working, and I also am working" (John 5:17), says Jesus, and he explains his role in this common work: "Very truly, I tell you, the Son can do nothing on his own, but only what he sees the Father doing; for whatever the Father does, the Son does likewise. The Father loves the Son and shows him all that he himself is doing" (5:19-20). This passage goes on to present the chief work of the Father through Christ as the bestowing of eternal life, as accomplishing a passage through the eschatological truth of judgment and into a new pattern of existence—a pattern only visible in this world as resurrection from the dead. It is this eschatological truth, the deathless reality of God's infinitely self-sharing life, that environs all creation and reveals the true intention and goal inherent in every creature. Thus this fourth moment of discernment leads to a provisional sharing in eschatological truth, in a capacity for judgment that springs from undivided pursuit of God's will: "I can do nothing on my own. As I hear, I judge; and my judgment is just, because I seek to do not my own will but the will of him who sent me" (John 5:30).

This form of discernment attains a judgment of the truth of things precisely because it seeks God's will in all things. Again, John's Gospel understands Jesus as speaking this truth that judges because he speaks as the Father has commanded him; and Jesus is convinced that what the Father commands is purely and absolutely life: "I know that his commandment is eternal life" (John 12:50). So we are talking here about a discernment of truth not in the sense of truth as the static essence of any thing, but truth as the living reality of each creature *existing in communion with its Creator.* This "eternal life" that judges and reveals the truth unmasks the falseness and aversion to life that has infected the world, but it does so because it illuminates all creatures with the light of their authentic existence as they were intended to know it in communion with God. John portrays Jesus as creating in his disciples a preliminary human form of this inbreaking eschatological life, a rediscovery of *reality as participation in divine communion.* Hence Jesus translates the Father's commandment for the disciples as his own commandment for them to love one another as he has loved them. In this way they themselves will become a visible sign of the divine communion within the structures of the world, for the Father, the Son, and the Spirit will abide in the community as the community abides in love (John 14). But more than this, the community itself will inhabit Jesus' own discernment of the truth of God's will; for as the disciples are formed in Jesus' own self-giving pattern of existence, he will begin to pour out within them a vision of that undying life:

> This is my commandment, that you love one another as I have loved you. No one has greater love than this, to lay down one's life for one's friends. You are my friends if you do what I command you. I do not call you servants any longer, because the servant does not know what the master is doing; but I have called you friends, because I have made known to you everything that I have heard from my Father. (John 15:12-15)

So we can best understand this fourth moment of discernment as springing from the community's participation in Jesus' relationship with the Father.[11] For John, this sharing is granted by the mutual desire of Jesus and the Father ("I will ask the Father, and he will give you another Advocate"), and it is no coincidence that the Spirit who indwells and teaches the community is precisely "the Spirit of truth" (14:16-17) who will declare to the disciples all that the Father has and gives to the Son and so "he will guide you into all the truth" (16:13). Once more we see that the truth is the clarifying radiance of that eternally self-sharing life that is God's own but given away in joy without limit.

The Fifth Moment: Discernment as the Contemplation of Wisdom

And that brings us to the goal of the discerning life, the moment (perhaps only implicit or touched briefly in the present life) when the perception of

God's will and the desire to embody that truth passes over into the delighted wonder of those who gaze upon the consummation of all creation in God, as the eternal life and divine wisdom they sought to discern all along. Such a beatific vision can only be understood eschatologically, for it cannot fully exist until the overcoming of the world's estrangement from God and the creation of a new heaven and a new earth.

Nevertheless, for our purposes, there is a very practical gain from considering this ultimate contemplative moment in discernment. For many of the writers we will study, this beatifying glimpse of eternal life seems to influence even now the way in which humanity knows truth. This eschatological vision or light from heaven breaks into the present world as the transfiguring light of Christ's resurrection and sets human thinking free from the constraints of fear and death: "So if you have been raised with Christ, seek the things that are above, where Christ is, seated at the right hand of God. Set your minds on the things that are above, not on things that are on earth, for you have died, and your life is hidden with Christ in God" (Colossians 3:1-3). This passage from Colossians goes on to show how a life that is already hiddenly present to heaven should now consider things on earth. The life of the world to come, a life of perfect communion and self-sharing love, transforms the present perception and action of believers. We could say that this contemplative dimension of discernment disposes believers to see and treat the world as it now exists, but with the freedom, confidence, and hope of those who already taste the eschatological banquet that God is preparing to make of the world's presently alienated and divided state: "Now you must get rid of all such things—anger, wrath, malice, slander, and abusive language from your mouth. Do not lie to one another, seeing that you have stripped off the old self with its practices and have clothed yourselves with the new self, which is being renewed in knowledge according to the image of its creator" (Colossians 3:8-10). This new knowledge is a vision of reality in motion toward the perfect communion in which present divisions that explode in "anger, wrath, malice, slander, and abusive language" are being overcome by the unitive power of the divine life. The preliminary form of this eternal life of divine communion is already present in the transforming power of Christ: "In that renewal there is no longer Greek and Jew, circumcised and uncircumcised, barbarian, Scythian, slave and free; but Christ is all and in all!" (Colossians 3:11).

So I am suggesting here that the fifth moment of discernment is a contemplative wisdom, born in the paschal mystery, touched by the perfect self-sharing of the divine communion, and able to reconceive the world in ways that hold it open to that limitless life for which it was created. Unless discernment is deeply oriented to this contemplative vision it is easily taken captive by the urgency of more apparently useful works of knowledge. The

paradox is that by turning too narrowly to the practical and useful a discerning mind is less able to envision the infinitely self-sharing love to which
all things are called; when that happens, the act of discernment shrinks to
the merely technical, procedural, or self-interested pursuit of knowledge.
The other side of the paradox, then, is that the more an individual or community holds discernment open toward contemplative wonder in God, the
more actually useful, insightful, and productive of real transformation its
discernment will be in the world as it now appears.

In this chapter I have sought to do two things at once, to outline the ever-
flowing rhythm of a discerning life and to show the integrity of that life as
grounded in the scriptural witness to God's reconciling work in Christ.
There is a certain genetic quality to the history of discernment that unfolds
after the New Testament period—certain characteristic features of each
dimension of discernment play themselves out in each new era. But more
importantly, I believe that these biblical vistas of the discerning life will provide the needed perspective to see the deeper theological and spiritual significance of the theories and practices to which we now turn.

TWO

The Historical Landscape
of Discernment: Christian Antiquity

In the previous chapter I offered a heuristic model of spiritual discernment, showing the interrelationships among its various forms and phases. I hope that will prove helpful as we turn now to the details of actual historical developments. This chapter and the next will survey chronologically (and, I fear, cursorily) some representative landmarks in the history of discernment.

Early Responses to 1 Corinthians 12:10

Patterns of spiritual discernment in Christianity spring from a wide range of biblical sources, extending well beyond actual verbal references to discernment per se. The actual phrase "discernment of spirits" (*diakriseis pneumatōn*) is found once in Scripture, at 1 Corinthians 12:10. In this crucial context, Paul is clearly warning the Corinthians of the need to think carefully about the source and origin of various charismatic or spiritual gifts often found in pagan cults and sometimes exercised in the Christian community (see chapter 5).

So while Paul lists discernment of spirits as one of nine such gifts, it takes on a certain special significance as the community seeks to clarify the authenticity of its spiritual life and to distinguish its gifts from non-Christian influences. Paul proposes three vital principles for identifying and understanding authentic Christian gifts: first, authentically Christian spiritual gifts never speak against but always affirm the lordship of Jesus (1 Corinthians 12:3); second, the variety and differences among the gifts should not obscure the unity of their source in the one divine giver of all good gifts (vv. 4-6); and third, the authenticity of the gifts may be discerned just insofar as they build up unity and desire for the common good in the Christian community (vv. 7, 12ff.). All this suggests that while the precise reference here is to discernment of spirits in the sense of identifying the true motivations of various forms of behavior, the particular context also points to the wider range of discernment discussed in the previous chapter. For example, understanding the proper use of discernment in the upbuilding of the community calls for a larger discerning sense of God's purposes in guiding the community and of practical wisdom in discerning how best to achieve that good.

In an important survey of patristic developments of this text from 1 Corinthians, Joseph T. Lienhard proposed three focusing questions that almost all the early writers address: Who is the primary recipient of this gift of discernment of spirits? What is meant by "spirits"? What are the criteria advanced for making this discernment?[1] Early responses to the first question suggest three possible trajectories. One view, associated with the more literal-minded exegetes in the Antiochene tradition, tended to locate Paul's reference to discernment of spirits so narrowly historically that it would appear to have little to say to those in any other circumstances or later generations. But the Alexandrian tradition exemplified in Origen (ca. 185–254) and Athanasius (ca. 296–373) reads Paul as remarking upon a charismatic gift of the Spirit that might be offered throughout the church's existence, though chiefly to those who through the ascetical life have prepared themselves to exercise the gift most acutely. Intriguingly, this view is taken up but transformed in the early monastic traditions in which discernment of spirits "ceases to be viewed as an exceptional gift or charism and is treated as a virtue, even a necessary virtue."[2] We will want to ponder further what might be the ramifications of this double shift in the perception of discernment: from rarity to frequency, and from charism to virtue. Finally, notes Lienhard, there was a tendency among Latin exegetes to link discernment of spirits with clerical office and to see it much less in charismatic or even ascetical terms.

On the second question, the interpretation of the "spirits" referred to by Paul, there is again an interesting range of views.[3] The Antiochene exegetes pointed more to the pagan religious and cultural influences at work upon believers as contrasted with the good or authentic spiritual voices of prophets within the church. Not surprisingly, the Alexandrians focus more on the cosmic powers and spiritual forces ranged for good and evil on either side of believers. Later writers emerging from desert traditions of spirituality develop this cosmic vision in much more personal terms, especially toward an awareness of demons who afflict those engaged in the ascetic life, that is, those whose costly struggles put them in direct contact and conflict with the spirits that normally operate within human lives more hiddenly.

Turning to Lienhard's third question regarding criteria of discernment, there are two approaches in patristic responses to the text of 1 Corinthians. If discernment is conceived as a distinguishing of spirits and influences upon and within believers, then the criterion is generally a form of psychological or existential experience: a sense of calm and freedom, joy and confidence, a sense of certainty, or a growing feeling of consolation. But if discernment has come to be practiced much more as the virtue of discretion, then the criteria are moderation, superior insight, and a maturity of judgment recognized by others.[4]

Let me summarize. In the authors Lienhard surveys, we find a noetic capacity that ranges between an inspired gift and a hard-won maturity. This capacity may include an awareness of the benign and malign cosmic and cultural influences upon the believing community, an ability to recognize the demonic provocations at work in one's own or another's psyche, and also a virtuous insight into the true significance of any given situation sufficient to guide one to mature judgment about how best to proceed.

Origen of Alexandria

Origen's teaching on discernment arouses believers from a prejudicial stupor into which their souls have fallen; it awakens them to the true ramifications of their choices by showing them the cosmic context of their earthly pilgrimage; and it intends to make them permeable again to the fire of divine desire. Let me take each aspect in turn.

Origen was a catechetical theologian, perhaps the greatest teacher of Christian faith prior to Augustine, and he worked in a period when Christians were still subject to imperial persecution. His thinking is acutely attuned to the struggles of non-Christians who were undergoing a conversion from one vision of reality to another. At considerable risk to his own life, he visited imprisoned converts and continued to teach and encourage them, even at their trials and executions.[5] He frequently advises that one should become more consciously aware of the mindset and images that hold dominion in one's life. This functions for him as a kind of minimal prerequisite for deeper spiritual growth and theological understanding, for apart from such awareness, one remains immured in a captivating and quite possibly distorting vision of life.

The human animal, he insists, not only undergoes a series of powerful natural movements in the mind and imagination, but it also has the capacity to become aware that this is going on and to *make a judgment* about such ideas and images. This faculty of reason permits humanity to "judge and discern between the natural movements, disapproving of and rejecting some and approving of and accepting others." To develop this capacity for assessing movements of thought is crucial, in Origen's view, because unless we "judge and determine how we ought to use them when they come," we have no freedom.[6] Origen holds this principle not only with respect to sense images or passions but also with respect to intellectual opinions that may have an unacknowledged dominance in a person's life. When, for example, Origen is going to discuss the meaning of desire in the Song of Songs or the consummation of all things at the end of time, he warns his readers that they should inquire after their own frame of mind before proceeding, lest they be carried away by their own prejudices:

> if a man is seized with a desire to read and learn about these matters that are so hard and difficult to understand, he must bring with him a perfect and instructed mind. Otherwise, if he has had no experience in inquiries of this kind, they may perhaps appear to him to be vain and superfluous; or else, if he has a mind full of prejudice and preoccupations in other directions, he may think these inquiries are heretical and contrary to the faith of the Church, not so much because he is convinced by reason as because he decides according to his own prejudices.[7]

We can see here the way in which Origen must have succeeded in peeling away the layers of his own and his students' motivations and dispositions, leading to a deeper freedom and readiness to learn. First there is the question of the prompting influence: why do I want to hear about all this in the first place? Do I have, perhaps, an ulterior motive such as a vain curiosity or a kind of intellectual lust that must inevitably distort my understanding by subjecting everything to my own particular desires? Or am I even aware of the preoccupations and prejudices that unconsciously govern my thoughts, and which the startling claims of the gospel may irritate?

But Origen is far from pessimistic about the chances of overcoming these ingrained perspectives and dispositions. Proper experience opens the mind to realities larger than the narrow grip of our own interests and makes it aware of both the beneficial and the detrimental influences operating upon us. Origen fosters such experience by training his students in a discerning attitude that constantly seeks deeper levels of meaning in everything. For example, in *An Exhortation to Martyrdom* Origen opens up the experience of persecution to these deeper and more cosmic levels. One can see the training process easily here, as Origen conducts his readers back and forth between the levels of meaning, building up a discerning facility that seems capable of plumbing one's experiences like the unexpected depths of a well.

The apparently private struggle over whether to maintain one's confession of faith actually takes place before a vast public: "A great theater is filled with spectators to watch your contests and your summons to martyrdom, just as if we were to speak of a great crowd gathered to watch the contests of athletes supposed to be champions."[8] And just before this passage, Origen had likened the testing of the persecuted to Israel's crossing over the Jordan River, and the crucial decision whether to be true to the Lord or return to a worship of idols. Suddenly one's experience becomes translucent to a searching light of discernment: one's confession of faith is rooted in an ancient heritage and knit together with similar acts of commitment of one's forebears in the faith; one's present struggle is not merely a personal yes or no but a vast public contest portraying the strength or weakness of Christian faith before the crowds. Then Origen opens up yet another dimension of reality to the discerning eye. For, he says, among the crowds who watch are many who believers had not realized would take so great an interest:

> The whole world and all the angels of the right and the left, and all men, those from God's portion and those from the other portions, will attend to us when we contest for Christianity. Indeed, either the angels in heaven will cheer us on, and the floods will clap their hands together, and the mountains will leap for joy, and all the trees of the field will clap their branches—or, may it not happen, the powers from below, which rejoice in evil, will cheer.[9]

We might say that for Origen discernment is at its most profound when it orients believers in this way to the widest dimensions of their existence and thus lays bare the cosmic nexus within which human choices are really being made. This dimension of discernment links reciprocally with our earlier discussion of discernment as requiring recognition of motivations and prejudices. A more conscious scrutiny

> "[I]f a man is seized with a desire to read and learn about these matters that are so hard and difficult to understand, he must bring with him a perfect and instructed mind."

of one's views and motivations sets one free to discern the wider cosmos within which one's life takes place; and conversely, a growing awareness of the eternal implications of one's choices alerts one to the bias and narrowness at work in one's views.

Discernment in Origen springs directly from the Alexandrian's vision of reality as a cosmic journey in which intelligent life has fallen away from communion with God and God seeks to accomplish the restoration of that fellowship. This cosmic drama is always unfolding even in the smallest choices. Discernment teaches one to recognize those wider and eternal dimensions in everything. Failure to recognize these ramifications and the impact of one's life decisions can lead one far astray and render one oblivious to the influences at work in life. For Origen, the struggles of humankind are set within the larger struggle of the wider creation, including not only the fields, floods, and mountains as in the quotation just above, but also, and far more influentially, the angelic powers both good and evil:

> Those, however, who have moved from their state of primal blessedness, yet not beyond the possibility of return, have been made subject to the rule and governance of those holy and blessed orders whom we have just described; and if they make use of the help of these and become reformed by their precepts and salutary discipline, they may return and be restored to their state of blessedness. . . . We must know, however, that some of those who fell from that beginning of which we have spoken above, have given themselves over so completely to a life of unworthiness and wickedness, that they are not only regarded as unworthy of this instruction and training whereby through the flesh the human race, aided by heavenly powers, is being instructed and trained, but on the contrary become adversaries and opponents of those who are being so trained and disciplined. The result is that all our mortal life is full of struggles and conflicts, since we are resisted and thwarted by those who can see no way back to the better state from which they fell, those, namely, who are called "the devil and his angels," and other orders of wicked beings whom the apostle enumerates among the opposing powers.[10]

Here we can see very directly indeed the mutual implication of discernment as distinguishing the influences at work within one's life and discernment as awareness of the cosmic dimensions of life. The angels, good or evil, are at work within a divine dispensation aimed at providing a "salutary discipline" and training for those capable of receiving it.

It would be anachronistic to think that for Origen one should recognize the influences impinging upon one's consciousness simply in order to decide and act more freely, that is, autonomously, by oneself. Indeed it is precisely turning *away* from fellowship and communion that has stranded rational creatures in their fallen state to begin with. In Origen's view, the blessed spirits have been sent to other creatures to restore in remedial fashion the very intelligence and vision that their loss of communion has deprived them of—and so to conduct them back toward that true freedom and wholeness which is nothing less than a joyful sharing in the common life of the Kingdom of God. Thus, Origen wants his students to discern the intention of the spirit that motivates one's thoughts and desires, not only to be more free of that influence in the case of a wicked spirit, but, on the contrary, to be all the more attentive and available to the guidance of that spirit, should it be sent from heaven. And says Origen, the more that instruction is fed upon, the more delightful it will grow, becoming the very feast that Wisdom has set for all who seek her—conducting such souls to be "instructed in that Jerusalem, the city of the saints" and so to discern at last the true fulfillment of all their thoughts in the heavenly city.[11]

By now we can at least begin to see the inherently eschatological dimension of discernment in Origen. His teaching consistently draws believers onward toward a greater vision of the truth of God. "I wish to turn those who yearn for the spiritual life in Christ away from praying for little and earthly things," he writes in a work on prayer, "and to urge those who read this treatise on to the mysteries of which what I said before were types."[12] Origen's typological exegesis of Scriptures is a consistent expression of his eschatological vision of reality, in which the present state of everything is only a hint or whisper of the consummation to come. This dynamic process by which, Origen believes, God brings the universe onward to its fulfillment—even weaving sinful distortions into the divinely providential design—needs to find its analogue in the discerning life. So Origen would not have his students rest content with "little and earthly things" when the mystery of God's life awaits. Origen suggests that souls who have settled into a narrow literalism or a poverty of low expectations have sunk into a state of barrenness. But "when they perceive the sterility of their own governing reason and the barrenness of their own mind," this discernment opens them to a new fruitfulness: "through persistent prayer they conceive from the Holy Spirit saving words filled with visions of the truth; and they give birth to them."[13]

Here is a fine example of Origen's own fertile analogical imagination at work: just as the divine breath hovered over the primordial silence in creation, just as the Holy Spirit overshadowed the virginal fidelity of Mary in the incarnation, so also the Holy Spirit is arousing and drawing the whole created order to a new state of fruitfulness, the consummate eschatological form of which is not yet apparent. And the transformation of the human soul is set in microcosmic analogy within this entire dynamic; here, significantly, we are dealing primarily with a new noetic fertility leading to an embodiment of truth. What those who pray *conceive* from the Holy Spirit are "saving words filled with visions of the truth." So the initial discerning recognition that one's own true life is fading into sterility can lead to an awakening, eventually to a prayerful glimpse of the mysteriously fecund depths of God's plan; this new discerning, this brief enjoyment of "visions of truth," leads to a process in which the hope one has conceived comes to birth as truth.

Origen likens this divine desire that re-animates and quickens all created life to a kind of "love spell." It is a sort of divine magic that sets the human mind free from the dark enchantments of fear, death, and hopelessness that afflict it. This "spell of love for God" has "power against the harshest sufferings and the deepest tortures."[14] Origen consistently links the power of discernment into the depths of God's mysteries with the intensity of the desire for God at work in a believer. Sometimes, he writes, one may consider the Scriptures longingly and yet little insight comes, for "these considerations seem scarcely able to produce a worthy desire in minds that hope for literal promises."[15] Discernment requires a mind stretched open by hope toward the ever greater mystery of God's promises. And yet, Origen argues, to recover this desire (which is led on by ever mounting hope) is to renew the naturally dynamic character of human being. For when we see some skillful work, "the mind burns to discover" all about it, but

> much more, and beyond all comparison, does the mind burn with unspeakable longing to learn the design of those things which we perceive to have been made by God. This longing, this love has, we believe, undoubtedly been implanted in us by God; and as the eye naturally demands light and vision and our body by its nature desires food and drink, so our mind cherishes a natural and appropriate longing to know God's truth and to learn the causes of things.[16]

The mind naturally loves the truth, for it springs from God and is the very food for which the mind hungers. For this reason, there is necessarily an ascetic dimension to discernment, a cleansing and cracking open of desire so that desire for God may renew its native role within the human journey and guide the mind to the *whole* truth it was created to desire, rather than some smaller more manipulable possession of one's own.

Origen outlines the necessary stages of this process, a retraining of the discerning eye and heart so that the vision of truth and the desire that fructifies that vision might recover their needed integrity and reciprocity. Origen parallels the revelatory wisdom bequeathed under the name of Solomon to a standard Hellenistic division of the sciences. The Book of Proverbs teaches the "moral science" and training in virtue "so that when a person has progressed in discernment and behaviour he may pass on thence to train his natural intelligence [with the Book of Ecclesiastes] and, by distinguishing the causes and natures of things, may recognize the vanity of vanities that he must forsake, and the lasting and eternal things that he ought to pursue."[17] Origen clearly sees a discerning component to each of these first two steps: one needs to progress "in discernment and behaviour" by forming a moral pattern of virtuous life that sets one free from small and self-regarding desire; then one moves to another level of discernment in which one sees the intelligible dimensions of created things and is thus able to distinguish the true purposes of everything and the true good to be pursued. These levels of training prepare one not for the extinction of desire but for its intended consummation, a subject taught in the Song of Songs. For Origen this is the "enoptic" science, the seeing-into science, that might also be called contemplation or an enraptured beholding of the mystical, the hidden beauty of God.

I want to suggest, then, that this third level of discernment in Origen is the implicit goal and dynamism at work within earlier stages of spiritual formation and draws them toward their fulfillment. It is the natural desire of intelligent creatures for the beautiful artistry of the creator; first the desire is purified, then it recovers its ability to distinguish the real goal, and finally it is enkindled by the fire of the divine desire to see into the heart of truth. This final beholding, says Origen, is practiced by Jacob, who "earned the name of Israel from his contemplation of the things of God, and saw the camps of heaven, and beheld the House of God and the angels' paths."[18] How does this loving perception grow to full life? The final step is accomplished, writes Origen, when the soul is aroused by heavenly longing. For then, "having clearly beheld the beauty and the fairness of the Word of God, it falls deeply in love with His loveliness and receives from the Word Himself a certain dart and wound of love."[19] We could say that this mystical and theological level of discernment (i.e., into the hidden truths of the divine life), is the "conception" within human existence of the divine desire; it is the vision of truth that humanity conceives as it glimpses the beauty of God. In pondering what manner of truth this might be, it is worth reflecting that such truth would be indistinguishable from the desire in which it is mediated and which alone can conceive it.

The Desert Elders

Love was at the heart of the desert fathers' world. Whatever diverse motives may have drawn them to the desert, whatever particular struggles occupied them during their sojourn there, the end of all their longings was ultimately expressed as love. The language, the attitudes, and the actions of the desert fathers were filled with this longing, with the desire to be touched and transformed by love.[20]

Douglas Burton-Christie's comprehensive insight alerts us to the link between Origen of Alexandria and the remarkable movement into the deserts of Egypt, Palestine, and Syria in the fourth century. In this period of early Christian history an astonishing range of persons sought a new form of ever deepening conversion, a new way of exposing themselves to the transforming divine desire of which Origen had taught. Living in the wilderness (Gk: *erēmia*) as hermits, practicing withdrawal (Gk: *anachōreō*) from society as anchorites, they sometimes gathered together in small groups to celebrate the Eucharist, and sometimes they formed larger and more established monastic communities. In every case, the goal was to search out the edges and limits of human experience, to discover by rigorous trial the purity, humility, and compassionate desire that would make them more available to God.

Athanasius of Alexandria composed a life of the pioneer of the desert hermits, Antony the Great of Egypt (ca. 251–356), that became exemplary throughout a good deal of the ancient Mediterranean world. Athanasius portrays Antony as bringing Christ's victory to bear upon human existence, restoring human nature to its God-intended purity, self-control, freedom, rationality, and goodness. After decades of contending with the evil spirits who try to undo and deceive him in every possible way, Antony emerges vibrant and balanced, having always kept "his mind filled with Christ and the nobility inspired by him."[21] In this way, Antony becomes the prototype of the spiritual father, whose personal experience has given birth in him to such a profoundly gracious and discerning mind that his very presence transforms and enlightens all around him, offering consolation to the sorrowful and unity to the divided.[22] Athanasius's heroic picture, for all its golden tinting, is nonetheless suggestive of the authentic power of a discerning life within the chaos of the world.

Antony's teaching about the evil spirits is represented as partly in accord with the views of Origen: the fallen spirits, in their bitterness and envy of other rational creatures who might ascend "thither from whence they fell," seek by all means available to them (mostly through the cunning of deceit and negative power of fear) to obstruct the path of believers; "thus there is need of much prayer and of discipline, that when a man has received through the Spirit the gift of discerning spirits, he may have power to recognize their characteristics: which of them are less and which more evil; of what nature is the special pursuit of each, and how each of them is overthrown and cast out."[23] Discernment is conceived of here as entirely a gift of the Spirit (though perhaps only granted to those prepared through "much prayer and discipline" to receive it); and it is envisioned as involving both the skill of identifying the variety of evil spirits, and the skill of knowing how each of them may be "overthrown." Whereas discernment in Origen was equally to sensitize one to the beneficial motions of good spirits, in the *Life of Antony* the emphasis has shifted almost entirely to the battle with demons.

When we turn to the numerous collections of sayings of other desert elders, there are signs of a shift from discernment as distinguishing the spirits to discernment as discretion about the means to combat them and to lead the ascetic life more generally. But before risking an over-tidy categorization of these pungent "words" from the spiritual elders, it will be good simply to consider a few of them and observe the subtle working out of discernment within each one.

In one saying attributed to Antony the Great himself, the saint remarks: "Some have afflicted their bodies by asceticism, but they lack discernment, and so they are far from God."[24] We may grasp something of the meaning of discernment in this saying by considering the story of a rather intense ascetic named Eulogius who ventured with his disciples to visit Abba Joseph, who was renowned for the greatest austerity. Eulogius, however, is greatly disappointed in the life conducted by his host, for there the abba and brothers who welcomed their visitors so hospitably seem to drink wine and never bother to chant the psalms at all. One of Eulogius's disciples, obviously feeling rather splendid about his own master's apparently superior austerity, even comments about it rather rudely, but no one answers him. On their return home, Eulogius and his disciples became lost during the night and had to return to Abba Joseph. They are astonished to hear fervent chanting of psalms (which the abba and brothers had in fact performed in secret while their guests were present), and when they are admitted, the drinking jar they immediately sought is only filled with highly unpalatable sea and river water not wine. "Coming to himself, Eulogius threw himself at the old man's feet" and asked to know the truth of his way of life. Finally, after much importuning, Abba Joseph said:

> "This little bottle of wine is for hospitality, but that water is what the brothers always drink." Then he instructed him [Eulogius] in discernment of thoughts and in controlling all the merely human in himself. So he became more balanced and ate whatever was brought to him and learnt how to work in secret. Then he said to the old man, "Truly, your way of life is indeed genuine."[25]

The humility and genuineness of Abba Joseph, who would never make a show of his piety before others, awaken Eulogius from the fantasy of his own perfection, and "coming to himself," he begins to be open to the deeper goodness at work in others. The result of Abba Joseph's instruction in discernment is that Eulogius "became more balanced." He accepts the moderate and unostentatious asceticism which is "balanced" and is no longer under a compulsion toward grandiosity—even, or perhaps especially, in ascetical greatness.

The same note is sounded by Amma Syncletica, a desert mother, who speaks of discernment as a sense of proportion and stability that is not easily carried away by extravagant impulses: "There is an asceticism which is determined by the enemy and his disciples practice it. So how are we to distinguish between the divine and royal asceticism and the demonic tyranny?

Clearly through its quality of balance."[26] Allied with this sense of moderate judgment is clear-eyed self-awareness and self-understanding: "Abba Poemen said, 'Vigilance, self-knowledge and discernment; these are the guides of the soul.'"[27] Clearly the desert elders envisioned discernment as an integral feature in an unfolding process of spiritual maturation. But while self-awareness is a vital element of this, it is far from self-preoccupation; indeed, compassion and attentiveness to others feature prominently among the direct references to discernment.

Very often the elder with real discernment is the one who seems to have less apparent ardent devotion, and the reversal in these stories happens when more patently pious monks suddenly realize that the elder with discernment was in fact acting with a keen regard for their own or someone else's spiritual needs, even to the extent of being held in disrepute or contempt. In one example, when a group of monks austerely refuse a host's kind offer of drink, one of them surprises the others by accepting; when they begin to rag him for his seeming laxity, he responds:

> "When I get up to offer drink, I am glad when everyone accepts it, since I am receiving my reward; that is the reason, then, that I accepted it, so that he also might gain his reward and not be grieved by seeing that no-one would accept anything from him." When they heard this, they were all filled with wonder and edification at his discretion.[28]

In an analogous story, an elder has for years accepted the blame for a violent act he did not commit, even doing penance for it. When the actual perpetrator finally confesses and the community rushes to apologize to the elder, he replies that he gladly forgives them. But then he adds, "as for staying here I shall not remain here any longer with you, for no-one here had enough discernment to show compassion for me."[29] What develops in the spirituality of the desert is not simply a conception of discernment as discretion and moderation, but rather discernment as understanding what, in any given instance, would really be for the building up and consolation of others and of the community. It is a new dimension of discernment, seeking a way to exercise authentically constructive compassion.

John Cassian

In about 385 a young monk named John Cassian (ca. 360–436) set out with his friend Germanus from Bethlehem for Egypt to learn about the amazing developments in the desert.[30] Thirty years later, Cassian was founding monasteries himself near Marseilles, and he wrote long accounts of his learnings among the desert hermits. The topic of discernment figures

largely throughout Cassian's teaching, which he presents in the form of dialogues among the desert elders.

In the second of Cassian's *Conferences,* which is directly on the subject
of "discretion," Abba Moses begins by quoting the passage from 1 Corinthians 12, referring to the gift of "the discerning of spirits." He then comments:

> The gift of discretion is no earthly or paltry matter but a very great
> bestowal of the divine grace. Unless a monk has sought this grace with
> utter attentiveness and, with sure judgment, possesses discretion con-
> cerning the spirits that enter into him, it is inevitable that, like a per-
> son wandering in the dark of night and in deep shadows, he will not
> only fall into dangerous ditches and down deep slopes but will even
> frequently go astray on level and straight ways.[31]

Moses' dramatic imagery (of benighted stumbling into peril) suggests
that while discernment may well be seen as divine charism, it is certainly a
universally *needed* gift for anyone undertaking an ascetic life. This is a point
worth pursuing, I believe, because it suggests something akin to a view Origen had emphasized: humankind is created for divine communion, and
while the capacity to return to that relationship is entirely a divine gift, it is
also profoundly and universally needed if humanity is ever to recover its
true form of existence. Discernment as distinguishing between spirits is thus
an element in the wider restoration of humanity's capacity to discern the
cosmic order and significance of all things—a discerning vision that flows
from the renewal of human companionship with God.

In this sense, then, we will see discernment of spirits discussed in Cassian
as a prerequisite to a more general (and more profound) discretion, that is,
a freedom from impulsive excesses and therefore an ability to discern the
proper order and ways of proceeding, concerning both matters small and
great. As Cassian continues the story of Abba Moses, the elder offers his
teaching on discretion by pointing away from himself to Antony the Great
(surely an example of freedom from self-regard in a teacher). All through
one long night, says Moses, Antony was addressed by a wearyingly unending series of elders who each thought he had the key to the ascetic life and
had found "sure steps to the summit of perfection" (II.2.1). The range of
proposals is interesting in itself, including fasts and vigils, contempt of the
world, solitude, and the duties of love and hospitality. At last Antony
speaks, agreeing that all these are very "necessary and useful for those who
thirst for God and who desire to come to him," but the fact is that even
those who are most advanced in these practices "are so suddenly deceived
that they are unable to bring to a satisfactory conclusion the work that they

have begun" (II.2.4). They are deceived, says Antony, because they lack discretion,

> which avoids excess of any kind and teaches the monk always to proceed along the royal road and does not let him be inflated by virtues on the right hand—that is, in an excess of fervor to exceed the measure of a justifiable moderation by a foolish presumption—nor let him wander off to the vices on the left hand because of a weakness for pleasure—that is, under the pretext of controlling the body, to grow soft because of a contrary lukewarmness of spirit. (II.2.4)

Significantly, there is no reference to good or evil spirits in this definition, only the suggestion that careening from the moderate mean into one extreme or the other necessarily involves one in various forms of distortion and falseness. Indeed this warning note about illusions and cloaked motivations is remarkably pervasive, and perhaps this is the link back to the need for discerning the spirits, since the evil spirits are in all writers characterized by mendacity, cunning, and deceit. In that case, we would indeed have a link between the references in the passage to self-inflated and foolish presumption (lack of discretion) on the one hand, and, on the other, to the beclouded mind of the would-be ascetic, easily mesmerized by deceptive pretexts and counterfeit motivations (inability to distinguish spirits). Thus discerning the "royal road" of "justifiable moderation" and discerning the spirits would be integrally related and equally necessary forms of clarity.

Cassian follows Antony's teaching with four telling examples offered by Abba Moses in corroboration of this view of discernment. In the first, a zealous solitary named Heron is said to have fallen prey to the devil's delusions because "he possessed little of the virtue of discretion and preferred to be governed by his own understanding of things rather than to obey the counsels and conferences of the brothers and the institutes of our forebears" (II.5.2). Discretion here is realized precisely in the communal wisdom that guards one from the particular idiosyncracies and excesses most subject to demonic manipulation. In this instance, Heron's personal tendencies toward great zeal and inflexible rigor secretly conduct him into a flattering self-regard, easily practiced upon by the enemy. "Deceived by this presumption, he welcomed with the highest veneration the angel of Satan as an angel of light" (II.5.3). The demon brings Heron's proclivities to a fever pitch by urging him to throw himself into a well from which his heroic virtue would eventually bring him forth completely unharmed. So "the deluded man hurled himself" into the well during the night "with the intention of demonstrating how deserving his virtue was upon emerging unharmed from there" (II.5.4).

When some of the brothers found him the next day and pulled him out with great difficulty, he was already near death and succumbed three days later; "but what is worse than this, he went along so stubbornly with his own deception that he could not be persuaded, even when faced with death, that he had been deluded by the cleverness of demons" (II.5.4). This story illustrates with a satisfying grimness the very core of Antony's definition of discernment as discretion: Heron is the classic case of one deluded by the excessive virtues of the right hand, so illustriously extreme in his asceticism that his virtue, instead of authentically opening him to God, becomes an obscuring fog of self-congratulation. Without the discretion of a justified moderation, mediated through the teaching and discernment of the community, Heron easily falls prey to demonic temptations to ever more extreme acts, and is no longer able to see reality—blinded as he is by his own stubborn magnificence.

The second story offers a variation on the first: two brothers carried away with ardent intentions to fast and not being "sufficiently motivated by prudent discretion" are discovered by desert nomads, nearly dead of starvation. When they are offered food, one of the brothers stubbornly refuses to compromise his fast and dies, but the other, "with the aid of discretion, corrected what he had thoughtlessly and foolishly begun" (II.6.2, 3). Significantly, Abba Moses concludes this story by pointing out that the discretion needed in this case was not only the wisdom to forsake what was "foolishly begun" but to recognize and receive the "divine inspiration" at work in the nomads who, remarkably, "had offered [the brothers] bread instead of the sword" (II.6.3). Again, we note the intermingling of an important relational dimension in this concept of discretion; part of what is needed in true moderation and discretion is the openness and humility to receive the good of another.

The third and fourth illustrative tales take up a different temptation to grandiosity: in these cases we have ascetics who are, perhaps unwittingly, led to succor the flame of self-regard by a mounting fascination with profound visions and revelations. In the first case, the man is carried along by the apparently wondrous gifts he had been given, and the honor showed him by this demon cloaked "in the guise of angelic brightness": "When these revelations were being received, his [the demon's] light took the place of a lamp in the man's cell every night" (II.7). Finally, when he was fully hooked by the glory of his stature, the man is ordered by the demon to offer his son as a sacrifice to God, "that by this sacrifice he might equal the dignity of the patriarch Abraham"; "so taken in was he by this idea that he would have committed the murder" except that the son saw him sharpening his knife "with unaccustomed care" and "fled away terrified" (II.7). In the second story a man is led into heresy and schism by the devil, who "wishing to draw him by frequent visions to believe in future deceptions, had, like a messenger of truth, revealed things that were perfectly true" (II.8.2). In both cases, the gifts of visions and magisterial acuity run parallel to the ascetical puffing up in the first two stories. Once more, then, we can see the close link between the need for discernment of spirits and the pursuit of authentically discreet moderation, grounded in humility. "True discretion is not obtained except by true humility," says Abba Moses at the conclusion of these four tales.

We have already seen hints regarding the intrinsically relational character of discretion, and this hallmark of humility highlights it even more clearly. For what Moses emphasizes, in Cassian's account, is humility as an antidote to arrogant presumption (leading to excess and grandiosity)—humility, in other words, as a willingness to place one's gifts and weaknesses *within* the community's life in God: "for by no other vice does the devil draw and lead a monk to so sudden a death as when he persuades him to neglect the counsels of the elders and to trust in his own judgment and his own understanding" (II.11.7). I think there is more here than a simple two-heads-are-better-than-one maxim; it has to do with a fundamental shaping of character, such that one longs to discover the truth and goodness of life precisely through the truth and goodness of friendship with others. The elders recognize both a safeguard and a positive gain in this discretion as humility.

Cassian's teaching on discretion portrays this form of discernment as the rescuing, truth-bearing, compassion of God at work within the community.

On one side, it opens up the lonely secret corners of the soul to the friendship of others; their presence to the soul frees it from the lurking and isolating power of the evil one: "for his harmful counsels hold sway in us as long as they lie concealed in our heart" (II.10.3). And more positively, this baring of one's heart to another kindles a new trust and compassion within the fabric of the world. In fact Abba Moses saves his most withering criticism for elders who are insufficiently gentle and encouraging to those who have laid open their souls for guidance. In one of the longest stories in the work, Abba Moses tells of a young monk who diligently confesses his impulsive desires to an elder. Instead of encouragement and healing, the elder "reprimanded him in the harshest language and declared that anyone who could be titillated by this kind of sin and desire was a wretched person" and unworthy to be a monk; he then dismissed the young man "in a state of terrible hopelessness, disconsolate to the point of deadly sadness" (II.13.4).

But when Abba Apollos, "the most upright of the elders," discovers the young man in despair, he consoles him and asserts "that he himself was disturbed every day by the same impulsive urges and seething emotions," and assures him that the attack would not be overcome "so much by intense effort as by the mercy and grace of the Lord" (II.13.6). Abba Apollos then rushed off to find the elder who had betrayed the young man's trust, and prayed that the elder would be afflicted by the same temptations for which he had so castigated the monk. Very shortly the elder raced "like a madman" from his cell, and Abba Apollos drew near questioningly: "Where are you rushing to and what is so childishly disturbing you that you have forgotten the gravity of old age?" (II.13.8). Apollos, seeing the old man's agony, calls off the demonic attack and delivers a lengthy rebuke ("learn to be compassionate toward those who struggle. . . . encourage them mildly and gently") that ends appropriately with a consoling reminder that no one could endure without the protecting and loving grace of God (II.13-11). The real drama, emotion, and crisis of this story very powerfully frame Cassian's teaching on discretion. It portrays this form of discernment as in no way a merely individualized virtue to be sought by adepts, but as the rescuing, truth-bearing, compassion of God at work within the community. It preserves humanity from isolation and excess, and it embodies within the usual structures of human relationships a new practice of communal honesty and affection that might well be said to reflect something of the divine truth and goodness.

My hunch is that we have begun to see in Cassian the signs of a gradual shift in the focus of discernment, a shift I would outline in three phases: first there is the more cosmic Origenian distinguishing between good and evil spirits; next there comes a narrower focus on recognizing only the demonic impulses leading to either the extreme of zealotry or the extreme of laxity; and finally to discernment as discretion, a broader more virtue-like capacity to find a balance in one's desires by holding them within the community's wisdom and compassion.[32]

John Climacus

Before we turn westward, it will be good to consider briefly the teaching on discernment that emerges in the generations following the desert elders. (The greatest figures in the immediately following generation are undoubtedly Evagrius Ponticus [345–399], who was one of Cassian's teachers, and Diadochus of Photike [mid-400s], both of whom we will turn to in later chapters.) Our last landmark figure among the Greeks was abbot of the monastery on Mount Sinai, having lived for forty years before that as a hermit. John Climacus (ca. 579-649) wrote the *Ladder of Divine Ascent* near the end of his life, and it crystallizes a good deal of the East's teaching about the ascetical life, becoming in later years the most widely used such handbook throughout Eastern Orthodoxy.

Employing the image of Jacob's ladder stretching between heaven and earth (Genesis 28:12), John structures his teaching as thirty steps ascending into the heaven of contemplation and union with God.[33] The first three "rungs" of the *Ladder* discuss the need for a break with the structures of the world; chapters four through twenty-six cover an ascending series of necessary virtues and freedom from vices, culminating in a final transitional chapter on discernment; the concluding four chapters are on stillness, prayer, dispassion, and love. Clearly discernment, then, functions in a pivotal role for Climacus (so surnamed in fact for his book); in his scheme, discernment reaches down to the roots of life, guiding Christians toward spiritual maturity, and it also stretches upward in greater and greater clarity toward the light of heaven. As one commentator remarks, all the virtues John teaches are not simply human character traits but divine attributes, in which humanity participates.[34] The role of discernment is to allow believers to sense the reality of these divine patterns of existence, so that their powerful holiness can permeate and transform human existence.

Accordingly, John begins his chapter on discernment with a comprehensive definition that highlights the evolving significance of discernment at different points in the spiritual journey:

> Among beginners, discernment is real self-knowledge; among those midway along the road to perfection, it is a spiritual capacity to distinguish unfailingly between what is truly good and what in nature is opposed to the good; among the perfect, it is a knowledge resulting from divine illumination, which with its lamp can light up what is dark in others. To put the matter generally, discernment is—and is recognized to be—a solid understanding of the will of God in all times, in all places, in all things; and it is found only among those who are pure in heart, in body, and in speech. . . . Discernment is an uncorrupted conscience. It is pure perception. (229).

John's definition is extraordinarily far-reaching and reveals the inner integrity of the several stages of discernment. Thus what could seem to be merely disparate skills or practices are always in motion toward the fullness of divine illumination; discernment as a virtue of the conscience (described as discretion and moderation in Cassian) is really a developing sensitivity to the divine life, the divine will and desire: "Let our God-directed conscience be our aim and rule in everything so that, knowing how the wind is blowing, we may set our sails accordingly" (230). The image is particularly apt. The Christian community in the ark of the church learns how to judge the right set of the sails and achieve maximum availability to the winds of grace. I wish especially to note this vision of the discerning life well, because when we come to consider (at the end of this book) the theology of divine illumination, Climacus's conception will be a useful corrective; for modern interpretations of the illumination theory of knowledge have proved, perhaps unconsciously, to be all too narrowly focused on the issue of epistemological certainty. But here we can see an understanding of illumination that grounds it not in concerns over justified warrants for beliefs but in the upward-reaching sensitivity of the conscience, allowing the divine pattern of life to commune with human knowing.

I think that what allows for this integrated vision of discernment (and hence the seeds for a properly theological conception of knowledge) is that the divine willing and knowing, love and truth, have not been abstracted from one another. Rather, Climacus senses that human perception relates to these aspects of the divine life differently at different stages. This means that for Climacus, the early stages of a discerning life must reach out for an understanding of God's ways that is rooted in a sensitivity to the divine *will,* for love can sense the divine pattern of life even when the soul cannot yet know the radiant *truth* of that life. Yet that illumination of the understanding, that coming to share in the divine self-knowing and truth, is not an *alternative* that must eventually wholly *replace* attunement to the divine will; John seems to hold rather that this growing radiance or clarity about the divine truth is the way God brings to light, now in the mind, that more "touching" awareness of God's ways which was already obscurely sensed by loving obedience to God's will.

> Whatever you do, however you live . . . let it be your rule and practice to ask if what you do is in accordance with the will of God. When we novices, for instance, do something and the humility deriving from that action is not added to the possessions of our souls, then the action, great or small, has not been undertaken in deference to the divine will. For those of us who are untried recruits in the life of the spirit, growth in humility comes out of doing what the Lord wants; for those who have reached midway along that route, the test is an end to inner conflict; and for the perfect there is increase and, indeed, a wealth of divine light. (242)

John thus proposes a test for each stage of spiritual discernment. For the basic level, the measure that indicates a true discernment of God's will is "growth in humility." This freedom from self-regard is the first sign of one's consciousness growing in grace, for one exists more and more toward the divine other, increasingly sensitive to "what the Lord wants" and adept at acting "in deference to the divine will." But as one advances, the divine will is less an *object* to be discerned, less over against the self, and there "is an end to inner conflict." At last, "the perfect" find their own dawning unity with the divine will now integrated with God's own reality, radiant as truth to the mind. Or, as John himself puts it more summarily, "Our eyes are a light to all the body. Discernment of the virtues is a light to all the mind" (244).

John Climacus offers us some final glimpses of this illuminative stage of discernment. This, he says, comes about when the divine will is no longer only a rule to which one submits in humility, but a light leading the mind into a fuller apprehension of virtue; this is the case of "the man who through illumination has come to possess God within himself both in things requiring immediate action and in those that take time" (245). In such a case, the divine will now resides "within" the soul, granting an illumined understanding regarding both short-term and long-term courses of action (or perhaps regarding matters for both action and contemplation). In the initial case, the mind has little direct cognition of the divine will, but through obedience and humility pursues the course of virtue. But for the one who "through illumination has come to possess God within himself," John foresees not simply an appropriate reliance upon virtue but a life springing afresh in each moment from the very fountain of virtue, a life alive and *intelligent* with the very ground and source of every virtue:

> There is the way of stillness and the way of obedience. And in addition to these there is the way of rapture, the way of the mind mysteriously and marvelously carried into the light of Christ. There are virtues, and there are begetters of virtues, and it is with these latter that the wise man has his dealings. The teachers of these parent virtues is God himself in his proper activity. (249)

The teaching of John Climacus holds all the stages of the spiritual journey in one compass. John forewarns us against any hard divisions between apparently active virtues and more contemplative ones, and he envisions discernment in various forms as active in all cases in the form appropriate to the needs of believers in any given state. Perhaps more than any thinker after Origen he highlights the way in which everyday acts of choice and moral deliberation are already translucent with the cosmic radiance of divine truth, beckoning believers from obedience and humility on toward rapture and communion.

THREE

The Historical Landscape of Discernment: Middle Ages to Modernity

Bernard of Clairvaux and Richard of St. Victor

Turning to medieval Latin thought about discernment we would of course want to note those two important carriers of early Christian wisdom about *discretio,* the *Rule of St. Benedict* (ca. 540) and Gregory the Great (ca. 540–604).[1] (The massively significant figure of Augustine [354–430], so influential in the development of Western thought, will appear in chapter 9, on discernment and illumination.) Though not a Benedictine himself, Gregory greatly furthered the role of the monastic life in the Christianization of Europe. Both Gregory and the growing influence of the Benedictines work within the general thinking about discernment we found in Cassian. Benedict envisaged the monastic community as, in many ways, a school of discretion as well as a school of charity—with the community focused on the moderation, balance, and the careful exercise of stability of life that had come to characterize discretion. Gregory's vast typological interpretations of Scripture held open an entire world of interior exploration and examination; the discernment of one's motivations and the pursuit of discretion in one's actions and judgments were intrinsic to his thought.

Over half a millennium later, we find the theme of discretion treated with a new artfulness and insight in two highly figural texts that allow the "personality" of Discretion to shine: the *Parables* of Bernard of Clairvaux (1090–1153) and the *Twelve Patriarchs* of his younger contemporary, Richard of St. Victor (?–1173).[2] Among the less-well-known works of the great Cistercian abbot, the *Parables* give us a taste of Bernard's playful side as a teacher of monks. As John Bunyan would do centuries later in *Pilgrim's Progress,* Bernard distilled the narrative world of the Christian gospel and the spiritual journey into a series of appealing allegorical adventures set in the context of his contemporaries—in his case, a world of kings, castles, knights, and even distressed damsels. Richard of St. Victor, teaching at one of the great conventual schools in Paris (possibly in the very year of Bernard's death), writes more studiously and develops a systematic analysis of the way to contemplation. Yet Richard too is highly imaginative, expanding traditional spiritual readings of the later Genesis stories; in this way he allows the narrative process of Scripture to energize an entire epistemological and spiritual structure. In Richard's case, the virtues and spiritual states he examines are not personified as courtly figures but as biblical characters: Jacob (the rational soul), his wife Leah (affection), Leah's handmaid Zelpha (sense knowledge), Jacob's other wife Rachel (reason) and her handmaid Bala (imagination), and their twelve sons and one daughter. The drama these figures enact portrays the journey toward the last-born child, Benjamin, ecstatic contemplation, whose mother Rachel (reason) comes to the end of her mortal life in giving him birth.

Both Bernard and Richard see the spiritual journey as fraught with crisis and the potential for grave misdirection. And in both writers, the figure who arrives to sort out the confusion and guide the characters toward the right path is Discretion. At first glance, it could appear that Bernard and Richard conceive of discernment as a merely negative virtue, a necessary check upon the ardor of more spirited virtues. We can see something of this dialectical view of discretion in two important passages from Bernard's sermons *On the Song of Songs*. Noting that true authority and true humility are only present in those who have "perfect discretion, the mother of the virtues," Bernard comments: "Without the fervor of charity the virtue of discretion is lifeless, and intense fervor goes headlong without the curb of discretion. Praiseworthy the man then who possesses both, the fervor that enlivens discretion, the discretion that regulates fervor."[3] This balance between fervor and discretion seems, in Bernard's view, to be a prerequisite for authentic spiritual growth.

In another sermon Bernard again posits for discernment a balancing role: "Zeal without knowledge is insupportable. Therefore where zeal is enthusiastic, there discretion, that moderator of love, is especially necessary. Because zeal without knowledge always lacks efficacy, is wanting in usefulness, and all too often is harmful."[4] Bernard, in good Augustinian fashion, is highly aware that human love all too easily becomes misdirected, self-regarding, and therefore unable to perceive the consequences for others. Discernment as discretion therefore acts, much as Cassian had suggested, as a clarity and wise judgment about the ends and means that love desires. But we should probably not take this in too utilitarian a sense. Bernard continues: "Discretion regulates every virtue, order assigns proportion and beauty, and even permanence. . . . Discretion therefore is not so much a virtue as a moderator and guide of the virtues, a director of the affections, a teacher of right living. Take it away and virtue becomes vice, and natural affection itself a force that disturbs and destroys nature."[5] In saying that apart from discretion nature destroys itself, the Cistercian abbot points unmistakably to its practical role in preserving spiritual life; but in arguing that discretion orders the spiritual life toward proportion and beauty, Bernard hints at the higher, transfiguring role discretion plays—distilling into the fervor of human seeking a touch of that wise ordering of all things whose ultimate reality is the beauty and logic of the divine life itself.

So when we turn to the allegorical tales of Bernard and Richard, we should be able to glimpse at least some sign of this higher, heavenly ordering aspect of discretion, as well as its more regulative and negative aspect of moderating earthly fervors. While we cannot examine the full panoply of virtues, vices, natural capacities, and graces personified in the narratives of the two authors, it will be helpful at least to give an indication of the sequence—so that as we discuss discretion in each case we can perceive its context. In Bernard's case, I simply offer a conflated outline, since the sequence varies slightly in each of the eight parables:

Bernard	Richard
Fear	Fear
Hope	Grief
Desire	Hope
Piety	Desire for Justice
Prudence	Imagination of Sensible Reality
Temperance	Contemplation of Intelligibles
Discretion	Abstinence
Boldness	Patience
Joy	Joy
Justice	Hatred of Vice
Reason	Shame
Prayer	**Discretion**
Charity	Contemplative Ecstasy
Peace	
Praise	

As we can see, discretion comes in at the middle turning point in Bernard and at the final crisis and transition in Richard. Bernard gives his parables a cosmic ring with overtones of the fall and an ongoing struggle for souls between God and Satan; he sets the monastic path firmly within a soteriological narrative. Richard is more concerned with the ordering of the affections so that they mature into true virtues and conduct the soul toward its desired consummation in divine contemplation.

What is the crisis that discretion comes to resolve in each writer? Bernard casts discretion very much in the role inherited from desert monasticism—the wise moderator both of excessive zeal and deficient devotion. The parables often begin with the fall of an individual or community, much grieved and mourned by God who sends servants to seek the lost. The first to arrive is usually Fear, who finds a truly abject child of God, all the more pitiable for remaining strangely unaware of his real state. In the "Story of the King's Son," Fear finds the boy in a "deep dungeon":

> He was covered with the prison dirt of sin and held fast by the bonds and chains of evil habit. He was unhappy, but unmindful, and though badly treated was still secure and smiling. With words and with blows Fear urged him to get out and return, but he so upset the poor boy that he fell to the ground, lying as one near death.[6]

The extremity of Fear's remedy looks to be nearly as bad as the disease! Bernard doubtless has a little fun here, perhaps at his own and many another's shocked response and prostration at the first moment of awakening to sin. The extreme gyration he paints is significant, however, for it foreshadows a central theme in all the parables, namely the desperate need humanity has for stability and wisdom (both of which find their strongest representative in Discretion)—lest the spiritual journey career perilously from one misadventure to another. Fortunately for the King's son, the next servant to find him is Hope: "He raises the boy's head and wipes his eyes and face with the cloth of consolation." As the boy awakens he begins to recognize the tender kindness of his comforter and asks if it is Hope: "Yes, I am Hope. I was sent by your Father to be your help, and not to leave your side until I bring you to your Father's house."[7] As moving as the scene is (and Bernard develops it quite extensively), Hope precipitously puts the lad astride a horse named Desire who gallops off wildly. "Borne along in headlong flight, they escaped; but danger remained, for they left without measure and without counsel."[8]

At this point a recurring trio of figures arrives to reorganize things: Prudence, Temperance, and Discretion. Together, these three provide the measure and counsel needed to moderate the wild swings between Fear and Hope. In a later parable, Discretion again appears in relation to Hope as a guardian of the aspirations and practices of Hope, lest they wander unwisely. While Discretion is rarely mentioned in the later struggles of the parables (usually some form of climactic conflict with evil in which Charity and Prayer play crucial roles), clearly Bernard doesn't think that anyone is likely to make sound progress at all apart from Discretion. Perhaps if we recollect that the Cistercian is, after all, personifying the affections and virtues of the human person, we can see Bernard assigning Discretion a primarily regulative function: it is not, in his view, the thrilling steed of Desire nor the heroic champion Justice, but it is the necessary good sense by which any of the virtues can flourish properly and so, at last, respond constructively to the help God sends. In a sense, I would argue, Bernard tells the parables from Discretion's own point of view. By letting his readers in on the larger picture that his primary characters cannot yet perceive, Bernard fosters the very sense of perspective, the ability to take the longer view, and so not be driven headlong by the moment's dominant experience—the very skills, that is, that discretion teaches.

Richard of St. Victor, by reserving the explicit role of discretion for later in his allegory, assigns it a more obviously momentous and determinative role. Indeed, the crisis to which discretion responds is both grave and troubling. For Richard has envisioned the journey of the soul toward divine communion as encountering a threat both from evil and, startlingly, from good. We might picture Richard's scheme as a dialectic in which the mind swings between a sequence of capacities toward the still point of true balance, self-knowledge, and the moment of complete availability to God—the birth of the last child, Benjamin, ecstatic contemplation. The whole journey is set within the framework of the sisterly and often conflictual relationship between Leah and Rachel.

Leah, representing the affections, needs the complementarity of Rachel, representing reason, in order to bring the affections to that ordered moderation which is true virtue. Conversely, Rachel/Reason needs the support of the virtuous powers of Leah in order to reach truth. The Holy Spirit draws each to fruitfulness, but only as they moderate and inform each other; and this is particularly important when the soul's affections are in danger of being carried away by desire for praise, "when the soul is affected in the proclamation of her own praise and is delighted in the perverse aura of popular favor," then reason must moderate the desire:

> The Holy Spirit in no way makes fruitful a mind that, when advised by reason, does not moderate appetite for vain praise. And so it is one Spirit who enriches each sister with an abundance of offspring since the same Spirit both illumines reason for cognition of truth and inflames affection for love of virtue. Therefore reason urges affection to moderate appetite for human favor under reason's guidance.[9]

I want to suggest, then, that while Discretion per se is not "born" (as Joseph) until much later in the sequence, the role of discretion as moderation and a judicious poise between swings of the soul's pendulum is in fact provisionally present all along the way.

Richard thus builds up a picture of harmonization and mutual support among the virtues, desires, and capacities of the soul. Each achievement of complementarity among the various "offspring" brings the soul a little more peace, clarity, and self-knowledge. As an example we can see the sons of Rachel's maid learning to work in consort with the sons of Leah's maid for the good of all:

> This is that house or city, viz., our conscience, in which the riches of spiritual goods abound when the sons of the above-mentioned hand-maids guard it with alert care: that is, when Dan and Naphtali [imagination of material and spiritual realities] are extremely busy with establishing the peace of the citizens and when Gad and Asher [abstinence and patience] courageously work in overcoming enemies. (xxxvi)

We could think of discretion as the gradual access within the soul of wisdom about itself, about how to balance its powers in ways that bring out the best attributes of each, so preserving the soul from running blindly toward extremes.

There is a deep and abiding potential, however, for the soul to miss the authentic still point of true balance. For each time discretion achieves a more refined level of harmony, there is a correspondingly more refined danger, a more polished counterfeit that falsely appears as the real balance that the soul desires. The danger is that the soul will falter in this most refined fashion, and so be held frustratingly off-kilter and always exhaustingly just off balance. Richard foreshadows this crisis by pointing out how easily a false intoxication with exterior praise is mistaken for true inner joy (xxxviii), and how easily a false self-righteousness is mistaken for true zeal for God (xli). With unmistakably painful personal familiarity (Richard at one point served as a long-suffering prior under an irascible superior), Richard points out how "many persons, because without doubt they are acting in a spirit of fury, think that they act with zeal of uprightness, and the things they enforce in truth from hatred of men, they think or pretend that they practice because of hatred of vices" (xli). In each case, the tragedy is that the authentic dynamism of the spirit, longing for God, is indeed moving the soul, but because of a lack of discretion the soul just misses the true still point of fulfillment:

> We know that the mind that fluctuates through various desires, which the tumult of worldly cares still disturbs, is not admitted to that inner joy and is not drinking from that torrent of pleasure. . . . Therefore he who desires or believes he is to be intoxicated by that cup of true

sobriety ought to restrain the fluctuation of the heart and to gather together the movement of the affections and thoughts with a view to the longing for one true joy. This truly is that blessed earth [the Promised Land], viz., tranquil stability of mind, when the mind is totally gathered within itself and is unalterably fixed on the one longing for eternity. (xxxviii)

In the case of counterfeit zeal, the desire for purity has been ever so subtly but cruelly misdirected—hatred of others has supplanted an authentic anger at vice. In the case of misdirected desires, the passionate longing for heaven has been subverted into a craving for various lesser desires that permanently prevent it from ever finding truly "tranquil stability of mind."

Richard's masterstroke, however, is to suggest that when the mind is able to touch the Promised Land of contemplation, "at least hurriedly and furtively by means of rare excursions," then "suddenly it receives a marvelous fortitude against all perils" because it "grows strong in the hatred of all vices" (xxxix). In other words, true inner joy and true zeal against vice emerge in mutual support of one another, and conduct the soul toward the authentic fulfillment of each and hence toward its goal. Again, as usual, this achievement of balance gives birth to a new level of self-awareness. For the last child born to Leah is a daughter, Dina, who represents honest shame (as opposed to mere embarrassment felt at damage to one's reputation). For Richard, true shame helps to balance the immediately preceding virtue and bring the soul that much closer to the desired still point: "for she [Dina/true shame] moderates the fury of a zealous soul much in every way, when the soul discovers in itself something by reason of which it should feel ashamed" (xlix). True shame, or conscience, as Richard eventually calls her, reveals to the soul the very faults in itself that it would like to condemn so emphatically in others; it is easy to see here how close we have come to discretion in the desert elders' sense of true humility in self-knowledge—and therefore a tender-hearted forbearance with the weaknesses of others.

As I have been warning, however, this brings us to the final danger point in Richard's view, for nothing is easier than for honest shame to be diverted by a growing preoccupation with public praise and honor for uprightness: "For since the beauty of shamefacedness is commended, praised and loved by nearly everyone, when Dina goes out, deserts her innermost dwelling, and quickly forgets the memory of her infirmities which was accustomed to make her humble, suddenly the praises of men embrace her and ruin her while they charm her with favors" (li). Alluding to Genesis 34 and the story of the rape of Dinah by Shechem, Richard thus speaks of the conscience being violently defiled by a preoccupation with public praise that overwhelms the soul. This sets loose a terrible new disorder in the soul, threatening to knock it completely off balance, swinging forever again between extremes—terrible inner remorse feeding a newly aroused obsession with the faults of others, leading either to pride at one's superiority or bitter annoyance at one's shortcomings, and so on and on.

> Often when we feel much shame because of our infirmities we begin to wonder if others feel these infirmities in themselves, and it seems that a certain kind of consolation comes to us if we discover in our degradation at least that we have companions. . . . [W]e begin to search out the pursuits of others more inquisitively, frequently survey-ing now a face, now a gesture and the deportment of the whole body, and we begin gladly to learn more about their secrets from the reports of others. (li)

Richard's psychological insight is striking. Here is an utterly unbalanced form of self-knowledge that does not grow out of a pacific desire for God but an itchy envy and judgmental degradation of self and others. Not sur-prisingly, Richard recounts the terrible revenge taken by Dinah's brothers in Genesis 34 as the continuing, violent, imbalance rocking the soul to ever greater extremes.

Richard has portrayed the inner turmoil of a soul in failure. The soul has been afflicted by a terrible sense of damage: "how much pain do you think pierces through the mind when it carefully considers the evil that it endured, the evil in which it engaged?" (lx). Dinah's brothers who inflict this pain are Simeon and Levi, whom Richard had earlier identified as the grief of peni-tence and hope of forgiveness; yet now, all unbalanced, they violently afflict the soul and direct it amiss—"fierce avengers . . . if only they had been as discreet as they were strong!" (lvi). These two brothers, says Richard, now begin to reproach and attack the soul with such vehemence that the mind falls prey to terrible self-punishment; soon the soul is undertaking all man-ner of extreme ventures that it could never complete, giving way to "immoderate sadness" and "indiscriminate abstinence," which destroy both the body and the mind (lvii). These "indiscreet" counsels that undo the soul bring to full realization Richard's admonition from the beginning, that all the affections and capacities must grow into ordered moderation in order to reach true virtue—or else they slide inexorably toward a vicious state: "And so in this way virtues are turned into vices if they are not moderated by discretion" (lxvi).

Thus at last, out of the bitterness of experience and painfully acquired self-knowledge, is born Joseph: "although he is born late, [he] is loved more than the others by his father. For who does not know that the true good of the soul can be neither acquired nor preserved without discretion?" (lxvii). In five swift chapters, Richard shows to full advantage how the main threads in his analysis of discretion are now woven together. Intriguingly, this picture of the full tapestry turns out to be more multidimensional than might have been expected; *discretio* in Richard emerges as a more full-bodied power of discernment than we saw in Bernard's treatment of the term. Let me briefly highlight the chief features that Richard now articulates.

First, discretion emerges only through a painful paradox: nothing is more needed for the full flourishing of the spiritual life. But on the other hand, nothing is less accessible to the inexperienced, for the wise governance and use of each virtue must be "learned by long use" before the soul develops a measured sense of the whole. While this insight is perhaps somewhat frustrating, Richard seems to offer it with a consoling air: Joseph's elder brothers "discover, as it were, by the ignominy of disgrace" how much they need to learn true discretion, and their immature adventures "beyond their powers" lead them to seek and find it by all the "more attentive pursuit" (lxvii).

Second, Richard suggests (in accord with earlier writers) that discretion is grounded in an ability to discern the spirits. For Joseph (discretion) is, after all, an interpreter of dreams: "in the very moment of temptation, true discretion discerns future dangers from their nature within the very phantasms of suggestions . . . [and] detects the ambush of imminent evils according to the confession of their own thoughts" (lxviii). Richard seems particularly aware here of the deceptive quality of these "phantasms" and how, necessarily, they require an insight that is itself not subject to the blandishments that other dimensions of the soul might find attractive or compelling. Perhaps this stability is the correlate of that still point of self-knowledge which we saw Richard advocating before; discernment of spirits would, in this sense, represent a freedom from the pendular swings that lead to exaggeration in the functioning of the other virtues. Richard does seem to have this in mind when he remarks that the other brothers (virtues) find Joseph's admonitions "excessively severe" and unappealingly devoid of the grateful applause that often secretly excites their usual efforts in virtue:

> Often the brothers of Joseph, when attempting something great while "well done, well done" is shouted on every side, are accustomed to extend their hands not only to useless but also to impossible efforts. Indeed, frequently affection of the soul is unbridled because of such shouting by flatterers, resulting in an immoderate audacity of presumption. Or rather, many times it is led by depraved intention of the mind to the crime of hypocrisy and is cast down. (lxix)

If the virtues are, in Richard's view, nothing less than ordered and moderated affections of the soul (vii), then whatever tends to excite those affections toward what is "useless" or "impossible," toward an "audacity of presumption," will eventually lead to a dulling, distorting, and depraving of intentions. Here again we can see the close link between discernment as distinguishing the spirits and discernment as discretion; recognizing the deluding voices, including perhaps especially the desire for public approbation, is integral to making wise judgments about proper and self-aware courses of action. Without the development of this skill, discretion and prudence degenerate, warns Richard, into mere hypocrisy, a harsh castigation of self and others that only feeds upon inescapable feelings of failure and inadequacy.

Richard seems, however, to recover the much earlier, Origenian, view that this discernment of spirits is not of malign influences only, but also of gracious ones. Indeed, the intimate kinship Richard sees between discretion and contemplation, between Joseph and Benjamin as brothers of the same mother (Rachel/Reason), testifies to the upward momentum of discretion in Richard's treatment. Discretion for Richard includes this positive openness to the upward call of God. It may include mundane tasks related to discipline and good ordering of life, but it does so in order to attend the more effectively to those inspirations and touches that lead the mind toward its consummate state in the contemplation of God. So discretion should assist the soul to examine carefully "by what thoughts it is attacked more, by what affections it is more frequently touched" (lxx). But this developing sensitivity to one's impulses means Joseph "must know not only his vices but also the gifts of grace and the merits of virtues. . . . [H]e ought to have at hand by what plan of temptations the evil spirit fights him; with what consolations of spiritual joys he abounds; how frequently the divine spirit visits him" (lxx). The role of experience in forming this capacity is clear; only trials, failures, continuing conversion, and delighted gratitude can build up in the soul this awareness of the particular "plan of temptations" or "consolations of spiritual joys" by which the soul is moved either to evil or to good.

> "When the mirror has been wiped and gazed into for a long time, a kind of splendor of divine light begins to shine in it and a great beam of unexpected vision appears to his eyes."

And this means that Richard envisions discretion as more than a tool for moderating passions; it becomes a mode of understanding the pattern of one's life, for discerning its most authentic direction, for recognizing "not only what sort he is but also even what sort he ought to be" (lxx). This concern for "what sort" of person one *ought* to be tells us that Richard is interested in discernment as self-knowledge in a very particular sense. He is discerning a self who is most real, most alive as, imperceptibly, the self begins to reflect and radiate the light of another:

> Whoever thirsts to see his God—let him wipe his mirror, let him cleanse his spirit. And so the true Joseph does not cease to hold, wipe and gaze into this mirror incessantly: to hold it so that it does not adhere to the earth after it has fallen down by means of love; to wipe it so that it does not become dirty from the dust of useless thoughts; to gaze into it so that the eye of his intuition does not turn toward empty pursuits. When the mirror has been wiped and gazed into for a long time, a kind of splendor of divine light begins to shine in it and a great beam of unexpected vision appears to his eyes. (lxxii)

Richard consummates this imagery by meshing his extended figural reading of Jacob's family with a figural reading (chapters lxxvi-lxxxiv) of the transfiguration of Christ (Matthew 17:1-8 and parallels). This is a rather splendid feat of hermeneutical acrobatics: Richard portrays the soul as image or mirror of God; from thence he conducts us via the soul's cleansing of this mirror (by means of discretion) to the radiant illumination of the mirror as "a kind of splendor of divine light begins to shine in it"; and thence by a final ecstatic leap to the ultimate epiphany of that divine light in the transfiguration. (Thus, incidentally, Richard fashions his text into a beautiful mimesis of the soul's own ecstatic journey.)

These ultimate stages of discretion are worthy of special note: it is not simply that Joseph must "hold" and "wipe" the mirror of the soul, stabilizing the passions and cleansing the impulses. No, Richard also ascribes to Joseph/Discretion the act of gazing "into this mirror incessantly . . . so that the eye of his intuition does not turn toward empty pursuits" (lxxii). Perhaps we could say that here Richard allows us to glimpse the hidden contemplative dimension present throughout a discerning life. For Jacob's children have struggled to discover the inner balance and learn by experience the discretion that alone gives life to their aspiration; and now we see that all along these efforts have been leading to the rediscovery, as it were, of the mirror of contemplation. The soul's journey to true self-knowledge, true discretion, has been restoring this mirror of truth to the mind's consciousness and cleansing from it "the dust of useless thoughts" (lxxii).

We might even think here of discernment as a profound orientation and affinity toward someone whose very name and nature has grown strangely obscure. Gradually, as discretion brings this deep momentum of the soul to clarity, the mind catches a glimpse of the radiant presence of the one it was created to know itself in knowing: "from the vision of this light that it wonders at within itself, the soul is kindled from above in a marvelous way and is animated to see that living light that is above it. . . . [F]rom this vision the soul conceives the flame of longing for the sight of God" (lxxii). Discernment brings about this strange translucency of the soul, radiantly apparent to itself at last, precisely as it is now filled with light and longing for another. So we have in Richard of St. Victor an account of discernment of very ample range, extending on into that rapturous yearning gaze during which the mind begins to kindle with the fire of contemplation. This theme of ardent desire, lifting discernment into a vision far beyond its previous vista, will burn even brighter in our next figure.

Catherine of Siena

Counselor to pope and prelates, comforter of countless laity and religious, Catherine of Siena (1347–1380) was gifted with both intellectual acuity and profound spiritual insight. In her brief life of thirty-three years she cared for the plague-ridden and sought reconciliation between antagonists both political and ecclesiastical. She became affiliated with the Order of Preachers (Dominicans) at age eighteen and in the midst of her remarkable range of public works also found time for a teaching ministry carried on through correspondence and finally through a mystical text written in the last three years of her life.

While most of the dimensions of discernment we have considered appear in Catherine's teaching, she unfolds one in particular with truly notable luminosity. Discerning God's will emerges in her thought as a profound transformation of human perception, rooted in the humility of true self-knowledge and achingly alive to the immensity of divine love. In her great work, the *Dialogue* (probably written in 1377–1378), Catherine recounts a vast conversation between God the Father and the soul. Catherine tells how, in response to each of four fervent petitions she offered—for the reform of the church, for the whole world, for the spiritual welfare of her spiritual guide, and for one unnamed—God drew her into ecstatic encounter and taught her.[10] The early sections of the work constitute a treatise on the virtues leading to spiritual perfection; and discernment appears as the "seasoning" of all the virtues, the one virtue that unites and makes possible all the rest (10).

Catherine begins her discussion of discernment in a mode quite similar to the monastic approach to discretion (her actual Italian is most often in fact *discrezione*): the virtues will be pursued in unbalanced and immoderate fashion unless governed by discernment. "If a soul were to do penance without discernment, that is, if her love were centered mainly on the penance she had undertaken, it would be a hindrance to her perfection" (9). Yet this passage already carries us beyond prudential moderation. It hints intriguingly of what we could see as a governing polarity in Catherine's vision of the spiritual life: the struggle within the soul between self-will and the attractive power of the divine will. So in the passage just quoted, the discernment is not simply a matter of judicious balance, but of an awakening love for the good that God longs to accomplish in the soul—as opposed to a love "centered mainly on the penance" undertaken, that is, a love focused on the important achievements of the self. Catherine teaches her readers to behold reality framed by a profound vision of God's love for the whole world. In many ways, we might simply identify this perception as the very ground of true discernment for Catherine.

Again and again in her remarkable oeuvre of letters, she holds this love before the eyes of her correspondents. Recognizing this love is the first step in the growth of discernment. Let me indicate how Catherine presents this love. "When we contemplate God stooped down to our very humanity," she writes to a Benedictine prior (whose monastery had been overrun by the plague), when we truly glimpse that immensity of divine love, then we are released from self-love and "left humbled in true and perfect self-knowledge."[11] It is almost as if, I think, Catherine pointed to a scale in the soul, so that as the true weight of the divine love begins to be felt, it completely outweighs the small and laborious efforts of the self on its own behalf. "We discover with what blazing love God's goodness is established within us, because we see that he loved us within himself before he created us" (I.120). Catherine relishes this theme of the Creator marveling in joy and yearning to bring the creatures into a distinct existence of their own beyond the mind of God, who eternally conceives them:

> Love, then, love! Ponder the fact that you were loved before ever you loved. For God looked within himself and fell in love with the beauty of his creature and so created us. He was moved by the fire of his ineffable charity to one purpose only: that we should have eternal life and enjoy the infinite good God was enjoying in himself. (I.132)

To enjoy this infinite divine good, the creature must, paradoxically, be given a chance to choose it freely, for only a freely desired love can share in the free giving and receiving that is the life of God. At the heart of Catherine's teaching is this trinitarian substructure of life lived in ecstatic delight in the other, freely giving life to the other; and this, of course, embeds within the fabric of *created* life an intrinsic orientation toward the divinely giving life in whose image it was created. This orientation or calling toward the perfection of divine self-sharing can only reach human consummation in a life that is not mesmerized by *itself* but is rather overwhelmed by the wonder of the divine Other who loves it—hence the constant conflict within the soul between self-love and love for God: "What heart is so hard and stubborn that it would not melt contemplating the affectionate love divine Goodness bears for it?" (I.132).

The whole spiritual life in pursuit of virtue is really, for Catherine, nothing other than an awakening and energizing of the self with this new center of its gravity, this new locus for its true identity, no longer in itself but in God. When it sees the vastness of the divine loving, which is the soul's real source and basis, then what it used to think of as its "own" seems of little account and becomes less and less a factor in the mind's ability to discern reality truly. Rather, the divine joy and desire and will, which are in fact the very ground of the soul's existence, kindle a wholly new form of perception:

> Once we are in its embrace, the fire of divine charity does to our soul what physical fire does: it warms us, enlightens us, changes us into itself. Oh gentle and fascinating fire! You warm and you drive out all the cold of vice and sin and self-centeredness! This heat so warms and enkindles the dry wood of our will that it bursts into flame and swells in tender loving desires, loving what God loves and hating what God hates. And I tell you, once we see ourselves so boundlessly loved, and see how the slain Lamb has given himself on the wood of the cross, the fire floods us with light, leaving no room for darkness. So enlightened by that venerable fire, our understanding expands and opens wide. And once we have experienced and accepted the light, we so clearly discern what is in God's will that we want to follow no other footsteps than those of Christ crucified. (I.266)

To explore Catherine's biblical metaphor, the fire of divine charity sets the soul's own desire ablaze with a fervor that "changes" the soul, kindling it up into one blaze with the fire of God's own loving. As this happens, human will begins instinctively to will as God wills. Catherine sees the human mind running to catch up, so to speak, discerning the truth which desire has already sensed as the divine goodness and love: "So enlightened by that venerable fire [divine charity kindling creaturely desire], our understanding expands and opens wide."

Catherine specifically links this new willing-as-God-wills with a new access of understanding. As self-love is overtaken and its hold on the soul is loosened by divine love, "we become able to discern God's holy will. And from that will is born a light" (I.120). This transformed perception sees everything now precisely in terms of God's will to bring the soul to blessedness. Everything that happens, every plan, every aspiration—all now become transparent, so to speak, to the divine will, because the soul enraptured by the divine will is increasingly attuned to that will, and it functions as the interpretive principle by which the soul considers everything. Writing to a monastic reformer, Catherine declares: "I long to see you enlightened with the true and wonderful light our souls need. I mean, I want you to open your mind's eye to see and contemplate God's supreme eternal will within

us, and to use that will as your standard of judgment" (II.384). Clearly we
have here moved well beyond discernment as either a discrimination of spirits or a discretion able to judge the virtuous mean between extremes.
Catherine describes a sense of understanding all things by discerning them
in light of God's will; and for her this means a form of knowing with several characteristics that we can now summarize: it is grounded in a passionate joy in God's love, it is increasingly free of self-regard, and it is also
consequently free of a denigrating or fearful attitude toward others:

> This is the dear vision that makes us wise. . . . It makes us careful, not
> thoughtlessly passing judgment on other people's intentions (as God's
> servants in their zealous love often do under pretext of virtue). This
> light makes us virtuous, no longer fearful. . . . So we rejoice in God's
> boundless charity and trust his providence to provide for our every
> need. God's giving is always well measured, and if he increases the
> measure he increases our strength. This we see and know when our
> mind's eye is enlightened and we come to recognize God's will, and are
> therefore made lovers of that will. I tell you, this light does not pass
> judgment on the intentions of God's servants or anyone else. No, it
> discerns and reverences the fact that the Holy Spirit is guiding them.
> (II.384-85)

Let me see if I can bring out in perhaps overly simple terms the underlying
logic of Catherine's complex insight: the deepest truth of reality springs
from God's self-sharing desire to bring all creatures to fulfillment; perception of this truth is obscured for a soul in the grip of self-will because its
principles of discernment (self-seeking) are diametrically opposed to the
self-giving divine will that *authors* (and structures) all life; therefore discernment of the truth of all things requires a soul enkindled with a new love
of God, such that the divine will becomes real (to the soul) in all its self-
giving delight, thus enabling the true discernment of the active leading of the
divine will (the Holy Spirit) in human life.

To a friar who had left his order, Catherine writes: "O dearest son, how
we need this light! In it is our salvation. But I see no way for us to have this
lovely light for our understanding without the pupil of most holy faith
which is within this eye. And if this light is clouded over or darkened by selfish love for ourselves, our eyes have not light and therefore cannot see. And
if we do not see, we do not know the truth" (II.507). Suzanne Noffke notes
that "for medieval physiology, the pupil *is* the light within the eye, not
merely an opening which lets in the light."[12] So for Catherine, faith in God's
saving love operates as the light permitting authentic understanding of reality. This is because the alternative principle of discernment, "selfish love for
ourselves," is incapable of perceiving and understanding the will and plan

of God in everything—a will characterized above all by the divine delight in the other and measureless self-sharing.

Catherine defines with considerable precision the impediments thrown up by self-love, and their continual short-circuiting of any authentic discernment of God's will:

> The wretched people who are without this light of holy faith do not know the truth. And why do the wretches not know this truth? Because they haven't got rid of the cloud of selfish love. So they don't know themselves and therefore don't hate themselves. And they don't know divine Goodness and therefore don't love him. If they do love at all, their love is imperfect, because they love God only to the extent that they see themselves getting pleasure and consolation from him, and they love their neighbors only to the extent that it is to their advantage. (II. 509)

Catherine says that if such persons knew themselves truly they would "hate themselves," which sounds rather problematic to our ears. But Catherine is immersed in the ancient rhetorical polarity between detachment and affinity found in the gospels (e.g., "Whoever comes to me and does not hate father and mother . . . yes, and even life itself, cannot be my disciple" [Luke 14:26]). For Catherine, there must be a complete abandonment of a self that is in any way achieved, accomplished, or formed by means of one's social, biological, cultural, or personal efforts—in order to recognize the infinitely greater gift of God's invitation to holiness, a calling that is the only true making of the self.

If we return to the *Dialogue,* it will perhaps be easier to see the meaning of this self-knowledge and humility. We began with a passage in which Catherine portrays God warning against doing penance "without discernment," that is, with love of the penance rather than of the real growth in holiness to which the soul is invited:

> . . . otherwise, if penance becomes the foundation, it becomes a hindrance to perfection. Being done without the discerning light of the knowledge of oneself and of my goodness, it would fall short of my truth. It would be undiscerning, not loving what I most love and not hating what I most hate. For discernment is nothing else but the true knowledge a soul ought to have of herself and of me, and through this knowledge she finds her roots. (*Dialogue,* chap. 9)

There are a number of crucial points here. Even the pious pursuit of virtue, exemplified in acts of penance, risks sliding into the most refined form of self-aggrandizement; for, unless it is pursued discerningly, that is, with an openness to the divine will grounding the soul, the penitential acts will leave the soul opaque to the divine life and trapped within the small compass of itself. When Catherine speaks of the soul hating itself and seeing itself with true humility, I think what she envisions is the radiant discovery, doubtless painful at first, that the soul is in fact a very poor maker of itself. And yet within its very existence is the vibrant, luminous touch of a true Creator whose delight it is to call the soul to its true own perfection—something it can never bestow upon itself but only receive.

We must recall that Catherine's letters so often include near their beginning a wondering praise of God's infinite delight and desire for the soul, with the suggestion that the soul cannot really understanding itself truly apart from perception of this divine charity from which it always springs. In the *Dialogue*, God remarks:

> . . . the soul gives glory and praise to my name for the graces and gifts she knows she has received from me. And to herself she gives what she sees herself deserving of. She knows that all that she is and every gift she has is from me, not from herself, and to me she attributes it all. In fact, she considers herself worthy of punishment for her ingratitude in the face of so many favors, and negligent in her use of the time and graces I have given her. . . . Such is the work of the virtue of discernment, rooted in self-knowledge and true humility. (9)

For Catherine, there must be a complete abandonment of a self that is in any way achieved, accomplished, or formed by means of one's social, biological, cultural, or personal efforts.

Discernment perceives the self as a gift; even humility springs from a puzzled sorrow that one could so ineptly respond to the mysterious potentialities of one's gifted existence. This true humility, therefore, is in no way focused on the self but on the marvel of divine giving; to see the self truly, even in repentance, is really to see the divine goodness and affection calling the self into existence and toward consummation. Discernment grows out of self-knowledge, in this sense, because it is the best practice for learning to see things as they truly are: in motion from God and toward God, mystically radiant with the divine goodness that delights to create them.

In her most richly complex presentation on discernment, Catherine offers an extended metaphor that shows how all the elements we have been considering relate to one another. The soul, she writes (*Dialogue* 10), is like a tree "made for love and living only by love," and the soul takes this divine love into itself through its root, which is its creaturely love. This is a good realization of Catherine's consistent teaching that the soul is most alive as it comes to love as God loves, so that its will is rooted in the divine will. This soul-tree stands in a circle within which its roots find complete nourishment, and this circle, says God, "is true knowledge of herself, knowledge that is joined to me, who like the circle have neither beginning nor end. . . . This knowledge of yourself, and of me within yourself, is grounded in the soil of true humility" which coincides with the circle of self-knowledge united with knowledge of God. Here, then, is Catherine's teaching that true self-knowledge grows out of the humility which recognizes itself as entirely God's loving gift. Finally, there is a branch carefully grafted and growing out of the side of this soul-tree, and the branch is discernment. Perhaps the fact that the branch is a graft (with resonances of Romans 11) is Catherine's way of reminding her readers that discernment, though it lives entirely upon the soul's humble self-knowledge rooted in divine love, nonetheless always remains a special gift and is not simply to be taken for granted as an inevitable and merely organic outgrowth of the spiritual life.[13]

As a final glimpse of the tightly woven fabric of Catherine's teaching, consider the serious social implications she sees entailed in a failure of discernment. In the middle of the *Dialogue*, Catherine recounts God's denunciation of those who have abdicated in their duties to accomplish the common good, in both church and state. Such people, says God, are like a "tree of pride with its offshoot of indiscretion" (121). Because they have failed to seek the nourishment of divine love, they are rooted in self-love and have no real discernment; their vision is preoccupied "by seeking higher office and adornments and delicacies for their bodies" (121). This leads to deeply ingrained injustice in their entire approach to life, for beginning with a fundamental inability to give true glory and gratitude to God, they constantly seek it for themselves, and this sets up a perpetual distortion in all their judgments. "They take to themselves what is not theirs and give me what is not mine" (121), with the result that such people are unable to discern the divine order or truth in human affairs and instead perceive everything only according to their own neediness. This "dark lack of discernment" leads to a state where such persons, having authority to seek the good and correct evil, do neither because they no longer see good or evil except in terms of what they can finagle for themselves:

> They do not pay me my due of glory, nor do they do themselves the justice of holy and honorable living or desire for the salvation of souls or hunger for virtue. Thus they commit injustice against their subjects and neighbors, and do not correct them for their sins. Indeed, as if they were blind and did not know, because of their perverse fear of incurring others' displeasure, they let them lie asleep in their sickness.

They do not consider that by wishing to please creatures they are dis-pleasing both them and me your Creator. Sometimes they administer correction as if to cloak themselves in this little bit of justice. But they will never correct persons of any importance. . . . [T]hey will, however, correct the little people, because they are sure these cannot harm them or deprive them of their rank. Such injustice comes from their wretched selfish love for themselves. This selfishness has poisoned the whole world. (122)

This powerful passage indicates the sweeping social vision that was integral to Catherine's spirituality. Discernment grounded in complete confidence in God's love contrasts very painfully with this counterfeit cunning; instead of perceiving and living for the divine truth in human relations, it has degen-erated into a fearfully conniving calculus of human power with little room for hope and even less for grace.

I have devoted little attention to Catherine's teaching on discernment as the distinguishing of spirits because that will be treated (in comparative terms) in the next chapter. But it would be fair to say that in many ways she represents the most multidimensional teacher of discernment we have so far encountered, analyzing aspects of each of the five moments of a discerning life explored in chapter one. Discernment for her is grounded and nourished in the divine love. It affords a revealing awareness of various impulses act-ing upon the soul. It provides a prudent ordering of a virtuous life toward its true goal. It constantly seeks and serves the divine will in everything. And it opens toward a kind of light for the soul, by which the soul is kindled into unity with the divine love.

Jean Gerson

Although he was born almost twenty years before Catherine's death, Jean Gerson (1363–1429) seems already to mark the advent of another world entirely. Chancellor of the University of Paris from 1395, Gerson played a major role in overcoming the internal schism of the church in the West. I introduce him here chiefly for two texts of his, *On Distinguishing True from False Revelations* (1402), and a briefer later summary of his thoughts, *On Testing the Spirits* (1415).[14] Few writers of his era had a bet-ter mastery of the classic sources on discernment, and Gerson regularly refers to them; and yet the atmosphere in which he takes up the questions of discernment is subtly shifting. It would be easy to focus on his system-atizing and academic tendency to order phenomena into discrete categories. Yet his pastoral concern and his own spiritual life are in no way left behind in his writing; the shift is subtler. It's as if, without intending it, our atten-tion is being gradually focused more on the *experiences* that discernment examines than on the *truth* that discernment seeks; or again, it feels as if the concern over whether one's experiences are legitimate is generating an ever more detailed experiential grid of analysis, so that method and analysis begin to dominate the foreground, and the divine agency, calling, and reality slips into the background in this analysis of human experience.

I begin with the later, more summary treatise (*On the Testing of Spirits*) as it sets a helpful frame. Gerson's first concern is to clarify what he articulates as four methods by which the discernment of spirits may take place. He contrasts the first two as, respectively, academic and experiential. So the first is "acquired from diligent and serious study of Holy Scripture," and uses relevant biblical texts as "norms" for discernment (§4). The second method relies on "interior inspiration" inculcating a "supernatural illumination" by means of which certain judgment about the validity of particular experiences may be attained (§4). The third method is also understood to be a matter of inspiration, but in this case it is a special charism of the Holy Spirit (as itemized in 1 Corinthians 12), and Gerson says that this method, "conferred through an ecclesiastical office by means of a special interior grace, is official" (§5). A good bit later in the treatise, Gerson adds what he refers to as "the fourth way of testing spirits" (§14). But this in fact turns out to be a further qualification needed for anyone proposing to take up the work of discernment:

> No one is capable of discerning spirits merely through skill and learning based on a knowledge of Holy Scripture alone . . . unless such a one has personally experienced in himself the various struggles of the emotions of the soul; unless he has flown to the heights of heaven, then fallen to the bottom of the abyss and has there seen in the depths the marvels of God. (§14)

It is interesting that Gerson applies this experiential prerequisite to those pursuing the "academic" method that draws on Scripture rather than the "charismatic" method conferred through ecclesiastical office (though office does often seem to induce experiences of "the various struggles of the emotions of the soul," so perhaps Gerson was simply being discreet!). In any case, we can see fairly clearly that the emphasis is on method and the personal gifts or experiences needed.

The second half of the treatise turns to the key questions that should structure a discerning investigation of spirits (Gerson offered the treatise at the Council of Constance to assist in considering the case for canonization of Bridget of Sweden). For convenience, I will simply enumerate them as follows:

1. *Who* has received the revelation, vision, or putative insight? Gerson rightly suggests that the person's health, sound judgment, dominant

passions or tendencies, maturity, personality, habits, education, and cultural background all be investigated. He concludes by warning, "above all, it is necessary to make sure that there is no hidden spiritual pride which escapes notice" (§24). Later he again emphasizes that the visionary's normal manner of life should be examined, especially to determine if there is a genuine simplicity and serenity at work or, by contrast, an inclination toward "continual conversations" and a spirit "itching with curiosity" (§48-51).

2. *What* is the content and meaning of the vision? Gerson insists that there be absolutely no hint of deception or falsity, for these would immediately indicate the handiwork of the "spirit of error." Of course, this begs the question since it is presumably the truth of the ostensible revelation that the process of discernment is meant to discover. Gerson seems to offer two chief criteria here: first, the vision ought to convey the authentic flavor of heavenly wisdom in being "chaste, peaceable, moderate, docile, in harmony with all good things, full of mercy and good fruits, without judging, without dissimulation" (following James 3:17) (§27); second, the vision ought to be consonant with Scripture yet in some way go beyond what can ordinarily be understood from Scripture, reason, or moral law, and this is because otherwise "a great number of Christians, having disregarded the study of Holy Scripture, would give their attention to such visions with their eyes and ears itching with curiosity," thus tending to render them even less attentive to the saving truths they need to learn from Scripture (§29). This point is noteworthy, I believe, in calling for discernment to include some consideration of the likely impact of an insight or new teaching upon the community.

3. *To whom* does the visionary choose to reveal the insight? Gerson's point here is again notably sophisticated and penetrating, for his real question is about the motivations that lead the visionary to speak: for instance, are there unexamined desires to receive approval, to be encouraged in acts of spiritual curiosity, or perhaps simply to have some audience for one's creeping self-preoccupation (§31-40). We could almost say that, for Gerson, discernment normally includes as a key indicator the kind of relationships that grow out of a person's choices or visions.

4. *Why* have the visions been given? Not only does the immediate impact of the vision need to be examined but also the unexpressed and unfolding influences: "The first effect may seem to be good, beneficial, worthy, and for the edification of others, which in fact becomes a scandal in many other ways" (§42). Once again, an important indicator of this likely trajectory of effects, says Gerson, is the

attitude of visionaries to those with whom they seek counsel about the vision. If visionaries are checked or received only very cautiously (as Gerson recommends) and nonetheless receive such counsel reverently and untroubled by their humiliation, Gerson sees that as a good sign of the likely healthy development and impact of the revelation upon the community.

5. *Whence* comes the animating impulse or spirit at work in the visionary? Gerson acknowledges the difficulty and question-begging aspect of this concern. Nevertheless he insists that the basic sources of spiritual motion can be placed into one of four categories—God, good spirits, bad spirits, or various elements within the human subject—and that experienced spiritual guides are able to discern the nature of the source by the kind of effect it has on the soul. Although he offers little amplification of this point, presumably Gerson would intend that the investigator correlate the authenticity and holiness of the vision to the identity of its animating source.

We will take up in more detail Gerson's own criteria for making this distinction between spirits, but this late treatise gives us a good sense of Gerson as a highly self-aware, methodologically astute practitioner of discernment. Perhaps more than any figure we have so far considered, he focuses attention on the conditions needed for proper discernment, especially the temperament, experiences, training, and office of the one seeking to discern. When we turn back to his earlier discussion, *On Distinguishing True from False Revelations,* we find Gerson expatiating upon the idea of crucial personal experience leading to the development of a personal capacity for discernment. He identifies three elements in the growth of discernment.

First, the ability to distinguish between spirits or between true and false revelations, can only be a charism, or gift.[15] Second comes a very interesting development, for instead of simply leaving this gift as defined by its functioning, Gerson feels drawn to identify it experientially. He does not do this as, for example, we find Catherine of Siena doing—by pointing to a life-direction in harmony with the divine will; rather, Gerson points to "a certain intimate taste" or a taste of "some kind of breath or odor within" oneself (350). While it would be anachronistic to speak here of a proto-modern turn to the subject, the new attention paid to the subjective states of the one discerning rather than the reality of the truth being discerned is certainly a harbinger. On the other hand, it must be said that the third element Gerson identifies in the growth of discernment is much more akin to the ancient form of practical judgment: "Why then should someone be surprised if a universal rule or certain and infallible teaching cannot be handed

over on this matter concerning discernment of spirits or the truth of revelations? This is more a matter of experience, dependent on a number of individual conditions, which are infinite, than a question of some technique"
(351). Yet even here, it is suggestive that Gerson feels compelled to register
a protest *against* precisely what will become a dominant modern desidera-
tum of all epistemological functioning, that there should be a universal
rationality, "some technique," a method, that guarantees "certain and infallible teaching."

I'm wondering if Gerson, rightly, opposes this momentum toward a
methodological algorithm in the spiritual life, but cannot help doing so
except by moving toward an analysis of inner subjective states—an analysis
that thinkers of a later era would tend to substitute for a participatory
encounter with the very truth the analysis was meant to discern. Perhaps
this seems a little far-fetched, except that the image Gerson chooses to illustrate his point (the difficulty of distinguishing dreaming from waking) figures so potently in the project of Descartes (see the first of the *Meditations*).
Gerson writes:

> A person frequently can think he is experiencing something while he
> is dreaming. He can believe that he is speaking, reading, and hearing,
> and by no means is dreaming. What will the person answer, except, "It
> is true, and in that case I am being deceived." But if you want to be
> even bolder and push the point even further, you can say, "And so
> now, my good man, you have no idea whether you are deceived?" Let
> him see whether he becomes speechless or if he can allege something
> of sufficient importance to free himself from this labyrinth. A person
> can only say that experiential knowledge alone of this wakefulness,
> which is quite different from dreams, is stronger and more vivid.
> Through this knowledge he does not so much have an opinion but
> knows and understands that he is awake. (352)

What is fascinating are the quite different uses to which Gerson and
Descartes put this image.[16] The two compatriots are equally concerned to
show that the great difficulty of distinguishing waking from dreaming ought
to make us realize how very dubious are many of our apparent certainties.
For Gerson, this does not mean that we are left only with uncertain opinions but that, if we abandon an arrogant curiosity and practice true humility, we can arrive at real knowledge and understanding (as he says just
above, a person of real experience *can* distinguish waking from dreaming
and "through this knowledge he does not so much have an *opinion* but
knows and *understands* that he is awake" [my emphasis]). But for
Descartes, of course, the dreaming vs. waking example is merely one step in
the development of his argument for systematic doubt in which the very

prudential, practical, and moral judgment Gerson goes on to advocate is pilloried and rejected as inadequate; the conversion and humility Gerson requires for true knowledge are in Descartes replaced by a very different method.

Gerson pays close attention to the conditions for the possibility of an authentically knowing self, questions of character, moral temperament, and willing intention. But, of course, whereas later thinkers would tend to locate the knowable truth precisely in those subjective conditions, Gerson is still attempting to convert the self to the reality beyond it. His work as a university chancellor seems to have given him a very clear picture of who would *not* be well equipped for discernment:

> He should not be the kind of person who is an eternal student that never comes to the knowledge of the truth, since he is wordy, garrulous, impudent, always making trouble and living in a bad way, more given over to feasting and wine tasting rather than judging his own actions carefully and conscientiously. For such a person every mention of religious devotion is a fable or a bore. (337-38)

Doubtless university life has changed entirely over the centuries. In any event, Gerson perceptively correlates a will for smaller pleasures with an obdurate dislike for anything liable to call out a larger and deeper commitment of the self. It is interesting that these deeper callings can only be sensed as illusory and tedious for such persons, Gerson says, as though the very faculty of recognizing truth had begun to grow enfeebled. In such cases, discernment is not the only casualty; there is a general degeneration of the patience and attentiveness that the mind needs to approach anything new. When something "obscure or foreign" is brought to such persons, "they immediately reject it with a derisive laugh and great anger, ridiculing it and dismissing it" (338). Perhaps Gerson has put his finger here upon a key impediment to discernment: a fearful or enervated close-mindedness that has little capacity to habituate itself to anything beyond the minute but gratifying certainties within its grasp.

Gerson immediately shows us those "who rush to the opposite vice," those who avidly suck in all "superstitious, vain, and illusory deeds and dreams of mad people" including "portents made up by those who are mentally ill or in depressed states of mind" (338). The chancellor seems to warn simply against credulity here, but again his sensitivity to the relationship between supposed visionary and would-be discerner goes farther. He is really warning about a kind of unconscious illness in the whole community of the faithful in which those who are unbalanced in some way are used by those eager for titillation or a cause to manipulate—and the latter go on enabling the former instead of really helping them. Again, discernment of truth would be supplanted in this case by a manufacture of sensationalist impact (not without parallels to our present day's fixation with "reality" television), an approach not to truth but to a mere commodity. In both the case of the jaded scoffer and the avid devotee Gerson gives us good illustrations of his special insight on discernment, a sensitivity to the atmosphere and relationships within which discernment is taking place.

Ignatius of Loyola

The founder of the Society of Jesus, Ignatius of Loyola (ca. 1491–1556), was (like Augustine of Hippo) drawn always beyond himself into an ever deepening conversion to God. Augustine's thought was marked by his overwhelming sense of God's compassionate humility in Christ, and thus began a remarkable transformation of that Neoplatonic itinerary of conversion that would always in some degree serve him as an intellectual and spiritual background. But in the case of Ignatius, the itinerary of conversion has become entirely configured to Christ. The yearning for contemplative unity with God has taken the form of a deep desire to discern and serve the divine will in all things. Few figures in the history of Christianity could be said to have woven a continuous, living act of discernment so entirely into the fabric of Christian existence.

Unlike such other important teachers as Richard of St. Victor or Jean Gerson, the guidance of Ignatius on discernment has been taken up into the unfolding life of the community he founded; and so a correspondingly vast literature has developed, ranging in focus from theological and historical analysis to contemporary pastoral development. Many fine books on Ignatian principles of discernment exist.[17] I will merely attempt to sketch briefly here the basic structure and hermeneutic for discernment that Ignatius devised (and in the next chapter will have more to say particularly about the discrimination between spirits). Ignatius himself was reluctant to put into print some guidelines he had been developing (since his own mystical encounter in 1521); these were in the form of a manual for those assisting persons to discern God's calling in their lives. The process of revision, however, was more or less complete in 1541, and what we now know as the *Spiritual Exercises* came into the world. It is important to remember that the *Exercises* are not a spiritual treatise or meditation intended for spiritual reading. They are series of notes intended for those who guide persons undertaking the actual pattern of retreat and meditation called the "spiritual exercises." Nevertheless, there is a deep structural integrity to the *Spiritual Exercises* and to the journey of growth in self-knowledge and discernment of God's will that the *Exercises* are meant to facilitate.

Perhaps I could say, by way of a simple synopsis, that persons who make the spiritual exercises (that is, who are guided on a retreat by a director making use of the text called the *Spiritual Exercises*) are invited to the following stages of growth, each step leading to and making possible what comes next:

(a) a new level of profound trust in God's love for them
(b) a new freedom from the dominating power of lesser attachments and motivations
(c) a growing attunement to Jesus' own sense of calling and mission
(d) a clearer perception of their own personal calling within God's desire for the world
(e) an ever greater sense of and desire to participate in God's love, which is ceaselessly laboring in all things.

This is certainly an oversimplification, but at least it indicates the fundamental dynamic that Ignatius seeks to nurture in the *Exercises*. And while Ignatius provides two specific sets of "rules" or further guidelines in distinguishing spirits, let me make use of this overly simple synopsis to show how spiritual discernment is at work throughout the overarching dynamic of the *Exercises*.

The first step (a) relies on an enhancement of one's ability to recognize or discern the ways in which God has been actively loving one throughout one's life, and indeed how God has created and destined one entirely to share in that love.[18] This would coincide, for example, with Catherine of Siena's unwavering intent to elicit such a recognition from her own correspondents, awakening them to a fundamental discernment of God's love for them as the basis for a more honest understanding of themselves. The second step (b) coincides with the discernment or distinguishing of inner motions and spirits per se.

> "[W]hile continuing our contemplations of his life, we now begin simultaneously to explore and inquire: In which state or way of life does the Divine Majesty wish us to serve him?"

The middle step (c) is the most characteristically Ignatian and makes a crucial contribution to the theology of discernment: attunement to Christ becomes the chief means by which a capacity for true discernment grows. The *Exercises* direct a good deal of attention to interior movements and impulses. Yet Hugo Rahner comments that even those very interior motions, termed "consolations" and "desolations" in the *Exercises*—seemingly all about states of subjectivity—are intended by Ignatius to be illuminated by one's growing familiarity with the ways of God in Christ: "the exercitant should not direct his attention simply to the movement of the

spirits going on within him, but rather to the love of God which both precedes and accompanies all movements of the soul—and he will do this by
continuing to contemplate the mysteries of the life of Christ."[19] The second,
third, and fourth "weeks" of the *Exercises* are devoted to meditations on
the life, death, and resurrection of Jesus, and to a discernment of one's call
in that context. So we could say that for Ignatius, the risen Christ in fact
becomes the guiding deliberative agent within the heart and mind of the one
making the exercises. This makes possible a discerning of God's will with
respect to one's own mission in life (d), and a gradually deepening discernment of God's love (e) as the radiant and attractive dynamism of the whole
universe.

All this suggests that while Ignatian discernment certainly includes both
distinguishing the spirits and the discernment of divine will, it also places
those modes within a larger discerning pattern of life. Let me, then, flesh out
the important relationship between these two modes of discernment (i.e., of
spirits and of God's will), in the larger context of the *Exercises*. If a fundamental goal of Ignatian discernment is to assist persons in finding greater
clarity and freedom in the service of God, there is ample need for an ongoing, subsidiary awareness of the impulses that tend to move one in various
directions. As one commentator puts it: "Failure to discern spirits correctly
can impede awareness of the Holy Spirit's guidance or bring one to see his
guidance where there is none."[20] Discernment of God's will receives direct
attention in the *Spiritual Exercises* in sections 135 and 169-189.[21] There we
find Ignatius first of all setting the election or decision to be made within the
context of Christ's life: "while continuing our contemplations of his life, we
now begin simultaneously to explore and inquire: In which state or way of
life does the Divine Majesty wish us to serve him?" (135). Through these
contemplations of Christ's life, Ignatius encourages those making a retreat
to allow their habits of mind and heart to be permeated by same Holy Spirit
who animates Jesus' own desire to do the Father's will.

The Gospels narrate a period in which Jesus is tested in the wilderness,
learning to discern between the impulses of the evil spirit and the authentic
impulses of the Holy Spirit. Ignatius intends those making the exercises
(usually called "exercitants") to develop something of the same sensitivity
to the source and origin of their impulses, precisely so that they may the
more easily recognize and respond to the authentic voice of the Holy Spirit
without being unconsciously influenced by negative impulses. It is useful to
remember, of course, that for Ignatius this process does not supersede the
normal rational reflection of the exercitant but is meant entirely to set that
reasoning free: the most likely time in which one would come to a decision
is precisely the time when "I am not more inclined or emotionally disposed"
to one side or the other (179), and when the perception of what would lead

to God's greater glory can be accomplished "by reasoning well and faithfully with my intellect" (180). It is in such periods of reflection that one's perception of the true end and goal of human existence could easily be clouded by interior movements, fears, desires, and so on, and hence the need for a developed skill in distinguishing between these "spirits." George Ganss usefully summarizes the matter:

> In discerning the will of God, a person asks questions such as: "By which option am I, with my personality and in my circumstances, likely to bring greater glory to God?" or "to serve God better?" or "to increase my supernatural life more and thereby bring him proportionally greater praise through eternity?" While engaged in such deliberations, he or she is likely to receive thoughts and impulses from the good spirit and subtle temptations from the evil spirit. Here recourse to discernment of spirits is needed, and perhaps also consultation with a counselor.[22]

It is *because* one is seeking the will of God, and learning to desire and discern it more amply that Ignatius believes one is the more likely to become aware of the lesser impulses that nudge and sometimes distort one's life. My suggestion, then, is that the *Spiritual Exercises* proposes a teleological dynamic of discernment, in which attention to the goal of the ever greater truth of God persistently brings to light the *reality* of present circumstances—a reality that, considered just in its own terms, can sometimes appear only obscurely, ambiguously, and subject to unrecognized factors of distortion. And Christ, in Ignatius's view, is the shining of that divine light of eschatological truth which illuminates the *present* structures of reality; for attunement to Christ's own desire to do the Father's will is the means by which one is able to discern the truth and goodness of God—including as they need to be discovered and enacted in any given moment.

I have been suggesting how Ignatius, in my view, allows the light of heaven to illuminate the struggles of earth. Perhaps it would help to exhibit this teleological momentum of discernment if we glimpse its impact upon the discerner herself or himself. Ignatian teaching on discernment is not a matter of discrete moments of clarity and judgment but leads to the transformation of a whole life, and therefore we can see the thrust of this structure of knowing as it comes to fruition in the larger pattern of a human life. More than almost any other figure we have studied, Ignatius attends to the whole dynamic of a person's life. Indeed, we might even say that Ignatius offers a hermeneutic of human life, an interpretive theory within which discernment can function properly. The particular "rules" that Ignatius offers (*SpEx* 313-36) for distinguishing between spirits are interwoven with reflections on a person's life trajectory. For the particular affects that one notices, whether consoling or the reverse, only reveal their true meaning if one interprets them in the context of a whole life-tendency: thus, in Ignatius's view, an experience of consolation and encouragement might well be an authentic motion of the Holy Spirit within the life of person who is genuinely seeking to grow in grace and holiness; but the same interior affects might bespeak the blandishments of an evil spirit at work within the life of one who is falling farther away from friendship with God.

From this basic awareness of a person's orientation, Ignatian discernment develops the virtuous character of the person: as the person's life is further attuned to Christ, her or his sensitivity to God's ways in the world is deepened and intensified. We could perhaps think of this as a patterning of one's present life more nearly after the rhythms of the life to come, the principles of which become more available as structures for present thought and action. The classical terminology for this speaks of the development of those long-term dispositions of character that make one more apt for the vision of God, namely the theological virtues of faith, hope, and charity. Julius Toner explains this as an interaction within the experience of the exercises, an interaction between the divine presence vivifying the believer's life (hence the growth of faith, hope, and love) and the believer's correspondingly intensifying sensitivity to the divine will.[23]

Another way to speak about this transformation wrought in the believer by discernment is to notice the (sometimes only implicit) role Ignatius ascribes to the Holy Spirit in the believer's growth. Ignatius sees the Holy Spirit as freeing and cherishing the deepest level of reality in every person, permitting each person to think and act more and more fully from the truth of herself or himself. Throughout the *Spiritual Exercises* we can find a wide range of references to God bringing the deepest and most authentic desire and perception to birth, and a great many of these may be ascribed to the Holy Spirit.[24] God "moves and attracts the will" (175), "guides and counsels us in time of consolation" (318), gives a taste of heavenly love to inspire right choices (184), and in general acts to clarify the real yearning of a person's life.

Indeed we could say that Ignatian discernment envisions the growth of a person whose consciousness has reached a fundamental integrity; unconflicted or baffled by ambiguous desires, such a person now perceives everything in terms of the great desire that is God's desire—fully recognizing her or his own freedom and personal consummation as flowing from service to that divine desire. For example, Ignatius suggests that if an exercitant "feels an affection or inclination to something in a disordered way" (e.g., if someone pursues some office "not for the honor and glory of God our Lord or for the spiritual welfare of souls, but rather for one's own temporal advantages and interests"), then the exercitant should not seek the office until and unless "the Divine Majesty has put proper order into those desires, and has by this means so changed one's earlier attachment that one's motive in desiring or holding onto one thing rather than another will now be only the service, honor, and glory of the Divine Majesty" (16).

This reorientation of one's desire might almost be said to *be* the basis of true discernment in Ignatius; thus discernment springs from that harmonious point where the human will and the divine will are fully in communion, allowing all things to be illuminated—for the human knower—by the divine knowing and loving of them. Ignatius's teaching on discernment is marked above all by an intrinsically trinitarian vision. As we have seen, the *Exercises* foster discernment by fostering an ever deepening intimacy with Christ and a knowledge of his own sense of being sent by the Father. This in turn leads to a greater ease in cooperating with grace, perceiving opportunities that serve the one great liberating desire of God. Such a person is, consequently, "free of egoistic desires and fears and ready to let go of unfounded prejudgments. Such a person is ready to be led by the Holy Spirit and to find God's will every day in every situation for choice."[25]

Ignatius embeds this transforming of personal character into the meditations proposed in the *Exercises*. Perhaps the most famous of these imaginative contexts for shaping a discerning heart comes in the "second week" of the *Exercises* with the meditation on the "Two Standards" (136-48). In this meditation, the exercitant is invited "to imagine a great plain in the region of Jerusalem, where the supreme commander of the good people is Christ our Lord; then another plain in the region of Babylon, where the leader of the enemy is Lucifer" (138). We will consider this meditation with different questions in mind in the next chapter, but for now it is useful just to note how Ignatius awakens in the exercitant's consciousness a deep sense of the hidden but nonetheless ever-present choice one makes in every thought and deed. Ignatius's meditation seems very strongly to parallel a number of Bernard's parables. In each case, a person is awakened to the larger spiritual context of her or his decisions and actions. In each case the villainous subterfuges of the evil spirit are exposed and contrasted with the seemingly difficult but loving invitations of God. Ignatius proposes imagining the "leader of all the enemy . . . seated on a throne of fire and smoke, in aspect horrible and threatening," who sends out minions everywhere "to set up snares and chains" (140, 142). In contrast, the meditation considers Christ taking his place "in an area which is lowly, beautiful, and attractive" (144). The meditation powerfully draws exercitants to consider under whose "standard" or flag they journey and struggle. All the elements we have noted in Ignatian discernment are here introduced and, so to speak, *practiced* in the time of meditation and reflection: there is an awakening to the divine love that calls one, an awareness of the conflicting impulses, a new polarization or transparency of everything to the divine will or its opposite, and, grounding it all, an invitation to the "lowly, beautiful, and attractive" milieu of Christ and his companions.

It strikes me how significant, in the history of Christian discernment, has been the use of various forms of narrative: the stories of Antony the Great and the other desert elders told and retold in Cassian, Evagrius, Diadochus, and Climacus, the parables of Bernard, the figural use of the Jacob stories in Richard of St. Victor, and the imaginative meditations of Ignatius, to name only the most obvious (and Bunyan's *Pilgrim's Progress* might be read as one long narrative of discernment). Stories take time and thus mimic the growth of life experience itself. They also famously involve the hearer or reader in a meaning that can only be appreciated by a certain vicarious participation, so that the meaning gradually distills itself in readers as they imaginatively practice the events of discernment themselves. Both these features are strongly present in Ignatian discernment, and again point to the crucial christological center of the *Exercises*. For it is the figure of Christ who in the *Spiritual Exercises*, as in Christian theology more generally, incarnates the heavenly love in a narratival, imitable pattern of choices and actions. This christological formation and ground of discernment, so important to Ignatius, performs a vital service for the theology of discernment: it holds the distinguishing of spirits and the most mundane practical judgment always open to the larger calling represented for Ignatius by Christ's imperative desire to do the will of the Father. In this way the active and practical exigencies of a discerning life are ceaselessly imbued with a contemplative momentum. Thus we might even say that every act of knowing bears within it the secret calling of what Ignatius would describe as the ever greater glory of God.

John Bunyan and Jonathan Edwards

In concluding these chapters of historical survey with a brief look at two great Puritans of different generations, we have, of course, not ventured very far into modernity at all. But besides pleading the constraints of time, space, and my own very limited expertise, I can perhaps offer one point suggesting the reasonableness (while admitting the inadequacy) of coming to a halt in the eighteenth century. John Bunyan (1628–1688) and Jonathan Edwards (1703–1758) do at least bring very clearly to light an important tendency in the modern development of discernment—even perhaps the most characteristic feature of discernment in modernity: an ever more central focus on interior states of subjective consciousness.

While it would be anachronistic (even painfully ironic in the cases especially of Ignatius and Edwards) to suggest that discernment is simply transforming into a variety of psychological analysis, there is an increasingly unavoidable sense in Gerson and Ignatius, Bunyan and Edwards, that the focus has shifted. Edwards's magisterial work, *A Treatise Concerning Religious Affections* (1746), emerges from the need (amidst the extravagant emotions of New England's Great Awakening) to discern the verity or falsity of one's own pious feelings and intentions. For Edwards, as much as for Gerson and for Ignatius, the analysis of one's inner life was in service to a greater objective obedience to God; yet, in America at least, the appealing voices of Romantic individualism and privatized religious belief beguiled that analysis of one's inner life off into a wholly new world of personal religious opinion and feeling. Reaction against Enlightenment empiricism and musty objective "evidences" for religious truth among the Deists only hastened the quest for a realm of one's own truth, in which discernment would become increasingly decoupled from an understanding of truth as public and communal.[26] The influential advice of John Locke concerning the proper relationship of religion and public life made the bearing of religion upon any truth larger than one's personal preferences nearly inconceivable.

Hence the insights of spiritual discernment regarding truth and human understandings of truth seem to tip over (in modern estimates) into an apparently antiquated form of teaching about emotional states and the often unsuspected influences of our subconscious mind. While I would by no means wish to suggest that the long history of Christian discernment has nothing to teach and learn from modern psychological theory, I am indeed suggesting that Christian discernment has manifestly sought truth in a much larger and ultimate sense.

Bunyan and Edwards, however their legacy may have unfolded, were intent to examine religious feeling precisely in order to discern the truth of one's status before God. The problem, put so clearly in *Pilgrim's Progress*, is that while one's personal destiny is fixed by God's eternal decree of election (either to grace or reprobation), only by careful examination of one's truest thoughts, feelings, and practice might one discern possible clues to whether one had been elected to grace or damned to hell.[27] As I will analyze Bunyan's great work in another chapter, let me here simply highlight some moments that shed light on the approach to discernment we will find roughly three-quarters of a century later in Edwards.

Among the many characters Christian encounters in *Pilgrim's Progress*, the brisk and breezy figures of Talkative and Ignorance provide particularly good foils for Bunyan on discernment. As Talkative draws apace with Christian and his companion Faithful, Bunyan describes him suggestively as "something more comely at a distance than at hand."[28] And indeed Talkative makes a very grand impression at first acquaintance, for his discourse is of the most godly kind and very insightful too. Bunyan suggests, however, that Faithful ought not have had quite so fine a sense of Talkative had he but noted the fatal inclination of the other, well, to *talk* about everything! It is not this that marks the authenticity of one's election to grace, for in reality, comments Christian, "Religion hath no place in his heart, or his house, or conversation; all he hath lieth in his *tongue,* and his Religion is to make a noise *therewith*" (emphasis original, 64).

As they go along, Christian and Faithful devise a little discernment process for their traveling companion. Faithful asks him "How doth the saving Grace of God discover it self, when it is in the heart of man?" (67). Predictably, Talkative is delighted with the question and immediately opens what sounds like a very improving homily on the topic, propounded all complete with headings and subheadings to be treated. He never gets far, however, for each time he begins his next section, Faithful calls him to account: Talkative says the first sign of grace is to cause an outcry against sin, but Faithful warns it must not only be an outcry but a true and transforming abhorring of it; next Faithful warns him against a mere knowledge of the gospel without action, distinguishing between "Knowledge that resteth in the bare speculation of things, and knowledge that is accompanied with the grace of faith and love, which puts a man upon doing even the will of God from the heart" (68). As Faithful goes on to clarify the marks of true conversion, he adds that the habits of sin and "abused reason" make one's mind likely to "mis-judge" the reality of one's conversion and therefore the concrete and costly works of a changed life are necessary indicators.

Considerably later in the story, after Faithful has been martyred at Vanity Fair (thus exemplifying his teaching), Christian is listening to his new companion Hopeful as he tells the story of his conversion. At first an awareness of his sinful life had provoked him to a great deal of amendment and a hunger for righteousness, but then he began to doubt of his true reformation for, he said, "I still see sin, new sin, mixing it self with the best of that I do" (114). Then Hopeful tells how he unburdened himself at last to their old friend Faithful: "And he told me, That unless I could obtain the righteousness of a man that never had sinned, neither mine own, nor all the righteousness of the World could save me" (114). Gradually he came to understand that this man was Jesus, so, following the counsel of Faithful, Hopeful began to study the promises of God in Scripture and to cast himself "over, and over, and over" before the mercy seat of Christ, but without sensing any response. About to give up all hope, Hopeful (appropriately) decided to persevere when the saying came into his mind: "If it tarry, wait for it, because it will surely come, and will not tarry."

Hopeful: So I continued Praying until the father shewed me his Son.
Christian: And how was he revealed unto you?

Hopeful: I did not see him with my bodily eyes, but with the eyes of mine understanding ; and thus it was. One day I was very sad, I think sader then at any one time in my life; and this sadness was through a fresh sight of the greatness and vileness of my sins: And as I was then looking for nothing but Hell, and the everlasting damnation of my Soul, suddenly, as I thought, I saw the Lord Jesus look down from Heaven upon me, and saying, Believe on the Lord Jesus Christ, and thou shalt be saved. But I replyed, Lord, I am a great, a very great sinner; and he answered, My grace is sufficient for thee. (116)

In this archetypal Puritan account of conversion, we can see the enormous power of religious emotion as the medium of spiritual truth for Bunyan. In his moving account of his own conversion, *Grace Abounding to the Chief of Sinners,* Bunyan told of an especially dire moment of diabolical torment. The "Tempter" threatened that though Bunyan was very zealous for mercy and God's righteousness at the moment, "I shall be too hard for you, I will cool you insensibly, by degrees, by little and little; what care I, saith he, though I be seven years in chilling your heart, if I can do it at last."[29] The threat is precisely that by cooling Bunyan's pious feelings, Satan would pry him loose from his confidence in Christ and thus at last reveal him to be among not the elect but the damned. Perhaps he would turn out, like Talkative, to be religious in word only but not in truth.

Yet Hopeful's account shows us how the emotional marker is not exactly solipsistic, for it brings to existential life the objective Scriptural words as now addressed personally to Hopeful by Jesus. He comments that the inward testimony of feeling and the sight of the "eyes of mine understanding" are aroused by the Father revealing his Son to Hopeful. And Christian immediately moves to confirm the authenticity of this experience by asking, "But tell me particularly what effect this had upon your spirit?" (117). Hopeful replies:

It made me greatly ashamed of the vileness of my former life, and confounded me with the sence of mine own Ignorance; for there never came thought into mine heart before now, that shewed me so the beauty of Jesus Christ. It made me love a holy life, and long to do something for the Honour and Glory of the Name of the Lord Jesus. Yea I thought, that had I now a thousand gallons of blood in my body, I could spill it all for the sake of the Lord Jesus. (117)

Hopeful's newfound desire to give his all for the one who gave his all for Hopeful will of course have to be tested for authenticity, but it is already considerably more realistic than a merely notional sense of sin.

Along with this ardency there comes to Hopeful a new awareness of his former ignorance, that is, his ignorance regarding the objective role of Christ in his salvation, for apart from that he really would be simply enjoying a heart strangely warmed. In one of Bunyan's many delightful touches, it is just at this point (when Hopeful has become aware of his ignorance) that a character named Ignorance overtakes the pilgrims. Sure enough, Ignorance places his greatest confidence in his feelings rather than in Christ's objective work of salvation. When Christian asks him, "Why, or by what, art thou perswaded that thou hast left all for God and Heaven?" Ignorance blithely responds: "My heart tells me so" (118). We can see the sticky problem for discernment in the ensuing exchange:

> Christian: The wise man sayes, He that trusts his own heart is a fool.
> Ignorance: That is spoken of an evil heart, but mine is a good one.
> Christian: But how dost thou prove that?
> Ignorance: It comforts me in the hopes of Heaven.
> Christian: That may be, through its deceitfulness, for a mans heart may minister comfort to him in the hopes of that thing, for which he yet has no ground to hope.
> Ignorance: But my heart and my life agree together, and therefore my hope is well grounded.
> Christian: Who told thee that thy heart and life agrees together?
> Ignorance: My heart tells me so.

At this point Christian throws up his hands in frustration at such blinding self-confidence, and one senses that Bunyan's own experiences as a pastor cannot be far away.

After remonstrating with Ignorance that his heart's belief must at least be found to accord with Scripture, Christian demonstrates that Ignorance in fact trusts more in his heart's righteous feelings *about* Christ than in Christ's own righteousness. Indeed Bunyan perceptively paints Ignorance as quite shocked that his companions would place their faith in an external act of Christ so apparently removed from real inner feeling about it: "What! would you have us trust to what Christ in his own person has done without us?" (121). At last Hopeful seems to recognize in Ignorance his own previous malady and breaks into the conversation with, "Ask him if ever he had Christ revealed to him from Heaven?" This gives Ignorance just the excuse he needs to play the calm and reasonable assurances of his own heart against the wild notions of Hopeful: "What! You are a man for revelations! I believe that what both you, and all the rest of you say about the matter, is but the fruit of distracted braines. . . . I have not in my head so many whimzies as you" (121). And shortly after this, Ignorance announces that the others go too fast for him and so he will keep his own pace and company.

Bunyan very poignantly depicts the predicament of authentic discernment, forced to depend on such a seemingly vulnerable combination of factors—an interior conviction of sin, an authentic experience of Christ's saving grace offered personally, an intense desire to serve Christ and suffer with him in truth if need be—whereas other less adequate forms of discernment in fact seem stronger and less questionable though this is merely the result of a narrower set of criteria for discernment.

We find Jonathan Edwards in no very different predicament when, in the face of the Great Awakening surrounding him, he sought to identify the hallmarks of genuine faith from emotionalism on one side or rationalism on the other.[30] This was not in Edwards's view merely a matter of individual discernment but had ramifications for the whole Christian community: "Tis by the mixture of counterfeit religion with true, not discerned and distinguished, that the devil has had his greatest advantage against the cause and kingdom of Christ."[31] Edwards wrote the *Religious Affections* first of all to clarify what was properly the *matter* for discernment and then to offer a series of twelve signs (which we will consider in the next chapter) by which to make discerning judgments.

The proper matter for discernment are the affections, namely those inclinations of the will either toward or away from things. In the view of Edwards, these inclinations of the will shape and direct our intellectual perception and understanding and in fact propel the whole human person: "Such is man's nature, that he is very inactive, any otherwise than he is influenced by some affection, either love or hatred, desire, hope, fear or some other" (101). We can see Edwards reaching for the same integrity of thought and feeling, knowledge and love, that was prized by Bunyan as the right sort of act by which to believe in Christ's redemption. For Edwards, this affection is not simply a feeling as in a narrowly emotional state, but is rather "a sensation of the mind which loves and rejoices . . . and that inward sensation, or kind of spiritual sense, or feeling, and motion of the soul, is what is called affection" (114). It seems characteristically modern that just when Bunyan and Edwards are most concerned to emphasize the objective historical redemption in Christ, they are simultaneously compelled to specify the subjective capacities for the apprehending and acceptance of that redeeming work. "He that has doctrinal knowledge and speculation only," warns Edwards, "without affection, never is engaged in the business of religion" (101). Perhaps earlier eras of Christian thought would have been less inclined to conceive that doctrinal knowledge *could* in fact ever be realized by the mind *apart* from the loving existential participation of the whole human person in the divine act of self-disclosure (by means of which the doctrinal knowledge is distilled into the human community).

In any case, Edwards works diligently to sketch a realm of human understanding and feeling in which the true saving knowledge of God can be realized. At the head of the *Religious Affections,* Edwards quotes 1 Peter 1:8 as follows: "Whom having not seen, ye love: in whom, though now ye see him not, yet believing, ye rejoice with joy unspeakable, and full of glory." This is in effect his text for the whole work, and it allows him to dilate for his readers upon the crucial question: what are the marks of authentic belief, of faith that is truly in communion with God? He notes carefully that though the feeling, the joy, that characterizes this act of believing is described as "unspeakable," yet is it also "full of glory," that is, it is not without intelligible witness or sign in the believer; it has a definite and radiant profile whose lineaments can be discerned:

> Although their joy was unspeakable, and no words were sufficient to describe it; yet something might be said of it, and no words more fit to represent its excellency, than these, that it was "full of glory." . . . In rejoicing with this joy, their minds were filled, as it were, with a glorious brightness, and their natures exalted and perfected: it was a most worthy, noble rejoicing, that did not corrupt and debase the mind, as many carnal joys do; but did greatly beautify and dignify it: it was a prelibation of the joy of heaven, that raised their minds to a degree of heavenly blessedness: it filled their minds with the light of God's glory, and made em themselves to shine with some communication of that glory. (95)

And Edwards immediately draws his conclusion; the doctrine "that I raise from these words is this: True religion, in great part, consists in holy affections" (95).

Here Edwards has moved into a very different idiom from Bunyan, or at least more innately metaphysical. Whereas Bunyan expresses this radiance of the heavenly light upon the pilgrims' path in terms of an occasional glimpse of Mount Sion in the distance, Edwards has envisioned this glory as a transfiguring of the believers' own minds: "it was a prelibation of the joy of heaven, that raised their minds to a degree of heavenly blessedness: it filled their minds with the light of God's glory, and made em themselves to shine with some communication of that glory." This most remarkable text is worth close attention: it suggests that at the very heart of all Edwards will say about the religious affections, he is in fact speaking of a divine illumination of the mind, a knowing that takes place as the human mind comes "to shine with some communication of that glory" of God. We will consider Edwards's kinship with illumination theories of knowledge in a later chapter, but for here it is useful to note at least that however much the great New Englander may seem to be parsing states of human subjectivity, he certainly intends those states as *opposed* to signs of an autonomous or solipsistic self—rather as signs of a self realized and consummated through friendship with God.

The difficulty, as Robert Jenson has shown, is that there is enough common work of the Holy Spirit (as Edwards puts it) assisting natural human principles of knowledge to foster a nearly perfect counterfeit of true religion, a religion in which God appears as the glorious affirmer of self-seeking and self-love. "Where Christianity is the available religion, this seeking will be very Christian and no less egocentric for that. It will then be the very benefits to *me* which God promises in the gospel, for the sake of which I will attach myself to him."[32] As we have seen just above, the very basis of authentic religious affection for Edwards is precisely a knowing that no longer judges according to its own needs and standards, but sees everything according to the radiance of God's glory. In other words, true religion understands everything more and more, as for Catherine of Siena and Ignatius of Loyola, purely by attunement to God's intention. God is loved for God's own glory, an element of which is indeed to redeem humanity; but the counterfeit religion Edwards wishes to expose loves God entirely for one's own sake— not for God's glory but for the glory God pours out for

---

Edwards seeks a self-consciousness grounded entirely in another, *not based securely or anxiously upon itself.*

---

oneself. In Edwards's view this mirror opposite of authentic faith can have very grave consequences, shrinking God and Christ to supporting roles in the self's own magnificent drama, and perhaps even eventually subjecting the soul in perversely idolatrous fealty to a false Christ:

> When this is the case with carnal men, their very lusts will make him [Christ] seem lovely: pride itself will prejudice them in favor of that which they call Christ: selfish proud man naturally calls that lovely that greatly contributes to his interest, and gratifies his ambition. And as this sort of persons begin, so they go on. Their affections are raised from time to time, primarily on this foundation of self-love and a conceit of God's love to them. (245-46)

This will be the mainspring of Edwards's approach to discernment, this probing and distinguishing of the animating spirit of one's love for God.

The basic principle throughout will be this, that the true saints "don't first see that God loves them, and then see that he is lovely; but first they see that God is lovely, and that Christ is excellent and glorious, and their hearts are first captivated with this view" (246). Again we can see that while Edwards will indeed be probing the inner subjective consciousness of believers, he seeks there precisely a self-consciousness grounded entirely in *another*, not based securely or anxiously upon itself: "In the love of the true saint God is the lowest foundation; the love of the excellency of his nature is the foundation of all the affections which come afterwards, wherein self-love is concerned as an hand-maid: on the contrary, the hypocrite lays himself at the bottom of all, as the first foundation, and lays on God as the superstructure" (246). For Edwards, the fundamental question of discernment will be (as Bernard of Clairvaux had also said) whether one loves God for God's sake or for one's own. And all the tests and questions of discernment will be to sense this deep and sometimes barely distinguishable tide within the affairs of a human life tugging toward God or toward self.

In this chapter and the previous one, we have explored an extended series of landmarks in the history of Christian spiritual discernment. My single aim has been to give as much sense (as is possible in brief compass) of the actual texture of these figures' practice and theory of discernment. My hope has been that, besides providing an overview of different approaches to discernment, these chapters would surface some underlying principles of Christian reflection about truth and how best it may be encountered. The constructive elaboration of these ideas will have to await the last chapters of the book, but in the meantime I propose to clarify them somewhat further by comparing many of the writers we have examined on four constitutive features of discernment.

FOUR

Constitutive Themes in Discernment

In the previous two chapters we explored some major landmarks in the historical development of spiritual discernment and introduced some of the most significant teachers. Along the way there have been a number of major issues and common threads, each of which could well merit a chapter to itself. We might have considered the changing sense of personal identity that a deepening practice of discernment brings with it. Or we could have examined the relationship between spiritual discernment and the virtues, or the cultural and ecclesial dimensions of discernment. And the list could grow! I have, probably somewhat arbitrarily, selected four such themes. I think they are reasonable choices because they at least qualify as constitutive issues. That is, it would be hard to imagine a form of spiritual discernment that did not, in some fashion, take account of these matters. As such, they will, I hope, provide something of a bridge between the more expository survey chapters that have come before and the more thickly described case studies that are to follow. In brief, the four constitutive themes are these: (1) formation or training for discernment; (2) distinguishing characteristic impulses; (3) the problems of deception; and (4) the role of an eschatological or teleological perspective in discernment.

Fostering a Discerning Mind

In a pioneering twentieth-century treatment of the mystical life, Anselm Stolz offers sage advice about matters of classification and structure that must concern us here. The problem, writes the Benedictine scholar, is that prior to early modernity most contemplative or mystical teachers assumed a theological perspective in analyzing their subject matter, so that degrees of prayer or stages of spiritual progress are given in terms of the nature of the divine activity involved at any given point. But our more recent interest in the psychology of inner states has led us to read these earlier formulations in anachronistically subjective terms. Even when older classificatory schemes are retained (e.g., union with God), they tend to be filled out in terms of inner experiential details in which their earlier users had far less investment.[1] Stolz's point here is not primarily critical but hermeneutical, and it will be a useful reminder for us as well; for given how significant inner states are to various discernment processes, it would indeed be easy to over-look the theological significance that the teachers we will be considering see in the patterns and structures they examine. So, for example, while we are in this section considering the personal transformations needed for a dis-cerning attitude to grow, it will be helpful to bear in mind that these are, for most of our authors, *primarily* accounts of the different ways in which grace may be at work in human acts and attitudes. They are attempting to find a language for the way God reconfigures the soul so that it may see the whole truth of things.

Let us begin this section, then, by noticing the attention our authors give to the unrecognized influence of various factors upon the mind. Indeed, their common concern seems to be that the mind very often simply assumes it is making an assessment of things in a quite transparent manner, unsus-pecting the impulses at work upon it. I suppose we might almost denomi-nate this as the first or propaedeutic step in forming a discerning mind, that is, becoming aware that one's thoughts are not entirely one's own. Origen writes of the mysterious and almost inconceivable depths inherent in his paradigm cases of discernment, namely, providence and scripture. His con-cern, however, is that just *because* the depths of these wonders are so far beyond our usual conceptions, the interpreter is very likely to constrict the reality to fit the preconception. "Just as providence is not abolished because of our ignorance . . . so neither is the divine character of scripture, which extends through all of it, abolished because our weakness cannot discern in every sentence the hidden splendour of its teachings."[2]

The first step in forming a discerning mind is becoming aware of the pre-conceptions and urgencies that conduct the mind toward an all-too-tidy consistency marked more by its narrowness than its wisdom. Sometimes Origen identifies this problem as "owing to the lack of thorough training, sometimes owing to rashness" (*First Principles* 4.2.2). In the commentary on the Song of Songs, Origen specifically mentions "evil thoughts and debased teachers" as undermining the soul's true vision of reality.[3] Origen assumes an underlying freedom and coherence in human thinking, such that the divine generosity would be naturally perspicuous to the mind. But *if* the mind is uncultured and narrow in its interests (or misled by "debased teach-ers"), and if it is easily moved by impulses of which it is unaware, then the bias with which it interprets reality will be quite imperceptible to it.

We see Cassian and Evagrius working with the same preliminary concerns. With playful subtlety Cassian's dialogue mimics the problem of the distracted mind: Abba Moses is discoursing gravely on the movement of the mind into contemplation of God when Cassian's companion Germanus breaks in vociferously:

> Why is it, then, that superfluous thoughts insinuate themselves into us so subtly and hiddenly when we do not even want them, and indeed do not even know of them, that it is very difficult not only to cast them out but even to understand them and to catch hold of them? Can the mind, then, sometimes be found free of these, and is it ever able to avoid being invaded by illusions of this sort?[4]

No one will ever accuse Germanus of insinuating *his* thoughts into the conversation too hiddenly. Yet while he asks a worthy question, Abba Moses's calm response hints, at least, that there is an unrecognized urgency buzzing around in Germanus himself, and that the concern he raises is best dealt with gently and without allowing the anxiety that speaks the question to gain too dominant a place. "It is, indeed, impossible," says the abba, "for the mind not to be troubled by thoughts, but accepting them or rejecting them is possible for everyone who makes an effort. It is true that their origin does not in every respect depend on us, but it is equally true that their refusal or acceptance does depend on us."[5] Moses points to the freedom of a self-aware mind to discern the appropriate response to the thoughts that arise.

But what generates this kind of self-awareness and the right disposition enabling one to respond to one's thoughts appropriately? Moses goes on to remind Germanus that the character of our thoughts can indeed develop in healthy or unhealthy directions.

> Therefore we practice the frequent reading of and constant meditation on Scripture, so that we may be open to a spiritual point of view. For this reason we frequently chant the psalms, so that we may continually grow in compunction. For this reason we are diligent in vigils, fasting, and praying, so that the mind which has been stretched to its limits may not taste earthly things but contemplate heavenly ones. When these things cease because negligence has crept in again, then, it is inevitable that the mind, by the accumulated filth of the vices, will soon turn in a carnal direction and fall.[6]

Abba Moses does not, it seems, recommend divine reading and ascetic practices simply as a way of quieting carnal clamor. He is advocating a real formation of the mind and heart that seeks to become "open to a spiritual point of view," which grows in "compunction," leading to a "mind which has been stretched to its limits." Formation for discernment requires a mind open to the divine "more," a gracious beauty and reality that stretches human thought and frees it (see the end of the present chapter). Perhaps we could even see this movement toward contemplation as the apprenticeship of the mind to the divine teaching, as the stabilizing and grounding of the mind in the divine principles of reality. This is the fruit of coming to "contemplate heavenly" things. And this is what forms a mind with the disposition and perceptions of things needful for an authentically discerning attitude.

Cassian's older contemporary Evagrius draws out these implications with considerable nuance. In his most famous summary of spiritual progress toward true theology (sharing in the divine self-knowing), Evagrius reports what he has regularly heard during his years with the desert elders:

> The fear of God strengthens faith, my son, and continence in turn strengthens this fear. Patience and hope make this latter virtue solid beyond all shaking and they also give birth to *apatheia*. Now this *apatheia* has a child called *agape* who keeps the door to deep knowledge of the created universe. Finally, to this knowledge succeed theology and the supreme beatitude.[7]

The stages of deepening participation in divine life are marked here by growing gifts of perception and insight. At the beginning level, one seeks clarity about and freedom from urgent desires and obsessions, and this comes through the gifts of faith and fear of God. This leads to a balanced and untroubled state (*apatheia*), which permits one to grow in availability (as Ignatius of Loyola was later to suggest) to the divine desire and will for all things (*agape*). This greater attunement to God then leads one to the first stage of contemplation, which Evagrius calls "natural" contemplation; it is a deepening perception and comprehension of the divine speaking in all natural things, an understanding of their unique inner principles (*logoi*). We can see how the stillness and attentiveness, and the freedom from self-preoccupation, required by this contemplative "listening" to the divine voice in creation would help form a discerning mind and prepare one to receive the gift of sharing more directly in the divine self-understanding and self-speaking (*theo-logia*).

Evagrius frequently clarifies the momentum of discernment toward contemplation. By contrast, he says, the demons are always hoping to suckle one passion or another within believers precisely so as to obsess and distract them: "for when man's irrational passions are thriving he is not free to pray and to seek the word of God."[8] Hence the ascetic life and practice of the virtues are recommended as aids to freedom and availability for reality: "We seek after virtues for the sake of attaining to the inner meaning (*logoi*) of created things. We pursue these latter, that is to say the inner meanings of what is created, for the sake of attaining to the Lord (*Logos*) who has created them."[9] Clearly, the hallmarks of a discerning mind in Evagrius's view are an imperturbable stability in the face of self-centered passions, a deep perception of the reality of things in themselves, and a desire and openness for the self-disclosure of the One who gives all things their reality and intelligibility.

Before considering this contemplative trajectory in discernment, it will be useful to see how integrally the pursuit of virtue features in progress toward contemplation; for as Evagrius says, "the virtues have knowledge as their fruit."[10] In some ways, this matter may sound strikingly odd to our ears, for modernity has prized theories of knowledge in which moral virtues have had little role. But for ancient Christians, for whom the full scope of discernment and knowledge ultimately reaches into a personal relationship with the divine giver of whatever there is to be known, the personal transformation of the would-be knower is essential. In this, Christians and Jews intensified the common ancient Mediterranean belief in an inextricable link between virtue and truth. In §89 of the *Praktikos*, Evagrius offers his outline of this perspective, highlighting which virtues may be cultivated in each dimension of the soul and what their role is in the pursuit of truth:

Part of the Soul	Virtues	Role
	prudence	to war against demons, protect the virtues, arrange matters as needed
the rational	understanding	to direct all things harmoniously toward perfection
	wisdom	to govern the contemplation of the intelligible structures of all things corporeal and incorporeal
	temperance	to permit exposure to the things that lead to fantasy while sustaining freedom from passions
the concupiscible or desirous	charity	to manifest the deep image of God to fellow humankind, even when under demonic attack
	continence	to refuse with joy every self-gratifying pleasure
the irascible	courage	to overcome fear of enemies
	patience	to endure affliction

throughout the soul	justice	to produce a harmony among the parts of the soul and their virtues

Evagrius understands the soul to be a battleground in which the passions, stirred up by demons, cloud the mind and render it undiscerning. The harmonizing of the soul begins by an awareness of its capacities and their strengths (virtues) so as to grow more aware of the movements afoot. "The spirit that is engaged in the war against the passions does not see clearly the basic meaning of the war for it is something like a man fighting in the darkness of night. Once it has attained to purity of heart though, it distinctly makes out the designs of the enemy."[11] So the practice and growth of virtue, Evagrius suggests, directly promotes a crucial first step in discernment, namely an awareness of the true origin of one's impulses and urgencies.

The goal of this ascetical progress in virtue is that charity which, as we saw above, Evagrius understands to be the "doorkeeper" to the house of knowledge. Or as Diadochus, writing a generation later, would put it: "All spiritual contemplation should be governed by faith, hope and love, but most of all by love. The first two teach us to be detached from visible delights, but love unites the soul with the excellence of God, searching out the Invisible by means of intellectual perception."[12] Diadochus here subsumes the various moral and intellectual virtues outlined by Evagrius under the first two theological virtues of faith and hope, which together instill in the soul such a sense (albeit inchoate) of life with God as to free it from present passions. But like Evagrius, he sees the birth of love (*agape*) as the motive force conducting the soul toward the contemplative goal of a discerning life.

Diadochus ascribes a far more prominent role to the Holy Spirit in the healing of the mind and strengthening of discernment. Indeed, he reckons the Spirit's intervention as a necessary liberation from the influence of the passions and their demonic sponsors: "Only the Holy Spirit can purify the intellect, for unless a greater power comes and overthrows the despoiler, what he has taken captive will never be set free" (§28). The powerful love and light of the Spirit begin to dwell in the soul, transforming its capacities and awareness:

Then we shall have the lamp of spiritual knowledge burning always within us; and when it is shining constantly in the inner shrine of the soul, not only will the intellect perceive all the dark and bitter attacks of the demons, but these attacks will be greatly weakened when exposed for what they are by that glorious and holy light. (§28)

Perhaps we could say that Diadochus restructures the discussion of virtue-formation in pneumatological terms. The virtues emerge in the soul and lead to self-awareness, knowledge, and discernment, but they are the shining forth of the Spirit's transforming presence. In fact, for Diadochus, our perceptive or discriminative faculty is now so torn between self-gratifying earthly pleasures on one side and God-oriented aspiration on the other, that the human mind is enervated and numbed. Only the "communion of the Holy Spirit" can unify and reinvigorate the soul; for unless the Spirit "actively illumines the inner shrine of our heart, we shall not be able to taste God's goodness with the perceptive faculty undivided" (§29).

The formative role of the Holy Spirit, not surprisingly, stems from the Spirit's particular mission as pouring out divine love and communion within creation. For Diadochus, this gift of a renewed ability "to taste God's goodness" is an absolute prerequisite. I think this is because such foretaste of life with God awakens the soul to the real truth and goodness of everything, precisely because the soul sees them all now in terms of their divine destiny rather than as potential possessions of its own: "our intellect, when it begins to act vigorously and with complete detachment, is capable of perceiving the wealth of God's grace and is never led astray by any illusion of grace which comes from the devil" (§30). Diadochus sees the mind as constantly subject to the suasion of demonic fantasy, false promises, and ultimately, obsession with an ever more impoverished inventory of gratifications—the "illusions of grace." But a mind awake to the true "wealth of God's grace" is no longer so easily captivated by fearful anxieties or possessive urges, for it gazes steadily and wonderingly upon the infinite divine generosity. And this gaze unifies the discerning eye, setting it free from any susceptibility to being tantalized and diverted from reality.

Diadochus also importantly distinguishes between a pleasant calmness, arduously achieved through self-control (which he believes is easily destroyed), and "the feeling of warmth which the Holy Spirit engenders in the heart," which by contrast is "completely peaceful and enduring" (§74). Whereas the attentiveness won through self-control is a good, it can be relied upon only with danger, since it is not only liable to grow depleted but is also easily manipulable by demonic thoughts of self-satisfaction and pride. "On the other hand, the feeling of warmth which the Holy Spirit engenders in the heart is completely peaceful and enduring. It awakes in all parts of the soul a longing for God; its heat does not need to be fanned by anything outside the heart, but through the heart it makes the whole man rejoice with a boundless love" (§74). Again love is described as the midwife of true knowledge, for this love aroused by the Spirit permits the mind to taste that divinely "boundless love" which is the very marrow of all truth.

Writing several centuries later, Catherine of Siena brings to light the inner integrity of the various subtopics of formation for discernment. She strongly confirms the synthetic role of love, desire, and the Holy Spirit in the progress toward a discerning mind. Very much like Diadochus, Catherine agrees that the practice of self-awareness and virtue is a prerequisite, but any real growth in discernment occurs only as the soul comes to feed more and more upon the divine love. In the *Dialogue,* Catherine describes God the Father as remarking that selfish love "is a cloud that blots out the light of reason"; in broadly Augustinian fashion, then, Catherine hears God describing the healing of the soul's memory, understanding, and will through their reorientation by divine love and away from self-centered love.[13]

The soul's grandeur is that it "cannot live without love"; indeed, "she always wants to love something because love is the stuff she is made of, and through love I created her," says the Father (§51). But this is also the problem, for if the memory is stuffed with *selfish* loves, gratifying vanities, and impatience at whatever impedes the self, then the understanding keeps working away on such things, being fed more and more upon less and less because of the will's enchantment by a false love:

> This love so dazzles the eye that it neither discerns nor sees anything but the glitter of these things. Such is their glitter that understanding sees and affection loves them all as if their brightness came from goodness and loveliness. Were it not for this glitter, people would never sin, for the soul by her very nature cannot desire anything but good. But vice is disguised as something good for her, and so the soul sins. Her eyes, though, cannot tell the difference because of her blindness, and she does not know the truth. So she wanders about searching for what is good and lovely where it is not to be found. (§51)

Catherine's analysis of the problem of discernment makes the role of the will inescapably clear: the soul's "blindness" stems from the dazzling allure of things. And, says Catherine, the world simply is going to be like this! So the real question is what fixates the soul on things that do not satisfy; and, as we have seen, Catherine unhesitatingly declares self-love to be the culprit. It seems to me that, implicitly at least, she is saying something like this: humankind is made by love for love, but precisely because this is so powerful a tide within human life, there is a strong tug toward whatever can satisfy it most quickly and in terms that the hungry self can have under its control. Paradoxically, these satisfactions are *too* easy for human love, which is created for a far greater communion, and so they leave humanity more and more immured in a delusional effort to get more of what satisfies less.

Catherine's proposed formation for an authentically discerning mind provides a profoundly trinitarian resolution. In brief, she says, it is necessary to retrain human love upon the one finite object that will not shortchange it but will instead hold it ever more completely open to a love beyond its grasp. And it is this restoration of human love to what we might call a trinitarian intensity that, Catherine believes, sets the mind free to discern truth once more. For Catherine, the starting place is not the soul's *own* awareness of itself but its enlightenment by the vision of *God's* love for it: "in knowing yourself you will come to know my mercy in the blood of my only begotten Son, thus drawing my divine charity to yourself with your love" (§63). Intriguingly, Catherine sets this process of the soul's rerooting in divine charity within the Great Fifty Days from Easter to Pentecost. She sees it as an unfolding of repentance for the various ways in which the soul has betrayed Christ, God's love made flesh, just as the first disciples underwent a deepening conversion during the time of the resurrection appearances.

> *"Once your understanding has received the light from the fire as I've described, the fire transforms you into itself and you become one with the fire."*

Their hearts are purged as "they persevered in watching and constant humble prayer until they were filled with the Holy Spirit" (§63). This intensified attentiveness to the Holy Spirit, "the flame of love," begins to open the inner discerning eye of the soul, so that it is not mesmerized by smaller loves but rather gazes within and beyond them to a previously unseen truth that recontextualizes them all: the divine bounty that gives and blesses all things.

> Affection is love's hand, and this hand fills the memory with thoughts of me and of the blessings I have given. Such remembrance makes the soul caring instead of indifferent, grateful instead of thankless. . . . In the dignity of [the soul's] existence she tastes the immeasurable goodness and uncreated love with which I created her. And in the sight of her own wretchedness she discovers and tastes my mercy, for in mercy I have lent her time and drawn her out of darkness. (§51)

We could say that for Catherine, the crucial theme of formation for discernment is conversion to God's love, not a self-preoccupied remorse but a genuine lifting up of the heart to feast again upon the fullness of God's mercy and abundance.

This encounter with the divine charity, says Catherine, "does to our soul what physical fire does: it warms us, enlightens us, changes us into itself."[14] The reciprocal influence of heart and mind, will and understanding, are carefully probed by Catherine. The blazing divine charity both enkindles and enlightens; perhaps we could even say that it reveals truth precisely because it transforms *human* loving into divine loving *in* humanity—and this loving as God loves makes possible a vision of reality as it is in truth. "So enlightened by that venerable fire, our understanding expands and opens wide. And once we have experienced and accepted the light, we so clearly discern what is in God's will that we want to follow no other footsteps than those of Christ crucified."[15] Fully as much as her forebears in teaching discernment, Catherine of Siena is concerned to see the conception and full maturation of the virtues as the fruits of this divine loving within the soul; but far more explicitly than the older desert traditions, Catherine roots the whole formation process in a growing attunement to Christ.

This becomes the measure and sure guide of formation, even as the experience of God's mercy in Christ is the motive force of the soul's conversion to truth: "Once your understanding has received the light from the fire as I've described, the fire transforms you into itself and you become one with the fire. Your memory thus becomes one with Christ crucified in that it cannot hold, enjoy, or think about anything except what the one you love enjoys."[16] We will explore in the next chapter what it means to "have the mind of Christ," as St. Paul put it, and to be formed in this way for a discerning life. But for now, Catherine's profound sense of Christ's own vision of reality is highly evocative and suggests the authentic matrix of discernment: "Through the flesh of Christ crucified, we suck the milk of divine sweetness, sweet light where no shadows fall. . . . This is what our enlightened understanding sees and contemplates as it gazes steadily into the eye of God's divine charity and goodness."[17] For Catherine, it would be fair to say, this is what it would be like to discern reality with the eyes of Christ: to gaze at all things, to know their truth, by gazing "steadily into the eye of God's divine charity and goodness."

Recognizing Signs and Distinguishing Spirits

If one had to specify the most central theme in the theology of discernment, surely it would be the struggle to recognize the source of the spirits or impulses at work in an individual or community. If we were devoting a whole treatise to individual teachers of discernment such as Ignatius of Loyola or Jonathan Edwards, we could easily spend the entire monograph on this topic alone. This leads me to a warning: because such magisterial thinkers devised quite highly articulated and contextualized schemes for distinguishing spirits, the present treatment of them will be less than ideal; for my goal in this section is not to itemize one person's list of criteria for discriminating between spirits and then another's, but to *try* at least to group similar criteria together for comparative purposes (which will necessitate taking them out of context). While a number of teachers of discernment do categorize all the signs of various influences directly in terms of their origins—from God, from the human mind and heart, or from the spiritual realm opposed to

God—this would jump over an important step for our purposes; for we are trying to consider what we might call the "presenting symptoms" with which discernment has to deal.[18] And we want to see how our representative teachers approach the problem of recognizing, by *means* of those symptoms, the source or direction of the influence at work.

One final and important preliminary observation is necessary. While there are certainly some signs that, because they point to fairly apparent concrete effects, are hard to mistake (e.g., an arrogant disregard for the common good in favor of one's own), there are some signs, particularly inner thoughts or feelings, whose significance cannot be readily discerned without some underlying hermeneutical context. The great teacher in this regard is Ignatius of Loyola. In the *Spiritual Exercises,* he begins his first set of principles to guide discernment with a sage admonition: attend to the context of a spiritual sign within a person's life-direction (nos. 314ff.). Good and evil spirits attempt to influence persons quite differently, depending on whether the person is already inclined toward conversion and love of God or toward one sin after another. Suppose someone experiences a wonderful sense of delight and expectation; this could be the motion of *either* a good spirit *or* a bad spirit, says Ignatius. We cannot discern which it might be apart from the broader hermeneutical frame of the person's life. If the person is headed toward the life of heaven, then the good spirit who would stir up the person all the more in that direction will likely pour out encouragement and hope; if the person is headed in a negative direction, then the sense of delight is more likely a sign of the evil spirit intending to secure the person's pleasurable compliance. And of course the converse would also be true.

	Actions of a good spirit	Actions of a bad spirit
on a person growing in love of God	encouragement, peace, consolation	anxiety, sense of futility, desolation
on a person turning away from love of God	remorse, stinging doubt about plans	anticipated pleasures, fantasies, excitement

As we can see from this oversimplified presentation, it would be quite easy to read the signs in the wrong fashion. Having said this, I will simply need to assume that Ignatius's important hermeneutical point will be kept in mind as we go along, without necessarily bringing it to bear on every conceivable instance.

As a very rudimentary structure for ordering the vast array of representative teachings on all this, I'm going to propose a rough division of signs into three categories (which inevitably overlap and are mutually implicating): the affective or attitudinal, the noetic or intellectual, and the relational or communal.

Affective Signs

In the *First Principles,* Origen presents one of the first systematic treatments of Christian teaching on distinguishing signs. After summarizing the common witness of the Scriptures and several late first-century texts, Origen emphasizes that the *result* of the influence of divine or demonic spirits always remains a matter of the believer's own choice: "Nothing else happens to us as a result of these good or evil thoughts which are suggested to our heart but a mere agitation and excitement which urges us on to deeds either of good or evil. It is possible for us, when an evil power has begun to urge us on to a deed of evil, to cast away the wicked suggestions and to resist the low enticements."[19] Origen goes on to say that the same is true in the case of a divine power; "our faculty of free will is preserved in either case." Origen clearly understands the influence to be active in the realm of one's desires and intentions, but in such a way that one could still choose how to respond.

This is important to Origen, for he sees it as one of the enemy's chief tactics to convince the soul that it really does *not* have the power to resist. "The opposing powers," he writes, afflict the soul with all kinds of losses, insults, accusations, and dangers, not simply in order to make the soul suffer but in order to provoke the soul "by means of them to fierce anger or excessive sorrow or the depths of despair."[20] For Origen, then, a vital clue in the affective realm, leading to the identification of the spirit at work, is precisely the impact of high emotional decibels upon personal freedom: if believers find themselves overwhelmed by anger or despair to the point that they feel *compelled* to act or think in certain ways, that is a very likely sign that they are being manipulated. Their present experiential state, in other words, is not the whole truth of reality; believers should remember their freedom and claim it. Indeed, he notes the preservation and enhancement of freedom and judgment as positive signs: "we learn to discern clearly when the soul is moved by the presence of a spirit of the better kind, namely, when it suffers no mental disturbance or aberration whatsoever as a result of the immediate inspiration and does not lose the free judgment of the will."[21]

Athanasius's *Life of Antony* points to a number of markers indicating demonic influence, chiefly incitements to whatever is a besetting temptation, unusual gifts of prophecy, a gyration between overzealousness and diffidence, and, above all, an overmastering sense of fear and threat.[22] By contrast, the presence of holy influence is announced very differently: "It comes so quietly and gently that immediately joy, gladness and courage arise in the soul. For the Lord who is our joy is with them [the good spirits], and the power of God the Father."[23] While the divine holiness may well evoke a sober fear or awe, it is a sign of truly holy influence if this fear is "taken away and in place of it comes joy unspeakable, cheerfulness, courage, renewed strength, calmness of thought. . . . Joy and a settled state of soul show the holiness of him who is present."[24] The impact of evil spirits is just the reverse: it is "fraught with confusion, with din, with sounds and cryings . . . from which arise fear in the heart, tumult and confusion of thought, dejection, hatred toward them who live a life of discipline, grief, remembrance of kinsfolk and fear of death, and finally desire of evil things, disregard of virtue and unsettled habits."[25]

The contrasting progression of feelings in either case is worth noting: the evil spirits seem to lead through fear and confusion to a state of sourness and unsettlement, while the good spirits move the soul chiefly through joy, peace, and stability in hope. Diadochus would later draw the same contrast; the energy of the Holy Spirit leaves the soul settled, the mind undistracted, and the whole person experiencing "uninterrupted joy."

> But if at that moment the intellect conceives any doubt or unclean thought, and if this continues in spite of the fact that the intellect calls on the holy name . . . then it should realize that the sweetness it experiences is an illusion of grace, coming from the deceiver with a counterfeit joy. Through this joy, amorphous and disordered, the devil tries to lead the soul into an adulterous union with himself. For when he sees the intellect unreservedly proud of its own experiences of spiritual perception, he entices the soul by means of certain plausible illusions of grace, so that it is seduced by that dank and debilitating sweetness.[26]

The subtle interaction between the mind and the feelings here is noteworthy: while the would-be contemplative is entranced by an inchoate sense of spiritual knowledge, the very pride being *felt* becomes the open door to demonic influence. Almost imperceptibly, the soul is made to shift focus from the divine reality whose contemplation brings stillness and joy to the joy it longs to experience, and thence to "that dank and debilitating sweetness" itself.

We might describe this reading of the stability/instability sign as also a shift from being grounded in God to a needier grounding in one's own *experiences* of God—experiences that are themselves easily switched to demonic simulations. Catherine of Siena confirms almost precisely the same insight about "whether there could be any delusion in . . . gladness."[27] The more a soul rejoices in a gift of new virtue or a consolation, the less the soul "is careful to discern with prudence where that thing came from" and thus "people who are very fond of spiritual consolation and find great pleasure in it hanker after visions and set their hearts more on the enjoyment of con-solation" than on God.[28] Catherine observes that in such conditions the soul could easily be manipulated by devilish influences.

The test is whether the gladness over spiritual consolations becomes enervating and self-cultivating with a painful "pricking of conscience," or whether it leads onward into a "burning desire for virtue and . . . humility"; the latter indicates that such souls truly "love the gift because of [God] the Giver, and not because of their own consolation."[29] Catherine develops, in this way, the full interpretation of a person's ongoing orientation, thus pointing to a form of discernment that goes beyond a scrutinizing of discrete moments and motions. As she records the Father in the *Dialogue:* "In my visitation [the soul] will find fear at the beginning; but in the middle and at the end, gladness and a hunger for virtue. When it is the devil, however, the beginning is happy, but then the soul is left in spiritual confusion and dark-ness."[30] We have a strong case of agreement here between Catherine and the early desert traditions of discernment; in both schools of thought, the nature of the spiritual influence only becomes discernible through the development of a life. Again, the direction of interpretation is beyond the purely interior into the realm of concrete effects and practices.

No single text in the history of spiritual discernment has led to more care-ful thought about this than the *Spiritual Exercises* of Ignatius of Loyola. Of special importance is Ignatius's use of the distinction between experiences of consolation and desolation in discerning both the animating impulses in one's consciousness and the authentic direction of one's mission in any given situation. As I noted near the beginning of this chapter, it would be crudely inaccurate to think that the consolation/desolation distinction simply *is* the criterion, for the distinction can only be brought to bear within the larger hermeneutic of a person's general direction in life. Furthermore, Ignatius follows other major teachers in regarding more external criteria such as Scripture and tradition as determinative. Given these caveats, the distin-guished commentator Jules Toner remarks on the "cardinal importance" of consolation and desolation for Ignatian discernment:

> Most, even if not all, of the motions which are relevant for Ignatian discernment of spirits can be in one way or another integrated into the total complex experience of spiritual consolation and spiritual desola-tion. . . . Discouragement is Satan's principal aim in his attack on a spiritually maturing person, and everything in spiritual desolation leads up to discouragement. . . . As we have also seen, consolation in particular has a cardinal value as a way in which the Holy Spirit encourages us and prepares us to receive and recognize his inspira-tions. On the other hand, spiritual consolation not fully understood can be used by Satan to deceive and mislead us. Further, we ourselves,

unless we understand how to respond, can misuse it to the frustration of God's purpose and to our harm.[31]

Toner points here to the delicate interplay in Ignatian discernment between interior affect, spiritual perception, and concrete actions. The central intention of Ignatius's two sets of rules or guidelines for the discernment of spirits is simply to facilitate this interplay by fostering better awareness of these affective markers and better interpretation of their significance. Or as Ignatius himself puts it (in titling the rules more suitable for the first "week" of the exercises): "Rules to aid us toward perceiving and then understanding, at least to some extent, the various motions which are caused in the soul: the good motions that they may be received, and the bad that they may be rejected."[32] George Ganss (following Toner) outlines the two sets of rules for discernment (sections 313-27 and 328-36 of the *Spiritual Exercises*) as follows:

> *Consolation, for Ignatius, is truly a grace from God, and should not be confused with general good feelings. It is characterized above all by an intensifying of the soul's ardent love for God.*

I. The first set: Fundamental principles for discerning spirits: the contrary actions of the good and evil spirits on regressing and progressing Christians (rules 1-2)
   A. Spiritual consolation and desolation (rules 3-14)
      1. Their nature (rules 3-4)
   B. Remaining open to the Holy Spirit during desolation (rules 5-14)
      1. Accepting the desolation as a test (rule 7)
      2. Counterattack by patience (rule 8)
      3. Examination of the causes (rule 9)
      4. During consolation prepare for desolation (rules 10-11)
      5. Style and strategy of the devil (rules 12-14)
II. The second set: The evil spirit in time of spiritual consolation (rules 1-8)
   A. Deception beginning during spiritual consolation itself (rules 1-7)
      1. Characteristics of the good and evil spirits (rule 1)
      2. Consolation without a preceding cause (rule 2)
      3. Consolation with a preceding cause (rule 3)
      4. Deception in consolation with a preceding cause (rule 4)
      5. How to detect such demonic deception (rules 5-6)
      6. Learning by reflection on experience (rule 6)
      7. Assurance and explanation (rule 7)
   B. Deception during the afterglow of spiritual consolation (rule 8).[33]

This is not the place to provide yet another commentary on these rules; what I would like to do is simply to analyze how Ignatius *utilizes* affective signs in discernment. The experiences of consolation and desolation that Ignatius attends to are in themselves much of a piece with the earlier accounts we have seen from Origen onward. We have the usual contrasts between anxiety or despondency as signs of the evil spirit, and courage, peace, and joy as signs of the good spirit (315). But Ignatius suddenly introduces, as I mentioned in the opening of this chapter, a canny second axis, so that the affective notes can be discerned far more discriminatingly by hearing them not only as they sound within the life of a progressing believer *but also* as they might be experienced in the life of one who is regressing spiritually. In this latter case of one regressing, the "affirmation" given by the evil spirit mimics the encouragement of the good spirit, but in a self-preoccupying and gratifying mode. Conversely, for one regressing, the good spirit's impulse is experienced as a feeling of uncertainty and misgiving (feelings more often associated with the evil spirit).

After establishing this existential interpretive framework (what matters for Ignatius is precisely one's actual course of life), the remaining rules of the first set attend for the most part to the consolation/desolation contrast and to the wisest response in each case. Consolation, for Ignatius, is truly a grace from God and should not be confused with general good feelings. It is characterized above all by an intensifying of the soul's ardent love for God, to the extent that the soul is increasingly free from the domination of any other needs or desires: "Finally, under the word consolation I include every increase in hope, faith, and charity, and every interior joy which calls and attracts one toward heavenly things and to the salvation of one's soul, by bringing it tranquility and peace in its Creator and Lord" (316). Provided that wise counsel has assisted a soul to recognize a genuine consolation (i.e., to discern that one is not simply being enticed further along a negative path), then insights and decisions arrived at during a season of consolation are worthy of adherence and respectful observance; for "the good spirit is chiefly the one who guides and counsels us in time of consolation" (318).

I think it would be fair to say that Ignatius retains, in his treatment of consolation, chief features of earlier teachers' views—that signs of positive spiritual influence include an interior freedom from compulsion, a genuinely humble desire for God, and an other-directed feeling of joy or peace. Where Ignatius presses the tradition further, I believe, is in his ability to harness this discerning awareness of spiritual consolation to a sense of mission: in other words, the new clarity about what animates one is not simply a good but ought to do some work in the arena of practical judgment and concrete availability for service. Here, I would argue, the completely central role of attunement to Christ (discussed in the previous chapter) in the *Spiritual Exercises* validates and encourages this intrinsic connection between clearer self-understanding and the freedom to give oneself more fully to reality.

Turning to Ignatius's treatment of desolation, we find many familiar features, but perhaps described with a new acuity. Ignatius seems to fathom the negative influence not merely as a lure into various self-debasing behaviors but as a painful erosion of authentic self-acceptance and freedom to act. Desolation, says Ignatius, includes,

> for example, obtuseness of soul, turmoil within it, an impulsive motion toward low and earthly things, or disquiet from various agitations and temptations. These move one toward lack of faith and leave one without hope and without love. One is completely listless, tepid, and unhappy, and feels separated from our Creator and Lord. (317)

Especially noteworthy is Ignatius's use of the theological virtues of faith, hope, and love as markers of either consolation or desolation. In the quotation above we see him suggest how desolation leads to the diminishment of these dispositions toward friendship with God; desolation, in other words, is in no way simply reducible to feeling unhappy, though it may include this. Rather, desolation is the affective symptom of life being lived in contradiction because it has become a life that "feels separated from our Creator." At first glance, this seems a fairly obvious conclusion for Ignatius to have drawn, but I think it highlights again the christocentric dynamic in Ignatius's thinking about discernment. For he has conceived the spiritual signs not simply as they bespeak some aspect of the soul but precisely as they indicate the soul's readiness or debility for participation in the mission of Christ.

Among the other more notable features of Ignatius's teaching are what we might call a certain dramatic flair for depicting the sinister. We have seen how the desert elders seemed to relish a good account of struggles with the devil, but Ignatius also employs this teaching device with considerable deftness. He pictures the "enemy" as a classic case of passive aggressor—easily cowed by a brave spirit but rapidly inflating to a "ferocity . . . almost without limit" if unchecked; if a "person begins to fear and lose courage in the face of the temptations, there is no beast on the face of the earth as fierce as the enemy of human nature when he is pursuing his damnable intention with his surging malice" (325). Similarly, Ignatius likens the evil spirit to a covert seducer who woos a person in secret and thrives in the shadows but is easily deflected by honesty and openness (326). Writing on the eve of modernity, Ignatius's concern that interiority not become a secret breeding ground for fantasy and deception sounds a particularly suggestive note.

Noetic Signs

Origen teaches, as we saw above, that spirits opposed to God and humanity seek to induce exaggerated and dominating emotions. But in his view even this aggressive vitiation of human freedom is not the ultimate goal. Rather, he argues, the opposing spirits seek thereby to induce believers who are in that worn-out state "to complain against God on the ground that he does not control human life fairly and righteously"; and that is not all: "Their aim is that by these efforts our faith may be weakened or that we may lose hope or be driven to abandon the true doctrines and persuaded to accept some impious belief about God."[34] So the deeper and more serious sign (because it may indicate a longer-term influence) is the gradual erosion of faith, a kind of theological instability in which emotional discomfort metamorphoses surreptitiously into intellectual distaste.

Origen seems to think that theological reflection marked by anxiety or anger, and a restless quest after more satisfying teachings, may well be driven by unhealthy forces. One can easily conceive of this taking the mirror-opposite forms of an uneasiness that longs for fundamentalist solutions or a frustration that ceaselessly achieves its own self-validation by condemning everyone else's beliefs. Origen points to a certain illusory assurance, even confidence, as possible signs that "false knowledge" is being "implanted in men's minds and souls are led astray while supposing that they have discovered wisdom."[35] By contrast, Origen implies that a sign of good spiritual influence may be a growing peaceful awareness of better things beyond one's ken; "a mind that is watchful and that casts away from itself whatever is evil calls to its side the assistance of the good."[36]

Antony the Great, in Athanasius's depiction, affirms this sense of serene enlargement of the mind as an indicator of good spiritual influence. In such cases "the thoughts of the soul remain unruffled and undisturbed . . . for the love of what is divine and of the things to come possesses it, and willingly it would be wholly joined with them if it could."[37] Perhaps we could say that the characteristic mental feature here would be an openness and hunger for union with the larger truth of God beyond the self, rather than an anxious pursuit of what the mind can grasp to itself.

Drawing on years spent among the desert elders, Evagrius formulated a summary list of the eight chief evil thoughts (*logismoi*) that beset the soul.[38] His searching analysis of their signs and symptoms reveals the near futility of categorizing them solely in any single section of our threefold division, but I think they are appropriately placed here for this reason: they all assume some passion stirring in the soul, but what chiefly interests Evagrius is how the demons use these passions to *distort and manipulate human perception of reality*. In each case this mental itch comes to obsess the mind to the point that all other thoughts are viewed through its perspective, thus leading the soul into deeper debasement of the understanding. Indeed, Evagrius concludes his analytical list by noting that "last of all" in the wake of pride there comes "the greatest of maladies—derangement of mind, associated with wild ravings and hallucinations of whole multitudes of demons in the sky."[39] Let me now sketch Evagrius's teaching on each "thought" in turn. As we can see, the common thread is a sense of deprivation and an anxious need to have something for oneself.

Evagrius: Eight Deadly Thoughts

1. *Gluttony* afflicts the monk with "concern for his stomach" and fixes the mind upon "the thought of a long illness, [and] scarcity of the commodities of life" (§7). Clearly Evagrius is not pointing to overeating per se as the real problem, but, rather, a gnawing sense that there will never be enough for oneself. Suddenly one is acutely aware of one's hunger, preoccupied with thoughts about how it may or may not be assuaged, and about how the spiritual life interferes with getting what one wants. The incipiently infantilizing tendencies are not far to seek. From this simple root, in my view, Evagrius spies out the secret growth of the whole tenacious system that evil uses to control the soul—a nexus of fear, anxiety, anger at the goods of others, and self-preoccupation. It is as though the mind begins, in this apparently simple-minded way, to be gripped more and more by a conviction of fundamental scarcity and closed off to a perspective of hopeful generosity and trusting patience. Evagrius suggests that one can fairly easily spot this creeping anxiety in its basic stages (the mind harbors images of people suffering and a weirdly enthralling fixation about getting sick!); the real problem is recognizing the warping and distorting influence that this thought has throughout the person's life.

2. *Impurity* or lust follows closely upon the soul's heightened sense of need and lack; one craving arouses another. Evagrius notes that "this demon has a way of bowing the soul down to practices of an impure kind, defiling it, and causing it to speak and hear certain words almost as if the reality were actually present to be seen" (§8). The emphasis on a slide into fantasy here is significant; for having begun to paint real life as intolerably stalked by scarcity, evil begins to lure the soul into an illusory world of lurid and yet never-fulfilling obsession. Reality becomes less and less real to the soul that must live upon fantasies.

3. *Avarice* very clearly displays this descent into anxiety and a compulsive neediness. This thought, says Evagrius, bespells the mind cringing among images of "a lengthy old age . . . famines that are sure to come, sickness that will visit us, the pinch of poverty, the great shame that comes from accepting the necessities of life from others" (§9). This last point is especially revealing, for it betrays the silken threads that, weblike, suspend the soul helplessly between specters of dependency and a deepening resentment of others. Soon the soul will be entirely unable to recognize the common goodness that may be discovered only in receiving all as a gift, including the gift of the other.

4. *Sadness* or melancholy is the direct result "of the deprivation of one's desires" that have now become so all-consuming (§10). Evagrius's analysis of the sign-value of sadness is particularly penetrating, I think, because he notes carefully how it *can* (if properly discerned) interrupt the soul's enthrallment: after all, the soul's fantasy world of catastrophic lack and compulsive need has been checked in some way that at least permits a sorrowful, and potentially repentant, mind. This would depend, however, precisely upon how the melancholy is understood. The person who has come to sadness can be helped to see the sadness as a genuine reaction of the soul to what were only illusory goods, and this opening can direct the mind's gaze perhaps toward the real good and real hope. But Evagrius warns that this will not be easy. Unless the soul is guided toward this opening, it will simply remain immured in a cycle of grief, anger, and blame; "so the miserable soul is now shrivelled up in her humiliation to the degree that she poured herself out upon these thoughts of hers" (§10).

5. *Anger* is the "most fierce passion" and "constantly irritates the soul . . . above all at the time of prayer it seizes the mind and flashes the picture of the offensive person before one's eyes" (§11). Evagrius highlights the transformation of the soul from one *occasionally* accosted by anger into a *persistently* indignant and embittered soul. In such cases, he advises, the mind is increasingly subjected to "alarming experiences by night . . . and the illusion of being attacked by poisonous wild beasts" (§11). Here at last the ravening "beast" of deprivation and compulsion has eaten the soul alive, transforming it into a hollow self, suffering from "a general debility of the body, malnutrition with its attendant pallor" (§11). Again, it is interesting that Evagrius does not point simply to actual events of rage or spite as the sign of this thought, but rather to a depth of bitter hollowness, less and less able to look freshly and hopefully upon the world, and increasingly enervated and worn out with the ceaseless bite of enmity.

6. *Acedia* or despondency is the very likely result of anger's attack; for Evagrius has begun to describe a being who has grown averse to real life and unable to draw any vitality or joy from the world. Evagrius remarks that this "noonday demon," who "makes it seem that the sun barely moves, if at all, and that the day is fifty hours long," is beyond doubt "the one that causes the most serious trouble of all" (§12). Unfortunately, the Latin tradition came to subsume acedia under sadness and therefore lost this pivotal sign of the soul's undoing. For Evagrius truly perceives this thought as the mark of a creature being subjected to another world, a mirror opposite to the creation of God's giving love, a world bereft of meaning or the excitement of discovery (indeed, Evagrius's final "thoughts," vainglory and pride, show this counterfeit self fully immured in a world whose power to bestow meaning now comes entirely from a false god). Besides diagnosing this

thought through the lassitude and tedium with which it infects everything, Evagrius highlights its deeper animating impulse of aversion to life itself: "[the demon] instills in the heart of the monk a hatred for the place, a hatred for his very life itself . . . . [S]hould there be someone at this period who happens to offend him in some way or other, this too the demon uses to contribute further to his hatred" (§12).

As I suggested above, this antipathy toward everything plunges the soul into an antiworld of restless self-assertion in a never-never land where conditions are never quite right. Acedia drives the soul "along to desire other sites where he can more easily procure life's necessities . . . and make a real success of himself." This hunger for validation in a world that no longer offers any satisfaction drives the soul to find it in ways that conflict with its reception as gift of God. I would argue that Evagrius's famous *apatheia,* or peaceful freedom, is the true confidence in God's providence of which acedia is the sour inverted form: instead of a joyful availability for everything that God gives (*apatheia*), the soul in the grip of acedia knows only a bored distaste for everything and a consequent need to manufacture pleasure and validation for itself out of whatever it can wring from other people. Evagrius notes, in fact, that if the soul can be liberated from this shadow world, it may already have been secretly prepared by God through its struggles to receive the gift of true *apatheia:* for "no other demon follows close upon the heels of this one," but rather "a state of deep peace and inexpressible joy arise out of this struggle" (§12).

7. *Vainglory* may thus turn out either to be a subtle and refined pursuit of the acedic soul for the praise of others or the subtle and refined search of the converted soul for the same thing! That is what, in Evagrius's view, makes vainglory and its final companion, pride, such crafty foes of authentic spiritual growth. When subject to vainglory, the soul is besieged with magnificent scenes of its own success and the praise it will receive. Although this fantasizing may be about more apparently pious and elevated objects than the mesmerism of lust, the effect is very similar: immuring the soul in a false world of necessity and hunger, and subject to traumatic frustration and grief when the fantasies are shattered. In fact, Evagrius warns that it is a particularly easy slide from vainglory to lust; for often someone whose hopes are dashed is "led off bound and is handed over to the demon of impurity," so that the habit of living in unreality is perpetuated (§13).

8. *Pride* is "the cause of the most damaging fall for the soul. For it induces the monk to deny that God is his helper and to consider that he himself is the cause of virtuous actions" (§14). Here is the full measure of that subverted desire for acceptance and love that has been so tragically uprooted from the good world of God's giving and lured down into the world of self-making.

Now the secret idolatry of the self, manipulated by the demons, is made plain. Everyone else, including God, is considered "stupid" because they do not realize one's true worth. So inverted has the soul become that it can no longer receive the vast outpouring of divine love that is ceaselessly offered. Thus it is driven to perceive all but itself as hopelessly uncaring, benighted to one's proper worth, and generally as useless beings. This complete distortion of reality leads, Evagrius predicts, to such cognitive dissonance and frustration that the mind finally becomes deranged.

Evagrius holds out hope for a discerning mind, advising one to take careful note of the seasons and symptoms of these besetting thoughts, and then "ask from Christ the explanation of these data he has observed" (§50). Because so much of the force of these eight demonic thoughts lies in their power to induce fantasy and a withdrawal from reality, I think we could say that, for Evagrius, discernment is truly a vigilance of the mind and its attendance upon the truth of the world. This joyful feeding of the mind upon the real is so important for Evagrius because it trains the soul for that full communion with Truth itself that he calls the contemplation of *theologia* or gazing upon the eternal self-expression of divine truth. As the spirit grows increasingly free from compulsions and illusions, it is "filled with reverence and joy at the same time"; when this occurs "then you can be sure that you are drawing near that country whose name is prayer."[40]

We can pursue further this topic of distinguishing healthy from unhealthy frames of *mind*. Both John Cassian, in the later patristic era, and Jean Gerson, in the later medieval era, offer probing tests by which to discern the true spirit animating one's thoughts and plans. Their common concern is not with obviously distorted intentions but with those apparently holy thoughts and perceptions that turn out to lead one astray. As a suggestive metaphor for this problem both Cassian and Gerson offer a traditional image of testing coins to discern whether they are true gold or counterfeit; the introduction of the latter, they both warn, leads to the debasement of the whole community's spiritual life.[41] Before we consider the two schemes for testing, here is a quick comparative glance at Cassian's four tests and Gerson's five (although they share some themes, the two schemes are not directly parallel).

Cassian	Gerson
1. Purity of the gold: Are thoughts genuinely purified by Holy Spirit or does impure human vanity still linger?	1. Weight of the coin: Do spiritual inspirations have the weight of true humility or are they puffed up with empty pride?
2. Real gold or imitation brass: Are thoughts being adulterated by "look-alike" interpretations or heretical tendencies?	2. Flexibility: Are thoughts and plans limber enough to be shaped by appropriate moderation and discretion or are they rigidly extreme?

3. Authentic image or the mark of a usurper: Are thoughts stamped with the image of true divine goodness or the sign of erring power?

4. Weight: Do the content and motivation of the inspiration confirm the authentic gravity of a stable spiritual life or do they lead toward a flighty instability and ostentation?

3. Durability or patience: Does the inspiration lead to endurance and humble perseverance or to obstinacy and arrogance?

4. Authentic stamp or counterfeit imprint: Does the inspiration conform to Scripture and a healthy moral development or does it depend on idiosyncratic views and special gifts?

5. True color of charity: Does the inspiration move one to sincere charity or is it animated by other more self-serving motivations?

Clearly these two discernment schemes have intriguing points of contact. Because Gerson's is worked out in far greater detail, I will follow his sequence and take up Cassian's points where they seem to offer the most illuminating parallels. Perhaps the most significant point of agreement lies in the two authors' common concern to examine the real *trajectory* of spiritual impulses. Both thinkers scrutinize the possibility

"If the coin in any, even the slightest matter, is different in its form and inscription from the royal mold, then without any doubt it is counterfeit."

that an apparently holy intention may either harbor an unsuspected malign influence within it or be easily susceptible to negative distortion and deflection.

Both Gerson's first and fifth tests relate to the affective roots of a new spiritual noetic, and so we can consider them together: the first searches for genuine humility at its basis, and the fifth for sincere charity.

Insofar as the first sign is concerned, if you know anyone who because of arrogant curiosity and vain praise and presumption of sanctity is eager to have unusual revelations, if he thinks himself to be worthy of them and delights in boastful tellings of such matters, then know that he deserves to be fooled.[42]

Gerson's concern is with the motivation at work: Is the person genuinely selfless in sharing word of the inspiration or in proceeding with a new plan, or is there an unacknowledged need for acceptance and praise distorting everything? Similarly with charity: "if love is true, chaste, and holy, it helps us inconceivably much in coming to know heavenly things. But if it is vain, in error, and lustful, it will fashion for itself different illusions, so that a person thinks he sees or understands matters of which he is wholly ignorant."[43] Here the noetic significance of the animating spirit is even clearer. An initial hunger for praise may lead to false inspirations and vitiate their sharing with the community; but a love that is overtaken with lust or self-serving needs renders the would-be visionary subject to illusions and false understandings. In each case, we can see how a constraining affective drive comes to dominate the mind. Cassian fully shares Gerson's scrutiny of the noetic shaping that affect gives to understanding. Perhaps we could say that for both authors this underlying affective matrix may be the best clue in discerning the likely authenticity and trajectory of a spiritual insight. Cassian points especially (as suspicious signs) to a curious need for ostentation, a sudden zeal for extreme ascetic rigor, and a pridefulness easily seduced by elegance and flattery.[44]

Throughout Cassian's and Gerson's treatment of these signs there is a strong emphasis on the intellectual miscarriage that threatens as a result of false spirituality. This is particularly clear in their respective tests regarding truth (in each case they use the metaphor of the image impressed upon the coin and whether it be that of the true ruler or another's). Gerson develops the metaphor by saying that "Holy Scripture is the location or workshop where the royal mold of the spiritual mint is kept. If the coin in any, even the slightest matter, is different in its form and inscription from the royal mold, then without any doubt it is counterfeit."[45] So in some sense, then, the lineaments of the scriptural "workshop" should be discernible in any authentic spiritual developments.

Cassian equally warns that a slightly skewed interpretation either of Scripture itself or of the scripturally inspired teaching of the elders leads to disaster; thus when Satan seemed to speak scripturally to Jesus during the tempting in the wilderness "he changed the precious words of Scripture by his clever use of them and gave them a contrary and harmful meaning, like someone who presents us with the image of a usurper's face under the guise of deceptive goal."[46] The surest indication, avers Cassian, that a "false impression" has been stamped upon a spiritual inspiration is the way it seems to shift its meaning from benign to baneful. Such intentions "appear very pious at first sight . . . but they are clandestinely fabricated by the fraud of demons" and lead to a self-defeating misunderstanding of one's vocation or of spiritual matters in general.[47]

Gerson brings a deep sense of the ambiguities involved and the difficulties of interpretation. Near the end of his discussion, he admits that it may be nearly impossible, even for the very learned, to detect the intellectual and doctrinal misdirections that lurk in false inspiration. What he recommends is a regular examination of the existential framework of the one whose inspiration is of concern. All spiritual insights are worthy of acceptance "so long as humility precedes, accompanies, and follows them, if nothing harmful is mixed in with them"; on the other hand, "if anyone takes his point of departure in such matters with pride and uses them as an excuse for displaying himself, then be suspicious of everything."[48]

Ignatius also emphasizes this theme of the putatively innocent beginning that unaccountably heads off in the wrong direction. Particularly in his second set of rules for discernment he points to a strange and unsuspected diversion of one's thinking. The evil angel, says Ignatius, can take on "the appearance of an angel of light"; in such guise the evil spirit "brings good and holy thoughts attractive to such an upright soul and then strives little by little to get his own way, by enticing the soul over to his own hidden deceits and evil intentions" (332). These subtle qualifications and alterations in one's intentions and perspective merit close scrutiny, says Ignatius; this echo of the ancient theme of stability and settledness, but now in the noetic realm, is characteristic of Ignatius. For him, the mark of spurious thinking is most often that, over a period of time, one can trace a kind of gathering obscurity or debasement in understanding so that one arrives at a "train of thoughts" conducing to "something less good than what the soul was originally proposing to do"; the same counterfeit thought process would be signaled "if it weakens, disquiets, or disturbs the soul, robbing it of the peace, tranquility, and quiet which it enjoyed earlier" (333).

These epistemological observations of Ignatius may strike us as threatening to foster a kind of stubbornness of thought. One has to remember that these remarks come in a phase of the *Spiritual Exercises* when a person is attempting to discern, and receive the grace to accept, one's true calling in life, so they are not meant in a generic way. Nonetheless, it would be fair to say that Ignatius does sense in vacillation and confusion of thought the marks of a negative influence and the need to recover balance, clarity, and a recollection of the evolution of one's thinking. More generally, we could say that Ignatius sees the noetic effects of spiritual desolation as a narrowing and obscuring of one's understanding, and a susceptibility to fearful prospects and imaginings that block out the reality of grace in one's life. By contrast, as Toner remarks, "the power to think truthfully, clearly, and comprehensively about spiritual experience is, like spiritual courage and energy, a gift of the Holy Spirit."[49]

It may seem peculiar to conclude this section on *noetic* signs by turning to Jonathan Edwards's magisterial treatise on the *Religious Affections* (which seemingly should be discussed in the section on *affective* signs). My contention, however, is that while there is certainly an affective component in what Edwards is discussing, the aim of his work is to test precisely the whole outlook and understanding of a person who seems to have these "affections" (for what Edwards means by "religious affections," see the section on Edwards in chapter 3 above). Edwards's great concern is with what Michael McClymond has well described as "spiritual perception," which he says "is one of Edwards's most encompassing themes," meshing "experiential manifestation with philosophical reflection."[50] The question, for Edwards, is whether this spiritual perception is authentically oriented toward God or is, usually unwittingly, animated by self-love. Because reality unfolds within trinitarian mutuality for Edwards, true spiritual perception must draw the soul beyond fixation on itself. As Robert Jenson remarks, "as reality is in fact mutuality, so dominant self-love and every illusion are the same."[51] This means that the aim in all of Edwards's twelve "signs" of true religious affection is fundamentally noetic, for he is searching for signs that the self has made contact with the real world and not simply the deep current of its own imagining and satisfaction. I will not attempt a detailed survey of all twelve signs in *Religious Affections* but will focus on a few of the most significant. By way of orientation, however, it may be helpful to list all twelve in sequence. Especially noteworthy is the fact that the last sign (the fact that truly gracious affections bear concrete fruits in practicing the Christian life) is roughly half again as long as all the previous eleven together. To give some sense of the proportion of Edwards's attention, I'll give the number of pages devoted to each sign in the Yale edition of *Religious Affections*.

Jonathan Edwards: Twelve Signs of Truly Gracious Affections

1. Indwelling by the Holy Spirit and new spiritual perception (42 pp.)
2. Loving God for God's sake and not one's own (13 pp.)
3. Appreciating the "loveliness of the moral excellency of divine things" (13 pp.)
4. An actual new growth of spiritual perception and authentic wisdom (25 pp.)
5. Conviction and certitude (20 pp.)
6. Authentic humility springing from the gospel (30 pp.)
7. A more Christ-like nature (4 pp.)
8. Sharing in Christ's gentleness (13 pp.)
9. A softened heart and an opened mind (7 pp.)
10. Symmetry, proportion, and balance in character (11 pp.)
11. Ever increasing hunger for God, not satiety (7 pp.)
12. Actual fruit in Christian practice (99 pp.)

We can synthesize the signs fairly, I think, by conceiving of them as the real, transformative, impact of divine life upon the believer. Encountering

God through the power of the Holy Spirit, the believer is given a new capacity of understanding (signs 1 and 4), a new object of knowledge (signs 2 and 3), and a new way of acting in harmony with this new vision of reality (signs 6-12). All this contrasts with the phenomena of inauthentic spiritual awakening in which believers remain, more or less unwittingly, focused on their own experiences and oriented toward their own needs, likes, and self-image.

First, then, a word about the new spiritual perception. Edwards argues that this is not simply an enlivening of normal, natural religious capacities but a creation of new principles for sensing, understanding, and responding to God. In an arresting metaphor, the New England divine says this new spiritual perception is not like a more intense form of a given sense (say smell) but rather like the development of a wholly new sense entirely (taste): "something is perceived by a true saint, in the exercise of this new sense of mind, in spiritual and divine things, as entirely diverse from anything that is perceived in them, by natural men, as the sweet taste of honey is diverse from the ideas men get of honey by only looking on it, and feeling of it."[52] Yet Edwards specifies his meaning here by saying that he does not mean a new faculty of nature but "new principles of nature," which he elucidates as a "habit or foundation for action, giving a person ability and disposition" to exert the whole person according to an entirely new mode (206). This leads, in Edwards's judgment, to an exercise of the mind "which is in its whole nature different" from that of a purely natural person; the true saint discerns something the latter cannot perceive at all (no question of *degree* is involved), "no more than a man without the sense of tasting can conceive of the sweet taste of honey, or a man without the sense of hearing can conceive of the melody of a tune, or a man born blind can have a notion of the beauty of the rainbow" (208). Edwards is painfully aware that "the devil can excite, and often hath excited such ideas" (216), and he takes care to distinguish these "external" ideas, or imaginary representations of things, from the true new spiritual sense which does not involve "picturing" things at all.

Another way of clarifying this distinction would be to say that counterfeit perceptions and insights are more graspable, more stimulating, and exciting to the believer, whereas authentic spiritual perception involve more light with less heat. They "evermore arise from some information of the understanding, some spiritual instruction that the mind receives, some light or actual knowledge" (266). Combining this point with Edwards's sense that authentic spiritual motions create a new noetic disposition or virtue, we could say that such authenticity is signaled by a genuine change in the kind of person the believer is. We would have someone who is not simply enjoying wondrous affections "let them be ever so high," but who actually grows wiser and more mature in understanding; by contrast, warns Edwards, "in many persons those apprehensions or conception that they have . . . have nothing of the nature of knowledge or instruction in them."

> As for instance; when a person is affected with a lively idea, suddenly excited in his mind, or some shape, or very beautiful pleasant form of countenance, or some shining light, or other glorious outward appearance: here is something apprehended or conceived by the mind; but there is nothing of the nature of instruction in it: persons become never the wiser by such things, or more knowing about God. (267)

Satan most easily appears as an angel of light to persons who are eager not for transformation and deeper wisdom but for display, "pleasant voices, beautiful images, and other impressions on the imagination"; indeed many, laments Edwards, "are deluded by such things, and are lifted up with them, and seek after them . . . especially when their pride and vainglory has most occasion for 'em, to make a shew of 'em before company" (290).

By contrast, the true gift of authentic spiritual perception is discerned as a new habit of knowledge or intellectual virtue, such that the mind of the saint really does sense and judge things with a new insight and wisdom. There are persons of high spiritual affection, notes Edwards, who seem to receive divine urges and promptings, but these operate upon them almost mechanically and without any development of wisdom or discretion (285). These apparently immediate divine dictates, says Edwards, have in them "no tasting the true excellency of things, or judging or discerning the nature of things at all" (285). Authentic spiritual perception has, on the other hand, as by second nature a true taste and relish for what is good. Edwards offers as examples of this authentic perception the case of a naturally good-natured person whose natural intuition teaches how to act benevolently, or the case of someone who is devoted to a close friend and is guided by friendship:

> He has as it were a spirit within him, that guides him, the habit of his mind is attended with a taste, by which he immediately relishes that air and mien which is benevolent, and disrelishes the contrary, and causes him to distinguish between one and the other in a moment, more precisely, than the most accurate reasonings can find out in many hours. . . . Thus it is that a spiritual disposition and taste teaches and guides a man in his behavior in the world. . . . So also will a spirit of love to God, and holy fear and reverence toward God, and filial confidence in God, and an heavenly disposition, teach and guide a man in his behavior. (283-84)

All this suggests that, as for many of the other writers we have considered, the sign of authentic spiritual growth is an enlargement of one's freedom, a deepening of one's own habit of wisdom through steady companionship with God.

This brings us to the second chief feature of Edwards on the signs of authentic spiritual perception: the growing delight in God for God's sake not for one's own. This is the new "object" of the mind. As we have already seen, Edwards notes how a new taste and relish for the divine holiness creates a growing internal compass and opens a new vision of reality: "when the true beauty and amiableness of the holiness or true moral good that is in divine things, is discovered to the soul, it as it were opens a new world to its view" (273). One can discern whether the soul has been truly drawn beyond its own self-interest in gazing upon God by examining the particular dimension of divine life the soul adores. If the soul's love for God is founded upon a joy in God's intrinsic loveliness, beauty, and holiness, this is a healthy affection. On the other hand,

> they whose affection to God is founded first on his profitableness to them, their affection begins at the wrong end; they regard God only for the utmost limit of the stream of divine good, where it touches them, and reaches their interest; and have no respect to that infinite glory of God's nature, which is the original good, and the true fountain of all good, the first fountain of all loveliness of every kind, and so the first foundation of all true love. (243)

Because, in Edwards's view, the divine glory in and of itself is the "first foundation of all true love," self-love (which inexorably turns God into an object of the soul's own gratification or fear or anger) leads away from true spiritual perception, and hence away from that authentic taste for the divine goodness that would otherwise guide the soul to wisdom. The awful problem, Edwards finds, is that self-love, through natural human gratitude, can lead to "a sort of love to God in many ways. . . . Men on such grounds as these, may love a God of their own forming in their imaginations, when they are far from loving such a God as reigns in heaven" (244).

Edwards foresees a dangerously slippery slope here: gradually such self-love encircles one very gratifyingly within the enchanting play of one's own experiences. Such persons have many fine elevations but they are suspiciously "wont to keep their eye upon themselves," indeed their minds are taken up with "admiring their own experiences: and what they are principally taken and elevated with, is not the glory of God, or the beauty of Christ, but the beauty of their experiences. They keep thinking with themselves, what a good experience it this! What a great discovery is this! What wonderful things have I met with! And so they put their experiences in the place of Christ" (251). At last such folk become the zealous and unbending votaries of the false god to which they have been subjected by self-love, and so "having a God who does so protect 'em and favor em in their sins" it becomes very necessary "to love this imaginary God that suits 'em so well, and to extol him, and submit to him, and to be fierce and zealous for him" (253).

Because Edwards believes that true spiritual perception is formed through encounter with the living reality of God, this devotion to the enslaving god whom one needs to burnish one's self-esteem can only deprave and distort one's spiritual vision. Reality can only be disclosed to one through friendship with reality's creator, and if the true maker of heaven and earth has been supplanted by the darling tyrant of self-preoccupation, then reality itself will be shrunken to fit the constricting grasp of one's need to be satisfied. So Edwards is, in fact, proposing as a test of spiritual growth the true object of one's love, whether it be a grace that appears "a profitable good to me, which greatly serves my interest, and so suits my self-love" or grace as "a beautiful good in itself, and part of the moral and spiritual excellency of the divine nature" (262-63).

The difficulty of applying this criterion leads Edwards to offer an extended series of auxiliary tests that might gauge the true focus of one's affections and the authenticity of one's spiritual growth within the realm of one's concrete deeds and actions. Indeed, in his lengthy exposition of the twelfth sign, Edwards meticulously considers how each of the previous eleven might take shape in actual Christian practice. But perhaps the clearest measure Edwards proposes is christological. "In the heart where Christ savingly is, there he lives, and exerts himself after the power of that endless life, that he received at his resurrection" (292-93), and this resurrection life, by the power of the Spirit, "makes a deep impression upon [believers'] minds, that they cannot forget him; and they will follow him whithersoever he goes" (395). And this, says Edwards, accounts for the practical implications of genuine spiritual perception, for a life drawn into the resurrection of Christ cannot help but be active with Christ.

This theme is explored also in signs seven and eight, where the authenticity of spiritual growth is pegged to the genuineness of one's Christ-like disposition. First, Christ's presence in the soul is not "so as violently to actuate it; but he lives in it; so that [the soul] also is alive" (342); this is the theme of genuine growth and transformation. But second, truly gracious affections "are attended with the lamblike, dovelike spirit and temper of Jesus Christ, or in other words, they naturally beget and promote such a spirit of love, meekness, quietness, forgiveness and mercy, as appeared in Christ" (344-45). On this matter, Edwards particularly indicts a pretended "boldness for Christ that arises from no better principle than pride" and is animated by bitterness and desire for "distinction and singularity" (352). These false affections lead to an unmistakable decline in real perception; for "false affections, with the delusion that attends them, finally tend to stupefy the mind, and shut it up against those affections wherein tenderness of heart consists" (358). Such impulses are very clearly distinguishable from a genuine charity toward one's enemies, patience with the erring, and a ceaseless practice of forgiveness—all of which Edwards ascribes to one indwelt by Christ—and all of which mark an authentically growing discernment of reality.

Relational Signs

As we will see in the next chapter, for St. Paul the most significant signs of healthy progress in life with God are indications of mutual upbuilding and edification. These are inherently relational signs. One scholar summarizes Paul's view: "the work of discernment has to do with the building of the *community identity* as such, rather than with the praise or condemnation of an *individual's behavior*. . . . The criterion is whether the interests of others as well as of self are served."[53] Even when Paul speaks of holiness, it is less as a criterion for discriminating the rightness of individual thoughts or acts and more accurately seen as a mark of the community's legitimate distinctness from the world. Put in the form of testing questions, such Pauline criteria ask about whether a teaching or communal practice helps to embody Christ's way of being or the world's usual *modus operandi*: "Does it relativize those distinctions between humans which in the world are used to foment fear and hatred, envy and competition, oppression and murder, or does it exacerbate them?"[54] Paul's regard for the shape of ecclesial life and its transforming momentum is perhaps insufficiently recollected as a criterion for distinguishing between spirits.

We saw already in the section on affective signs above how Antony the Great noted in those afflicted by evil spirits a hatred toward others who lead a disciplined life. This seems to have been a developing theme in ancient desert spirituality. Negative influence betrays itself through a kind of inner isolation from others, suspicion of them, and a need to instruct or manage them. Whereas a healthy impulse is marked much more by a genuine and deep interest in others, in and of themselves, rather than as the objects of one's own need. *The History of the Monks of Egypt* makes an intriguing connection between negative influences that "take our attention captive" during prayer and a parallel failure to attend patiently to human others. Such people tend to "behave as if they were superior to those on whom they have bestowed something," and whenever they pick up some tidbit of learning "at once they want to become teachers."[55] On the other hand, a mind fully hospitable to the other—both divine and human—is a good sign of healthy spiritual growth:

> A mind which has checked anger, put down fury, avoided deceit, banished envy, and not only does not disparage its neighbour but does not even allow itself to think or suspect any evil of another and which takes to itself the joys of a brother and reckons his sadness as its own, a mind which observes these things and those like them opens itself to the Holy Spirit and, when he has entered and illuminated it, there will always grow therein the fruits of the Spirit which are joy, happiness, love, patience, long-suffering and goodness.[56]

This rather comprehensive passage suggests how important the relational criterion might be in discerning the influences at work. For it clearly combines both affective and noetic elements, and it also alleviates the difficulty of attempting to read interior movements and impulses whose true valence is not always apparent in isolation from their effect in a person's life. The patterns and struggles of community life doubtless provided a considerable test of the spirits animating members' lives. A life that "takes to itself the joys of a brother and reckons his sadness as its own" discloses a person whose life has been genuinely opened toward that fullness of self-sharing which is the trinitarian life itself; it is a life truly animated by the Holy Spirit. We see a very similar criterion of the soul's health in Evagrius's *Chapters on Prayer:* "Happy is the monk who views the welfare and progress of all men with as much joy as if it were his own."[57] Here again, it is the intrinsic mutuality with which one perceives reality that marks the presence of a holy influence—as compared to the negative influences manifested by anger, fear, and the reduction of others to players in one's own various dramas.

Perhaps the most comprehensively relational sign comes from Jonathan Edwards, who points directly to the impact that believers' behavior has upon one another and upon unbelievers. By very obviously mingling tares among the wheat, says Edwards, "the devil gratifies himself," exposing the saints themselves to all manner of muddled examples of what Christianity is really about and encouraging doubters to think of Christianity as pointless and pathetic. Edwards's view is not simply that Christians are sometimes easily deluded about the validity of their religious practices and feelings, but rather that it's a strong sign of counterfeit religion whenever Christians become a stumbling block to one another.

> By this means [the devil] damps and wounds religion in the hearts of the saints, obscures and deforms it by corrupt mixtures, causes their religious affections woefully to degenerate . . . and dreadfully ensnares and confounds the minds of others of the saints, and brings 'em into

great difficulties and temptation, and entangles 'em in a wilderness, out of which they can by no means extricate themselves. By this means, Satan mightily encourages the hearts of open enemies of religion, and strengthens their hands. . . . By this means, he brings it to pass, that men work wickedness under a notion of doing God service, and so sin without restraint, yea with earnest forwardness and zeal, and with all their might. By this means he brings in, even the friends of religion, insensibly to themselves, to do the work of enemies, by destroying religion, in a far more effectual manner, than open enemies can do, under a notion of advancing it. (*Religious Affections,* 88)

With this damning observation Edwards draws attention to what *ought* to be an obvious sign to believers, namely, the debilitating force of their own conduct upon one another. Yet somehow, as Edwards insightfully notes, the very zeal and earnestness at work seem to blind the saints to the fact that they are "destroying religion" even "under the notion of advancing it."

Indeed, says Edwards, the whole process can become so absorbingly vituperative that the various parties not only fail to see how they are harming one another, but even that they—brother and sister Christians—have been turned into warring factions.

By this means the devil scatters the flock of Christ, and sets 'em one against another, and that with great heat of spirit, under a notion of zeal for God; and religion by degrees, degenerates into vain jangling; and during the strife, Satan leads both parties far out of the right way, driving each to great extremes, one on the right hand, and the other on the left, according as he finds they are most inclined. . . . And in the midst of this confusion, the devil has great opportunity to advance his own interest, and make it strong in ways innumerable, and get the government of all into his own hands, and work his own will. And by what is seen of the terrible consequences of this counterfeit religion, when not distinguished from true religion, God's people in general have their minds unhinged and unsettled, in things of religion, and know not where to set their foot, or what to think or do; and many are brought into doubts, whether there be anything at all in religion; and heresy, and infidelity, and atheism greatly prevail. (89)

Surely it would be hard to miss all that as a sign of malice afoot! But Edwards's point is precisely that, so enmeshed in the struggle are all, they they see what is the undoing of one another as a great and doubtless terribly important insistence on all the right things. Edwards draws attention to an especially sinister feature of this scenario, which may account for its hiddenness in plain view, namely, the degree to which it conducts believers into a frantic mirroring of one another's extreme tendencies, so that the whole community is thrown into a polarization, action and reaction, that becomes mindless and tidal. As we saw above, Edwards's patient elaboration of a series of criteria for discerning healthy spiritual perception was designed to forestall such an emergency discernment as he describes here. But few teachers of discernment could surpass Edwards in recognizing the communal and social impact of a failure in discernment.

The Problems of Deception

As we have frequently noticed, teachers of discernment offer a good deal of counsel about the problems of deception. They all analyze ways in which believers, often through their own good intentions and convictions, are led astray into false positions or attitudes. The writers we have studied do not often attempt to proportion the blame for this slide into a delusory spirituality, for they are sure that both the self and the larger powers of mendacity loose in the world are entitled to share the blame. Nevertheless, as Origen constantly emphasized, the self does not entirely forfeit its freedom and responsibility; therefore, a discerning awareness of at least the most common snares and patterns of deception should assist the self in the struggle to abide in truth. At the usual risk of overschematizing things, I have provisionally grouped the various types of deception into three general categories. The first is the broadest assortment and might in general terms be described as an exaggeration and distortion of believers' aspirations. The second category includes various types of false knowledge, often related to a gratifying estimation of one's own perceptiveness. And the final category comprises varieties of despondency and doubt about oneself and one's relationship to God. The common thread in all three, and a constant observation of our thinkers, is the mendacity and falsifying tendency of evil.

Exaggeration and Distortion

In discussing natural proclivities toward various flaws, Origen makes a useful distinction between what damage the self does through intemperance and what "hostile powers" can make of this opening that intemperance has given them.

> When we indulge these [desires] to excess and offer no resistance to the first movements towards intemperance, then the hostile power, seizing the opportunity of this first offence, incites and urges us on in every way, striving to extend the sins over a larger field; so that while we men supply the occasions and beginnings of our sins, the hostile powers spread them far and wide and if possible endlessly.[58]

Origen advises that one can recognize this aggravating demonic exaggeration by the sense of compulsion and suffering it brings with it, quite beyond the negative impact of one's own tendencies. Describing, as an example, the snowballing momentum of avarice, Origen points to the demons' ability to harness the longing and drive people relentlessly by means of it: "their passion is succeeded by a mental blindness and, with the hostile powers stimulating and urging them on, money is now not merely longed for but even seized by force or acquired through the shedding of human blood."[59] Origen very significantly fingers the darkening "mental blindness" as a grim sign of the violence to come.

Not only potentially sinful desires are subject to this manipulation but also, perhaps especially, religious forms of zeal and holy intentions. Cassian tells the story of Heron, among many others (*Conferences* II.v), whose intense rigor of discipline becomes the plaything of demonic temptation to grandiosity and overextension, to the point of nearly exterminating himself in an overweening display of his ascetic prowess. John Climacus puts this with great clarity: "It often happens that our enemies deliberately inspire us to do things beyond our capacities, and their objective is to make us falter, so that we abandon even what lies within our power, and make ourselves ridiculous to our enemies."[60] The fatal impulse in this exaggeration is away from what would be manageable and, while not perhaps extraordinary, good and decent. "Demons," Climacus warns, "often prevent us from doing what would be easy and valuable for us. Instead they like to push us into trying what is harder."[61] Perhaps we could see in this incitement toward what is seemingly magnificent the counterfeit of God's grace, inspiring believers into a reality they cannot themselves conceive. The mark of authentic grace, as opposed to this excess of zeal, would be a peaceful humility and acceptance of whatever may come of the effort, rather than an incipient fear of being made risible.

We have already seen, in the section above, how Ignatius warns of the devil's masquerade as an angel of light—the chief goal of which is to seduce the soul into a subversion of its own best intentions (*Spiritual Exercises* 332ff.). Toner's commentary points out how concerned Ignatius was about this possibility that active and inspired Christians might be undone by an exaggeration of their own generosity. "Little by little," comments Toner, the evil spirit "will try to lead the intended victim to some harm to himself or others: to neglect of meditation and contemplation; to exhaustion and, if the works do not go as the person planned, to resentment, discouragement, withdrawal from dedication to a life of service to God's people."[62] The use of one's own good intentions in this way seems even more subtle than an obvious appeal to self-esteem, yet there is undoubtedly a connection. The passionate attachment of the self to its special project (no matter how worthy) becomes the fulcrum by which the evil spirit, in Ignatius's view, can pry the soul into "impetuous desires for immediate great undertakings, altogether beyond the reach of the person being tempted, for which he or she has neither the gifts nor the training. What disaster could follow is not hard to imagine."[63] Such manipulation would lead before long to the grimmer form of deception discussed at the end of this section, namely, the slide into despondent feelings of one's uselessness and abandonment.

False Knowledge

We saw above (in the section on noetic signs) that Origen warned of the demonic flattery of pseudo-sophisticates, "by which false knowledge is implanted in men's minds and souls are led astray while supposing that they have discovered wisdom."[64] Origen discerns a suspicious intersection of the human thirst for knowledge and the demonic thirst to receive the unwitting obeisance of humankind, thus deflecting humanity's thought away from truth and humanity's worship away from the Author of truth at the same time. To some extent, Origen is even willing to allow that the "spiritual powers" of this world are themselves blinded by their own pride and so prevented from seeing the truth about God. He remarks that it is a real question whether the ideas of pseudo-wisdom with which the powers "strive to indoctrinate men are introduced into our minds by the opposing powers with the desire of ensnaring and injuring us" or whether these powers simply wish us to see everything according to their own (misperceived) understanding of truth; in fact, Origen says, the latter is probably "more likely."[65] In some ways this is a more tragic, if less melodramatic, vision: the different realms of knowledge all systematically distorting others in their hunger to know the truth—which they tragically misperceive. In the famous *Homily 27 on Numbers,* Origen is considerably less charitable, describing the hostile powers there as burning with impotent rage whenever a believer turns to Scripture for truth:

> since they had darkened human minds with the darkness of ignorance and had gained their object that God might be unknown and the zealous pursuit of divine worship might be transferred to them. What a blazing fire of torments is brought upon them when they see the darkness opened by the light of truth and the clouds of their deceit dispersed by knowledge of the divine Law! For they possess all who live in ignorance.[66]

Perhaps we could say that, as God is the creator of the real, so the hostile powers can only receive homage by luring believers farther into unreality and fantasy.

This view would seem to be well supported in the desert literature, where the demons are regularly described as having a mastery of simulation and misrepresentation, assuming appearances of many kinds so as to manipulate believers (e.g., *Life of Antony* §25). Similarly (as we saw in chapter 3), the desert elders are wary of special gifts of prophecy and knowledge whose origins may be suspect. Here it is a case of showing the truth, but only in order to fabricate a lie, namely, the spurious wisdom of the recipient of the "gift" who then becomes attached and self-impressed. "The demons, however, do this not from any care for the hearers, but to gain their trust, and that then at length, having got them in their power, they may destroy them" (*Life of Antony* §31).

Catherine of Siena points to a different sort of noetic darkening, not so much a pseudo-wisdom as a constricting of vision to meanness. As she memorably describes such folk: "their wretched little souls are filled with thanklessness, the source of all evils" (*Dialogue* §31). More than most other writers we have studied, Catherine identifies a degradation in human understanding with a debasement in human virtues. She traces this "thanklessness" of the soul to the stultifying effects of self-love, which suborns any virtuous effort to the decrees of self-interest and so gradually hardens the soul to the living presence of God's bounty and beauty. In this passage from the *Dialogue*, the Father explains to Catherine the noetic debilitation of those trapped in self-love.

> And now these who have drowned in the river of the world's disordered love are dead to grace. . . . Because they are dead they remember nothing of my mercy. Their minds neither see nor know my truth (for their sensitivity is dead, and they see nothing but themselves, and that with the dead love of selfish sensuality). . . . They become unbearable to themselves. They who wanted to rule the world find themselves ruled by nothingness, that is, sin—for sin is the opposite of being, and they have become servants and slaves of sin. . . . Do you know where this tree of death [the fallen soul] is rooted? In the height of pride, which is nourished by their sensual selfishness. Its core is impatience and its offshoot is the lack of any discernment. . . . Had they been grateful for the blessings they received from me, they would know me. And in knowing me they would know themselves, and so live in my love. (§31)

In this remarkable passage, Catherine probes the hidden links between self-love, ingratitude, and loss of discernment. Because God, as Truth, is generosity itself, reality can only be perceived as one shares in this free bestowal in which one gratefully receives all and lives in this giving love. But the awful paradox of self-love is that the soul, desperately seeking to satisfy itself, is converted to a grasping and ungrateful frame of mind in which "sensitivity is dead" and nothing of divine mercy can be remembered; as a consequence, the world and the self "become unbearable," for reality cannot be touched and known by such a "dead love."

Perhaps this state of noetic blindness is the full-blown condition of that gradual slide into delusion of which Ignatius warns. Catherine focuses directly on the root motivating defect in one's thinking, namely, a self-love that is insensitive to God's generosity. Ignatius, by contrast, attends more to *method* by which the evil spirit "little by little" conducts the mind toward a dead end. Especially throughout the "second set" of Rules for Discernment, Ignatius urges a persistent and patient attention to the gradual development and evolution of one's thinking—always keeping in mind that "it is characteristic of the enemy to fight against [consolation] by using specious reasonings, subtleties, and persistent deceits" (*Spiritual Exercises* 329). Even after an authentic gift of profound consolation, one's own reasoning process can lead very subtly away—sometimes with demonic prompting—from the actual inspiration; soon, warns Ignatius, "we form various projects and convictions which are not coming immediately from God our Lord" (336). Toner comments that in such cases, the evil spirit "brings about the gradual isolation of a proposed truth from balancing truths, and thus he leads his victim to a sort of destructive obsession. Through an intricate process of conceptual, imaginative, emotional associations which begins from the spiritually consoling thoughts, he leads a person to wrong conclusions."[67] The common thread in both Catherine's and Ignatius's analyses is the fatal absence of any real self-critical awareness or doubt that one's perceptions are valid. Yet the goal nonetheless is precisely to lure the soul into the opposite extreme, that is, a crushing doubt that equally fails to connect with reality.

Despondency and Doubt

The teachings of the desert elders are particularly sensitive to this dimension of deception, for they often encourage believers not to be led by demonic impulses into a quite unnecessary despair. Antony the Great, says Athanasius, enjoined his listeners to be wary of thoughts seeming to accuse their consciences; the demons, he says, "do this not for the sake of piety or truth, but that they may carry off the simple to despair; and that they may say the discipline is useless, and make men loathe the solitary life as a trouble and a burden."[68] In the *History of the Monks of Egypt* we read of intended schemes employed by the enemy to bring monks to despair. The tipping point is often the very worthiness and laudable achievement of the monk, into which the demon drips a tincture of self-congratulation. In the case of one such ascetic, "because he persevered with his prayers and made progress in the virtues, he came eventually to trust in himself, placing his reliance on his good way of life."[69] Once the demon has effected this subtle shift in the ground of the ascetic's hope, the way is prepared: an overwhelming temptation is dangled, the monk falls, and "in the morning he got up, dragging behind him the miserable experience of the night. He spent the whole day in lamentation, and then, despairing of his own salvation, which is something he should not have done, he went back to the world."[70] Like the other categories of deception, this mugging by despair relies upon a barely perceptible adjustment in perspective and focus, from God to self, and this is enough room for the power of the unreal to dominate the mind.

Perhaps we could think of this as a subversion of identity, so that a believer's true self—as known and loved by God—becomes obscured by the false self suggested into being by demonic temptation. This false self, apparently so antagonistic to God's good pleasure, provokes one to despair. Just as Christian in *Pilgrim's Progress* is horrified to find himself uttering gross blasphemies (without realizing they are really being whispered in his ear by demons), so the self has regularly to struggle against the creeping thought that it is a hopeless case, incorrigibly wicked, abandoned by God. It is quite important here not to read anachronistically, that is, to assume that this talk of evil itself speaking into the soul like a ventriloquist is simply an unrecognized form of psychological projection in which the self conveniently splits off and externalizes that which its more conscious ego judges worthy of condemnation. Such a reading would, I think, betray a conventionally modern solipsistic self; whereas the spiritual traditions we have been studying have an understanding of the self as a far more mutually engaged and relationally constituted being.

The self in this view is the locus of many voices and interventions. Diadochus, for example, argues that because of "the primal deception, the remembrance of evil has become as it were a habit" (§83). Rather than encouraging humanity to flourish through communion with reality and its giver, the demons, says Diadochus, gradually refocus the mind on the self (which is easily accepted) and then upon a false self that apparently doubts God's intentions and its own.

> The intellect, being highly responsive, makes its own the thoughts suggested to it by the demons through the activity of the flesh. . . . The flesh delights endlessly in being flattered by deception, and it is because of this that the thoughts sown by the demons in the soul appear to come from the heart; and we do indeed make them our own when we consent to indulge in them. (Diadochus §83)

"The intellect, being highly responsive" makes the thoughts of others its own; in a sense, then, the deception of despair is a moment when evil's illusory magic succeeds in suggesting into being that which is not. The work of discernment, argues Diadochus, is precisely to release the believer from this spell and help in the rediscovery of the true voice that has all along been calling the human being into full personhood.

Sometimes, however, the voices are difficult to distinguish. Bernard of Clairvaux describes a scene in one of his parables in which a soul, having been rescued from slavery by the good spirit Fear, encounters someone else along the road back to Jerusalem. The enervating spirits of the enemy had all been driven from the soul by Fear of God, but one of their number still waits in ambush: Sadness. This enemy spirit tells its comrades, "Do not be afraid of Fear. I know what is to be done. I shall go and, as a lying spirit in the bends of the roads, pretend that I am Fear's friend. I understand humans; to deal with them you need cunning, not force. Wait and see for yourselves."[71] Then Sadness crept back into the way, and "he met the man and engaged him in friendly though malign conversation and thus began to lead him astray"; soon "they were very near the place where Sadness could cast his victim into the pit of despair" when the true King ordered Hope to the rescue.[72] By pretending to be a friend of liberating Fear of God, the destructive spirit Sadness can insinuate himself, Bernard suggests, and so finally substitute an obsession with one's own failures in place of attentiveness to God. In the brightly lit world of the parable, Bernard is able to mock such Sadness and easily show its weakness in the face of God's true champions, Fear and Hope. Yet Bernard would not have conceived the story in this way were the surreptitious troubling of Sadness not all too easily mistaken for authentic fear of God in the healthy sense.

Almost identical teaching is offered in a letter written by Catherine of Siena:

> If we are in the midst of diabolical temptations and our eye is afflicted with this blindness, we are so deluded that, when the devil puts these illusory thoughts and suggestions into our heart, we think we have been rejected by God. This leads us to discouragement, which in turn makes us give up the practice of prayer because we imagine God does not find us acceptable—and we become [so] despondent we can't stand ourselves. . . . All this, and a multitude of other bad things happen to us because we haven't thrown off the cloud of selfish love either spiritually or temporally. We don't, therefore, recognize the truth.[73]

Catherine's discernment is both traditional and acute. She links demonic illusion with despondency and traces both to the leverage given them by self-love. Her point is not simply that the faithful should be alert to such false suggestions (i.e., about their unacceptability to God), but rather that as long as they are focused on themselves at all, they cannot "recognize the truth." The divine love cannot be scrutinized in terms of various degrees of human need, and once the mind has been beguiled into thinking about everything in precisely those very terms, then every deception can be practiced upon it. As she writes in *The Dialogue* (§44), "The soul, if blinded by selfishness, cannot recognize or discern what is truly good and profitable for soul and body. So the devil, evil as he is, when he sees that the soul is blinded by sensual selfish love, proposes all sorts of sins to her. . . . It seems to them [souls gripped by this delusion] that following me, that is, keeping to the bridge of my Son's Word, would be a great burden. So they fall back, afraid of thorns." In Catherine's view, human desire is so powerful an element in discernment that, if it can be affixed to the small, tangible, and graspable goods that the world proposes to the soul, then these small and precarious desires can be used to delude and manipulate the soul. Even, perhaps especially, persons who seek God can be led into a false world of seemingly painful obstacles that focus their attention on their own fear and frustration in the search for God. This self-preoccupation then blinds them to the immeasurable love with which God calls them, and can even occlude it so entirely as to leave them enslaved and deluded by fear.

Light from the Kingdom to Come

It would be a very defective portrait of Christian discernment that ended on such a string of sinister observations. In this last section, then, I would like to offer a brief balancing glimpse of a theme we will explore more fully in the final chapter of this book, namely, the present power and guidance that flows into discernment from what Christians think of as the life to come. If we were, like Origen, to think of Christian life as a journey, then perhaps we can imagine this role of heavenly light within discernment as a distant but mysteriously powerful vision of the journey's end. Growing from virtue to virtue, says Origen, the soul "begins to watch and to look for the future hope . . . little by little it grows, while it is more nourished by hope than worn out by toils"; and so the soul comes to be guided by the view it has of "grandeur of the things to come" (*Homily XXVII on Numbers* §9). We might liken this hope to an unseen compass within the discerning mind, providing a clearer sense of direction. Evagrius says to a person who truly wants to pray: "Have heaven for your homeland and live there constantly" (*Chapters on Prayer* §142). It is as if one could see and move about within the landscape of eternity, and those actions would be translated into an earthly life as prayer and discerning vision.

I think we can, in fact, see something very like this in Bernard's *Parables*. Very often one of the characters (usually Prayer) speaking with the "Lord" of the kingdom (i.e., God) will be explaining in some detail what is going on with those who sent him, but as he speaks, Bernard's readers would have gradually sensed a familiar sound to his speech—for Bernard has these messenger figures speak almost entirely in "Scripture-speak," that is, their speech is a beautifully crafted mosaic of phrases from throughout Scripture employed as a fully coherent communication. The effect of this is very moving, for Bernard's hearers would have had the sensation that the language of Scripture in which they had for so long immersed themselves in worship and study was actually the normal language of heaven, indeed that they had been engaging in heavenly communication all along without necessarily realizing it. This sense of heavenly life mysteriously operating within apparently earthly patterns is central in Bernard's *Parables* and shows how the perspective and outlook of heaven might shape and transfigure the view of things on earth. Hope, which may spring up within a human heart on earth, appears in the *Parables* as heaven-sent, and Hope's guidance always overcomes the inordinate or dominating fears the characters suffer (see chapter 3).

This light from heaven may also be figured in terms of the intimate tasting of love. Diadochus assures that "if we fervently desire holiness, the Holy Spirit at the outset gives the soul a full and conscious taste of God's sweetness, so that the intellect will know exactly of what the final reward of the spiritual life consists" (*On Spiritual Knowledge* §90). Here the noetic feature is interestingly heightened, even while the discerning capacity is operative at the deep level of a transformed appetite: the mind judges all things in light of its "taste of God's sweetness" and so discerns, by means of its own innate (but transformed) desire, what is right and good. For Catherine of Siena, it is precisely by a taste of that loving union with

> *Persons who seek God can be led into a false world of seemingly painful obstacles that focus their attention on their own fear and frustration in the search for God. This self-preoccupation then blinds them to the immeasurable love with which God calls them, and can even leave them enslaved and deluded by fear.*

God which God intends for the soul that the soul is set free from its preoccupying service to self-love. The Father tells Catherine that the blessed in heaven behold God in a way that supremely satisfies them. "How do they have this pledge in this life? Let me tell you: They see my goodness in themselves and they know my truth when their understanding—which is the soul's eye—is enlightened in me" (*Dialogue* §45). This presence of God's goodness within the patterns of the soul's earthly life illuminates everything for the soul, because it satisfies (without satiating) the hunger that would otherwise degenerate into self-love. "Having lost their own selfish will they clothe themselves in mine" (§45), and this frees the mind to perceive every-thing according to the divine giving and mercy rather than within an econ-omy of fear and hopelessness.

As we have heard some serious warnings from Jonathan Edwards in this chapter, we may properly close with his famous and glorious account of divine radiance. Just as Catherine observes the transformation of perception made possible by a glimpse of the heavenly goodness, so Edwards remem-bers with perfect freshness a time in his youth when a sense of the joy of life in Christ opened his eyes to the mysterious depths of divine glory in every-thing. My suggestion is simply that such a vision of heavenly goodness radi-ating within earthly life brings discernment to life and habituates the judgment to a heavenly frame of reference. After telling his father about his experience of "conversing with Christ" in what felt like mountains or "some solitary wilderness," Edwards recalls:

> I walked abroad alone, in a solitary place in my father's pasture, for contemplation. And as I was walking there, and looked up on the sky and clouds; there came into my mind, a sweet sense of the glorious majesty and grace of God, that I know not how to express. I seemed to see them both in a sweet conjunction: majesty and meekness joined together: it was a sweet and gentle, and holy majesty; and also a majestic meekness; and awful sweetness; a high, and great, and holy gentleness. After this my sense of divine things gradually increased, and became more and more lively, and had more of that inward sweet-ness. The appearance of everything was altered: there seemed to be, as it were, a calm, sweet cast, or appearance of divine glory, in almost everything. God's excellency, his wisdom, his purity and love, seemed to appear in everything; in the sun, moon and stars; in the clouds, and blue sky; in the grass, flowers, trees; in the water, and all nature.[74]

PART TWO

Case Studies
in Discernment

FIVE

Discernment and the Paschal Mystery: St. Paul and Desert Spirituality

Now it is time to offer the first of three case studies in which we can see more precisely something of the noetic potential of Christian spiritual discernment. I begin by considering the death and resurrection of Christ as the fundamental context of discernment. My interest is in discovering how the paschal mystery seems to recreate human perception and understanding. What could it mean to partake, in St. Paul's words, in "the mind of Christ" (1 Cor 2:16)? My goal is to explore this theme as it unfolds in St. Paul and comes to a new expression in the two greatest theorists of desert spirituality, Evagrius Ponticus (346–399) and Diadochus of Photike (mid-400s). These writers, taken together, suggest what it might mean to share in the mind of Christ, to heal and awaken human rationality from grasping and jealous habits of mind by flooding the whole person with the light of the limitless divine abundance that is the very ground of the mind's activity. Persons whose entire existence has become attuned to this abundance no longer understand anything "according to the flesh," as St. Paul puts it; that is, they no longer understand reality in terms of a fundamental lack compelling all to anxious self-seeking but are instead awake to the endless mercy of God's giving life.[1]

By way of setting the scene, consider the following observation from Evagrius: "Spiritual fat is the obtuseness with which evil cloaks the intelligence."[2] Here we notice immediately the indissoluble link that this tradition sees between knowledge and spirituality, between vision and the moral life. Behind this conviction, I believe, lies the thought that reality is inaccessible to minds that have fallen into certain debilitating conditions. In our own time, we would likely grant the analogous claim, for example, that prejudice or bias can blind one to the true merits of another person. Racism is an obvious example. And from roughly two centuries after Evagrius, we can see the later development of this perspective in the early Byzantine Maximus the Confessor (580–662). He interprets our passage from 1 Corinthians

2:16 on the "mind of Christ" by declaring a mystical participation in Christ to be the basis for discerning reality:

> The mind of Christ which the saints receive according to the saying, "We have the mind of Christ," comes along not by any loss of our mental power, nor as a supplementary mind to ours, nor as essentially and personally passing over into our mind, but rather as illuminating the power of our mind with its own quality and bringing the same energy to it. For to have the mind of Christ is, in my opinion, to think in his way and of him in all situations.[3]

Learning to think as Christ thinks is a central theme I will be exploring carefully. But for the moment simply note again the fact that this tradition clearly sees the transformed disposition of the knower as crucial to the functioning of discernment. Moreover, Maximus implies that such a transformation is not a replacement of the human mind with something else; it is an illuminating and energizing of the human mind in all its human rationality, an exercising of it according to a certain "way" (tropos) of thinking that makes the discernment of truth possible. So along with the ascetical dimension of discernment, I want to highlight also this mystical dimension—a disposing of the mind to understand all thing by sharing in the mind of Christ, sharing in that divine fullness from which all things come.

I hasten to add that while one *might* conceivably make a genealogical claim about the historical links in the development of this tradition of thought, I shall not attempt to do so. My concern is to explore this unfolding teaching about discernment as a way of thinking about what it means to think. So I examine first what our authors have to say about the ascetical aspects of discernment, then consider their awareness of a painful transition to a new pattern of mind, and finally turn to the mystical aspects of discernment as a form of intelligence grounded in the abundance of divine life.

Clearing Away Incorrect Diagnostic Schemes

The texts we are considering call for an important preliminary: in order to discriminate in a healthy way between what is true and what is false, or to understand what is good or right, one has first to become suspicious about one's own critical instincts. The very faculty of judgment one brings to bear on a given situation may, itself, have become mesmerized by an incorrect diagnostic scheme.

As we saw in earlier chapters, the desert fathers were particularly acute observers of this problem. They placard before us the tendency to slide into comfortably measurable criteria of judgment and the numbing ineptitude that results.

Abba Lot went to see Abba Joseph and said to him, "Abba, as far as I can I say my little office, I fast a little, I pray and meditate, I live in peace and as far as I can I purify my thoughts. What else can I do?" Then the old man stood up and stretched his hands toward heaven. His fingers became like ten lamps of fire and he said to him, "If you will, you can become all flame."[4]

In this little encounter we can see the tidy conventional appraisal of a spiritual adept exposed as a self-satisfying and yet ultimately frustrating norm. Abba Lot's seemingly moderate, prudent, and wise scheme for discerning his progress has left him feeling curiously restless, never quite accomplishing as much as he feels he perhaps ought to be, or else covertly pleased with himself and yet oddly in need of another's approbation. Abba Joseph will surely have an improving refinement to make to the scheme, an exquisitely appropriate modification that will set Abba Lot up perfectly. But Abba Joseph in fact will have nothing to do with Abba Lot's criteria for discernment. Instead his radical availability to the fire of the Spirit opens before us the unfathomable promise of divine grace, which cannot even be conceived within the categories of the conventional scheme of spiritual improvement.

In a similar way, St. Paul confronts Corinthians who are busy judging, evaluating, discerning, and comparing themselves according to a variety of apparently satisfying critical schemes. There is the measure of one's baptismal lineage ("Each of you says, 'I belong to Paul,' or 'I belong to Apollos,' or 'I belong to Cephas'" [1 Cor 1:12]). There is the measure of class status and cultural sophistication ("Consider your own call, brothers and sisters: not many of you were wise by human standards, not many were powerful, not many were of noble birth" [1 Cor 1:26]). There is the (probably) proto-Gnostic measure of spiritual elitism (the *psychikos-pneumatikos* distinction Paul subverts in 1 Cor 2:14).[5] But in Paul's view all these schemes of discernment are only binding the Corinthians ever more inexorably within a constricted measure of what is truly important. They cannot "receive the gifts of God's Spirit, for they are foolishness to them"; indeed the gifts of divine outpouring are utterly unapparent and ungraspable within such categories (1 Cor 2:14).

It would be easy enough to blame such cognitive distortion on the fallenness of reason per se, or the sheer incapacity of the unaided human mind to appreciate the divine activity in its midst.[6] But I suggest that Paul is not so much attacking human criteria of discernment as pointing out how inadequate are the ones in use currently in Corinth. Paul is proposing another criterion that requires just as much deployment of human rationality, intelligence, and skill to apply it and use it as a noetic norm. As we know, the criterion Paul holds up is God's rescuing action in Christ, the message or word of the cross. Paul, however, is not holding it up as a pristine norm of faith as against all merely rational human norms; he is holding up the cross as a criterion provided by the loving action of God as compared with criteria provided by the envious rivalry of factions. Indeed J. Louis Martyn has even made a strong case that one of the factions Paul is most concerned to undo is precisely the spiritual elite and culturally sophisticated group who feel that they have a far more spiritual, more faith-based, and divinely inspired criterion of discernment than do the ordinary members of the church in Corinth.[7] Against such a false criterion of discernment, Paul (like Abba Joseph with his fiery witness to the power of God) points to a divine act of generous love and away from the more conventional religious tests of spiritual progress.

The fifth-century bishop Diadochus of Photike picks out exactly this kind of distinction between divine generosity and factional envy. The former provides the right mind for proper discernment, he says, because when the mind focuses on God's generosity, "it no longer needs the praise of men"; furthermore, focusing on the deeds and words of God "keeps the mind free from fantasy (*aphantaston*), transfusing it completely with the love of God."[8] By contrast, conversation grounded in the "wisdom of this world always provokes self-esteem; because it is incapable of granting us the experience of spiritual perception, it inspires its adepts with a longing for praise, being nothing but the fabrication of conceited men."[9] Here, suggests Diadochus, is an authentic diagnostic question: is your life truly attentive to what God is doing, or is it unconsciously driven by concern with your own status and how others perceive you? It is intriguing and important that Diadochus links this latter compulsion for worldly regard with a tendency toward fantasy, an ego-gratifying fabulation to cocoon the self or social group in an illusory world more reassuring than real. This is the kind of cognitive blindness that true discernment heals and false discernment breeds and legitimates.

Specifying the Problem in Corinth

Soon we shall want to analyze the noetic dangers that true discernment unmasks. But to make sure I don't lead us down the wrong path about all this it will be useful to verify my characterization of Paul's targets in Corinth. For a good part of the twentieth century, the dominant view among New Testament scholars pointed to a putative theological argument between Paul and a range of misguided religious tendencies—usually Jewish, or Hellenizing, or Gnostic, and sometimes all three at once. In these interpretations the tendency was then to see Paul as arming himself with a defiant assertion of divine revelation against all human rationality, or with a kind of existentialist faith against all secular reason.

More recently, scholars have noticed a good deal of head scratching and embarrassing pauses whenever one asks for detailed proof of the actual existence of one or another of these religious tendencies in the church at Corinth. They have also begun to notice that Paul's argument here, as contrasted with that in the Letter to the Galatians, does not really focus on particular, erroneous theological views but rather seems more concerned with the mutual antagonism and painful disunity of the local church. Thus 1 Cor 1:10 is seen as the real theme of the letter: "Now I appeal to you, brothers and sisters, by the name of our Lord Jesus Christ, that all of you be in agreement and that there be no divisions among you, but that you be united in the same mind and the same purpose." Correlate with this is the emphasis throughout the letter on love and edification for the sake of the Body, climaxing with the great praise of love as the ultimate basis of understanding and wisdom in 1 Corinthians 13.

So what about Paul's rejection of human wisdom and his taunting "Where is the one who is wise? Where is the scribe? Where is the debater of this age? Has not God made foolish the wisdom of the world?" (1 Cor 1:20). Part of the emerging consensus is that in such passages (even including the yet more searing indictment of human noetic malfeasance in Romans 1:18ff) "the issue is not noetic fallibility or weakness but human rebellion against the creator God. . . . What humankind has denied is the basic reality of God. . . . [T]he rebellion against the true God has created a false world within which false gods play their role as securing and validating the very falsity itself."[10] The result of this alienation from God is that the validating criteria of wisdom are given not by the beneficent Creator but by needy, compulsive idols that require full adherence in order to grant validation of one's status, worth, and position. A number of scholars now identify the driving force in all this as the social and cultural divisiveness that simultaneously validates and enslaves the various social strata of the church.[11]

What Paul is trying to pry the Corinthians loose from, then, is the structure of their relations with one another. The letter reveals a climate "of intense rivalry involving a cross-section of people from different socio-economic and cultural backgrounds."[12] How do these cultural divisions figure into Paul's concern about noetic functioning? Recall Diadochus on the suspicious links between worldly "wisdom" or talk, the persistent need felt by such mental dispositions for the applause of others, and the tendency of such persons to fall into fantasizing. A whole range of epistemological vices begins to spring up in such a climate. Conceit, bragging, boasting, envious comparisons, arrogant attachment to one's own positions, prudish disdain for the new ideas of others all "create conditions in the community that make difficult the pursuit of knowledge and the exercise of practical reason."[13] In such an atmosphere of noetic self-importance and rivalry, it is not surprising to hear Paul say, "God chose what is foolish in the world to shame the wise . . . so that no one might boast in the presence of God" (1 Cor 1:27-28).

If one, then, also factors in the particular high-culture avoidance of anything that might be sniffed at as servile, slavish, or weak, and the corresponding attachment to power and beauty, rhetoric and sophistry, as markers of one's social status, cleverness, and supposed refinement (all things eagerly pursued in the social-climbing atmosphere of Corinth), it becomes urgent for Paul to point out that his teaching absolutely refuses any contest in this arena:[14]

> When I came to you, brothers and sisters, I did not come proclaiming the mystery of God to you in lofty words or wisdom. For I decided to know nothing among you except Jesus Christ, and him crucified. And I came to you in weakness and in fear and in much trembling. My speech and my proclamation were not with plausible words of wisdom, but with demonstration of the Spirit and of power, so that your faith might rest not on human wisdom but on the power of God. (1 Cor 2:1-5)

As Paul admits (1 Cor 4:6ff), he has spoken about himself in passages like this as though the real issue were a contest about which of the various apostles to Corinth (Paul, Apollos, Cephas) was the greatest; but in fact he has been speaking this way as a mirror to the whole church, as a lesson against the rivalry and self-important envy that afflicts them: "so that none of you will be puffed up against another. For who sees anything different in you? What do you have that you did not receive? And if you received it why do you boast as if it were not a gift?" (1 Cor 4:6-7). So I suggest, following this reading of the conflict in Corinth, that the problem is not with human reason per se as opposed to faith, but rather the problem is the Corinthians' prideful self-deception: "They exaggerate their true status and abilities, glorying in themselves. And that is why the concept of boasting is central to the understanding of Paul's critique."[15]

If we are correct in identifying the problem this way, then two important points follow. The first regards the faith and reason question, as we have just seen. To quote Paul Gooch again, "worldly wisdom, though opposed to the true knowledge of God, is opposed not as philosophy against faith but as human conceit that shuts itself up against truth. Paul's critique of such wisdom requires the opposite of an irrationally extreme fideism; it asks for right reasoning and for the cognitive modesty appropriate to all human intellectual activity."[16] The second point concerns the precise pathology of this temptation toward noetic error (perhaps we could even call it the "logic" of distorted reason), and the possibility of discerning what is really at work there. To this we now turn.

Envy's Aversion to Truth

What we see now is how the word of the cross might be the authentic measure of discernment, how it might permit a liberating recognition of the compulsive idols that drive one away from truth and deeper into fearful and arrogant fantasies. In 2 Corinthians, St. Paul continues his critique of the church's ceaseless sizing-up of one another: "We do not dare to classify (*ankrinai*) or compare (*synkrinai*) ourselves with some of those who commend themselves. But when they measure (*metrountes*) themselves by one another and compare (*synkrinontes*) themselves, they do not show good sense" (2 Cor 10:12). Here Paul uses the same terminological field we saw him employ in 1 Cor 2:14 to talk about proper spiritual discernment. And, as I have argued above, it is exactly Paul's point that this measuring and comparing of one another is a dangerously false principle of discernment. Envious rivalry in cultural and spiritual advancement, in Paul's view, only renders the parties to the scheme blind and without understanding, stuck in that conflictual and rapacious mentality that he calls thinking according to the flesh: "as long as there is jealousy and quarreling among you, are you not of the flesh and behaving according to human inclinations?" (1 Cor 3:3).

> "My speech and my proclamation were not with plausible words of wisdom, but with demonstration of the Spirit and of power."

The desert fathers provide a number of probing analyses of this mentality. What they uncover there is a toxic seepage among envy, anger, fearfulness about the frustration or loss of one's own desires, and a grimly deepening need to best others in order to restore one's own self-esteem. In a classic statement reported by Evagrius, an abba remarks: "I have this reason for putting aside pleasure—that I might cut off the pretext for growing angry. For I know that anger constantly fights for pleasures and clouds the mind with passion that drives away contemplative knowledge."[17] In intensely compact form this saying captures the abyss we are trying to fathom: first, there is the anxiously possessive pursuit of pleasure, the power to gratify one's drives and thus manifest one's status; second, there is the fear and anger that floods in whenever the success of others dims our splendor; and throughout all this the mind is increasingly clouded and rendered insensible to truth.[18]

Evagrius developed a diagnosis of minds debilitated by fearful envy (an analysis later adapted by John Cassian and Gregory the Great). Out of many years of practice among the desert hermit colonies and conversations with them, Evagrius formulated perhaps his most characteristic insight, namely, that one could, with time, begin to recognize the various illusions that the mind ceaselessly throws up around us.[19] Evagrius's interest was not simply in exposing the prevaricating self but in freeing it to appreciate the infinitely greater joy of real life. In the more juridical atmosphere of the West, what came to be called the "seven deadly sins," were in Evagrius's formulation merely eight kinds of powerful *logismoi*—thoughts, picturings, considerings: "It is not in our power to determine whether we are disturbed by these thoughts, but it is up to us to decide if they are to linger within us or not and whether or not they are to stir up our passions."[20] Evagrius's concern is not so much that we one might tend to overeat or have sex too much or be terribly listless, but rather that each of these is the symptom of a deep and repetitive mental fidget which, unless overcome, is going to distort and cloud the mind.

Each of these fantasies is going to play on a particular aspect of the personality so that one is unable to get beyond the clamor of the will at all; everything and everyone else comes to be apprehended now, if at all, only in terms of the most atavistic needs and fears. So the thought of gluttony afflicts the monk with fears that he might undergo a long illness and a lack of caring physicians; "these things are depicted vividly before his eyes."[21] Or the *logismos*, the mental itch, of sadness drives one to a terrible homesickness, or tantalizes with memories of lost joys:

> Now when these thoughts find that the soul offers no resistance but rather follows after them and pours itself out in pleasures that are still only mental in nature, then they seize her and drench her in sadness, with the result that these ideas she was just indulging in no longer remain. . . . So the miserable soul is now shriveled up in her humiliation to the degree that she poured herself out upon these thoughts of hers.[22]

Evagrius consistently spies out this subtle power of these obsessive thoughts, whether gratifying or catastrophic, to disable and stunt the mind. It is significant that in every case there is a fundamental *anxiety about scarcity,* a fear of somehow not getting what one is convinced one must have. Just as "sadness tends to come up at times because of the deprivations of one's desires," so too vainglory stirs up in its apprentices a desperate craving "to make their struggles known publicly, to hunt after the praise of men."[23] What makes these observations so telling is that they are not simply the automatic disdain of a stoic for any desire whatsoever. Rather they reflect a sense that there is an enormous abundance that is real and available, yet hidden from minds in the grip of this mentality of deprivation.

Such painful dissonance between a mind constricted and itching and a mind awake to divine mercy is most poignantly evident in another story from the desert. It concerns a monk and a virgin who visit an elder and during the night have carnal relations. After they leave the old man's cell the next day, they are overcome again but this time by a kind of malign curiosity, wondering how the elder could have failed to notice what they had done. So they went back to his cell and learned that he had, in fact, been aware of everything: "They said to him, 'What were you thinking at that time?' He said to them, 'At that time my thoughts were standing where Christ was crucified, and weeping.'" And the two, profoundly shaken by the elder's compassionate grief, are converted.[24] The elder's mind, fixed on Christ crucified for sinners, is free from the need to assert his own virtue in an act of angry condemnation, free from the fear of losing his own reputation; the cross in this narrative represents God's powerful mercy breaking into the itching, pusillanimous needs of the fallen world, holding open the possibility of a wholly other disposition grounded in the generosity of divine action.

Discernment and the Paschal Mystery

How does the cross work to uncover the mechanism of these thoughts and set the mind free from them? If Evagrius is right, a persistent fear of lack and scarcity is what drives the eight deadly thoughts. Perhaps we could say that for Evagrius the noetic effect of sin is not felt directly in the reason of humanity but in the will: a heart alienated from God grows blind to divine generosity, trust atrophies, love grows cold, and the mind succumbs to a fearful need to compensate itself. In such circumstances, reality comes to be interpreted as a realm of scarcity in which the hungry self must extract goods from others that it no longer knows how to receive freely from God. One might well expect people in the grip of such thoughts to pursue an antidote to this fear through a wonderful elevating of the mind to bliss, and indeed it seems to have been just such an escapist mentality of pseudo-spiritual accomplishment that Paul critiques at Corinth. Alexandra Brown argues that for Paul these spiritual seekers were only practicing a more refined form of running away, a form that left them all the more subtly but deeply controlled by fear and the need to boast of superior social status:

The *psychikos*, whose intent is to rise *above* the world actually remains enslaved to it. Having received *gnosis* without *pneuma*, the psychics remain ignorant in the clutches of the world and its wisdom. Because they fail to receive the Spirit, they do not perceive *what is revealed* (2:9-10) by the Spirit, namely, the crucified Christ. They therefore misperceive the critical interpretive power of the cross for eschatological life in the present.[25]

The paradox Paul has been able to discern because of the cross is this: the more the pseudo-spiritual seek to evade their fears by assuming a higher status and comparing themselves with others, the more they remain enmeshed in the idolatry to which fear and rivalry subjects them.

The word of the cross, however, is a word that brings to nothing this mentality because it is news about God's action to *embrace* the very status (slavery, humiliation, and death) that the pseudo-spiritual most fear. Jesus accepts this status and, by his death, destroys the power of death to frighten and dominate those who place their whole trust in God. Or as Hebrews 2:14 puts it:

> Since, therefore, the children share flesh and blood, he himself likewise shared the same things, so that through death he might destroy the one who has the power of death, that is, the devil, and free those who all their lives were held in slavery by the fear of death.

At the risk of oversimplification, I am suggesting that the cross becomes the basis of discernment because it grounds the mind in reality free from the distortions of fear, envy, and anger—all of which have as their ultimate bogey-totem the shame and humiliation of death itself. To suggest, as Gooch does, that Paul's preaching of the cross encourages a proper epistemological modesty is perhaps something of an understatement, but it is, I think, nonetheless correct. It will be helpful, however, to see a little more definitely how this new noetic environment that Jesus creates might be able to reshape the minds of those who come to share it.

Perhaps the simplest way to put it is like this: Jesus' entire personal identity, Christians believe, is the immediate expression of his loving relationship with the one he calls Abba, and therefore his personhood and his way of thinking are not distorted by the envious fears of the world. Jesus creates a community in which persons whose thinking *is* so distorted, who suffer from an undiscerning mind (*adokimon noun*, Rom 1:28), find themselves called out of their old personhood by sharing in Jesus' loving relationship with the Father: "for you did not receive a spirit of slavery to fall back into fear, but you have received a spirit of adoption" (Rom 8:15). As minds are renewed by confidence in God's loving generosity, it becomes possible again to discern (*dokimazein*) truly "what is good and acceptable and perfect" (Rom 12:2). This transformation from a mind possessed by fear and envy to a mind alive to the immensity of divine love is, Paul believes, only possible by way of the cross: "joint heirs with Christ—if, in fact, we suffer with him so that we may be glorified with him" (Rom 8:17). Believers who suffer with Christ lose all status, all claims to cultural, biological, moral, or spiritual superiority. Their minds are freed from the paralyzing magic of a self-esteem plucked from the envying approbation of the world. They rest their sole confidence in the resurrection of Jesus, that is, in the glory or recognition that comes from the Father. James Alison, developing the perspective of René Girard, has put all this with remarkable clarity. Commenting on John 5:41ff. ("I do not accept glory from human beings. . . . How can you believe when you accept glory from one another and do not seek the glory that comes from the one who alone is God?"), Alison writes:

> That is what Jesus was suggesting: in order to receive your reputation, your being noticed and recognized, by God, you have to be prepared to lose the reputation which comes from the mutually reinforcing opinion and high regard of those who are bulwarks of public morality and goodness and find it among those who are held as nothing, of no worth. . . . The order of this world has its own glory, which depends on mutually rivalistic imitation, and is a glory or reputation that is grasped and held onto with difficulty. Being enveloped in the order of this world prevents us from beginning to act in solidarity with those of poor repute, because if we do so we lose our reputation. But those whose minds are fixed on the things that are above, that is, who have begun to receive their "I" from their non-rivalistic imitation of Jesus, already begin to derive their reputation from the Father and not from their peers. This they learn to do in the degree to which, doubtless with much difficulty, they learn to give little importance to the reputation which people give them and thus become free to associate with those who have no reputation, just like the one who was numbered among the transgressors.[26]

So the new mind that is thus freed into the infinite resource of God is, paradoxically, not preoccupied with spiritual achievement, it has no boast except the cross; but in fact a truly discerning mind is free to understand all the dimensions of reality, including those the world despises and rejects.

Interruption: The Noetic Transition of the Cross

A painful transition is unavoidable here. Not only because, as Alison points out, those who have begun to derive their self-worth from God will likely not fit in well with the world's schemes of approval, and hence come to seem to others and perhaps to themselves like dismal failures. But beyond this, as the mind shares more deeply in the mind of Christ, there is the painfully growing awareness of how broken the world is and how immense is the divine compassion and justice in the face of this. Diadochus remarks that "at the outset, the soul in pursuit of theology is troubled by many passions, above all by anger and hatred"; this happens not because the demons are arousing evil thoughts but precisely because the soul "is making progress":

So long as the soul is worldly-minded, it remains unmoved and untroubled however much it sees people trampling justice under foot. Preoccupied with its own desires, it pays no attention to the justice of God. When, however, because of its disdain for this world and its love for God, it begins to rise above its passions, it cannot bear, even in its dreams, to see justice set at nought. It becomes infuriated with evil-doers and remains angry until it sees the violators of justice forced to make amends. . . . Nevertheless, it is much better to lament the insensitivity of the unjust than to hate them; for even should they deserve our hatred, it is senseless for a soul which loves God to be disturbed by hatred, since when hatred is present in the soul spiritual knowledge (*gnōsis*) is paralysed.[27]

There is a noetic blindness caused by self-preoccupation, says Diadochus, but there is another more subtle form of mental constriction that can only be healed by an even more radical abandonment and handing over of all into the purposes of God. It is relieved, says Diadochus, not by an impatient insistence on one's own rectitude of judgment but by a steady holding of all things up into the plenitude of God's grace.[28] But in the initial stages of this transformation, such perception of plenitude may be nearly entirely eclipsed by the perception of injustice and consequent anger.

Evagrius had prescribed for this period a time of patience, stillness, waiting, attention to the other—to use his term, *apatheia*. It is an ascetical process of self-stripping which, paradoxically, does not annihilate but rather liberates the self from its compulsions, from the "higher" temptations to attack violence with more violence, to combat injustice with an insidiously self-approving indignation. Part of the problem is that the self's survival instincts train us to think in very purposeful, utilitarian ways about what surrounds us. As Paul had warned the Corinthians, however, the really real is not reducible to something we can use or appropriate for ourselves— even perhaps in the service of righteous indignation. Rather, the divine strength is likely to appear in our newly impatient frame of mind as mere foolishness, a painfully enigmatic cross. For Evagrius, this means that often we may not be able to experience much of reality at all. The real may accost us only in an experience of futility and darkness. Origen had suggested that ascesis and moral discipline would lead one to a clearer vision in which we begin to sense the true heart of things in themselves (rather than as fantasized by us). But this clarity is a difficult vision in which most of the world of our striving appears as pointless, in vain: "when a person has progressed in discernment and behaviour he may pass on thence to train his natural intelligence and, by distinguishing the causes and natures of things, may recognize the vanity of vanities that he must forsake, and the lasting and eternal things that he ought to pursue."[29]

So in addition to the possibility of anger and hatred being stirred up, there is a danger that in reaction to its frustration with the world's wrongs and its own inability to right the world perfectly, the soul may sour into what Evagrius calls acedia, a depressing sense of futility. Diadochus comments:

> When the soul begins to lose its appetite for earthly beauties, a spirit of listlessness (*akedia*) is apt to steal into it. This prevents us from taking pleasure in study and teaching, and from feeling any strong desire for the blessings prepared for us in the life to come; it also leads us to disparage this transient life excessively, as not possessing anything of value. It even depreciates spiritual knowledge itself, either on the grounds that many others have already acquired it or because it cannot teach us anything perfect.[30]

It is important to see that these twin problems of impatience and dryness are set loose because believers have begun to enter into the paschal mystery and have caught a glimpse of what the world looks like through the eyes of Christ. The convenient older noetic is no longer accessible, but a new vision is not yet at work either.

As J. Louis Martyn puts it, the cross remains an epistemological crisis. Paul's criticism of the Corinthians is that instead of abiding there with Christ on the cross, trusting in the unimaginable hope of the Father's love, they seek a perfectly graspable, religious wisdom of their own. But the only authentic

> new way of knowing is not in some ethereal sense a spiritual way of knowing. It is not effected in a mystic trance, as the pseudo-apostles had claimed, but rather right in the midst of rough-and-tumble life . . . life in the midst of the new-creation community, in which to know by the power of the cross is precisely to know and to serve the neighbor who is in need.[31]

Martyn's point here would seem to confirm the views of Alison I considered above, namely, that if believers place their sole confidence with Christ in the Father's love, the new vision that begins to open before them can no longer fit within the confines of their own grasp. They will not be able to enter into the paschal mystery *and* retain a perspective or judgment that somehow relies on their own sense of self-worth, or status, or moral accomplishment. Any attempt to do so will only turn the mystery of Christ's dying and rising into a new datum to possess, rather than the noetic framework within which one now exists. As one New Testament scholar puts it: "The epistemological point is inseparable from the eschatological one and therefore epistemology cannot be reduced to a matter of individual subjectivity."[32] Paul seems to understand the death of Jesus as opening up a new order of reality in which everything is charged with a different polarity, a new meaning. "It is a way of knowing granted not to the natural person, but to those who are able to discern the eschatological significance of Christ's death and who view reality in terms of its consequences."[33] As I have been suggesting above, such a conversion would transform both one's identity and derivation of self-worth and also one's relations to others. Being drawn into the paschal mystery will take the form of a difficult and fumbling new way of seeing one another and of living for the sake of one another: "we are convinced (*krinantas*) that one has died for all; therefore all have died. And he died for all, so that those who live might live no longer for themselves, but for him who died and was raised for them" (2 Cor 5:14-15).

This loving holding of the other into the rescuing love of God may, therefore, be the foundational practice needed to ground a truly eschatological noetic. Perhaps that is something of what we find in the non-anxious humility and patience of the desert fathers in the face of many faults and weaknesses. Again and again we see them learning, almost like a new skill or language, how to interpret and understand the neighbor against the horizon of Jesus' self-giving on the cross. Somehow the fabric of reality, in this new state of being, can best be touched and sensed in the delicate practice of relationship with the other; the possibility of gradually coming to discern the fullness of the new reality and entering into it hangs upon the experiment of this new way of relating to the other. Anthony the Great is recorded as saying, "Our life and our death is with our neighbour. If we gain our brother, we have gained God, but if we scandalise our brother, we have sinned against Christ."[34] The neighbor here is revealed as a test, a discernment of the degree to which one is beginning to live into the new reality opened up by the cross. And this new reality, marked so utterly by relationship with the other, becomes a crucible in which old patterns of relationship are undone and new ones learned, grown almost, from the organic self-giving of Jesus. Abba Poemen comments on how this new relational pattern of life may begin to unfurl among the disciples of Jesus:

> "Greater love hath no man than this that a man lay down his life for his friends" (John 15.13). In truth if someone hears an evil saying, that is, one which harms him, and in his turn, he wants to repeat it, he must fight in order not to say it. Or if someone is taken advantage of and he bears it, without retaliating at all, then he is giving his life for his neighbor.[35]

One can see very frequently in these stories the struggle between the old order in which the truth of one's rectitude and of justice must be asserted and the new order unfolding in the working of Jesus' death and resurrection, in which vindication and moral worth and righteousness are not achieved by blotting out the other but by resurrection, by the Father's infinite loving of the other into the new state of being—a state barely discernible by those whose minds are not yet filled with a sense of the divine plenitude.

So, for instance, when some righteous brethren come to Abba Poemen with complaints about others who irritatingly nod off during the liturgy, they expect him to provide a judicious correction of the slumberers and certainly the admonition to wake them up. But Poemen replies, "For my part when I see a brother who is dozing, I put his head on my knees and let him rest."[36] Here the new reality begins to dawn, one suspects, in a very confused way upon the minds of the righteous brothers who must feel both chastened and yet perhaps attracted by this gentle care. And likewise, there must be a peculiar shift out of the polarities of self-condemnation and self-justification for the brother who startles awake in embarrassed exhaustion but finds his head cradled consolingly in the lap of the Abba. The attractive and converting dimensions of this divine generosity are limned even more explicitly in the stories of thieves who find more than they had bargained for among the elders. For having plundered one of the old men, he took up a little bag they had missed and struggled after them, "crying out: 'My sons, take this, you forgot it in the cell!' Amazed at the patience of the elder, they brought everything back into his cell and did penance, saying, 'This one really is a man of God!'"[37] In all these stories the old order of reality marked by need, condemnation, and rapacity is overtaken by an endless resource that not only grounds everything in mercy and forgiveness but makes an outpouring gift of the very thing which before could be perceived only as a scarce commodity to be grasped and possessed as one's own.

Discerning the Fullness of Reality: The Mind of Christ

As this new order of reality begins to unfold, what noetic shifts and epistemological possibilities begin to appear? In the section just above I have considered some of the ascetical yet exhilarating experiences likely to develop in the transition from the old order mentality to a mind marked by the paschal mystery. Now we want to consider what might legitimately be called the mystical dimensions of the new noetic, as minds awaken (like sleeping brothers cradled in the arms of Abba Poemen) to the hidden presence of the divine abundance.

The apostle Paul asks the Corinthians to notice something that God is doing within and among them. Indeed, we could even say that throughout the letters he consistently points to God as the prime noetic agent, the one who calls and knows the Corinthians and thus engenders knowing in them. He seeks to awaken them to the ways in which God's life is reconfiguring the noetic possibilities of the believing community. He helps them open themselves to this new process of perception, a process in which God the Holy Spirit translates the loving generosity of God in Christ into the very patterns of the community's thought. To "have the mind of Christ" means, I will argue, to think within the framework of Jesus' own fidelity and joy with respect to the Father's abundant life; it also means, therefore, to be drawn into God's own humanly incarnate form of knowing.

Part of the problem facing Paul is that while the Corinthians were committed to the Gospel, they also, perhaps unconsciously, tended to transpose the status ideals of their society into the framework of the church. So Paul is working hard to "resocialize" the members of church, recalling to their minds their ecclesial formation and identity "in terms of their response to the 'word of the cross.'"[38] Paul's talk of God's wisdom secret in a mystery (1 Cor 2:7) seems to fit well with "the contemporary Jewish terms used to speak of God's eschatological design for the salvation of his people."[39] It is this wisdom in a mystery that is at work reconciling the world in Christ, but, as Paul deliberately emphasizes to the Corinthians, it is precisely this hidden dimension or depth of reality that the "rulers of this age" fail to discern. They have not been recreated by sharing in Jesus' dying and rising. By contrast, says Paul, "we have received not the spirit of the world, but the Spirit that is from God, so that we may understand (*eidōmen*) the gifts bestowed on us from God" (1 Cor 2:12).

Putting this all together with the joyful climax in 2:16, "But we have the mind (nous) of Christ," we can see Paul holding before the Corinthians a vision of the divine generosity: this vision is what most crucially marks the Spirit-filled mind of Christ. It is a vision utterly free from fearful grasping, and in its confidence in the Father's love it is the outpouring (Spirit) of that divine generosity within the constraints of the broken world. This seems indeed to be what Paul is getting at in his parallel use of *nous* in the famous passage in Philippians 2: "Let the same mind be in you that was in Christ Jesus, who though he was in the form of God, did not regard equality with God as something to be exploited, but emptied himself. . . . [T]herefore God also highly exalted him." Paul calls the Philippians, like the Corinthians, to let themselves be sharers in a common mind, the mind of Christ. He urges them to immerse themselves in Jesus' non-anxious confidence in the divine resource which makes him free to live as the perfect embodiment of that giving life; in the context of the present world order, this giving can only be seen as folly, humiliation, and death. Yet the true power and boundlessness of the divine generativity is manifest in the resurrection of Jesus, whose life beyond the power of death redounds "to the glory of God the Father" (Phil 2:11).

Clearly, then, the "mind of Christ" is not an alien rationality that displaces native human reason, but is rather a pattern of rationality constantly held open by faith to the wideness of God's mercy. In an important discussion of Paul's use of *nous* in 1 Cor 2:16, Robert Jewett summarizes his results as follows:

> If it [the mind of Christ] is the basis on which the church is to be united (I Cor. 1:10) and if it is the plan of salvation revealed in Christ, then it must be more than an individual rational capacity. . . . I would say that *nous* is a complex of thoughts and assumptions which can make up the consciousness of a person. It is quite different from a purely rational capacity, from the power of judgment and decision which the Greek idea presupposes. . . . It is a constellation of thoughts which is given in the gospel and as such it provides the basis for unity in the church.[40]

This particular pattern or "constellation of thoughts" gives access to a new way of discerning reality. It seems that these thoughts also are too large, as it were, to be thought individually; the mind of Christ seems irreducibly relational in its constitution. Indeed, we have seen reason to think that participation in the mind of Christ is fundamentally a relational activity, a noetic event that transpires in the communion of love.

Diadochus explicates this relational framework by teasing out the new role of compunction in those who are growing spiritually. Their knowledge, he says, is contingent on their sensitivity to those around them and their consequent readiness to seek out in loving humility those who are alienated from them. "For spiritual knowledge, consisting wholly of love, does not allow the mind (*nous*) to expand and embrace the vision of the divine, unless we first win back to love even one who has become angry with us for no reason."[41] Perhaps we might understand this view by considering that this noetic relational matrix of reconciling love instantiates within the world something of the divine communion that is the very basis of reality. And so when one begins to think about everything in this profoundly reconciling way, one is intuitively more capable of perceiving the truth of life. This is, I believe, what Diadochus is saying when he comments,

The "mind of Christ" is not an alien rationality that displaces native human reason, but is rather a pattern of rationality constantly held open by faith to the wideness of God's mercy.

> The qualities of a pure soul are intelligence devoid of envy, ambition [lit. zeal] free from malice, and unceasing love for the Lord of glory [note the direct contrast with the powers of the age who do not love and cannot understand the Lord of glory, 1 Cor 2:8]. When the soul has these qualities, then the intellect (nous) can accurately assess how it will be judged.[42]

The noetic significance of love cannot be overestimated here. For Diadochus, faith and hope help the soul to find freedom from worldly compulsions, "but love unites the soul with the excellence of God, searching out the Invisible by means of intellectual perception (*aisthēsei noera*)."[43] Again, I want to suggest that this not be taken solely in an individualistic sense, but that we instead see Diadochus's social and relational concern operative here; in that case the knowledge that love makes possible is a discernment of the relational ground of all things, their existence in and through and for communion with God and by means of participation in God's triune life.

What Kind of Knowledge?

Does this mean that we have worked our way back into a purely spiritual "faith-knowledge" that has no relevance outside the idiomatically religious sphere? There are two important preliminary points to be made here.

First, if the universe is trinitarianly constituted, then thinking with the mind of Christ will, as I have suggested, make possible a perception of reality in its truest depths. This need not mean that a Christian scientist, for example, will discover something *other* than quarks or whatever subatomic particles are discoverable; rather, a Christian scientist would discern such particles in their true identity as expressive events, outpourings, in the infinite exchange of love that is the divine life. Even the apparent necessities of nature are ultimately gratuitous, luminous with freely giving love of the Trinity.

And second, the fact that Paul applies the mind of Christ principally to ecclesial life and the overcoming of its mutually divisive misperceptions need *not* mean that the mind of Christ is preoccupied, as it were, with church in an exclusive sense. For the church is simply those bits of the whole creation called up into a new pattern of relationship in which, however faintly and fitfully, something of the divine pattern of relationship can be recognized and sought. The church exists in the process of undergoing new creation not instead of the rest of the universe but only as a sign to the whole creation of what God has in store for everything. And that means that the particular pattern of communal thinking identified as the mind of Christ is the pattern of knowing and loving in which all creatures are called to share. Practicing it in its provisional ecclesial form is meant to draw more and more of the creation into this mind. So when Paul or others talk about the mind of Christ in terms of the church's life or its decision-making, we ought to think of this as a kind of dry run for the rest of the creation, not as a peculiar tribal activity of a coterie.

Knowledge as Communion

Let me now attempt to bring the points I've been making to their conclusion. Throughout this chapter I have highlighted in various ways the old-fashioned and quaintly unmodern point that moral and intellectual virtues are integrally related. St. Paul, Evagrius, and Diadochus have all maintained that vicious minds are not capable of perceiving much beyond the anxious and manipulative grasp of their own fears and desires—and whatever they do espy of such greater reality they soon misperceive as either a potential object of possession or a bitter obstacle and focus of aggression. As the Letter to Titus describes such a state, folly or incomprehension is its very first characteristic: "For we ourselves were once foolish, disobedient, led astray, slaves to various passions and pleasures, passing our days in malice and envy, despicable, and hating one another" (3:3).

I have suggested how the process of conversion away from such a state leads to ascesis and to a clearer vision of one's "evil thoughts," to use Evagrius's term, and how such a recognition goes hand in hand with an opening of the mind to the boundless gratuity of God in Christ. But as we have moved through the noetic significance of sharing in the paschal mystery, the communal dimension of graceful knowing has become more and more apparent. The mind of Christ is an irreducibly relational and communally knowing "subject."

So when Diadochus explores the growing transparency of the mind to God, we ought not to read this apart from the communal context he certainly presupposes. Take this beautiful mystical passage, for example:

> He who loves God consciously in his heart (lit., who perceives God in the heart by love, *aisthēsei kardias agapōn*) is known by God, for to the degree that he receives the love of God consciously in his soul, he truly enters into God's love. From that time on, such a man never loses an intense longing for the illumination of spiritual knowledge (*gnōseōs*), until he senses its strength in his bones and no longer knows himself, but is completely transformed by the love of God. He is both present in this life and not present in it; still dwelling in the body, he yet departs from it, as through love he ceaselessly journeys towards God in his soul.[44]

This dilation of the human being in love with God ceaselessly whets the appetite for a truth that itself becomes the knower ("until he senses its strength in his bones"), realizing this truth in a love that sets the knower free from self-preoccupation and available to the other ("no longer knows himself"). Because the reality in which the knower participates is itself a radically self-sharing and freely loving existence, this mystical journey toward

God in the soul cannot be solipsistic. Indeed, the self-forgetting desire for the other that characterizes this state of spiritual knowing finds its real embodiment in the neighbor; this relational pattern of existence is the framework for true knowledge. It is not surprising that Diadochus immediately follows the passage just quoted with this one:

> When a man begins to perceive (*aisthanesthai*) the love of God in all its richness, he begins also to love his neighbour with spiritual perception (*aisthēsei pneumatos*). This is the love of which all the scriptures speak. Friendship after the flesh is very easily destroyed on some slight pretext, since it is not held firm by spiritual perception. But when a person is spiritually awakened, even if something irritates him, the bond of love is not dissolved; rekindling himself with the warmth of the love of God, he quickly recovers himself and with great joy seeks his neighbour's love, even though he has been gravely wronged or insulted by him. For the sweetness of God completely consumes the bitterness of the quarrel.[45]

I note here the intimate conjunction between spiritual perception or discernment and the divine love. This love is the ground of the deepening steadfast knowledge of the neighbor and sets flowing a renewable understanding of the other. We could even say that the divine loving inhabits the human relationship, making it possible, and bringing to light within it the amiable truth of the other which God alone (sometimes!) can know. It is precisely this feasting of the perception upon "the love of God in all its richness" that sets the mind free from fearful self-preoccupations and enmities, filling it with the divine abundance and so preparing it to risk the truth of the other, rather than merely the fantasized objectification of the other.

This kind of knowledge is one with the discernment shown among the desert fathers. It is an acute insight into the shape of God's loving design for the other. It is an awareness of the right patterns of activity by which to embrace the destiny of oneself with another, by which to allow God's call to self and neighbor to take flesh and come to life in the world. The test of this knowledge is found, therefore, in its unity with the relational life within which it can alone come to perception. If it builds up the body (cf. 1 Thess 5:11), then it is authentic and not spurious knowledge. Commenting on Paul's critique of false knowledge in 1 Corinthians, Luke Timothy Johnson observes:

> Any knowledge claiming to provide a liberty that can proceed in action heedless of the consequences to others only "puffs up" (1 Cor 8:1) the individual while running the risk of destroying the community. . . . Paul therefore speaks of edification as that expression of the

"mind of Christ" (1 Cor 2:16) in which each person looks not to his or her own interests but to the interests of others.[46]

This freely self-giving love of Christ becomes, by the power of the Holy Spirit, the very structure of a new kind of talking and thinking and being with one another. The whole thrust of Paul's address to the Corinthians is to submit their divided and factionalized communal life to the unifying relationality let loose upon the world in Christ.

Alexandra Brown joins Johnson and others in noting the close association in Paul's writings between the cross event and a particular state of mind. To share with one another in the "mind of Christ" or to "let the same mind be in you that was in Christ Jesus" is, for Paul, to perceive reality within a matrix of reconciliation, service, unity, and humility.[47] My most basic conviction about all this is that the reason this sharing in Christ's mind so frees the community to live for one another is because sharing in Christ's mind is knowing, in the provisional form possible in this life, something of the glory of the Father's love as the very foundation of one's existence. And when Diadochus dilates on the gift of contemplation, or, as he calls it, *theologia,* I think it is really the church's sharing in Christ's relationship with the Father that he is describing.[48]

Again, we might see something like this in Paul's reference to the building up of the church as the temple of the Holy Spirit (Ephesians 2:19-22), the earthly locus and form of the heavenly exchange of love that is God's life. And as that exchange takes place, the new act of knowing occurs, a knowing which is, of course, a being known, a lifting of the world, even in fragments, up into the life by which God knows and loves God. Such a relational ground of knowing is not without analogies. A rose, for instance, has a vast number of specifiable data about it which one can know, and yet all these are understood anew and differently when the rose is given by someone to a friend; when it is taken up into their mutual life, indeed becomes a cherishable dimension of their life, it is knowable in a new way. Jesus has taken up the believing community into his life with the Father. This community, in the Gospel of John, becomes by Jesus' sending of the Spirit the dwelling place of God. Here the truth of the creation (that it is the beloved of God) may begin to radiate through the world. Because Jesus lives from the Father in a way that destroys death he makes possible a communal life that is not driven by the fear of death. Because Jesus lives, the disciples live also: "On that day you will know that I am in my Father, and you in me, and I in you" (John 14:19-20). In the words of James Alison,

His life will be seen in their capacity to live beyond (rather than live toward, i.e., moved by) death. It is by their coming to live beyond death . . . that they will know the complete mutual implication of the

Son and the Father, because they will themselves be caught up in the making real and visible of that mutual implication. . . . By the disciples' loving imitation of Jesus' self-giving, they will creatively make present Jesus' sonship, and thus the divine paternity, in the world that does not know it.[49]

So knowing with the mind of Christ is not simply an acquisition of truths but "an expanding possession of the believer by the Father and the Son creating eternal life in the midst of this world through the creation of an imitative adhesion" by the believing community to the practices that identify Jesus' relationship with the Father.[50] "Those who love me will keep my word, and my Father will love them, and we will come to them and make our home with them. . . . This is my commandment, that you love one another as I have loved you" (John 14:23; 15:12).

This has three crucial implications. First, the faith, in the sense of the ideas by which the mind knows and seeks to understand what God has accomplished in Christ, becomes a new cognitive framework by means of which the Holy Spirit "will guide you into all truth" (John 16:13), re-structuring the mind and prying it open to the infinite, deathless reality of God. This sets the believing community free to enact a new pattern of relationship, free from the fear, envy, and enmity that are death's instruments in controlling the mind.

Second, because of the nature of the reality in question, the divine life, the "ideas" by which the mind apprehends such a reality are not purely conceptual; that is, they of course have a conceptual form by means of which they are present in the mind of someone trying to think about them, but the forms by which this divine reality makes itself known seem to be primarily relational events, acts of mercy and love. So, for instance, the truth of the Incarnation is actually something one cannot grasp within the bounds of an individual mind but which unfolds its reality within the new practices of communal life that the Incarnation establishes within the network of the world's life.

And third, the effect of this new communal pattern, the mind of Christ, continuously woven into the fabric of the world, is that the world begins to know everything differently; indeed as the world is drawn into the new life that Jesus is establishing in its midst, the world is not simply thinking differently but finds that its thoughts are not solely its *own* at all, but God's, that the pattern of relational activity by which it has come to think everything, bringing everything eucharistically into this communal event, is the trinitarian event of God's knowing and loving.

SIX

Discerning a Divine Calling: Vocation and Truth in *Pilgrim's Progress*

In the previous chapter we examined the unfolding power of the paschal mystery in illuminating human perception. For a second case study I want to return to a figure we noticed briefly in chapter 3, the seventeenth-century Puritan writer and preacher, John Bunyan. Probably no Christian writing, apart from the Bible itself, has been more widely translated and read than Bunyan's allegory, *The Pilgrim's Progress from this World to that which is to Come* (1678). Upon the Restoration of the crown and episcopal authority in Britain, Bunyan was among the first Puritans imprisoned for refusing to desist from unauthorized preaching. He remained a prisoner from 1660 to 1672. During those twelve years he struggled to discern the truth of God's calling to him, and this led him to considerable insight regarding vocation as a bearer of truth. In this chapter, then, I explore *Pilgrim's Progress* as a way of examining the discernment of calling, and calling as a way of thinking about truth.[1]

Vocation as the Calling to Exist

If we think of vocation simply in terms of our own particular choice of a career in life, then Bunyan must seem an odd tool for exploring the discernment of truth. *Pilgrim's Progress* is, after all, about a journey from damnation to salvation and involves a fairly dire *critique* of the very world in which, presumably, most persons are trying to follow their individual callings. But suppose what we usually think of as "vocation" were really only an emerging thread in the developing pattern of a human live. Religious thought tends to think of vocation this way, not simply in a narrow and technical sense (vocation as job), but as calling in the deepest sense— calling out of illusions and pretenses, calling into the fullness of each person's authentic identity.

149

In more overtly theological terms, we might see vocation as a dialogue.[2] On one side there is God's calling everything that exists into the fullness of being. And on the other side there is the "response" that each thing makes to that calling, in the first place simply by coming *to be,* but also by coming to be very particularly the *kind* of being that each thing is. When the things in question have some degree of mindfulness about them, then this dialogue between divine calling and intelligent, voluntary response is more exhilarating and more challenging, involving as it does abilities to feel and reason, to choose and reject, to commit and evade. God's calling to human beings, as Rowan Williams comments, "happens from birth to death, and what we usually call vocation is only a name for the moment of crisis within the unbroken process."[3] It might make sense to regard a whole life as a pilgrimage in response to divine calling, and one's particular vocation as a journey into those patterns of life that allow one to be truthfully and wholly the persons God is calling into being. But what that might mean at any given moment is not always clear: "crises occur at those points where we see how unreality, our selfish, self-protecting illusions, our struggles for cheap security, block the way to our answering the call to be. To live like this, to nurture and develop this image of myself, may be safe, but it isn't true."[4]

To pursue one's vocation in this sense, then, means becoming more real, moving beyond a kind of stymied, half-life caricature of oneself. It would mean moving beyond a response to calling that is merely a biological drive to go on existing and toward a listening, responding, choosing, delighting personhood. This kind of personhood involves the risk of setting out from the self given to us by our biology, or constructed for us by our culture, and embracing the call to relationship with others who stretch us beyond the limits even of what we thought of as our selves, and on into a deeper truthfulness of being. This is the calling, the vocation, that religious thought understands as the calling into being by virtue of a calling into relationship with God.

If we take vocation in this broader sense, then Bunyan gives rise to helpful reflection. For he dramatizes the journey into the truth of one's being precisely as a pilgrimage into a more truthful response to God's calling—a pilgrimage, that is, into a less fearful, less driven, less illusory, and more personal form of existence. Bunyan is adept at unmasking the artificial stopping points, the inauthentic concretions of selfhood, that mesmerize and numb persons. And he illustrates what we might call path-finding vocational skills. These habits of discernment and interpretation permit one to read the world not as a concatenation of mute objects and opaque events but as the landscape of a journey with discernible landmarks, inspiring vistas, and a population of important companions for the way.

Allegory in a Reifying World

It is not coincidental that allegory was so popular a genre among Puritan writers. *Pilgrim's Progress* and many other works in the same vein were designed to pry open the range of meanings inherent in everything, and to do so in a world increasingly ill at ease with ambiguity. Founding figures in the new science of early modernity like Francis Bacon were happy to employ allegory as well. But Bacon's allegorizations of ancient myths were designed to cloak the real political and scientific implications of his teaching; they are essentially a rhetorical training in subtlety and calculation. Bunyan's allegory, by contrast, is more nearly a narratival metaphysics; *Pilgrim's Progress* is a way of recovering entire dimensions of meaning that, in Bunyan's view, were being washed out of the picture.

Early modernity is marked by an epistemological crisis, by an urgent "search for new forms of language to replace traditional logic and rhetoric."[5] For Bacon, for Hobbes, and for the influential founders of the Royal Society, language had been too much infected with the teleological momentum of Aristotelian logic and the seemingly artificial plausibility of the rhetorical tradition. For language to be useful again it would need, in their view, a nominalizing purification, a pruning away of all metaphorical and analogical penumbra. And the point of this was not simply to chasten language but to purge our conception of the reality that language names. Hobbes is very clear about wanting to jettison all the linguistic habits of thought that might conduct the mind toward anything infinite, anything not subject to knowledge of the senses.[6] Establishment religious thought, despite its occasional opposition to Hobbes, was of a very similar view. Archbishop Tillotson (himself the son-in-law of one of the founding members of the Royal Society) argued strenuously for the elimination from religious discourse of all "sublime notions and unintelligible mysteries, with pleasant passages of wit, and artificial strains of rhetoric; and nice and unprofitable disputes, with bold interpretations of dark prophesies."[7]

And yet Bunyan was convinced that it was precisely the work of puzzling over such dark mysteries which could fit the mind to encounter a truth not graspable by a plain, discursive, nominalizing rationality. In the "Apology" which prefaces *Pilgrim's Progress*, Bunyan addresses himself as if directly to Tillotson:

> Solidity, indeed becomes the Pen
> Of him that writeth things Divine to men:
> But must I needs want solidness, because
> By Metaphors I speak; was not Gods Laws,
> His Gospel-laws in older time held forth
> By Types, Shadows and Metaphors?[8]

The practice of figural reading trains the mind to search for hidden depths of meaning in ordinary life. To discover a hidden purpose in your life, to "read" the choices you make in terms of that goal—these are vocational habits that allegory is able to teach in a way that more discursive argumentation cannot. This is so partly because of how the interpretive task of allegory forms the mind, but it is also true in a more ontological sense: what Bunyan draws to our attention may in fact not *be* apprehensible apart from an analogical frame of mind. Or as Bunyan puts it in his preface to the second part of his work:

> And to stir the mind
> To a search after what it fain would find,
> Things that seem to be hid in words obscure,
> Do but the Godly mind the more alure;
> To study what those Sayings should contain,
> That speak to us in such a Cloudy strain.
> I also know, a dark Similitude
> Will on the Fancie more it self intrude,
> And will stick faster in the Heart and Head,
> Then things from Similies not borrowed. (139)

For Bunyan, this "fancie" is a creative, imagining faculty capable of receiving a "dark Similitude" and being drawn thereby into a new level of understanding and insight. "Words obscure/Do but the Godly mind the more alure," and so conduce toward a multidimensional sense of the world. For Hobbes by contrast, such fancy or imagination "is nothing but decaying sense."[9] Hobbes's materialism and nominalism have no conception of the imagination playing a constructive role; it is in his view but the ever fainter impression left on our senses of whatever is now absent from us. This is important to Hobbes because he fears that any interpretive openness about the world leaves a dangerous opening for challenges to the epistemological dominance of the state. The modern world badly needed to shut down rival visions of reality if it was to achieve peace and order.[10] But what if rival visions are precisely what we need in order to hear an authentic calling, one not, perhaps, engineered for us by the culture? All this is instructive because it may help us to understand why discernment seems such a challenge for us today, why vocational awareness seems inaccessible: when the mind reifies the world, sees everything as reducible to one datum after another, then the world becomes opaque and mute. It becomes extremely difficult to sense any "more" to the world if it has no more interpretive depth to it, no more quality of sign-fullness.

This is excruciatingly demonstrated by a later writer of Puritan descent, Daniel Defoe. Defoe's *Moll Flanders* (1722) arrives a generation after *Pil-*

grim's Progress (1672), and its warning against the mainstream cultural absorption of a Hobbesian frame of mind is searing. *Moll* is the original "Pilgrim's Regress," depicting the rapid descent of the anti-heroine into a moral autism of confused identity, loss of purpose, and persistent duplicity. For when nothing has any enduring significance, everything becomes capable of meaning anything, all is simply what you make it: everything is reducible to different denominations in one common coinage and available to the largest purse. Whereas Bunyan's pilgrim still struggles toward discernment, Moll's submersion beneath the unrecognizable significance of her endlessly compromising circumstances reduces her efforts at personal and vocational judgment to a suspiciously amusing charade of excuses for debauchery.

Moll's ability to notice and respond to authentic personal vocation is reduced to the flatness of a materialist biological drive in which her conduct is merely the result of whatever appetite or aversion is most immediately brought to bear upon her at any given moment. The sustaining vocational directionality of Bunyan's Providence (figured in such characters as the Evangelist, Faithful, and the Shepherds) has been replaced in Defoe by a series of characters who can imagine no end for Moll other than the basest devices of their own desires, and who teach her to hope for nothing better. Our ambivalence about doctrines of predestination today perhaps obscures their positive function in vocational discernment; as one commentator puts it, weaken predestination "and you are heading toward Defoe."[11] Perhaps we could say that Bunyan's allegorical thinking brings out the providential, directional function of predestinarian Puritan thought; for it illuminates life in terms of a guiding calling and goal—or at least serves as a marker, holding open the world to a meaning from beyond it. Certainly the absence in *Moll* of any hope of that transparency of life to its deeper meaning reminds us of how painful the loss of a discerning capacity can be.

Bunyan's use of allegory, therefore, is an important step in retraining the mind to navigate life not as one thing after another but as invested with meaning and directionality, irradiated with a light of eternal significance. In fact, we could say that by conceiving life allegorically in terms of pilgrimage, Bunyan is not merely telling us about the possibility of our lives' deeper meaning, but he is engaging us in a literary practice of sign-reading, path-finding, depth-discovering—all of which are important skills in vocational reflection.[12]

Learning to Recognize Illusion

Having considered the implications of Bunyan's chosen genre, let me now attend to the critical faculty he seeks to teach. Later I will focus more directly on the more positive skills of vocational discernment.

Bunyan spent over a third of his adult life in prison for continuing to preach without a license, so he knew very well that his interpretive vision of life was threatening to both the cultural and individual status quo. The world does not especially like to notice the "more" of God's invitation. Bunyan wants to make sure that his readers reckon with their tendencies to illusion about this. He wants to warn us about the power of counterfeit goals to beguile us from efforts toward vocational authenticity. Real calling as a divine gift is, in Bunyan's experience, likely to be heard by the world only as a repugnant threat to its autonomy. The interpretive space, the graceful multidimensionality of life lived toward a radical call, is perceived as a dangerous mark of epistemological instability by a reifying world; just as the same calling renders us politically unstable, unwilling to confine our loyalties to the state. Because Bunyan is so aware of this he makes the recognition of "substitute" callings an important part of his teaching on discernment.

We might begin with the most obvious attacks on vocation and move toward an awareness of the subtlest. Undoubtedly the most overt threat to Christian and his own self-understanding comes from the "foul fiend" Apollyon. This monstrous figure (whom Bunyan adapts from biblical references) assails Christian with a telling combination of frightful appearance and a cunning reasonableness; he is shown to be the pilgrim's hateful adversary but also his secret, unacknowledged master. When Christian announces that he has come from the City of Destruction, Apollyon exults malignantly: "By this I perceive thou art one of my Subjects, for all that Countrey is mine; and I am the Prince and God of it. How is it that thou hast ran away from thy King? Were it not that I hope thou maiest do me more service, I would strike thee now at one blow to the ground" (47). There is a horrible shock here as Christian is made to realize who *claims* at least to have been the dominant power in his life so far.

> "All this is true, and much more, which thou has left out; but the Prince whom I serve and honour, is merciful, and ready to forgive."

Even more disconcerting, however, are Apollyon's well-oiled counsels, charmingly accommodating and even consolatory in tone: he fears Christian will find his new calling a hard one, promises good things upon Christian's undoubted return to his old King, and assures him that "it is ordinary for those that have professed themselves his [Christ's] Servants, after a while to give him the slip; and return again to me; do thou so too, and all shall be well" (47). Here is the strangely comforting poison of despair, holding before us a hopeless picture of our apparently inevitable failure and so giving us permission to skulk back cozily into the old and familiar servitude, forsaking any effort to test the real depths of our calling.

Apollyon tightens the noose further with an excruciatingly accurate rehearsal of all the ways in which Christian has already been unfaithful to Christ (and is therefore unlikely to persevere in his calling). The fiend saves his most insidious swipe for last: "and when thou talkest of thy Journey, and of what thou has heard, and seen, thou art inwardly desirous of vainglory in all that thou sayest or doest" (48). Even Christian's highest calling, says Apollyon, is morbidly tainted with self-preoccupation. But Christian answers freely and fearlessly, "All this is true, and much more, which thou has left out; but the Prince whom I serve and honour, is merciful, and ready to forgive" (48). Surely if Christian *had* tried to argue with Apollyon, finding mitigation for this or that little infidelity, Christian would have been lost. He would have been swept into a collaboration with all his weaknesses, and gradually brought to a destructive choice between a ceaseless and exhausting denial of truth or else a paralyzing state of self-condemnation. Vocational judgment is not possible, Bunyan seems to suggest, if we pretend that flawed motivations are entirely absent from our journey; but neither can we let our shortcomings be the measure of our hope. The hope of our calling lies quite beyond ourselves: "the Prince whom I serve and honour, is merciful."

In the episode of Apollyon, Bunyan alerts his readers to the danger of a distortion of their calling; he does this by depicting the menacing power of the world, both in its beguiling calls to a false and lesser goal and by its insinuations that the pilgrim has really been seeking only these lesser goals all along anyway. Apollyon is depicted finally as a bully who begins by using believers' own self-doubts against them and then escalates to naked threats of violence in order to keep would-be pilgrims back in their accustomed places.

The underlying systematic structure of control, which Apollyon merely personifies, becomes even more apparent in the famous adventures of Christian and Faithful at Vanity Fair. In this great sequence, Bunyan shows what difficulty the world has even to *imagine,* let alone pursue, a vocation beyond the commerce of the world. For what Bunyan unmasks here are the commodifying structures of the world, which seek to convert every desire to a purchasable form and thus constrain all our aspirations and goals to the limits of a worldly purse: "at this Fair are all such Merchandize sold, as Houses, Lands . . . Kingdoms, Lusts, Pleasures, and Delights of all sorts, as Whores, Bauds, Wives, Husbands, Children, Masters, Servants, Lives, Blood, Bodies, Souls, Silver, Gold, Pearls, Precious Stones, and what not" (73).

The fact that the pilgrims refuse to enter into the "commerce" of the Fair creates a terrible hubbub. Their refusal to name a price or quantify their callings in commodifiable terms is a threat to the world system; for their refusal opens the eyes of some "that were more observing, and less prejudiced than the rest" (75) to the possibility that there may *be* real goals not fully attainable on the world's terms. And thus it shows the very idea of vocation to be a sign of transcendence, a marker of an ungraspable calling to "more" in a system that would like to assimilate everything and everyone within the scope of its own measures, converting a vocational "more" into a quantifiable excess.

At Vanity Fair no one attempts to convince the pilgrims, as Apollyon sought to, that their goals are really only pious expressions for worldly ambitions; rather, here Bunyan simply depicts the stark incomprehension of any ideals that might threaten to extend beyond material terms. The pilgrims are regarded frankly as dangerous lunatics; they are beaten, put on public display in cages, and tried on trumped-up charges with a parade of false witnesses. Bunyan's magnificent trial scene, presided over by Lord Hategood and receiving testimony from such sober citizens as Envy, Superstition, and Pickthank, portrays the world's vicious discomfort with authentic vocation as rooted in bitter pusillanimity. The world's soul is literally too small (*pusilla anima*) to embrace the glory of a hope beyond its own tight-fisted management and control. If it cannot buy and sell the thing, it despises it. Christian and Faithful threaten to open the world's eyes to the real depths of its desires, depths it prefers not to notice because they lie beyond its own powers.

One of the paradoxes that Bunyan repeatedly explores is that a deep and wonderful calling, which seems so foolhardy, dubious, and deadly to the world, is really the only thing capable of prying open the world's otherwise continually constricting hopes. Conversely, the goals that the world holds out as worthy callings, says Bunyan, inevitably collapse into vain and ever-narrowing pursuits of self-interest. While most of us might wish to affirm the naturalness of religious belief and its perfect congruence with true human happiness, Bunyan always points to the danger of our authentic callings being suborned by lesser ones.

The climate was not auspicious for Bunyan's warnings. Bishop John Wilkins, one of the founders of the Royal Society, had written a highly influential work, *Of the Principles and Duties of Natural Religion,* which appeared just three years before *Pilgrim's Progress*, and emphasized how harmoniously religious faith and human success might go together. His goal, he wrote, was

> to persuade Men to the Practice of Religion, and the Virtues of a good
> life, by shewing how natural and direct an influence they have, not

only upon our future Blessedness in another World, but even upon the Happiness and Prosperity of this present Life. And surely nothing is more likely to prevail with wise and considerate Men to become Religious, than to be thoroughly convinced, that Religion and Happiness, our Duty and our Interest, are really but one and the same thing considered under several notions.[13]

Bunyan seems to be satirizing Wilkins's argument pretty directly when he presents numerous self-declared pilgrims who, despising Christian's risky and difficult route, keep falling by the wayside into more pleasant paths. One good example is By-ends, who claims as his relatives a Mr. Smoothman, Mr. Facing-bothways, and Mr. Any-thing. Having discoursed upon his enviable relations, By-ends adds blithely:

Tis true, we somewhat differ in religion from those of the stricter sort, yet but in two small points: First, we never strive against Wind and Tide. Secondly, we are alwayes most zealous when Religion goes in his Silver Slippers; we love much to walk with him in the Street, if the Sun shines, and the people applaud it. (81)

Vanity Fair, suggests Bunyan, is the state of the world when it has finally accommodated all its real hopes in this way. First, there is a barely perceptible debasement of authentic calling into a more immediately prosperous counterfeit version, and then at last comes total incomprehension and antagonism toward any call that refuses to fit in. By-ends and his friends Mr. Hold-the-world, Mr. Mony-love, and Mr. Save-all accuse Christian of being rigid and censorious, a threat to liberty. And yet as their own conversation continues, Bunyan depicts them as falling progressively into the most laughably self-serving platitudes imaginable. "Tis best to make hay when the Sun shines," opines Mr. Hold-the-world cheerily to his friends:

you see how the Bee lieth still all winter and bestirs her then only when she can have profit with pleasure. God sends sometimes Rain, and sometimes Sunshine; if they be such fools to go through the first, yet let us be content to take fair weather along with us. For my part I like that Religion best, that will stand with the security of Gods good blessings unto us; for who can imagin that is ruled by his reason, since God has bestowed upon us the good things of this life, but that he would have us keep them for his sake? (83-84)

For Bunyan, a world in which the depths of authentic vocation are left unexplored is a world in which the profoundest hopes become unhearable and one's calling degenerates into crassness. And this loss of deep vocational acuity leads to a real epistemological numbness, an inability to conceive of or interpret reality beyond the bounds of the obvious and the quantifiable.

Bunyan seems to be telling us that if what is truly great can only be present in this world in the form of our human yearning for it, then should that longing be falsely satiated we will suffer a terrible absence of what is real beyond all measuring. Platitude assumes the place of wisdom.

The Self Becomes Its Own Prisoner

Bunyan deepens the paradox still further, for he shows this vocational autism, which tries to be happy by hearing nothing beyond the clamor of self-aggrandizing desire, as always at risk of falling yet more grievously into nihilism and despair. It is as if the self, deprived of a real calling *beyond* itself, becomes the prisoner of its own anxieties and doubts. If the human will exists in a mere echo chamber of its own desires, in which the authentic voice of the other has been silenced in favor of an "other" that is merely my own self-interest projected outward, then my will becomes, paradoxically, self-annihilating. Nowhere is this clearer than in the episode of Doubting Castle and its lord, Giant Despair.

Christian falls subject to this terrible figure through nothing but his own self-seeking will. Bunyan sets the scene with astuteness. Christian and his new companion, Hopeful (Faithful having given his life for his calling at Vanity Fair), have been enjoying a period of refreshment and consolation beside the River of Life. But as they take up their journey again they discover to their sorrow that their Way parts from the River: "Now the way from the River was rough, and their feet tender by reason of their Travels; So the soul of the Pilgrims was much discouraged, because of the way. Wherefore still as they went on, they wished for a better way" (91). Yet this desire to make joy their possession leads them to a false path and a way that is no way at all. They see a delightful meadow on the other side of a fence and immediately Christian cries out, "Tis according to my wish . . . here is the easiest going" (91). And of course it is delightful walking, but with nightfall a tremendous storm and flood overtake them, and in their lostness they fall asleep. With the morning they are awakened by the "grim and surly voice" of the owner of the grounds upon which they have trespassed, Giant Despair. In his "nasty and stinking" dungeon they are kept for days without any light or food or drink. "In this place, Christian had double sorrow, because twas through his unadvised haste that they were brought into this distress" (93).

Bunyan is very subtle at this point, for he allows the fairytale-like conventions to play themselves out realistically, testing the reader's ability to read between the lines. The giant terrorizes them, and they are starving, with their wounds untreated, and so on. Yet gradually it appears that the giant's power over them is somehow linked to their own fear; he browbeats them with the hopelessness of their plight and urges them to take their own lives: "for why, said he, should you chuse life, seeing it is attended with so much bitterness" (94). Now Christian begins to succumb, and the voice of Despair becomes indistinguishable from his own thoughts.

Bunyan had hinted at this most sinister ventriloquism once before. When Christian was passing through the Valley of the Shadow of Death, one of the demons had crept up so covertly and close to him that the horrible blasphemies and dismally obsessive murmurings that the demon was whispering into Christian's ear seemed to him as if they "proceeded from his own mind" (52). Bunyan's vision is quite telling. The supposed bastion of rational judgment and enlightened self-interest, the human self, turns out to be much less stable than we might like to think; the isolated ego, busily pursuing its own path, is far more susceptible to unperceived motivations than it usually admits. But whereas in the episode of the whispering demon Christian is still being accosted, albeit covertly, from without, now in Doubting Castle the threat has truly found its interior nest and begins to incubate in the pilgrim's own heart. All vocational judgment begins to be undermined, infested with despair, and these thoughts really are now proceeding from the pilgrim's own mind. The self, having been led into decay and debasement through the pursuit of counterfeit goods (the beguilingly soft meadow) is left in a vacuum. The voice that had continually *called* out to the self, made it alive and awake to a reality beyond itself, has been walled out, and the self now feels itself cut off and tyrannized by its own fears.

It is at this point that Bunyan makes movingly clear how truly vocation can only ever be a communal journey. Human beings may each have to travel as individuals, but they are lost if they travel alone. Just as Christian has reached the point of irrevocable despair, Hopeful comforts him, reminding him of all the great wonders he has seen and passed through already. And most importantly he simply calls Christian "My Brother," and says: "Thou seest that I am in the Dungeon with thee, a far weaker man by nature than thou art: Also this Giant has wounded me as well as thee; and hath also cut off the Bread and Water from my mouth; and with thee I mourn without the light" (95). In spite of the world's attempts to divert the pilgrims by falsely constricting their callings within the limits of the self's own natural desires, that self is not quite left entirely alone; there is always a fellow sufferer whose presence holds open a door out of the self that the world has tried to construct for it, whose voice is the voice of a calling beyond the limits of what was *thought* to be selfhood.

Encouraged by Hopeful's words, Christian joins him in praying through Saturday night "till almost break of day" (96). Then suddenly in amazement, Christian cries out that he realizes he has all along had in his possession a key "called Promise, that will, (I am perswaded) open any Lock in

Doubting-Castle" (96). Perhaps Bunyan sets this moment of liberation deliberately in the time sequence of Saturday vigil to resurrection morning, suggesting how Christian's recovered fellowship with Hopeful draws him again more deeply into a community of new life that has learned to live precisely by living no longer for itself alone but for another who has suffered with and for it.

Clearly for Bunyan, the deepest cause for concern about vocation relates to this very intrinsic tendency it has to fall prey to solipsism and to a culture that holds itself together precisely by holding us apart, by abetting isolation and obsessive self-interest. If calling is to remain clear and healthy, and vocational discernment to remain robust and free, they will need a fellowship that permits everyone to discover the true depths of their "own" callings in mutuality with one another.

Communities of Vocational Discernment

It would take us beyond the bounds of this chapter to examine all the instances in which Christian is taught or inspired by others to have a deeper understanding of his calling. But leaving aside such memorable figures as the mysterious Interpreter and the kindly Shepherds of the Delectable Mountains (see chapter 1 above), let me consider just the great episode of Christian's visit to the Palace Beautiful.

This extended episode comes immediately prior to two of Christian's most desperate trials (Apollyon and the Valley of the Shadow of Death) and provides the formation and encouragement in his calling without which he would have very likely perished. Taken as a whole, the episode comprises three distinct sequences: an initiatory trial, a dialogue on experience, and a confirming immersion in the historical and communal context of the pilgrim's calling.

There are possibilities of friendship and mutual support and unexpected refreshment all along the way.

The episode begins in extreme ambivalence: night has fallen on Christian, he has just been warned of ravening beasts ahead, and yet "while he was thus bewailing his unhappy miscarriage, he lift up his eyes, and behold there was a very stately Palace before him, the name whereof was Beautiful, and it stood just by the High-way side" (37). We can sense very well the tension and conflicting emotions that beset the early stages of any vocational journey. An image or foretaste of the hoped-for goal is in sight, but at the same time there are considerable hindrances, chief among them the fear and uncertainty about whether one can truly sustain the journey, or whether it would be better to turn back. This all comes to a climax as Christian approaches the gates, and Bunyan intensifies the significance of the moment for the reader by informing us that the lions Christian hears roaring are actually chained, although because of the darkness Christian is not able to see this.

By letting us in on the actual state of affairs Bunyan is training the reader; he is conjoining the ability to see the real truth of things (the chains hidden by the darkness) with a reasonable ground for hope and confidence (the lions cannot actually harm us), and by linking these in the reader's mind Bunyan teaches us a basic vocational stance: namely, that the more deeply we perceive the circumstances of our lives, the more we will realize the true basis for hope. In other words, this time of testing is not just an occasion for scaring off the fainthearted but is really a means of forming confidence and endurance even in the face of what we cannot yet see how to cope with or understand. The entire episode is strongly reminiscent of the Parables of Bernard of Clairvaux we considered in chapter 3, and suggests the enduring role of narratival "practice" in forming discernment. Indeed, Christian's chief task at the Palace Beautiful is to tell his narrative under the clarifying scrutiny of the virtues.

The confidence needed for such growth in discernment, says Bunyan, is most likely mediated by others: Christian was on the point of turning back, "for he thought that nothing but death was before him" (37), when the Porter at the gates sees him and calls out to say that the lions cannot harm him. Watchful the Porter briefly questions Christian, informing him that "This House was built by the Lord of the Hill . . . for the relief and security of Pilgrims" (38). Watchful's presence and help are the beginning of Christian's new sense that he is not alone in his journey, that there are possibilities of friendship and mutual support and unexpected refreshment all along the way.

Watchful calls out one of the household, "one of the Virgins of this place, who will, if she likes your talk, bring you in to the rest of the Family, according to the Rules of the House" (38). This young women is named Discretion, and she does indeed introduce Christian in turn to her sisters, Piety, Prudence, and, at last, Charity. It is quite possible that Bunyan was consciously deploying these figures in their accustomed traditional roles. Certainly there is a kind of logic in having the pilgrim exposed first to two of the Gifts of the Holy Spirit, Discretion and Piety, and then move on to two Virtues, culminating in Charity. Christian needs literal inspiring, gifting with grace, before he can begin to realize within his calling the strengths of the virtues. In any event, Bunyan does portray the sisters as conversing with Christian in a friendly and loving manner that draws out from him some crucial features of his journey so far, features upon which he needs to reflect more deeply. One of Bunyan's foremost modern interpreters explains the vital importance of this examination of Christian's experience:

> A basic element in the expressions of the Puritan's interest in past experience was the profound belief that experience formed the kind of rational whole in which God's activity could be descried as an explication and confirmation of biblical statement. In his private experience, as much as in the Word, the Puritan discerned God's voice speaking instruction and doctrine. Indeed, insofar as he made edifying use of his past, he tended to read it as *logos,* as an elaborate allegory of intelligible statement.[14]

There is a very clear progression in the kinds of questions the sisters put to Christian, designed to move him to a new awareness of the divine meaning implicit in his journey, and so help him intuit the deep structure of his calling.

Discretion begins by asking Christian to reflect on the most basic features of his life hitherto, helping to hold before his mind's eye the fundamental shape of his calling. Her questions lead him at last to a realization of how much he longs now to rest there. And in silent, poignant response, "she smiled, but the water stood in her eyes" (39). Perhaps this woman of good counsel is moved by the authenticity and yearning she senses in the pilgrim, glad that he will, at least for the time being, have a chance to explore and confirm the true depth of his calling. Piety's questions are much more detailed and seem designed to clarify and savor the very real changes and insights that have come to Christian's life already. All this corresponds to Bunyan's advice to readers given in the preface to his own autobiography:

> It is profitable for Christians to be often calling to mind the very beginnings of Grace with their Souls. . . . Yea, look diligently, and leave no corner therein unsearched, for there is treasure hid, even the treasure of your first and second experience of the grace of God toward you. Remember, I say, the Word that first laid hold upon you; remember your terrours of conscience, and fear of death and hell: remember also your tears and prayers to God; yea, how you sighed under every hedge for mercy. Have you never a Hill Mizar to remember? Have you forgot the Close, the Milk-house, the Stable, the Barn, and the like, where God did visit your Soul?[15]

Just as Bunyan's allegorical vision in *Pilgrim's Progress* teaches the reader to see the underlying meaning in everything, so this meditation on experience teaches pilgrims how to read their lives as the landscape of a journey, to recognize at last the pattern and shape of God's calling out to them.

With this foundation of trust and hope, it becomes possible to ask with

Prudence rather more probing and analytical questions. "Do you not think sometimes of the Countrey from whence you came?" she begins (41). Her questions invite Christian to be honest about the ways in which negative movements seem to hinder him, but also to recognize what contrary motions seem to help him: "Can you remember by what mean you find your annoyances at times, as if they were vanquished?" (41). What helps Christian most to get past the resistances are the thoughts of what Jesus had given him and the future to which he is being drawn. Thus it is reflection on features we might characterize as external gift and definite future that help to alleviate the interior doubts and feelings of helplessness or unworthiness. Significantly, Prudence's last question leads Christian to achieve some interior appropriation of that confidence and joy: "And what is it that makes you so desirous to go to Mount Zion?" (41). This moment of reconnecting with the deep desire of his heart again leads Christian to break out in tender affection toward the one who is the source and ground of his calling. It is just at this moment, when Christian has reached some clarity about his deepest feelings and the role they play ("For to tell you the truth, I love him, because I was by him eased of my burden" [42]), that Charity takes over the dialogue.

It is not surprising that Charity's questions are the most probing and in some ways most painful of all, for they direct Christian away from himself and toward those whom he has left behind. Her questions force Christian to consider whether the dissonance between his calling and his commitments to his family is really inescapable or is the result of a failure in charity on his part. Asking why the pilgrim has come without his wife and children, Charity demands to know whether Christian had truly made every effort to bring them, and whether the former pattern of his life did not render his new sense of calling simply unintelligible to his loved ones: "But did you not with your vain life, damp all that you by words used by way of perswasion to bring them with you?" (42).

We can see here the aptness in depicting *Charity* as the one who sets our calling in the context of our relationships. Her questions reframe the pilgrim's sense of vocation, enlarging it, and investing it with a mature sense of the costs and sorrows of an authentic pursuit of calling. For in the end, Charity does not disclose so much a lack of love in the deepest heart of Christian but rather a more general and universal need for love. We know that in part two of *Pilgrim's Progress*, Bunyan would indeed recount the happy journey of Christian's family to join him; but at this point Charity finds that Christian's vocation must be to set out ahead of them, and by the painful separation to force both himself and his family to cast themselves all the more entirely upon the charity of God. The urgency of vocation is truly pressing, and it can only avoid hardening into fierceness and zealotry (cf.

Richard of St. Victor in chapter 3) if it understands itself in the milieu of a universal love. There are no easy algorithms for calculating the justness of this step or that in the working out of an authentic vocation, and sometimes it will be necessary not to *cease* loving one's own but perhaps to place our little love in the context of a much greater love and trust that that greater love can alone supply what is most truly needed. Surely we see such difficult stages of awareness in the vocations of most married folk and vowed religious with respect to their families of origin. None of us can manipulate precisely the perfect balance of "mine" and "theirs" in the pursuit of our callings, we can only, Bunyan suggests, be terribly mindful of the need to test the love that moves us and remember that our callings never leave those around us unaffected.

We come to the final portion of Christian's stay at the Palace Beautiful by way of a lovely transition. From the poignant conversation about Christian's family left behind, Bunyan takes us immediately into a new kind of fellowship: the family of the House gathers Christian with them to their Table "furnished with fat thing, and with Wine that was well refined; and all their talk at the Table was about the Lord of the Hill" (43). In this way the ecclesial and indeed eucharistic fellowship makes possible the pilgrim's transfer from one life to another, from one basis of relationship to another, from one kind of hope to another. And though Christian is indeed eager the next day to begin these momentous passages, the Family politely urges him to stay, to strengthen and confirm the new life that has begun to take root in him.

For three glorious days the sisters immerse Christian in the many wonders and "Rarities" of the place. They show him marvelous records of all the many good things wrought by the Lord of Hill and of all the fellow pilgrims whose lives had been changed. They bring him into the armory and let him see and handle the strengths of faith and the "engines" used by faith's champions of old (Moses's rod, Gideon's trumpet, and David's sling among them!). They take him to see incredible views in the Delectable Mountains and Immanuel's Land in the distance beyond. And, of course, they continue to talk with him about the experiences of his calling and how to interpret it all. In these many ways we could say that the sisters of the Palace Beautiful afford Christian a formational community in which his authentic vocation can be nurtured and clarified and shaped. They give him a history in which his calling's deepest significance can become clear and its solipsistic tendencies overtaken by the light of a communal struggle and a corporate hope.

What Is "Vocation" in *Pilgrim's Progress*?

Perhaps it is this mingled thread of struggle and hope that weaves the vocational theme together in Bunyan—the struggle to see and speak honestly about calling, and the hope that keeps calling fresh and lively. Bunyan's own experiences of religious persecution, coupled with his sense of the self-deluding sinfulness of humankind, make him a highly critical interpreter of vocation. Few could have a more discerning eye when it comes to picking out the distorting influence of culture and self-interest upon vocation. So while the source and ground of one's calling is very strong, a vocation is, in Bunyan's view, always a living, changing, growing, and provisional dimension of one's being. Its unfolding is never mechanical or fixed; and if it is subject to negative misshaping, so by the same token the living out of a calling is also open to new clarity, intensification, and maturation.

We have also seen that, for Bunyan, it is this divine ground of calling that alone can fund the certainty and perseverance needed for vocational fruition. While it is the self which grows into truth by leaving earlier versions of itself behind, the growth, the pilgrimage, are sustained by the caller who remains always other. And this otherness, which must ever be the proper milieu of vocation, is figured in Bunyan by the many occasions when the pilgrim would certainly perish without companionship. Vocation emerges in Bunyan as a fully social phenomenon, in which the deep trajectory of the self becomes perspicuous in terms of the mutuality of calling. Perhaps it is ironic that a thinker like Bunyan, so alive to the relational and the divine as the authentic milieu of truth, would need to discern that truth within so profoundly personal a setting. Yet, perhaps because of this very feature, Bunyan may afford some relief for modernity's tendency to prioritize the knowing subject over the truth that the subject knows. For while no one could imagine Bunyan ignoring the contextual and subjective constraints on knowledge (so dominant in modernity's thinking about truth), ultimately, I believe, Bunyan moves beyond any solipsizing tendencies of modern critical thought. He does so because he finds truth unfolding itself not within the putatively inner structures of an individual consciousness but within the social and historical patterns of a life journey, a pilgrim's progress.

SEVEN

The Trinity and Discernment in John Henry Newman

One of the most characteristic features of Christian thought, at least in its premodern expressions, is apophasis—a surrendering of one's images, concepts, and speech in silent wonder before the illimitable self-disclosure of God. The Word, who always speaks more than humans can say, the Spirit who radiates a love beyond all earthly form—these historical missions of the divine life, Christians believe, are revealed in an economy of salvation that manifests its truth by carrying its human collaborators into a reality that both consummates and transcends their normal patterns of understanding. This knowing by way of unknowing is, paradoxically, quite unanxious and unembarrassed about its seeming poverty of knowledge, for it is happy to know by *participation* in truth, by coming to share in the knowing and loving that are the life of God.[1]

We have seen how this transformation of mind develops in Paul and desert spirituality (chapter 5), and we have noted how discernment turns out to be a central practice in this Christian approach to truth. From this standpoint, truth unfolds itself in the contours and relationships of a life, and not solely within the confines of a graspable datum of thought. In the previous chapter on Bunyan we considered this discernment of life-shape, of vocation, as a fundamental practice of knowledge and truth-seeking. But what happens when the pressure for definitive conceptual knowledge is too great, when there is no more room for patience with mystery as a quality of truth? In this chapter I consider modernity's impatience with mystery and the efforts made by John Henry Newman to rediscover mystery, and his correlate recovery of discernment as a path such truth-seeking might appropriately take.[2]

Fleeing Apophasis, Avoiding the Trinity

The apparent anxiety driving Descartes's rush toward absolute certainty provoked one of his critics to remark: "Your new method denigrates the traditional forms of argument, and instead grows pale with a new terror, the imaginary fear of the demon which it has conjured up. It fears it may be dreaming, it has doubts about whether it is mad."[3] It is a curious if not surprising feature of the modern quest for clear and distinct ideas that the more decisively all ambiguity is shunned, the more intolerable, even fearsome, becomes every aspect of real mystery. If it cannot be exposed as specious reasoning or ridiculed as abstruse "scholastic" wrangling, it comes to be reviled as a dangerous threat to human freedom and flourishing.[4] But, as Alciphron amiably reassures his friends in Berkeley's dialogue: "Fear not: by all the rules of right reason, it is absolutely impossible that any mystery, and least of all the Trinity, should really be the object of man's faith."[5]

Alciphron's comfortable dismissal of mystery to the contrary notwithstanding, my suggestion in this paper will be that the more real mystery is not only tolerated but actually lived into, the more religious certainty comes to light and truth becomes embodied in a human life. Bishop Berkeley himself was pointing in this direction (though at the time few seem to have grasped the significance of his suggestion). Berkeley's spokesman in the dialogue, Euphranor, responds to Alciphron by arguing that the words in which Christians speak of mystery ought not to be interpreted so positivistically, as though they simply and directly framed distinct ideas or could point directly at some reality. Rather, he proposes, it may be that such words are signs by which a life comes to be regulated and put into a right relationship with a reality that lies beyond any easy coining into intellectually manipulable concepts:

> Whence it seems to follow that a man may believe the doctrine of the Trinity, if he finds it revealed in Holy Scripture that the Father, the Son, and the Holy Ghost, are God, and that there is but one God, although he doth not frame in his mind any abstract or distinct ideas of trinity, substance, or personality; provided that this doctrine of a Creator, Redeemer, and Sanctifier makes proper impressions on his mind, producing therein love, hope, gratitude, and obedience, and thereby becomes a lively operative principle, influencing his life and actions, agreeably to that notion of saving faith which is required in a Christian.[6]

The rationality of mystery, suggests Berkeley, is discovered not by some algorithm capable of reducing all language to either simple ideas or quantifiable things, but by a transformed life, a living apophasis in which the reality of divine mystery is known only as it becomes embodied in the slow and patient work of learning to live by grace.

But for this understanding of mystery to be recoverable in Western thought, however, something of a turning point would have to be reached:

the point at which skeptical doubt about the capacity of reason has been deepened and stretched into a new appreciation for real mystery and a willingness to explore its meaning and significance—not by analysis into simple propositions but by the experiment of living. To arrive at such a new perspective would not be easy, for by the end of the seventeenth century, disputes about the nature and validity of the doctrine of the Trinity—the paradigmatic mystery—had rendered trinitarian thought so antagonistic and wearisome, in the general climate of opinion, that the very mention of the Trinity seemed in danger of becoming (as it clearly was for Alciphron) a "free thinker's" favorite bogeyman.[7]

Perhaps there was something instructive for Christian thought when Hume, in the *Dialogues Concerning Natural Religion*, contrived to make the dogmatist Demea an unwitting ally of the skeptical Philo against the erstwhile rationalist theologian Cleanthes. Though poor Demea realizes too late the true spirit of Philo's agreement with him, Philo's earlier employment of Demea's views is suggestive: "None but we mystics as you [Cleanthes] were pleased to call us, can account for this strange mixture of phenomena, by deriving it from attributes infinitely perfect but incomprehensible."[8] As the supposedly assured results of rationalist theology are inexorably dismantled by Hume, it becomes clear that the skeptic is tellingly aware of how indigestible any real sense of divine incomprehensibility must be in Cleanthes' rationalist system. For Hume, it may be safe to say, this intractability simply leaves belief in God all the more obviously in doubt. But for a more religious mind, it might recall a way of speaking about and understanding God that seemed to have been lost among the deists and freethinkers, a way of living in relationship with mystery that patiently exposes the mind to what it cannot grasp.

It may not be surprising that rationalist thought should have little room for the mystery of the Trinity, or that a more deeply skeptical turn of mind such as Philo's (and Hume's) should appropriate the incomprehensible itself as an acid solvent for complacent rationalist verities. But would I be warranted at all in thinking that there is some positive connection between a robustly trinitarian approach to God and apophaticism? I want to suggest that various examples of rationalist theology, whether of the Eunomians in the fourth century or of the deists in early modernity, ought to make us suspicious of a god whose philosophically pristine ineffability is so highly touted.

Gregory of Nazianzus certainly argued that it was precisely his Eunomian opponents who had defined deity into a conveniently manipulable conceptualization: for, he says to them, you "cannot even take the measure of yourself, and yet must busy yourself about what is above your nature, and gape at the illimitable."[9] By contrast, Gregory proposed that the lan-

guage for God (unbegotten and ingenerate) being used by the Eunomians
was not a simple idea that neatly *describes* the divine nature but rather a
sign for the trinitarian relationship of the Father in respect of the Son and
the Spirit. For Gregory, when we move forward on a trinitarian basis, such
language initiates us into a true apophasis, for it opens before us the truly
incomprehensible abyss of the trinitarian life, the understanding of which is
not discoverable as ideas we have about it but as the life we come to share
within it.

And there is certainly an analogy in the case of early modern deism.
Archbishop Tillotson's remote and chilly references to the doctrine of the
Trinity hardly portend a new embrace of radical apophaticism but rather an
extreme distaste for it. For Locke, the doctrine of the Trinity was either a
foolish piece of mystification or else a pretended logical model that simply
failed to make real sense.[10] Perhaps what's at work here is what John Coulson, drawing on Coleridge, has called the difference between an analytic use
of language and an older fiduciary use of language. The analytic language
brought into being through the efforts of thinkers like Bacon and Hobbes,
for the sake of the new philosophy, needed a complete one-to-one correspondence between word and idea or thing. But with religious language,
like poetry, "we are required to make a complex act of inference and assent,
and we begin by taking *on trust* expressions which are usually in analogical, metaphorical, or symbolic form, and by acting out the claims they
make."[11] This life of being formed by the incarnate, embodied imagery of
religion is in a very real sense apophatic, for it does not permit the language
to be fixed into a noetic possession but trusts the language to lead one, by
the very means of its incarnate imagery, into deeper and deeper communion
with reality. It is not the encapsulation of reality but its promising deferral—
for the sake of a truer encounter beyond the reifying conceptual grasp of the
knower.

So in what follows, I want to consider John Henry Newman as a particular case of this mutual implication of trinitarian and apophatic thought. I
believe that what allows Newman to risk a real exposure to apophasis is his
inclination to root the deepest form of apophasis not in a radical skepticism
tout court but more particularly in the Incarnate Son's yearning to know
and do the Father's will, even from within the deepest depths of human
alienation from God. Newman's apophatic tendency (if such it may be
called) is thus recontextualized in the trinitarian mission of the Son. It is not
a bare or contentless apophasis, but an apophasis that is itself the super-
expressivity of the infinite relations of the divine Persons, and the incarnation of that relationality in the broken and distorted language of a fallen
world. The recovery of negative theology and of a trinitarian habit of
thought seems integrally related in Newman. And, I wish to suggest, it is not

at all coincidental that the practice of truth-seeking Newman pursues shows strong parallels with various forms of discernment.

Insensibility to Mystery

It may be easiest to begin exploring these themes in Newman by noticing first of all what he wants to overcome: an obtuse and clumsy insensibility to the reality of mystery. This debility arises even when we think of everyday features of life. For we are often in danger of stepping away from the wholeness and mutifaceted nature of our own involvement with life's details. We forget the sensitive network of encounters, impressions, and feelings in which our own thoughts originally occurred. So, I believe, for Newman we easily tend in later reflection to climb up into an abstract and artificial judgment about things, a partial view that marches brusquely forward as though everything had been decided but whose concrete grounds in the congress of actual things and real life have been rendered imperceptible and mute. The gravity of this problem is twofold: first, we fall into the habit of thinking that this abstract and explicit form of reason is the true measure of reality; and then second, when, as it often does, it is unable adequately to warrant on its own terms what we really hold as true or even to notice the rich actuality of life in which we have met truth in the first place, we are tempted to a despairing or else cynical skepticism and a flight from the very reality in which the mind would find its true enjoyment.

So in the last of the *University Sermons,* Newman pleads with his listeners, first, not to mistake their rational constructions of reality for the thing itself, but then also not to despair when they realize that their tools of thought have been only that, no more. Our abstract reasonings in general, or even doctrinal formulations in particular, might be compared to mathematics:

> Various methods or *calculi* have been adopted to embody those immutable principles and dispositions of which the [mathematical] science treats, which are really independent of any, yet cannot be contemplated or pursued without one or other of them. The first of these instruments of investigation employs the medium of extension; the second, that of number; the third, that of motion. . . . They are, one and all, analyses, more or less perfect, of those necessary truths, for which we have not a name, of which we have no idea, except in the terms of such economical representations. . . . They stand for real things, and we can reason with them, though they be but symbols, as if they were the things themselves, for which they stand. . . . While they answer, we can use them just as if they were the realities which they represent, and without thinking of those realities; but at length our

instrument of discovery issues in some great impossibility or contradiction, or what we call in religion, a mystery.[12]

Newman's argument is, as it were, a positively apophatic one. There is a
utility to reasoning in general and to doctrinal reasoning in particular, but
such forms of rationality are best employed not as ends but as means, as
"instruments of discovery" for exploring into an unimaginable depth of
reality which the reason alone can barely even perceive, let alone grasp.

It is for this reason that he is so impatient with the kind of self-satisfied,
short-circuited way of thinking about religion that fails to recognize this
"economic" or regulative or analogical character of our language. Such
interpretive flatness renders its exponents immune to a transforming
encounter with divine reality; or else its mortally attenuated version of
divinity inevitably disappoints and is rejected, often leaving potential believers mistakenly sure they have tried religion and found it wanting. Newman
imagines the religiously insensible blundering around heaven itself: "They
would walk close to the throne of God; they would stupidly gaze at it; they
would touch it; they would meddle with the holiest things; they would go
on intruding and prying, not meaning anything wrong by it, but with a sort
of brute curiosity."[13] In this passage, Newman picks out the correlate of a
merely analytic approach to religious thought, namely a reductionist
approach to reality in general. If, in other words, language has ceased to
conduct its speakers toward a deeper dimension of life and has now become
merely opaque and univocal, then it will be increasingly difficult for people
to conceive of reality itself as extending beyond the necessity of nature and
on into mystery.

The "intruding and prying" that Newman describes as a well-intentioned
but "brute curiosity" sounds very like the new approach to reality that
Newman knew stemmed from the rise of modern science, and specifically
from the anti-teleological thought fostered by Bacon. Newman is far from
opposing science per se, but he is more than uncomfortable with the
assumption that scientific patterns of rationality ought to be the world's sole
approach to truth—even the basis for a religious apprehension of reality.
Newman quotes Bacon as approving Democritus against Aristotle because
the former "never meddled with final causes."

> Lord Bacon gives us both the fact and the reason for it. Physical
> philosophers are ever inquiring *whence* things are, not *why;* referring
> them to nature, not to mind; and thus they tend to make a system a
> substitute for God. . . . The study of Nature, when religious feeling is
> away, leads the mind, rightly or wrongly, to acquiesce in the atheistic
> theory, as the simplest and easiest. It is but parallel to that tendency in
> anatomical studies, which no one will deny, to solve all the phenom-

ena of the human frame into material elements and powers, and to dispense with the soul. To those who are conscious of matter, but not conscious of mind, it seems more rational to refer all things to one origin, such as they know, than to assume the existence of a second origin such as they know not. . . . If we come to [nature] with the assumption that it is a creation, we shall study it with awe; if assuming it to be a system, with mere curiosity.[14]

Newman was to make a very similar point years later in *The Idea of a University;* namely, that while science is a crucial part of the circle of knowledge, neither it nor its methods can operate in persistent isolation from religion. In such cases the native human desire to understand and to know is deprived of that larger vision which alone prevents it from degenerating into an omnivorously reductionistic curiosity.[15]

In the latter case, warns Newman, such thinkers "conceive that they profess just *the* truth which makes all things easy. They have their one idea or their favourite notion, which occurs to them on every occasion. They have their one or two topics, which they are continually obtruding, with a sort of pedantry."[16] Most noteworthy here is Newman's diagnosis that such minds, who have "clear and decisive explanations always ready of the sacred mysteries of Faith," edge over time toward inflexibility and, above all, isolation: "Narrow minds have no power of throwing themselves into the minds of others."[17] It is this deformation of the person, this incapacity for sympathy and relationship that strikes Newman as the most serious issue. In his view, personal formation is the foundation for truthful religious knowledge. That is because religious knowledge itself seems most capable of advancing truthfully in persons whose personal training and habits of mind enable them to be profoundly and honestly present to God, listening and sensitive to the reality of the other. In the absence of such a personhood, religious knowers become "proud, bashful, fastidious, and reserved," their particular moral character rendering them stiff and remote from the living encounter with the personal truth who is God: "it is because they do not look out of themselves, because they do not look through and beyond their own minds to their Maker, but are engrossed in notions of what is due to themselves, to their own dignity and their own consistency."[18]

Personal Formation for Religious Knowing

Newman's comment above about the difficulty of not being able to look *through* one's own mind to the Maker suggests how entangled, in his view, are the two dimensions of our question. For it isn't at all simply a matter of how the subject knows an object, but much more concretely, how the divine reality (the object) itself shapes and forms the mind of the subject who draws near seeking understanding. Newman's analysis, in other words, of the problem of modern insensibility to mystery leads him to the conclusion that there must be some practice of apprehending religious reality which modern rationalism has overlooked. And this has meant that rationalism, oblivious to the role that this practice and formation of the mind plays in giving a truthful vision to faith, has tended therefore to see religious belief as merely a weak or uncritical form of reason. What this practice of personal formation is we must now explore, and its underlying ground in trinitarian apophasis is what I will discuss in the final section.

We can see Newman chewing over this problem about the mental habits appropriate to religious knowing in some of his comments on John Locke in the *Grammar of Assent*. It is characteristic that Newman prefaces his argument with the personal reflection that he has "so high a respect both for the character and the ability of Locke" that he feels "no pleasure in considering him in the light of an opponent"of his own long-cherished ideas.[19] But nonetheless, Newman is quite sure that something has gone badly astray somewhere between Locke's admission, on the one hand, that sometimes "probabilities" rise to the level of complete assurance, and on the other hand, Locke's warning against ever "entertaining any proposition with greater assurance than the proofs it is built on will warrant."[20] With apparent reluctance, Newman concludes that Locke's logical inconsistency here is the symptom of an unreal and narrowly theoretical view of the human mind. "Instead of going by the testimony of psychological facts, and thereby determining our constitutive faculties and our proper condition, and being content with the mind as God has made it, [Locke] would form men as he thinks they ought to be formed, into something better and higher."[21] It is interesting not only that Newman feels he is being truer to the empirical reality of human beings than is Locke, but also that his reading of human capacities is more able than Locke's to find consistent room for the *limitations* of the mind—limitations which in Newman's view have a very important and positive role. For while he criticizes Locke's misguided design to "form" the human mind into "something better and higher" than God has made it, Newman designedly uses this same term, thus hinting very definitely that what is at stake here is a quite different approach to mental *formation*.

But what kind of formation of mind could find a useful role for the *absence* of knowledge? For Newman this is really a question about epistemological culture, about the habits and practices by which we almost instinctively try to understand something. Consider, first, a negative example in which an inadequate formation of "religious understanding" short-circuits what is, in Newman's view, an essential feature of healthy religious knowing. When, for instance, Newman considers what it would mean for a university *not* to teach theology as a distinct discipline, he wonders whether the partisans of such an approach really do mean the same thing as he does when they talk about "God." If God is powerful or skillful, "just so far forth as the telescope shows power, and the microscope shows skill," then we are really only talking about "Nature with a divine glow upon it."[22] In such a case, says Newman, he can quite understand why it would be a waste of time to include theology among the university disciplines, because we would be talking about a discipline of knowledge whose capacity for astonished wonder had been rationally circumscribed to become a mere affectation, at best a pious emotional response to what is entirely graspable, manipulable, and determined by all the other branches of knowledge. It would be "just as we talk of the *philosophy* or the *romance* of history, or the *poetry* of childhood, or the picturesque, or the sentimental, or the humorous, or any other abstract quality, which the genius or the caprice of the individual, or the fashion of the day, or the consent of the world, recognizes in any set of objects which are subjected to its contemplation."[23] In such a culture of knowledge there is no real room for the radically new or the other or the incomprehensible; everything is massively clear, explicable, quantifiably appreciable. Most significantly, the personal formation inherent to such a culture would be that of the religious genius, the exquisitely cultivated appreciator of the sublime. This kind of formation does *not* really have a use for the ability to encounter the unknowable.

By contrast, Newman is envisioning a different kind of formation. Whereas a rationalist religion may be based on "evidences," such evidences are flat, all their meaning is on the surface; they have nothing luminously unknowable about them and elicit no personal commitment in the process of knowing. Newman has in mind a process of formation in which real knowledge is gained only by a willingness to go on pursuing what cannot be grasped, by a humble attention to what cannot be reduced to simple facts or distinct ideas, and by "that instinctive apprehension of the Omnipresence of God and His unwearied and minute Providence which holiness and love create within" the one who desires to understand.[24] It is this intuitive sense of divine presence that informs the religious sensibility and makes it an instrument of knowledge. But there must be, in Newman's view, some structure or process whereby the forming of this moral and religious sensibility takes place, a patterning that knits knowledge together into wisdom and shows the relationship of many impressions to one coherent whole. Apart from that concern for the whole, the religious mind as easily degenerates into superstition, prejudice, and bigotry as into rationalism or indifference.[25] An "instinctive apprehension of the Omnipresence of God" must be sustained by a formation in holiness that liberates the mind, leaving it sensitive to the overwhelming reality of the divine mystery and thus freeing it from the temptation to reduce this sense of God to partial, one-sided bigotry on the one hand or pale, rationalist abstractions on the other.

There is reason to think that Newman was not entirely out of step with his age in his concern that the formative power of mystery not be reified. Edward Sillem, in his analysis of the sources of Newman's philosophical views, quotes from the *Discourses on Painting and the Fine Arts* delivered by Sir Joshua Reynolds before the Royal Academy in 1786. What is especially intriguing from our point of view is that Reynold's language foreshadows Newman's in two ways: it speaks of the formation of a habitual reason or faculty of judgment that works with the whole of a person's experience of life, and it connects that formation process particularly to the apprehension of visible forms and expressions, and to the impressions they make upon the mind. Half a century later, we see Newman working toward a parallel insight, namely, that the wholeness of real wisdom often leads us to a perception we cannot adequately explain on simple rational grounds, precisely because our vision has been shaped by countless impressions made upon us throughout the course of life, and particularly by those impression-making sacramental forms of the Christian life that draw us into a participatory process of knowing.

So, for example, Reynolds writes:

> . . . there is in the commerce of life, as in art, a sagacity which is far from being contradictory to right reason, and is superior to any occasional exercise of that faculty; which supersedes it; and does not wait for the slow progress of deduction, but goes at once, by what appears a kind of intuition, to the conclusion. A man endowed with this faculty, feels and acknowledges the truth, though it is not always in his power, perhaps, to give a reason for it; because he cannot recollect and bring before him all the materials that gave birth to his opinion. . . . This impression is the result of the accumulated experience of our whole life, and has been collected we do not always know how or when. But this mass of collective observation, however acquired, ought to prevail over that reason, which however powerfully exerted on any particular occasion, will probably comprehend but a partial view of the subject. . . . If we were obliged to enter into a theoretical deliberation on every occasion, before we act, life would be at a stand, and art would be impracticable.[26]

In Reynold's view, the formation process for this faculty of perception is cumulative and existential; it shapes the personal character in ways that give one the capacity for intuitive insights beyond the more pristinely deductive process of analytical reason. And this means that such a faculty of habitual or intuitive perception will have to accept in humility its inadequate "knowledge," its inability to justify its insights on purely rational and discursive grounds. Indeed, Reynolds warns his listeners that if they attempt to pin down "by a cold consideration" the impressions that great things produce upon the mind, they will lose the very possibility of that greatness being infused into their own art; the artist will be tempted to "reconsider and correct" the very ideas that had inspired him, "till the whole matter is reduced to a commonplace invention."[27]

What is so striking in Newman is the degree to which this kind of approach is transposed into moral and spiritual and theological terms. For the impression which converse with God has upon us is unveiled, of course, not in a painting or statue but a life of holiness and loving attentiveness to the ever-greater concreteness of God's life. And yet the aesthetic and spiritual patterns of formation are parallel. Just as overmuch "cold consideration" tempts the artist to reduce concrete originality to a merely "commonplace invention," so too a believer may be tempted to reduce the spiritual life to pious good manners or a merely notional acceptance of religious propositions.

So in a sermon on the "Moral Effects of Communion with God," Newman suggests that the words and acts of the church's life of prayer initiate believers into a converse with the Kingdom of God, and that in countless untold ways this shapes the believer's spiritual sensibilities, awakens and heightens many moral qualities that might otherwise have lain dormant or grown distorted. One who prays habitually "is no longer what he was before; gradually, imperceptibly to himself, he has imbibed a new set of ideas, and become imbued with fresh principles. . . . As speech is the organ of human society, and the means of human civilization, so is prayer the instrument of divine fellowship and divine training."[28] Again like Reynolds, Newman suggests that if one attempts to reduce every insight or inspiration that emerges from this formation to a purely rational basis, then the living reality of the insight will be lost. In such a case, "the next world is not a reality to him; it only exists in his mind in the form of certain conclusions from certain reasonings. It is but an inference; and never can be more, never can be present to his mind, until he acts, instead of arguing."[29]

Here we begin to see the crucial paradox at work: namely, that the only possible presence of the divine reality to the human mind is that of an absence, an eluding of the grasp of purely rational inference and argument. And this presence, in Newman's view, becomes available only to the one who begins to *act*, to live concretely in converse with the divine life. So there is a crucial dialectical relationship between the cataphatic and the apophatic, between the concrete form by which the person comes to know

God and the surpassing of all conceptual knowledge as the same person acts more and more within the very patterns and converse of God's life.

From his studies of the Fathers, especially of Alexandria and Cappadocia, Newman had certainly been exposed to this dialectical paradox of cataphatic and apophatic, word and silence, and to the way in which it comes to be embodied in the dynamic of a lived spiritual journey.[30] Hans Urs von Balthasar comments on this same existential dialectic in Gregory of Nyssa, remarking that for the great Cappadocian the representations of God in the cosmos become empty or dead if they are reified into simple rational concepts; the signs of God are only truly cataphatic, truly expressive of God, if they transport the beholder beyond themselves to the very abyss of apophasis: the vertiginous awareness of the infinite richness of divine life. If that is possible, that is, if the soul learns not to foreclose the signifying power of the sacramental sign but rather is drawn into a never-ending journey by means of it, then the cataphatic and the apophatic are most truly themselves, truly in a dialectical relationship that gathers momentum within the believer's life. Balthasar usefully highlights a distinction in Gregory's thought between the cataphatic *content* of a divine sign and the apophatic *movement* that is aroused by the sign. The "vision" or growth in understanding is, importantly, not identified with an intellectual grasp of the sign per se but with the transforming action and movement in pursuit of its ever-receding divine surplus of meaning.[31]

We often see Newman making a similar distinction, most famously perhaps in his *Apologia* account of how "carried away" he was by the "broad philosophy" of Alexandria:

> Room was made for the anticipation of further and deeper disclosures, of truths still under the veil of the letter, and in their season to be revealed. The visible world still remains without its divine interpretation; Holy Church in her sacraments and her hierarchical appointments, will remain, even to the end of the world, after all but a symbol of those heavenly facts which fill eternity. Her mysteries are but the expressions in human language of truths to which the human mind is unequal.[32]

But while the mysteries of holy church may only be expressions "of truths to which the human mind is unequal," they are clearly nonetheless, in Newman's view, the divinely appointed means for forming the mind and drawing it into that converse with eternity which alone can illuminate the mind with truth. The church's sacramental life becomes, in Newman's reading, the matrix for this dynamic dialectic of cataphatic and apophatic, for the soul's awakening and arousal to a pursuit of truth in the highest sense.

We can see at least preliminarily, I think, three fundamental aspects to this sacramental dialectic of formation: (1) Christ is mysteriously present to believers through the concrete forms and practices of the church's life; (2) the minds and hearts of believers are transformed by their participation in these habits of worship, service, and teaching, and this transformation is consummated by the power of the Holy Spirit knitting believers more and more completely into the grace and ministry of Christ; (3) the truth of God and the reality of believers' own vocation are mutually disclosed in this process, but in a way which sustains in believers an availability of spirit and a longing movement toward the infinity of divine truth. I am suggesting, in other words, that the personal formation of mind envisioned by Newman has a fundamentally trinitarian matrix. The deepest kind of knowing and understanding of reality consists, for Newman, in being drawn by the Holy Spirit into the mission of the Incarnate Word and in coming to share in his relationship with the Father.

In respect of the first point, this is no more than Newman's own particular formulation of Christianity's basic sacramental theology, namely, that the church's life is a way of living into the mystery of Christ's presence. "The Ministry and Sacraments, the bodily presence of Bishop and people, are given us as keys and spells, by which we bring ourselves into the presence of the great company of Saints," says Newman, suggesting how by participation in the church's life one enters into the life of Christ's Body.[33] Newman argues throughout his sermons that the life of the church is a process of fitting believers for heaven. And this is especially true of the sacraments: "In these is manifested in greater or less degree, according to the measure of each, that Incarnate Saviour, who is one day to be our Judge, and who is enabling us to bear His presence then, by imparting it to us in measure now."[34] The transforming presence of Christ is sensed by believers in a way that roots them in the saving action of Christ on their behalf: "We recollect a hand laid upon our heads, and surely it had the print of nails in it, and resembled His who with a touch gave sight to the blind and raised the dead. Or we have been eating and drinking; and it was not a dream surely, that One fed us from His wounded side, and renewed our nature by the heavenly meat He gave."[35] Newman's language in this and similar passages seems evocative of a believer's confusion in the presence of a consolation quite beyond the ability of the mind to calculate or control.

And that is suggestive of the second feature of this formation process, namely, the Spirit's role in forming and renewing the life of believers. The sacramental economy of the Christian life is the concrete and objective

> *"Man's progress is a living growth, not a mechanism."*

framework within which believers encounter and are formed by the presence of Christ. The Holy Spirit works within this process to draw believers
through the sacramental forms and into a living participation in that reality
which the signs betoken. The church's "sacraments are the instruments
which the Holy Ghost uses" to realize and effect in believers the new life
opened before them by Christ.[36] It is a life that progresses by way of the cataphatic, the shaping impression of the forms and images of the sacramental
economy. These external signs of Christ's ministry form believers into a new
body, a new pattern of life, which is animated by the Holy Spirit, who fills
each and every member with the mind of Christ. And it it this latter
indwelling by the Spirit that draws believers on toward the apophatic journey into ever-deeper trinitarian relationality.

Observing this process of formation is quite central to the epistemological concerns of this essay. For my argument has been all along that far from
seeking to evade the skeptical (even Humean) critique of rationalist
thought, Newman has found a way of deepening it. He has extended it
down into an even more profound critique of rationalism by opening up
that skeptical dissatisfaction into the endlessly yearning apophasis of trinitarian life. I'm arguing indeed that the formation of mind, for Newman,
takes place precisely as one is rooted more and more deeply by the Spirit
into the life of Christ.

We can begin to see the apophatic consequences of this move in regard
to the third element of Newman's framework, namely, a way of knowing
that is structured by the ever-more of Christ's own mission as the Word of
the Father. Needless to say, such an organic and developmental vision of
knowing truth would be highly consistent with Newman's usual lines of
thought. His regular concern is for the "realizing" of the mind, for the
patient training up into actuality of what was by nature merely provisional
in our capacity to know and understand truth. And in Newman's view this
process requires humility in the face of what we cannot know, and a wisdom that frees us from the urge to commodify truth into the coinage of our
own rational certainties. This is true even at the most elemental level in our
natural pursuit of knowledge, as Newman points out in the *Grammar of
Assent*:

> Instead of devising, what cannot be, some sufficient science of rea-
> soning which may compel certitude in concrete conclusions, [we are
> left] to confess that there is no ultimate test of truth besides the testi-
> mony borne to truth by the mind itself, and that this phenomenon,
> perplexing as we may find it, is a normal and inevitable characteristic
> of the mental constitution of a being like man on a stage such as the
> world. His progress is a living growth, not a mechanism.[37]

In Newman's view this humble reliance on "the testimony borne to truth by the mind itself" is not a liability; it is a sign of the crucial importance of the mind's proper and healthy formation and of its necessary and indeed salvific reliance upon communion with God. A little later in the same passage we can, in fact, see Newman very characteristically pushing on with this observation about the normal and natural limits of human knowing and the significance of the mind's formation—pushing on with it into a recognition of the divine matrix of human knowing. As an undeniable marker of our need for communion with God, says Newman, we see how difficult it is to understand the highest and most religious truths. This is in order

> that the very discipline inflicted on our minds in finding Him, may mould them into due devotion to Him when He is found. "Verily Thou art a hidden God, the God of Israel, the Saviour," is the very law of His dealings with us. Certainly we need a clue into the labyrinth which is to lead us to Him; and who among us can hope to seize upon the true starting-points of thought for that enterprise, and upon all of them, who is to understand their right direction, to follow them out to their just limits, and duly to estimate, adjust, and combine the various reasonings in which they issue, so as safely to arrive at what it is worth any labour to secure, without a special illumination from Himself?[38]

The particular language Newman adopts here (direction, follow, estimate) is noteworthy: it is the language of practical pathfinding and speaks of a kind of habitual knowledge or skill only available to someone long practiced and experienced in the task. And as we have seen, Newman has a very definite sense of how this practical skill, which is nonetheless a "special illumination," is received and activated by the mind, for it is none other than—at least in its most complete form—the event of the Spirit realizing in us the mind of Christ, a mind well habituated to the vast hiddenness of God.

It is very much as if the skill and pathfinding knowledge of Christ, the pioneer of faith, were to become available to the believer. By the Holy Spirit, believers have access to Christ's approach to reality: "you must use His influences, His operations, not as your own (God forbid!), not as you would use your own mind or your own limbs, irreverently, but as His presence in you. All your knowledge is from Him; all good thoughts are from Him; all power to pray is from Him."[39] Newman's warning not to mistake the Incarnate Word's mystical presence and understanding for the believer's own merely confirms how completely, in his view, must be the identification of the believer's mind with Christ's.

But Newman is not implying here that there is a kind of vague or amorphous religious tinge given to human understanding. Rather, the power and wisdom that come to shape the believer's mind are shaped very concretely by the historical pattern, the earthly formation process, so to speak, of Jesus' own mission. "What was actually done by Christ in the flesh" during his earthly ministry is "really wrought in us."[40]

> Or to express the same great truth in other words; Christ Himself vouchsafes to repeat in each of us in figure and mystery all that He did and suffered in the flesh. He is formed in us, born in us, suffers in us, rises again in us, lives in us; and this not by a succession of events, but all at once: for He comes to us as a Spirit, all dying, all rising again, all living. . . . His whole economy in all its parts is ever in us all at once.[41]

Newman delineates this mystical indwelling of Christ in the believer quite carefully in terms of the most crucial, identifying patterns of Christ's mission, in terms of the events that mark and shape him as the one he is. Christ's vision of reality is not just in general terms "divine"; it is a vision of reality in terms of the paschal mystery, of the Word's infinite relationship to the Father in the Spirit, a relationship wrought out in the terms of a broken human world.

Participation in Trinitarian Apophasis

So far I've been arguing that the sacramental economy of personal formation is itself, in Newman's view, the extension of the Incarnation, and that the moral and spiritual formation of the mind is rooted through Christ in an ever deepening participation in the trinitarian life. But what kind of knowing, what kind of formation of mind, would this lead to? Let me try to answer this question in two ways. First, by drawing some final conclusions regarding Newman's notion of knowing—in particular his view that the kind of knowing we come to through personal formation is a moral and spiritual wisdom, a practical discernment or *phronēsis* (to use the term he adopts from Aristotle) and not a general metaphysical clairvoyance. It is, in other words, the kind of knowing that judges rightly about the fitness and truthfulness of actions and ideas (what our earlier Christian writers call "discretion"). And second, I want to flesh out a bit further the sense in which this discerning quality of mind is itself sustained by an apophatic journey into the ever greater mystery of God's trinitarian self-giving.

I have already argued above that the mind's capacity to know is, for Newman, shaped most definitively within the trinitarian framework of the church's life. Moreover, this is hardly the place to rehearse the extensive literature on Newman's teaching about *phronēsis* and the illative sense (the term he deploys in the *Grammar* to refer to our capacity to judge truly).[42]

What I want is merely to give a sense of how a mind formed within this trinitarian pattern of life might in fact discern what is true and know what is right. I'm arguing, in other words, that the various notions of discernment and the illative sense that we find throughout Newman's work are best understood in terms of their trinitarian matrix in his thought.

Nothing could be clearer in Newman than the link between one's moral and spiritual growth and the capacity to know truly. And, as we have seen, this link is grounded in the believer's growth into the mind of Christ. This shapes the process of knowing and discernment in important ways. In the last of the *University Sermons*, Newman had argued that while "the Christian mind" certainly "reasons out a series of dogmatic statements," it cannot do this simply by treating the doctrines merely as "logical propositions"; rather, such a mind must reason "as being itself enlightened and (as if) inhabited by that sacred impression which is prior to them, which acts as a regulating principle, ever present, upon the reasoning, and without which no one has a warrant to reason at all."[43] Newman is saying here that the living reality in question so impresses itself upon the mind and patterns its thoughts as to provide a kind of intuitive vision and discernment that alone can properly regulate the deliberations of reason.

By the time of the *Grammar of Assent*, Newman had been able to work out a kind of taxonomy for this power of discernment. Starting from a provisional sense of the divine, humanity in the image of God is led either to the realization of this image in a fully sensitive and perceptive conscience or else to the degeneration of this conscience to the level of a stifled whisper. Whether this sensitivity to God's will "grows brighter and stronger, or, on the other hand, is dimmed, distorted, or obliterated, depends on each of us individually."[44] Intriguingly, Newman supposes that the more frequently people ignore or act against this apprehension of God, the more it "may become almost undistinguishable from an inferential acceptance of the great truth, or may dwindle into a mere notion of their intellect."[45] This is an inverse variation on Hobbes's view of the imagination as but a "decaying" sense of reason; for Newman is here suggesting that in certain cases the operation of deductive reason itself may be but a decaying remainder of the deeper and truer intuition of the religious imagination!

As Newman goes on to chart the course of "a mind thus carefully formed upon the basis of its natural conscience," he observes a steadily increasing sensitivity to the divine presence and activity in all things. Newman says that a mind so formed is able to arrive at a "theology of the religious imagination" that "has a living hold on truths which are really to be found in the world, though they are not upon the surface. . . . It interprets what it sees around it by this previous inward teaching, as the true key of that maze of vast complicated disorder; and thus it gains a more and more consistent and luminous vision of God from the most unpromising materials."[46] This rather beautiful passage highlights the vital connection between the capacity to interpret reality truly and the capacity to intuit the presence of God in all things; indeed for Newman these two capacities in fact converge to a single apex.

> When men begin all their works with the thought of God, acting for His sake, and to fulfil His will, when they ask His blessing on themselves and their life, pray to Him for the objects they desire, and see Him in the event, whether it be according to their prayers or not, they will find everything that happens tend to confirm them in the truths about Him which live in their imagination, varied and unearthly as those truths may be. Then they are brought into His presence as that of a Living Person, and are able to hold converse with Him, and that with a directness and simplicity . . . so that it is doubtful whether we realize the company of our fellow-men with greater keenness that these favoured minds are able to contemplate and adore the Unseen, Incomprehensible Creator.[47]

Here we can see more clearly than ever how for Newman right discernment is the organic growth within a human person of the mind of Christ; for discernment seems to be modeled upon and grounded in Christ's own desire to act for the Father in all things, to interpret the will of the Father in all things, and to remain through all things in "converse with Him."

That this is the case can be seen from Newman's *University Sermon* of 1832 entitled "Personal Influence, The Means of Propagating the Truth." Here he had already imagined what the personal formation of a "Teacher of the Truth" would be like, and as he goes along sketching out the training of such a person, it becomes clear that he has been describing Jesus' own life. Intriguingly, Newman allows for a developmental process of formation: each period of personal growth brings with it new tests, new occasions to discern truth by listening for God's will in situations of increasing complexity. "In him the knowledge and power of acting rightly have kept pace with the enlargement of his duties, and his inward convictions of Truth with successive temptations opening upon him from without to wander from it."[48] The capacity to apprehend the truth, Newman suggests, is only truly realizable within a steady desire to hear and serve the Source of all truth. It is this desire that the Teacher must plant in the heart. "It is not a mere set of opinions that he has to promulgate, which may lodge on the surface of the mind; but he is to be an instrument in changing (as Scripture speaks) the heart, and modelling all men after one exemplar; making them like himself, or rather like One above himself, who is the beginning of a new creation."[49] And to make others like himself is for Christ also to plunge them into the same human incomprehension that he faced, but more importantly, it is to conduct them toward that ineffable converse with the Father which is the very life of the Incarnate Son.

This is the final piece of our picture, the piece which must to an extent always remain ungraspable. For if a proper human understanding of the truth of all things is grounded ultimately in Christ's personal sensitivity to God's will in all things, it is also an understanding of truth that always remains open to the incomprehensible mystery of divine self-sharing. Over and over Newman contrasts the inexplicable condescension and incomprehensibly loving humility of God in Christ and in the saints with the banal, utilitarian perspective of human nature turned away from God. Public opinion has enough vestigial religion wafting about in it to prevent most people from expressing "their repugnance to the doctrine" of voluntary self-giving, says Newman, "but you see what they really think of Christ, by the tone which they adopt toward those who in their measure follow Him."[50] Newman then acidly ventriloquizes the world's observations: "Here is a lady of birth; she might be useful at home, she might marry well, she might be an ornament to society, she might give her countenance to religious objects, and she has perversely left us all; she has cut off her hair, and put on a coarse garment, and is washing the feet of the poor."[51]

> As believers come to share in the mystery of the Incarnate Son, they find themselves beginning to understand his humility and self-giving love from within.

Exactly the same kind of incomprehending obtuseness, says Newman, obtrudes itself in the very manner in which the world attempts to reason about Christian doctrine. As perhaps the most famous example, he points to the way in which the worldly mind attempts and fails to make sense of the Incarnation, precisely because it stands outside the living reality of the Son's relationship with the Father and so perceives only an argument, apparently quite illogical, about how the Creator could also be a creature. By contrast, says Newman, "how different is the state of those who have been duly initiated into the mysteries of the kingdom of heaven!"[52] Those who have begun to share precisely in the mystery of the Incarnate Son's life, in his relationship with the Father, have the key to enter into the meaning of the doctrine:

> We are able indeed to continue the idea of a Son into that of a servant, though the descent were infinite, and, to our reason, incomprehensible; but when we merely speak first of God, then of man, we seem to change the Nature without preserving the Person. In truth, His Divine

Sonship is that portion of the sacred doctrine on which the mind is providentially intended to rest throughout, and so to preserve for itself His identity unbroken.[53]

It would seem to the merely rational inquirer that the clearest and simplest approach would yield the most adequate answers; God is supposed also to be human; but these are mutually exclusive terms, ergo the doctrine is irrational. The paradox is that the more one participates in mystery, the more permeable one's thought is to the incomprehensibility of the trinitarian life, the more one is able to grasp or at least be grasped by the truth. Newman's point is that as believers come to share in the mystery of the Incarnate Son, they find themselves beginning to understand his humility and self-giving love from within, to recognize that it embodies and echoes in fragile human terms the infinite and incomprehensible self-giving of the eternal Son.

Newman's diagnosis of human knowing leads him to suspect an underlying cause for both rationalism on one side and bigotry and superstition on the other. Small-mindedness in all its forms stems from a refusal to remain available to mystery—above all to the ground of mystery, the incomprehensible love which is God's infinite existence. The sheer prodigality of God's giving is overwhelming to the mind. Christ, says Newman, made his whole life "a free offering to His Father, not as forcing His acceptance of it. From beginning to the end it was in the highest sense a voluntary work; and this is what is so overpowering to the mind."[54] The problem, Newman believes, is that this divine extravagance is fundamental to reality, and if we persist in trying to evade it we distort our perspective about everything. The absolute self-giving of Christ

suggests to us, as by a specimen, the infinitude of God. We all confess that He is infinite . . . but, we ask, what is infinity? . . . the outward exhibition of infinitude is mystery; and the mysteries of nature and of grace are nothing else than the mode in which His infinitude encounters us and is brought home to our minds. Men confess that He is infinite, yet they start and object, as soon as His infinitude comes in contact with their imagination and acts upon their reason. They cannot bear the fulness, the superabundance, the inexhaustible flowing forth, and "vehement rushing," and encompassing flood of the divine attributes. They restrain and limit them to their own comprehension, they measure them by their own standard, they fashion them by their own model.[55]

It is just this intolerance for mystery with which we began, and here we see Newman explaining why it is so injurious to the human mind. The very reality of the universe encounters us ceaselessly with this "outward exhibition of infinitude"; and if human rationality has no room for the apophasis set loose by such an "inexhaustible flowing forth," then humankind will inevitably, and defectively, fall to measuring reality by a false scale. Participation within the mystery of the Incarnate Son's infinite self-giving is, in Newman's view, the crucial formation of healthy human minds, lending them the moral wisdom and, above all, the tolerance for mystery that constitute right judgment.

In the history of apophatic thought, John Henry Newman may not immediately spring to mind as a leading exponent beside such figures as Dionysius the Pseudo-Areopagite or Meister Eckhart. And yet I have tried to show how Newman's concern for the right course of human understanding led him to a new engagement with the mystery of the Trinity—not simply as a doctrine to be itemized but as a way of thinking about the real, as a matrix for the formation of human mindfulness. And it was from that perspective, I believe, that Newman was able to rediscover the indispensable function of an apophatic trajectory. He saw the importance of grounding all human knowing within the eternal trinitarian converse of God's own infinite knowing and loving of God. This rediscovered apophasis functions regulatively for Newman in every act of mind, shaping its habits of interpretation, preserving it from shrinking the real to quantifiable dimensions, and sustaining that suppleness of thought that springs from wonder at the superabundance of God's life.

PART THREE

Discerning Truth

EIGHT

Aesthetic Vision and Intelligible Beauty

What Is There to See?

This chapter and its companion, chapter 9, represent the culminating (and constructive) reach of this book. It is time, therefore, for me to draw together what I hope I have been able to show regarding the noetic potential of spiritual discernment, and thereby advance an argument about the spirituality and theology of truth, and human knowledge of truth. This chapter will focus on the reality given for the mind to see; the next chapter will focus on the mind in the process of seeing, knowing, and being known.

Perhaps the most basic question that all the varieties of spiritual discernment have sought to answer is this, "What is there to see?" And their universal answer has always been, "Far more than you think!" From Origen's effort to show his catechumens the cosmic implications of their decisions to Ignatius of Loyola's attempt to awaken retreatants to the deep desires that animate their lives, the teachers of discernment have sought to hold the human spirit open to a larger dimension of reality than it commonly bothers to notice. We have seen Paul and the developing desert spirituality hold out the power of the paschal mystery to "free those who all their lives were held in slavery by the fear of death" (Hebrews 2:15), and so liberate them from an anxious spiritual and mental poverty. In that case, what there was to see was the resurrection of Christ. We have considered John Bunyan's struggle to rediscover the truth of human life *beyond* an early modern commodifying, nominalizing, and miniaturizing of aspirations. In Newman we saw a new effort to train the human mind in hospitality to mystery, to wait upon a knowledge that is not quite its own to possess, yet all the greater for that.

If truth is the very food upon which the mind feeds to live, then the mind will grow stunted if it looks out at nothing but the world as it sometimes appears. The problem is that, on the one hand, frequent failures of perception (both moral and intellectual) lead to a gradual shriveling of what the mind is willing to count as reality worth its trouble; and, on the other hand, the mind is so eager to possess what reality it can perceive that it ceaselessly risks another version of reduction, in this case to more manageable (but inevitably less truthful, less beautiful) proportions. In both cases, we have types of degeneration into a fantasizing poverty of perception, either a fantasy of dismal expectations or a fantasy of paltry private possessions.

Take the first case, in which a sinful gap between human *possibility* and human *performance* begins to shrink the human vision of reality. As Bernard Lonergan once remarked:

> While it may happen that after each failure to carry out ideal aspirations man repents and reasserts the primacy of the ideal over the real, of what ought to be over what is, it may also happen that after repeated failure man begins to rationalize, to deform knowledge into harmony with disorderly loves. . . . Moreover, this deformation takes place not only in the individual but also and much more convincingly in the social conscience. For to the common mind of the community the facts of life are the poor performance of men in open contradiction with the idealism of human aspiration; and this leaves the will a choice in which truth seems burdened with the unreal and unpractical air of falsity.[1]

Lonergan suggests here that humankind badly needs a vision capable of overturning the degenerative and falsifying tendencies of human truth-finding.

And what about the other shrinking of reality, to fit the constraints of manipulable possession? St. Augustine is always an acute observer of this tendency to partiality and bias, to a reality no larger than one's own control:

> What happens is that the soul, loving its own power, slides away from the whole which is common to all into the part which is its own private property. By following God's directions and being perfectly governed by his laws it could enjoy the whole universe of creation; but by the apostasy of pride which is called the beginning of sin it strives to grab something more than the whole and to govern it by its own laws; and because there is nothing more than the whole it is thrust back into anxiety over a part, and so by being greedy for more it gets less.[2]

The bishop of Hippo points to a fearful, anxious need to make certain of possession. The grim irony of this impulse is, of course, that the tighter the grip, the narrower the grasp: "and so by being greedy for more it gets less."

Augustine's suggestion is that while the grip of human reason is essential to productive life in the world, it needs frequent airing out and refreshing journeys up into the high country of wisdom. This exposure to the freely given and immeasurable outpouring of divine light relaxes the mind's self-defeating grip on its own small certainties. Otherwise the mind begins to draw back from the common joy of life in God and grows "busy reasoning in a lively fashion about temporal and bodily things in its task of activity, and along comes that carnal or animal sense with a tempting suggestion for self-enjoyment, that is for enjoying something as one's very own private good and not as a public and common good which is what the unchangeable good is."[3]

Modern prowess in technical knowledge can be a great public good. Augustine is alert, however, to the proclivity of such knowing to close in upon reductive analysis and the manipulable atoms and particles of reality, and hence lose sight of a beauty in form that points beyond itself and eludes any individual grasp. And as we saw in the last chapter, some of the most characteristic achievements of modernity have sprung precisely from a reduction of reality to manipulable pieces analyzed in pristine dissociation from their consummate form or end. Besides the temptation to a false and narrow mastery of the created order, this can also lead both to a loss of contact with beauty that has been anatomized and atomized, and to an unconscious slide into a cocoon of fantasy and simulation. We can now represent reality by reducing it to the on–off switching of digitization, to reality represented in univocal bits of data that can be rearranged at will into our own choice of simulacra.

I am not here intending to inveigh against modern scientific successes at all, only to note with some wariness the fact that an increase in technological power and control over nature seems to be attended by a potential loss of contact with the wholistic forms of beauty and a corresponding capacity for simulation and worlds of our own making. Such a combination is (unintentionally?) hinted at in the great utopia of that founder figure of modern natural science, Francis Bacon (1561–1626). In *New Atlantis,* a member of the secret society of scientific philosophers that rules the utopian island (which mysteriously turns out to be as large as the North American continent), reveals in brief form many of the great experimental works that he and other members of the College of Six Days Work undertake. In keeping with the name of their institute, the philosophers there seek out the principles governing the created order so as to manage it for human benefit. "We also have parks and inclosures of all sorts of beasts and birds, which we use not only for view or rareness, but likewise for dissections and trials; that thereby we may take light what may be wrought upon the body of man."[4] The astonished listener is then told how the investigators remove parts of the animals to see when death occurs, try various poisons and chemicals upon them, and manipulate their growth—all to "take light what may be wrought upon the body of man."

> Also we make them [the animals] differ in colour, shape, activity, many ways. We find means to make commixtures and copulations of different kinds; which have produced many new kinds. . . . We make a number of kinds of serpents, worms, flies, fishes, of putrefaction; whereof some are advanced (in effect) to be perfect creatures, like beasts or birds. . . . We have also perspective-houses, where we make demonstrations of all lights and radiations; and of all colours; and out of things uncoloured and transparent, we can represent unto you all several colours . . . also all colorations of light: all delusions and deceits of sight, in figures, magnitudes, motions, colours. . . . We have sound-houses, where we practise and demonstrate all sounds, and their generation. . . . We represent small sounds as great and deep; likewise great sounds extenuate and sharp; we make divers tremblings and warblings of sounds, which in their original are entire.[5]

"Which in their original are entire" is a telling phrase. The capacity to reduce reality (by dissection or "putrefaction") from its original entirety, thence to reconstruct new "perfect creatures," is closely accompanied by a fascination with "all delusions and deceits" in manipulation and control of appearances. It goes without saying that spiritual discernment is, at the least, likely to question the impulses at work in the advancement and use of such capacities and the honesty of the world they fabricate. The leader of this Baconian research utopia concludes his

"Our chief illusion is our conception of ourselves, of our importance which must not be violated, our dignity which must not be mocked."

speech with a brief paragraph insisting that "we do hate all impostures and lies," yet the skill and avidity with which the College has replaced the natural beauty of form with a simulated perfection of its own devising casts a chill over his reassurances. This is especially so given that he began his address by declaring the goal of the College to be "the enlarging of the bounds of Human Empire, to the effecting of all things possible." "All things possible" (contemporary debates about human cloning?) suggests a frame of mind that would perhaps benefit from some considered discernment.

The teachers of discernment have always pointed out that reality has a way of making itself known, of shining out so as to awaken the self from its manipulations and fantasies. In Origen and Evagrius we saw a certain developmental ordering of a discerning mind: moral pedagogy leads to natural contemplation, seeing the truth of things, and this leads to what these writers called *theologia* proper, or the contemplation of God by participation in the divine life.[6] All this suggests that we might want to consider insights from those who have examined this nexus between moral growth, aesthetic discernment, and the perception of the really real.

Spotting the Greedy Cunning Self at Work

"I am not saying," Brendan went on, "that you are necessarily wrong in wanting to leave the priesthood. I am saying that you should wait. The spiritual life is a long strange business and you've got to be quiet and docile enough to go on learning. . . . And now that you've got an inkling of what's really involved you're appalled, or the ego in you is appalled. It's like a death sentence. It is a death sentence. Not pain, not mortification, but death. That's what chills you. That's what you experience when you say there is no one there. Up till now you have seen Christ as a reflection of yourself. It has been a comfortable arrangement. . . . You are in a dream state. Ordinary human consciousness is a tissue of illusion. Our chief illusion is our conception of ourselves, of our importance which must not be violated, our dignity which must not be mocked. All our resentment flows from this illusion, all our desire to do violence, to avenge insults, to assert ourselves."[7]

So says a priest, Brendan, to his younger colleague Cato in Iris Murdoch's novel *Henry and Cato*. Throughout the work, Murdoch probes the idea that "ordinary human consciousness is a tissue of illusion." She traces Cato's high-minded illusions and dramatizes his calamitous confrontation with a real world (including his own real and unexamined self) that he had thought to recreate according to his own predilections. Murdoch lays bare certain subterranean patterns in the self here, and I want to take up her analysis, not only for the moral ascesis she proposes as the prerequisite for seeing the whole, but for her insights about the power of beauty to speak to the mind and arouse it to yearn for a larger truth.

In the prologue to his commentary on the Song of Songs, Origen of Alexandria had warned (see chapter 2) that what he is about to discuss is liable to be dangerously misconstrued by the spiritually immature. Origen fears that such a reader "will twist the whole manner of his hearing" away from the costly demands of real love and toward a more manipulable satisfaction of one's own "carnal desires."[8] The great Alexandrian's concerns would have been readily understood by another Murdochian character, Fr.

Damien, the offstage spiritual advisor to yet another self-deluding seeker, Bellamy James, in *The Green Knight*. Murdoch brilliantly evokes the frustrated attempts of Fr. Damien to break through poor Bellamy's hopelessly exaggerated fantasies of himself as a profound mystic:

> Your recent letters are becoming, it seems to me, increasingly more expressive of Byronic romanticism than of the spiritual ecstasy which I believe you imagine yourself to be experiencing. . . . The greedy cunning self has many ways of deceiving; as I know well in my own imperfect struggles! [Damien in fact abandons his religious order later in the novel.] . . . I begin to feel that our correspondence may be engendering in you simply illusions, and that anything I say to you becomes in you illusion.[9]

The covert work of the "greedy cunning self," turning spiritual truth into self-gratifying illusion, is precisely what Origen and Damien are worried about. But how to get at it, how to unmask it?

Just to remind us, Origen had pointed out, quoting the Letter to the Hebrews (5:14), that the reality of the spiritual truth he is trying to describe will only be apprehensible by those "whose faculties have been trained by practice to distinguish good from evil."[10] It is worth noting that the word translated as "faculties" is *aisthētēria,* the plural form of the faculty of *aisthēsis,* whence derives our word "aesthetic." So in this basic form there is a kinship between aesthetic judgment and moral sense; *aisthēsis* is a capacity to discern, to recognize, to perceive what appears, to apprehend it in its radical distinction between good and evil, real and illusory. Origen therefore goes on to preface his commentary with the outline of a classical pedagogical training scheme designed to build up this aesthetic and moral discernment, and therefore to set the mind free for the apprehension of truth.

Murdoch, it seems to me, shows us very well how beauty, and the practice of its apprehension in aesthetic form, helps us to think more *truly.* In her rich chapter on "Imagination" in *Metaphysics as a Guide to Morals,* Murdoch pauses summarily at one point to say, "I have been talking about the way in which our moral experience shares in the peculiar density of art, and in its imaginative cognitive activity."[11] Murdoch here shares with early Christian spirituality the sense that our ability to know truth and do good is rooted in a capacity to see, to discern, which is perhaps best explored in aesthetic categories. The Good, the True, and the Beautiful are not only convertible, of course, but our separated reflections upon them turn out to be much assisted when we open ourselves to their mutual illumination. For this reason, I think, Murdoch rightly returns with real persistence to the aesthetic categories of vision and void, fantasy and imagination, in order to understand how we become better and how we know more truly.

The reality we're seeking, says Murdoch, can rarely if ever be glimpsed truthfully, fully, and without distortion, except perhaps by truly saintly persons. And this is our problem, for if we are to allow the Good some foothold in our thought we have to have *some* way of picturing it, talking about it. If this is healthy and virtuous, it is a kind of imagining that never tries to stop our gaze, to turn glitteringly idolatrous. "Virtue is dynamic and creative, a passionate attention directed toward what is good . . . a power working at a barrier of darkness, recovering verities which we somehow know of, but have in our egoistic fantasy life 'forgotten'" (*MGM* 320). The hitch is that, as Murdoch always reminds us, "the human mind is naturally and largely given to fantasy," and this because our ego is "somewhat mechanically generating narrowly banal false pictures" (*MGM* 322, 321). If the real is *beyond* our grasp, then we must remake the real (as do Cato and Bellamy), magicking for ourselves the perfect match for our needs:

> Neurotic or vengeful fantasies, erotic fantasies, delusions of grandeur, dreams of power, can imprison the mind, impeding new understanding, new interests and affections, possibilities of fruitful and virtuous action. If we consider the narrow dreariness of this fantasy life to which we are so much addicted the term "unimaginative" seems appropriate. (*MGM* 322)

Perhaps we could, as Murdoch occasionally does herself, talk about this fantasizing tendency as the mental correlate of our biological drive for sheer persistence. It is common to see the world with ourselves at the center, in rivalry with everyone and everything else for whatever there is to be had; and the mind dresses up this survival instinct in the most fascinating and intriguing ways. But Murdoch suspects that while this fantasizing tendency, which turns the world into a series of possessible objects for ourselves, may be rather ordinary and common, it is not, in fact, the real truth about us.

As she puts it, "What I have called fantasy, the proliferation of blinding self-centered aims and images, is itself a powerful system of energy, and most of what is called 'will' or 'willing' belongs to this system."[12] But in her view, this self that is thus hypnotized into being is neither the truth of the self nor capable of perceiving reality in its fullness. Murdoch's prescription, like that of Evagrius, is patience, stillness, waiting, attention to the other, self-questioning. It is an ascetical process of self-stripping which, paradoxically, does not annihilate but rather liberates the self from its obsessions and fears. I think something like this is intended in the response of the desert father who was asked, "'Why am I afraid when I walk into the desert?' And he answered, 'Because you are still alive.'"[13] As Brendan had tried to say to Cato, spiritual growth is a kind of death sentence. Discovering the real means learning to let oneself loose from the clingy, grasping, anxious, self-preoccupied ego. "Make a hole in your world, you may see something through it," suggests Brendan (*HC*, 175).

Seeing through a Hole in the World

Evagrius, following Origen, had proposed that as the soul becomes more aware of the power of the evil thoughts in its life, it may become freer, quieted, less stirred up and muddled and tricked by these fantasies, and so more able to notice the depths of reality. But this is not necessarily a comforting vision. Looking through a hole in the world may mean that one's world has ruptured fairly irreparably. Part of the problem is that the self's survival instincts train us to think in very purposeful, utilitarian ways about what surrounds us. But apprehending the *really* real would mean precisely *not* being able to *do* anything with it or to it. The real is not reducible to something we can use or appropriate for ourselves, and therefore, since that is our most characteristic mode of meeting reality, we may not at first be able to experience reality at all. The real may accost us in an experience of futility and darkness.

Origen says that ascesis and moral discipline lead one to a clearer vision in which we begin to sense the true heart of things in themselves (rather than as fantasized by us). But this clarity is a difficult vision in which most of the world of our striving appears as pointless. Origen's gesture toward the disillusioned voice (Ecclesiastes) also has its parallel in Murdoch:

> The Good has nothing to do with purpose, indeed it excludes the idea of purpose. "All is vanity" is the beginning and the end of ethics. The only genuine way to be good is to be good "for nothing" in the midst of a scene where every "natural" thing, including one's own mind, is subject to chance, that is, to necessity. That "for nothing" is indeed the experienced correlate of the invisibility or non-representable blankness of the idea of the Good itself. (*SG* 71)

Looking through a hole in the world may be experienced as staring into the void, as Murdoch well understood. And yet she also agrees with Origen (and above all Simone Weil) that this void, this "invisibility," may also be the only form the Good can take in our world. Looking into the void, the hole in the world, may with patience and courage lead to a new kind of vision; even the darkness may teach one to "see" in a new way.

Murdoch reflected movingly on this spiritual moment of transition in her depiction of Cato's plight in an abandoned air-raid shelter in which he's being held for ransom. His fall from the fantasy of perfect spiritual mastery and priesthood has been precipitated by having fallen in love with the young tough who has now kidnapped him. This dizzying decapacitating of Cato's intellect and ego makes possible his tentative, groping discovery of a simpler, more real world literally at his fingertips.

> The darkness was total. Cato's eyes had not "got used" to it. Rather they had been filled with it, rinsed with it, so as to feel finally without the capacity of light. . . . Plunged in continuous darkness he felt strangely muddled and had to try hard to keep the most ordinary processes of thought from wandering aside into fantasy. It was not exactly like going mad, it was more like a gentle disintegration of a tentacular thought-stuff which had never, it now seemed, had much cohesion, and which now floated quietly away into the dark. . . . His sense of touch, he found, now became a sort of life-line of significance. He explored his quarters again and again in the dark, feeling up and down the walls and along the door. (*HC* 284-85)

As Cato's world is darkened, he begins to notice at last how easily his thoughts have always tended to verge off into fantasy. He experiences the prying loose of the "tentacular thought-stuff" by which his self had seemed so coherently to grasp the world. In fact, he senses, this stuff, these clear and distinct ideas—the loss of which had seemed so damaging to his spirituality—now seems never to have "had much cohesion" anyway. As Brendan had been trying to tell him, there are worlds beyond the concepts, and relationships more real than our ideas of them could ever be.

Murdoch plunges her readers into this darkness with Cato. She teaches us to feel with him the panic as the known world is made to dissolve: the numbing grief of this ungraspability is there, certainly, yet also the real presence of an unseen world, brushed only fleetingly by the painful, almost pitiful, groping of mind in a new mode. Here is the mystery of a reality that reaches us almost imperceptibly along an unexpected "life-line of significance," a new pattern of apprehending the real no longer purely according to the unspoken agenda of the ego. This is a very authentic depiction, in my view, of spiritual growth. Murdoch sometimes refers to Eckhart and John of the Cross, and I think she shares with them the insight that a newer, deeper presence to reality may only be experienced by the self as a mysterious laming and disabling, a groping about in what is barely deliverable to the conceptualizing mind at all. It is striking that when Cato, for one brief moment, is able to light a single match, the light is overpowering to him at first, and yet he still manages to catch a new glimpse of reality:

> After a moment's hesitation and with a violent heart-beat he drew the precious match firmly down the wall. The sudden bright light was for

a second almost an agony and he closed his eyes and nearly dropped the match. Then when he opened his eyes he seemed to be looking into a weird picture. The wall, very close to him, was a dark but rather radiant green, and Cato felt that he had never in his life seen such a wonderful colour. (*HC* 286)

Cato's green night of the soul pours out within him the hint of a new freedom, even in his terrible lostness and confinement, a joy in the reality of something entirely detached from himself, the sheer reality of that radiant green, so real, so much a gift from beyond himself and all his own mental patterns: "and Cato felt that he had never in his life seen such a wonderful color."

Murdoch tellingly suggests that this moment of new vision is also, quite in spite of Cato's literal isolation, able to break through the dreadful loneliness and solipsism in which he has been captive long before his physical incarceration. For as he gazes at the radiant green of the wall, Cato suddenly realizes his eyes are seeing something else: names and drawings and dates, dozens of them all over the wall, all the signs of real people who had in fact used this very place as an air-raid shelter during the World War II bombing of London. These real people, completely unrelated to Cato, were here too; and somehow by their very ordinary and funny, even childlike names—Jeff Mitchell, Tommy Hicks, Peter the Wolf—Murdoch conjures for the reader the camaraderie and simple heroism and humor with which they have invested the place. The moral courage and steadfastness of that generation have broken into Cato's world, Murdoch makes clear. Though the situation seems hopeless, Cato thinks now that "he must not give way, he must take the initiative and try to save himself. It was a soldier's duty, if taken prisoner, to try to escape"; and when he thinks of what he has done to his friends by cravenly writing a letter begging for ransom he sees now that "it was such a dishonourable awful thing to do"(*HC* 287) and that he must no longer consent to live in a convenient daze, a hazy drugged state, which is after all the precise description of that self-preoccupied world of wish-fulfillment and fantasy that Murdoch is teaching her readers to recognize and leave behind.

The Sovereign Reality of Beauty

There is, then, this unceasing path of demythologization, of liberation from the constricting illusions of our own fantasies. "The spiritual life," writes Murdoch, "is a long disciplined destruction of false images and false goods until (in some sense which we cannot understand) the imagining mind achieves an end of images and shadows (*ex umbris et imaginibus in veritatem*)" (*MGM* 320). She knows that we "live by moving beyond our images and can recognise this effort of deliberately moving out into a 'blank' or 'void.' This could be a kind of prayer, or part of an artist's discipline" (*MGM* 329). But Murdoch is not an iconoclast. She also knows that "we live normally by metaphors and pictures," and that "there is a continuous breeding of imagery in the consciousness which is, for better or worse, a function of moral change" (*MGM* 329). Cato's self- preoccupation is interrupted in the darkness by a glimpse of wartime patience in suffering, and this in turn generates a new, somewhat less pathetic way of perceiving himself: the good soldier does not give up trying to get free. Murdoch teaches us to notice that our imagination matters enormously to our moral and spiritual growth. Cato is, at least briefly, able to imagine himself in a morally different light. As our "sight" is set loose from egoistic fantasy we are enabled to see reality both more truly (the other person who is not just there as an object of our own desires) and also more transcendentally (the green that Cato sees is "radiant")—transcendental vision in the sense that the ego no longer possesses, reifies, and opacifies the world but leaves it more porous or transparent to the Good.

What seems absolutely vital to me here is the connection Murdoch is making between seeing the real in a *non*-grasping way and being enabled and nurtured in this capacity precisely by the ordinary goodness of reality that is finally able to beckon to us—no longer frozen and enchanted by our fantasizing picture of it. We need, in other words, to practice this life-giving imagining of the really real, free from ego, because reality itself is nourishing to us, liberating. The good person, in some sense, lives in a much larger world than the egoist because, says Murdoch, "he can see more of life. (He returns to seeing, now *really* seeing, rivers and mountains as rivers and mountains)" (*MGM* 325). This seems akin to what Origen and Evagrius would call the second stage of spiritual growth, namely, natural contemplation, *theōria physikē*: seeing things as they are in themselves and delighting in the truth and reality of them, the overflowing abundance of them set loose by the withdrawal of the ego's constricting grasp ("seeing, now *really* seeing, rivers and mountains as rivers and mountains"). It is as though there is a kind of density and nourishment in this actuality of life that nourishes the continuing growth of the imagination, a nourishment not available in the simulacra which fantasy ventriloquizes for its own gratification.

In seeking to understand this nurturing power of good imagination Murdoch points to Paul's advice in Philippians 4:8: "Finally, beloved, whatever is true, whatever is honorable, whatever is just, whatever is pure, whatever is lovely, whatever is gracious, if there is any excellence, if there is anything worthy of praise, think about these things."

> There are moral illuminations or pictures which remain vividly in the memory, playing a protective or guiding role: moral refuges, perpetual

starting points, the sort of thing St Paul was talking about at Philippians 4.8. A Christian may think here of Christ upon the cross. But at a simpler level the story of his birth, complete with shepherds, kings, angels, the ox and the ass, may be a good thing to have in one's life. Buddhists speak of "taking refuge." Such points or places of spiritual power may be indicated by a tradition, suggested by work or subjects of study, emerge from personal crises or relationships . . . a sudden vision in art or nature, joy experienced as pure, witnessing a virtuous action, a patient suffering, an absence of resentment, humble service, persistent heroism. (*MGM* 335)

There are numerous instances of these "moral illuminations" in Murdoch's novels, and her organic presentation of them weaves them subtly into the imagination of her readers, prying open an awareness of their real possibility and a kind of expectation of them in our own life.

Perhaps one of the most gracious and deservedly well-known of these moments of vision comes during Dora's visit to the National Gallery in *The Bell*. In this novel, Dora (an aspiring artist of sorts) has joined her increasingly estranged husband at a lay community of quite idiosyncratic religious seekers, who themselves are living in association with an enclosed contemplative order of nuns.

Sometimes the possibility of a higher spiritual reality and position is really more than some of us can even remotely sense; the call into a deeper place in life may seem damaging or threatening.

At this point in the novel, having left behind her very difficult husband and the strange muddles of the lay community, Dora finds herself moving among the familiar pictures "as through a well-loved grove."[14] Art as the imitation of nature is more than an interesting debating point for Murdoch, and I would say that many of her very beautiful evocations of the ordinary natural world function every bit as transfiguringly as this account of the power of art. Dora, perhaps because of her many previous visits to the Gallery, finds herself growing immediately detached from her frantic anxiety; she begins to be able to watch "with compassion" the other visitors, whose anxious peering is no longer necessary for her: "Dora did not need to peer. She could look, as one can at last when one knows a great thing very well, confronting it with a dignity which it has itself conferred" (*B* 190). The sovereign reality of beauty, embodying the mysterious form of truth, has been able to train Dora's gaze and to confer upon her quiet seeing a real share in its own dignity.

This scene is especially good training in aesthetic vision because Murdoch contrasts it tellingly with the immediately prior chapter when such illumination is offered but, because of spiritual immaturity, remains only a painful obscurity. Dora's flight to the Gallery is preceded in the story directly by an adolescent boy's frightened and obsessive little foray into the nun's monastic enclosure at the abbey. Toby, a boy on the cusp of adulthood, is a quintessential Murdochian naive quester, barely aware of his own impulses or his impact on others, searching for a truthful sense of himself while careening blindly from infatuation to puzzlement. In this scene, Murdoch shows us Toby's fantastic imaginings and projections of what might lie behind the cloister walls: "He wondered what would happen if he were found; and his imagination hesitated between a picture of nuns fleeing from him with piercing screams and nuns leaping upon him like bacchantes" (B 177). He is shocked and disappointed when all he finds is more of the same landscape from whence he's come.

Murdoch comments in more than one instance that sometimes the possibility of a higher spiritual reality and position is really more than some of us can even remotely sense; the call into a deeper place in life may seem to us only damaging or threatening (cf. MGM 331). By showing us Toby's inability to receive the gift of the solitude and ordinary beauty of the nuns' space, Murdoch is sensitizing us to the parallel shortfalls in our own spiritual imagination. The beauty of the enclosure seems remote, exotic, taboo to Toby, who can only perceive it through the fog of his own desires and fears. In reality it is a simple space of quiet goodness, touched as the genuine ordinary often is in Murdoch, with a sacramental depth, freshness, and vibrancy.

Having scrambled over the cloister wall, Toby at last passes on into what his ego can only see as a forbidden and dangerous realm; in fact, Murdoch shows us a peaceful and homey scene of two nuns, complete with lawn mower, quietly tending the community's cemetery: one of the nuns comes over to Toby, "her long habit sweeping the grass. Paralyzed with shame and alarm he watched her approach" (B 178). Toby's self-preoccupied trance renders him entirely impervious to the nun's simple kindness and her personal reality: she immediately speaks his name, invites him to enjoy the swing, beams upon him, shows him that the gate to the enclosure has never been locked at all, and hints that he would be welcome to visit again—and all in a lilting, affectionate, Irish voice (reminiscent for Murdoch of her own childhood?)—but Toby only hangs his head in shame. It is a truly sweet and poignant little scene, and I can't help feeling that Murdoch is urging the reader to mourn for Toby's inability to enjoy, if only for a moment, some honest, kindly, pure-hearted goodness (so different from the tortured, self-deceiving, self-obsessing morass being offered him by the other characters who populate the lay community!).

By contrast to Toby's blinkered visit among the nuns, Dora's journey to the Gallery is more nearly an authentic pilgrimage. In what must surely be one of Murdoch's finest novelistic passages, Dora muses in the presence of these great paintings:

> Dora was always moved by the pictures. Today she was moved, but in a new way. She marvelled, with a kind of gratitude, that they were all still here, and her heart was filled with love for the pictures, their authority, their marvellous generosity, their splendour. It occurred to her that here at last was something real and something perfect. Who had said that, about perfection and reality being in the same place? Here was something which her consciousness could not wretchedly devour, and by making it part of her fantasy make it worthless. . . . [T]he pictures were something real outside herself, which spoke to her in kindly yet in sovereign tones, something superior and good whose presence destroyed the dreary trance-like solipsism of her earlier mood. When the world had seemed to be subjective it had seemed to be without interest or value. But now there was something else in it after all. (*B* 190-91)

This remarkable passage is really a manifesto for the reality and power of beauty as the shining of truth into the world, sovereignly free and able also to *impart* freedom and new vision to others. The whirl and self-preoccupation of Dora's thoughts is transfigured by the paintings' "marvellous generosity"; they are able to give themselves to her, and yet they bestow "something which her consciousness could not wretchedly devour." Murdoch teaches us a good deal in this text not only about what there is to see in the world (beauty) but also about its capacity to constitute meaning and truth (intelligibility) within the mind and life of its beholder. The goodness of this beauty is, in Murdoch's view, "superior" and more real than the dismal shrunken version of reality for which we often settle; Dora realizes that this "presence" has "destroyed the dreary trance-like solipsism of her earlier mood."

Here is the paradox Murdoch teaches us to discern and live by, that when we perceive the world as nothing but the commodity of our own subjectivity, far from lavishing us with value, the world grows anemic and thin. But when we have learned to attend to its depths, its density, its fullness beyond our powers of imagining, then we really begin to be *addressed*:

> The idea of reverence is common to what are usually thought of as religious and moral attitudes, connected with art, love, respect for persons and for nature, extending into religious conceptions of the sacred or the holy. . . . Teach meditation in schools. . . . Morality, as the ability or attempt to be good, rests upon deep areas of sensibility and cre-

ative imagination, upon removal from one state of mind to another, upon shift of attachments, upon love and respect for the contingent details of the world. (*MGM* 337)

Murdoch suggests that this "removal from one state of mind to another" is indeed made possible for Dora at the end of her musing: "She remembered that she had been wondering what to do; but now, without her thinking about it, it had become obvious. She must go back to Imber [the community] at once. Her real life, her real problems were at Imber; and since, somewhere something good existed, it might be that her problems would be solved after all" (*B* 191). The real world and the good are found in the same place, and Dora's practice of attention to beauty has made possible her liberation from her "dreary trance-like solipsism"—long enough at least for the reality of the good to gain a purchase in her life again.

Union with the Real

No one is more aware than Murdoch of how tenuous this foothold of reality and goodness is in our lives, and how easily we fantasize ourselves back into a trance-like spell. A great deal of her later novel *The Green Knight* has to do with this strange sliding of vision into false magic and the soporific paralysis of fantasy. Perhaps most dramatically of all, in this novel Murdoch depicts the avatar of goodness himself, Peter Mir, moving through a strange process of recovering his mind and moral vision, as he moves from a revengeful desire for justice (to be extracted from the character who wronged him), to the *anamnesis* of mercy, and finally into an eros-driven celebration of unions and reconciliations. And yet, as these progressive revelations take place among the characters, Murdoch teaches us to beware a too-tidy, too fabulously magical solution to everything: the deep cultural myths and religious images—Cain and Able, Grail legends, Arthurian romance, the sacrificial death of Jesus—all rumble away quite observably and therefore perhaps self-critically in the background. For when Murdoch has Peter Mir himself taken away near the end (apparently a runaway psychiatric patient), she is surely forcing us and her characters to face the truth: that all this can only be a sign, an icon, a sacrament and we must—no matter how much like poor Bellamy we might long to adore and to abandon ourselves to a magical and possessible version—always let the signs point beyond themselves and not try to possess them too tightly.

Near the end, with the announcement of Peter Mir's death, the characters gather (eucharistically) and find themselves toasting him: "As they, more solemnly did this, Clement said suddenly, 'How strange, do you remember that drink which we had at Peter's place before dinner, that "special"? Now we see what it was—it was a love potion!' And Joan said, 'It's as if all spells are broken and we are all set free!' Everyone laughed, then became solemn" (*GK* 448). As Murdoch says, "religion is always menaced by magic, and yet faith can redeem and transform magic" (*MGM* 337). Peter's troubled passage through the characters' midst has indeed cast spells; it has also, thanks to his modeling of new vision and moral illumination, broken spells and set free. The characters have come to a new kind of faith, a trust in the reality of their lives, a knowledge that is perhaps only accessible and only articulable through their personal transformations and above all through their new honesty in relationships with one another.

Murdoch is sober about the artist's own obligation to face the truth, not give in to easy, self-gratifying solutions and totalizing representations. Indeed she forthrightly declares that one can judge the goodness of a novel by the freedom from the writer's own ego displayed by the novel's characters.[15] In this regard I think it would be a mistake to condemn the characters of *The Green Knight* as mere somnambulist stick-figures for the particular points Murdoch is making. Such a view overlooks two important features: first, the characters are indeed bespelled by their fantasies and Murdoch teaches us to feel *frustrated* at the very agony of their enchantment and so to discern elements of analogous unclarity in our own lives; but second, and perhaps more importantly, I sense that in this novel more than almost any other, Murdoch is also letting us, as it were, see behind the stage curtains of her own inventive mind the great mythic themes upon which she was drawing. She was inviting us in, welcoming us as collaborators in the process of imagining how beauty might shine as liberating truth into a spellbound world. Sometimes, she writes,

> what is wholly transcendent and invisible becomes partially, perhaps surprisingly, visible at points where the "frame" does not quite "meet." This image describes certain kinds of experience where it is as if, to use another image, the curtain blows in the wind (of the spirit maybe), and we see more than we are supposed to. . . . Here again the activity of the artist or thinker may be taken as an image (or analogy) of, or a case of, the moral life. . . . The artist or thinker concentrates on the problem, grasps it as a problem with some degree of clarity, and waits. Something is apprehended as *there* which is not yet *known*. Then something comes; as we sometimes say from the unconscious. It comes to us out of the dark of non-being, as a reward for loving attention. (*MGM* 505)

Perhaps, in her way, Iris Murdoch has been rewarding us for whatever degree of "loving attention" we could give, teaching us the painful pleasure of apprehending truth as it comes to birth not conveniently as a manipulable object but as the creative transformation of our own life and thought.

This is in some ways the most difficult act of discernment, the recognition that the great truth we so longed to grasp, to make *appear* as beauty, to display, is more likely to make itself felt in a new quality of our regard for others, our reverence for life, our courage and loving perseverance in the face of suffering and death: "There is much that cannot be expressed but can only be experienced or known after much training" (*MGM* 318). And yet there is even in this inarticulacy still the promise of something wonderful beyond what words could say. Origen argues that the eros that has driven the soul through purgation and illumination will finally reveal its true name at last. The highest state of mystical knowledge is, of course, a state of union with the One whom the soul has all along been seeking:

> The soul is moved by heavenly love and longing when having clearly beheld the beauty and fairness of the Word of God, it falls deeply in love with his loveliness and receives from the Word himself a certain dart and wound of love. . . . If, then, a man can so extend his thinking as to ponder and consider the beauty and the grace of all the things that have been created in the Word, the very charm of them will so smite him, the grandeur of their brightness will so pierce him as with a chosen dart—as says the prophet [Isaiah 49:2]—that he will suffer from the dart himself a saving wound, and will be kindled with the blessed fire of his love.[16]

The level of natural contemplation, when the self, freed from egoistic fantasy, has been able to behold the truth of the world, has in Origen's view a crucial role in what follows. For this nurturing vision of the real, as we likewise saw in Murdoch, unleashes upon the soul the bright love of its source; patience, waiting, loving attention is rewarded not only with a glimpse but an embrace of truth. At this point the self begins to love with the love of the Word and therefore to intuit reality no longer as object but as known and cherished from within.

I believe that Murdoch is pointing us very much in this direction when she quotes Dante and in her comment about the highest inspiration of the artist "who on the border-line of what can be expressed, with trembling excitement and quickening pace, reaches his goal by a path which he cannot later remember or explain" (*MGM* 319). If discernment is at least in some sense a clarity about reality at deeper and deeper levels, than Murdoch is teaching us a constructive, imagining, discerning skill, that leads us into the fullness of the other and helps us to recognize when abandonment to this other is right and true and when it is merely illusory.

> The last lines of the *Paradiso* express both the joy and the helplessness of this condition in which ultimately the soul surrenders its desire and its will to the harmonious movement of love. This is the apotheosis of

the imagination where words and images fail and the concept, which implies some kind of striving or separation, comes to an end. (*MGM* 319)

Learning to Feel the Obedience of the Universe to God

I want now to probe Murdoch's suggestions about the potential gifts of an aesthetic vision of reality. What exactly *is* the power of the beautiful, and how does it transform human perception? Murdoch's own responses to these questions were at least partially influenced by her reading of the French intellectual, Jewish by birth and drawn toward Christianity, Simone Weil (1909–1943). (It is intriguing that Murdoch, who had a hand in introducing Weil's writing more widely in the English-speaking world, concludes a 1956 review of Weil's *Notebooks* with this quotation from that text: "To be able to study the supernatural, one must first be capable of discerning it."[17]) Weil, along with Murdoch, rekindles awareness of an aesthetic vision that perceives the world as a cosmos, as—even in its suffering and chaos— invested with an intelligibility and beauty that ceaselessly bids for a *responsive* intelligence, a beholding, and a transforming of the beholder.

The prerequisite for a reawakened sensitivity to divine presence, says Weil, is to recover a non-mechanical model of the universe, to perceive it again as shot through with an unfathomable artistry. "One can never find enough visible finality in the world," writes Weil, to think that it is really nothing but a usefully consumable object.[18] The beauty of the world seems to point toward something beyond any apparent end within the world; like a work of art, the universe has arrangement and completion "without any imaginable end," or else one must say that "the end is completely transcendent."[19] Weil's point is that if one gradually learns to forgo merely using, consuming, and possessing the world, then its peculiar beauty begins to grow luminous again, precisely because it is the very nature of the beauty of the world that it *cannot* be consumed, and that it is most vibrant, most evocative, most resonant when in all its mysterious ungraspability it points quite beyond itself. A work of true art (like the paintings that Dora encounters in Murdoch's *Bell*), one that is not mere kitsch or commercial decoration, has this sort of "end" or non-possessable finality. "Exactly the same is true of the universe and of the course of the universe, of which the end is eminently transcendent and not representable, since that end is God Himself."[20]

Iris Murdoch depicted, as we saw above, the numbing enchantment of the possessive ego, draining the world of life and reality in grasping service to the ego's fantasizing uses. She also portrayed mysterious moments of awakening and new discernment, usually the result of some crisis, in which reality inscribes its true form (often very harshly) upon the unwilling ego. Simone Weil often speaks of this "affliction" that either destroys the soul or sets it free. It is a painful exposure to the waves of necessity and circumstance that gradually wash into the soul some recovering memory of a truth and reality quite beyond its own manufacture.

Humankind is like an apprentice learning a trade, and when an apprentice suffers from unaccustomed ways of using muscle, the workmen "have this fine expression: 'It is the trade entering his body.' Each time we have some pain to go through, we can say to ourselves quite truly that it is the universe, the order and beauty of the world, and the obedience of creation to God that are entering our body."[21] There are some patterns of reality so deep and so ungraspable that they only become known to us, to begin with, by their gradual patterning of our own being, taking up residence within us like the painstaking acquisition of the skill of a sculptor. It is as if there were a secret to this beauty so profound it can only be known by the muscles and nerves of the hands that serve it, while it remains hidden from the mind that perhaps too easily suborns it to smaller self-gratifying ends.

Weil works throughout her essays to reveal the hidden order and mysterious beauty of the creation—a terrible and dangerous beauty that, when humanity encounters it genuinely is often experienced as an overwhelming force. The paradox, says Weil, is that the universe's beauty lies precisely in the fact that it *cannot* be easily submerged in our small plans but remains obedient to a higher (divine) order. Humankind usually experiences this as brute natural necessity.

> Seen from our present standpoint, and in human perspective, it is quite blind. If, however, we transport our hearts beyond ourselves, beyond the universe, beyond space and time to where our Father dwells, and if from there we behold this mechanism, it appears quite different. What seemed to be necessity becomes obedience. Matter is entirely passive and in consequence entirely obedient to God's will. . . . In the beauty of the world brute necessity becomes an object of love. What is more beautiful than the action of gravity on the fugitive folds of the sea waves, or on the almost eternal folds of the mountains? The sea is not less beautiful in our eyes because we know that sometimes ships are wrecked by it. (*WG*, 76)

If someone were to attend with sufficient patience and reverence to the order of the world, this primordial obedience of matter to a calling beyond the world would show itself like a secret code embedded in ordinary speech.

Weil recommends "the contemplation of relationships of arithmetical and geometrical quantity" as helpful in training the soul to attend to this deeper level of reality. "This contemplation attains its whole fruit when the incomprehensible ordering of these relationships, and the marvellous concordances which one finds in them, make one feel that the very enslavement, which is necessity, or law, upon the plane of the intelligence, is beauty upon the plane immediately above, and is obedience in relation to God."[22] I believe that what Weil proposes here is in almost exact agreement with the plan for "natural" contemplation of the divine *logoi* or principles as we have seen it in Origen and Evagrius. It is a process of training, requiring preliminary moral ascesis, so that the ego is free from self-preoccupied fantasies and available to attend to the principles of divine ordering in the cosmos.

Weil, as much as Origen or Evagrius, is aware that this kind of pure attention is very rare.

> We live in a world of unreality and dreams. To give up our imaginary position as the center, to renounce it, not only intellectually but in the imaginative part of our soul, that means to awaken to what is real and eternal, to see the true light and hear the true silence.[23]

In Weil's view, this birth of a new awareness of reality unclouded by self-preoccupation is to "empty ourselves of our false divinity" and "to discern" that "the true center is outside the world" ("FLG," 100). When this self-emptying is freely chosen and given in an act of genuinely loving attention to the other, then, says Weil, it has a miraculous impact on the perceptive capacity of the soul, for it reconfigures human patterns of existence into harmony with what Weil believes to be (as I will show in a moment) the divine pattern of self-emptying by which the whole universe exists and which is, therefore, its fundamental law and signature.

> A transformation then takes place at the very roots of our sensibility, in our immediate reception of sense impressions and psychological impressions. It is a transformation analogous to that which takes place in the dusk of an evening on a road, where we suddenly discern as a tree what we had at first seen as a stooping man; or where we suddenly recognize as a rustling of leaves what we thought at first was whispering voices. We see the same colors; we hear the same sounds, but not in the same way. ("FLG," 100)

Weil sees this transformed capacity of knowing as quite unsensational yet radical, for it is not a matter of seeing fantastic visions but of seeing the ordinary imbued with an utterly new significance right in its very ordinariness. It is, she says, like the difference between holding a newspaper upside down (and seeing only strange shapes) and holding it right way up (and seeing words); suddenly the universe of apparently mechanical necessity is intelligible—while maintaining the very same patterns—as a cosmos, as an unfolding activity of obedience ("LGA," 78). Or it is like two people, one of whom knows how to read and the other of whom does not, both looking at the same sentence printed several times in different colors of ink. The one who cannot read will mostly notice the different colors, but the one who can read will recognize the same message in each case. "Whoever has finished his apprenticeship recognizes things and events, everywhere and always, as vibrations of the same divine and infinitely sweet word" ("LGA," 78). "Every event that takes place is a syllable pronounced by the voice of Love himself."[24]

So what Weil is describing here is a training in familiarity with the divine rationality implicit in the created order; it is an apprenticeship in contemplative discernment sufficient to allow one to recognize the divine word, the beauty of the divine self-sharing, in the ordinary colors of the world:

> For anyone who has arrived at this point, absolutely everything here below is perfectly beautiful. In everything that exists, in everything that comes about, he discerns the mechanism of necessity, and he appreciates in necessity the infinite sweetness of obedience. For us, this obedience of things in relation to God is what the transparency of a window pane is in relation to light. As soon as we feel this obedience with our whole being, we see God. ("LGA," 77)

As the non-possessive ego has learned to let things be freely themselves, the secret message encoded in the being of all things begins to grow radiant, clear, and beautiful. Weil's example, as we have seen, for discussing this is the way the same event or feature of nature can be viewed either as brute necessity or as obedience to a higher order.

Let me propose two questions for tracing out the logic of her position: first, what precisely is it about this contemplative stance of giving space for the other that opens one's eyes to the inner truth of reality? And second, why might Weil choose as her prime example the difficulty of reading the laws of nature as traces of God, especially when natural necessity seems to function so autonomously, automatically, apparently bereft of any divine presence?

The answer to both questions, I believe, lies in Weil's radically trinitarian interpretation of the mystery of creation. As I signaled above, Simone Weil conceives both the order of all being and the order of all knowing to be integrally related and to spring forth together from a ceaseless divine act of free self-sharing. Every existing reality is, precisely in its very own autonomous, "natural" existence, an event of the divine love, which itself exists in an eternal, trinitarian pattern of making space, giving freedom, to the other. And in this sense the real meaning, the noetic value or sign-fulness of every creature is already intrinsic to itself ("Every event that takes place is a syllable pronounced by the voice of Love himself"), for it exists as a moment of the eternal act wherein the Father makes space for the Son, and the Son accepts to be this Word of the Father's self-renunciation, and the Spirit simultaneously cherishes this loving distancing and bridges it.

In her analysis of friendship, Weil had argued that authentic friendship, while marked by an intense mutual desire and love, must be equally marked by a pure intention to preserve the freedom and consent of each other. For apart from this free mutual consent, there can be no real love but only domination of various kinds, leading to an eventual decay in the personhood of each. She adds that where one desires another but is unsure whether the affection is returned, the lover must "suppress his own affection, out of respect for the free consent which he should not desire to force" ("FLG," 134). Whenever a pure friendship develops it is a kind of miracle in which both desire and freedom, intimate union and distance, are preserved. Genuine lovers who desire each other must also, if they are equally true friends, ceaselessly preserve a distance, a space, in which each other can continue to be herself or himself:

> Pure friendship is an image of the original and perfect friendship that belongs to the Trinity and is the very essence of God. It is impossible for two human beings to be one while scrupulously respecting the distance that separates them, unless God is present in each of them. The point at which parallels meet is infinity. ("FLG," 137)

In Weil's view, then, the divine Persons of the Trinity are constituted, so to speak, by their mutual embrace and mutual space-giving consent. The Father eternally desires the Other and makes space for the Other to be *genuinely* Other, the Son, who exists with the freedom to consent to the Father's love.

As we have just seen, in the case of creaturely friendship, this mutual preservation of the freedom for consent, for genuine otherness, requires a freely accepted form of self-renunciation. And for Weil, this self-renunciation is infinite within the Trinity: the Father infinitely renounces the need to be "all" in order to make space for the Son, who equally does not count equality with God a thing to be grasped but empties himself as the perfect image of the Father's self-giving love. And the Holy Spirit personifies the infinite joy, desire, *and* freedom-preserving space for the other:

> The love between God and God, which in itself *is* God, is this bond of double virtue: the bond that unites two beings so closely that they are no longer distinguishable and really form a single unity and the bond that stretches across distance and triumphs over infinite separation. The unity of God, wherein all plurality disappears, and the abandonment, wherein Christ believes he is left while never ceasing to love his

Father perfectly, these are two forms expressing the divine virtue of the same Love, the Love that is God himself. ("LGA," 74)

Weil interprets the historical events of Christ's life and death as the crucial interpretive key, the historical manifestation that reveals the eternal self-giving rhythm of the trinitarian life.

Now comes the most significant step in Weil's logic. For she does not, as one might expect—given her profoundly Platonic inclinations—see the cosmos as simply a pale, finitized copy of the God from God, the Son. Rather Simone Weil (much more like such Christian Neoplatonists as Maximus, Eriugena, Bonaventure, or Eckhart) understands God as creating the universe *within* the relational structures of the eternal triune self-sharing. "This universe where we are living, and of which we form a tiny particle, is the distance put by Love between God and God. We are a point in this distance. Space, time, and the mechanism that governs matter are the distance" ("LGA," 75). The world, in other words, comes to exist as a moment of that infinite act of loving by which the Father chooses not to be all for the sake of there being an *other*, and the Son chooses to imitate that self-renunciation by loving the Father from across an infinite distance. By the same act in which the Father and the Son "make space" for one another, so also they make space for the *creaturely* other, the universe. Indeed, Weil believes that if God did not leave us the freedom and consent of creaturely distance, we would not only be completely without the ability to *choose* to love freely in response, but we would be simply overwhelmed: "It is God who in love withdraws from us so that we can love him. For if we were exposed to the direct radiance of his love, without the protection of space, of time and of matter, we should be evaporated like water in the sun; there would not be enough 'I' in us to make it possible to surrender the 'I' for love's sake."[25]

The paradox of creation, for Weil, is that while God gives the creatures space to exist freely in the apparent absence of God, the real fulfillment of their being lies in freely choosing (as God does) to live for the neighbor and for God, to choose a renunciation of the putative autonomy. Like the divine Persons of the Trinity, human persons are in this sense constituted precisely by giving way to the other. While this is a dying to a possessive self, it is a free consent to love the other, and it turns out to be the liberation of an authentic, relational, self: "We have to die in order to liberate a *tied up* energy, in order to possess an energy which is free and capable of understanding the true relationship of things."[26]

The problem of creaturely existence is that very often its apparent autonomy beguiles the creatures into settling down and refusing the signals of transcendence, gradually becoming blind to the invitation to a larger life of communion. As this happens, the distance and freedom within which creation exists (the distance between the divine Persons) hardens for creatures into an isolation and alienation, a distance across which they no longer know how to love.

> God created through love and for love. God did not create anything except love itself, and the means to love. . . . He created beings capable of love from all possible distances. Because no other could do it, he himself went to the greatest possible distance, the infinite distance. This infinite distance between God and God, this supreme tearing apart, this agony beyond all others, this marvel of love, is the crucifixion. Nothing can be further from God than that which has been made accursed. This tearing apart, over which supreme love places the bond of supreme union, echoes perpetually across the universe in the midst of the silence, like two notes, separate yet melting into one, like pure and heart-rending harmony. This is the Word of God. The whole creation is nothing but its vibration. When human music in its greatest purity pierces our soul, this is what we hear through it. ("LGA," 72)

This remarkable passage merits careful elucidation. Humankind has been created "capable of love from all possible distances," thus sharing the self-renunciatory logic of the triune life. But whereas in the bliss of eternal trinitarian life this loving union can stretch across an infinity of otherness and freedom (between the Father and the Son), this same pattern of freedom and consent can and does become distorted within the creaturely realm. Then the distance becomes a "supreme tearing apart," and the beautiful obedience of matter to the divine dulls into opacity, seeming no more than brute mechanical necessity. But the Son who is the very image of the beautiful pattern of self-sharing now journeys into this far country, this distance-become-alienation, and there enacts and reveals again the true pattern of self-sharing love for the other that is the very logic of universal existence.

This is why Weil chose as her prime example of contemplation the struggle to see a beautiful obedience within natural necessity. When the self has grown possessive and small, it thinks it has finally grasped its freedom and autonomy; but for Weil, when someone "turns away from God, he simply gives himself up to the law of gravity. Then he thinks that he can decide and choose, but he is only a thing, a stone that falls" ("LGA," 75). In such a condition one can no longer discern the beauty of the order of the universe, and the light of its obedience to God cannot penetrate the mind that has grown subject to the laws of mere self-preservation and aggrandizement. Like one who does not know how to read, such a person sees the shapes of the world, but without recognizing their meaning or significance or beauty.

And yet, Weil suggests that by attending to Christ on the cross, by following that way, one begins again to notice the perfect beauty of self-renouncing and self-sharing love. The eternal pattern of divine life, radiant within the structures of creation, becomes luminous again.

> God created the universe, and his Son, our first born brother, created the beauty of it for us. The beauty of the world is Christ's tender smile for us coming through matter. He is really present in the universal beauty. The love of this beauty proceeds from God dwelling in our souls and goes out to God present in the universe. ("FLG," 104)

Christ, as Bonaventure said, becomes appreciable as the logic, the structure of a mind awake to the universal rhythm of self-sharing trinitarian life. Murdoch and Weil have proposed training an aesthetic vision in order to discern an intelligible beauty in the cosmos. In Weil, the sovereign beauty of reality finds a name and face, identifiable on the cross. Reality asserts itself here in a way that manifests both human flight from truth and antagonism toward it (the crucifixion of Jesus); but also the unfathomable goodness of the truth of reality, sovereignly unwilling to leave humanity unexposed to the radiance of truth (the resurrection of Jesus).

"This tearing apart echoes perpetually across the universe in the midst of the silence, like two notes, separate yet melting into one, like pure and heart-rending harmony."

This truth secretly accomplishes that paschal journey in all creaturely reality, enacting a self-renunciation and hiddenness that permits humankind the freedom to ignore the truth of reality, distort it, even crucify it. But it also reveals in this paschal journey that it is radiantly, sovereignly alive, the deep truth whose unconquerable risenness illuminates the truth of the world precisely in authoring the world's freedom to be itself and to consent freely to become real as it is restored to communion with this ever-giving and forgiving source of its truth.

What I am groping to suggest, albeit awkwardly and allusively, is that the intelligible structure of reality (its quality of being true) is consummated and revealed for humankind in the death and resurrection of Christ. For there, Christians believe, the one through whom all things came into being (John 1:3) enacts in visible, historical form that very same pattern of divine self-renunciation from which (as Simone Weil thought) all creation flows. And in the risen Jesus, creation encounters the very same one who patiently waits for acknowledgment and recognition as the ground of truth, and whose offer of communion across the distance, unrecognition, and alienation of sin recreates a discerning heart, one capable of joining in freely chosen and desired communion with truth and so at last coming to discern it:

He walked ahead as if he were going on. But they urged him strongly, saying, "Stay with us. . . ." So he went in to stay with them. When he was at table with them, he took bread, blessed and broke it, and gave it to them. Then their eyes were opened, and they recognized him. (Luke 24:30-31)

NINE

Illumination and Truth

In the previous chapter, I began to push our reflections on discernment to their widest scope. We turned to the analogy of aesthetic judgment and examined the resonant power of beauty to call forth that judgment. This exposed how easily our minds are diverted from the full depths of truth in things. But we also considered, guided by the thoughts of Simone Weil, how the deep level of truth can be recovered and permitted to shine forth intelligibly once again as humanity discovers its place within the Trinity. Now it is time to see how discernment grows within that trinitarian structure of reality, and how truth discloses itself within human communal life. Let me briefly indicate the four points I will make in this concluding chapter.

First, I want to show *why*, exactly, Christians have believed the universe to be intelligible, "hear-able" as divine speech or perceptible as divine artistry (as Simone Weil had suggested). Second, I want to examine a classic Christian notion (sometimes called the illumination theory of knowledge) about how this deeper truth of reality is known; this should help us to envision not only the upward reach of discernment but also its fundamental orientation toward encounter with God. Third, I shall suggest how this deeper discerning of all things—as they are illumined by God's own knowing of them—reveals a unique role for humanity in what Christians believe to be the divine purpose in creating a universe at all. Fourth and finally, I hope to indicate the inherently communal pattern of life in which truth embodies itself—a eucharistic knowing and encounter with truth that mirrors the trinitarian self-sharing from which all truth flows and which leads the universe from division and fear to unity and love.

Reality Has the Character of a Word

If I were attempting to trace the historical *origins* of the ideas I am about to unfold, I would certainly begin with the earliest encounters of people with Jesus. I would want to delineate how his presence—in his earthly ministry, in the resurrection appearances, and in the sending of the Spirit—

always seems in the Gospels to open persons to a greater reality and awareness of truth (as in the Emmaus story we recalled at the end of the previous
chapter). Karl Barth argues that the appearance of Christ plunges those
whom he encounters into a new kind of understanding, a new way of apprehending reality that participates in (or "repeats" in human fashion, to use
Barth's language) God's own activity:

> Recognition of this man [Jesus] can obviously take place only as a new
> act of cognition, i.e., one which shares in the newness of His being. It
> must therefore be aware of the divine act of majesty which is the
> ground of His being in the cosmos. It must attach itself to this. It must
> follow and accompany it. It must repeat it. . . . This means that in and
> with His self-disclosure He induces and initiates the human seeing and
> interpreting which attaches itself to the divine act of majesty in and by
> which He has His being.[1]

My suggestion is that discernment arises precisely out of this "new act of
cognition" induced in the community by its affiliation with Jesus. I think we
could then show how the interaction of Jesus' followers with what they
identify as the Holy Spirit leads them into an ever deepening encounter with
the *truth* in Christ (see, e.g., John 14–17), and, indeed, how this leads the
community in time to formulate a way of talking about God as Trinity,
about God as an eternal activity of existing, knowing, and loving. Here,
however, I must confine myself merely to tracing out the logic of the ideas
themselves without attempting to examine in detail the stages of their history. From the standpoint of logical ordering, it would clearly be best to
begin with the beginning, and in this case, even before the beginning.

A large range of Christian thinkers in many eras have understood the
beginning of all things to exist *before* their beginning in time. In this view,
all things have a primordial existence as God knows and desires their eventual coming to be in time and space. But since they exist as God's ideas or
thoughts, so to speak, these creatures-to-be have a matchless intensity and
purity and vivacity and truthfulness from all eternity, because "they" are
nothing less than God thinking and loving (just as, for example, one's ideas
are oneself in the act of knowing and feeling something about what one
knows). In his homilies on John's Gospel, Augustine (to pick a notable
example) explains the basic point as follows:

> A carpenter makes a box. First he has the box in design; for if he had
> it not in design, how could he produce it by workmanship? But the
> box in theory is not the very box as it appears to the eyes. It exists
> invisibly in design, it will be visible in the work. Behold, it is made in
> the work; has it ceased to exist in design? The one is made in the work,
> and the other remains which exists in design.[2]

Augustine wants his hearers to realize that the theoretical box, existing in the design-idea of the artisan, is distinct from the wooden box on the shelf, yet that theoretical or ideal box has a crucial relationship with the wooden box. It is the living *truth* of the box in the maker's mind that gives the wooden box its own reality. If the wooden box rots, says Augustine, the enduring truth of the box in the mind of the artisan can form a new wooden box. It is this creative idea of the artisan that has life and authors things.

Then returning to his text (John 1:4), "That, which was made in Him, is life," Augustine applies his analogy: "Because the Wisdom of God, by which all things have been made, contains everything according to design before it is made, therefore those things which are made through this design itself are not forthwith life, but whatever has been made is life in Him"; and as Augustine had noted earlier: "If, then, Christ is the Wisdom of God, and the Psalm says, 'In Wisdom hast Thou made all things'; as all things were made by Him, so all things were made in Him."[3] In Augustine's teaching, then, all the creatures that have ever or will ever or could ever exist in time and space have an eternal form of existence in God's knowing of them. And this knowing of what comes to be is, of course, God simply knowing God-self, knowing God's authoring plan or creative Wisdom. This Wisdom by which God knows Godself (as planning and providing for all creation) is God's eternally begotten Word, the incarnation of whom Christians believe is Jesus Christ. So Augustine is saying that the Father knows and expresses himself in the Word or Son, *and* that included in that eternal activity of knowing is God's knowing, simultaneously, all the creatures.

At the risk of getting far ahead of myself, let me gesture at why this is worth thinking about. First of all, it is going to mean that the deep structure or truth of all things, the fullest potential of what they each have it in them to be, is something God from all eternity knows and loves. Second, it means that because there *is* in fact a deep pattern or recognizable truth inherent in all things, they are actually knowable, intelligible, and even the partial discovery and recognition of this truth by creatures capable of it is going to be an experience of profound joy; for it will be like hearing a recognizable word addressed to someone by the very source of one's own life and existence. And third, it is going to mean that the more believers come to participate in God's *own* desire to know the Word of truth, that is, to participate in God the Holy Spirit, the more they will come to know and love the truth of all things as God does.

But to pick up where we left off: Augustine's view is that the divine ideas or reasons (*logoi* in Greek) are the productive, veracious, ground of the created universe's intelligibility. In a sense we could even say that they are the loom upon which all creaturely thought is woven, for any act of intelligence is a response of mind to this deep truth in which all things consist and come to be. We can find Origen teaching quite similarly about the noetic dimension of creation. He notes that the eternally begotten Word of God is the divine Wisdom in whom "there was implicit every capacity and form of the creation that was to be. . . . [S]he [Wisdom] fashions beforehand and contains within herself the species and causes of the entire creation."[4] For Origen, this divine Wisdom is not only the Word by which the Father eternally speaks the divine life and truth, but is the crucially revealing Word who unveils the truth of all creatures:

> For wisdom opens to all other beings, that is, to the whole creation, the meaning of the mysteries and secrets which are contained within the wisdom of God, and so she called the Word, because she is as it were an interpreter of the mind's secrets. . . . This Son, then, is also the truth and the life of all things that exist; and rightly so. For the things that were made, how could they live, except by the gift of life? Or the things that exist, how could they really and truly exist, unless they were derived from the truth?[5]

Origen very explicitly grounds the veracity of the universe in the truthful self-knowing of God, and he points to an intrinsic generosity and bounty in that divine knowing. For not only does Wisdom form the intelligible structure of all things, but she seeks to open to all other beings "the meaning of the mysteries and secrets which are contained within the wisdom of God." Wisdom is a Word who can become the "interpreter of the mind's secrets." Origen hints here at the communal and indeed communion-like nature of the event of knowing (which we will consider in more detail in the final section of this chapter); for the understanding of all things is likened to a passage into mysteries and an interpretive exegesis, both of which for Origen have their true locus in the church's life of catechesis and worship. The "mind's secrets" that Wisdom interprets are discovered as dwelling first in the divine mind but reflected in the creatures and recognized in gratitude by finite minds who are open to Wisdom's teaching. So the event of knowledge turns out to be a communal event of self-sharing.

Along the same lines, we find Maximus the Confessor (ca. 580–662) teaching that the practice of virtue leads to a growing "recognition with understanding of the more spiritual principles of things," and that this growth comes about precisely because of the divine self-speaking:

> The word of God is like a grain of mustard seed; before its cultivation it appears to be very small, but when it has been properly cultivated it shows itself to be so evidently big that the noble reasons of creatures of sense and mind come as birds to rest in it. For the reasons of all things are set in it as finite beings, but it is limited by none of these

beings. . . . The grain of mustard seed is the Lord, who is sown by faith in the Spirit in the hearts of those who receive him.[6]

With characteristic dexterity Maximus recontextualizes the Christian Neoplatonism of Origen in a yet more entirely christological context. The mustard seed of the Gospel is the true resting place of all the *logoi* (the reasons) of things, in which believers who have cultivated the gospel life are able to sense the harmony and fittingness of all the creaturely truths as they nestle together in the full-grown seed. And this overarching *Logos* in whom all the *logoi* find their true meaning and relationship is for Maximus none other than Christ the Lord implanted within the community by the Spirit. The eternal Wisdom of Origen and Augustine, says Maximus, gives itself to be sown in our very midst as a seed growing secretly; it grows up into a tree whose fruit (the cross from which hangs the crucified Lord) discloses the truth of the world. Again, it is worth noting for future reference the intrinsically communal nature of the truth-event in Maximus; it is as all the reasons of the creatures come *together* in the seed/Lord that their truth and identity is discoverable.

Jumping ahead several centuries to Thomas Aquinas (ca. 1225–1274), we find the Angelic Doctor's commentary on John's Gospel carefully following the very passages in Origen and Augustine we considered above. Thomas agrees with his predecessors that things considered in *themselves* may be alive but are not necessarily life itself. Yet when all things are "considered as they are [eternally] in the Word, they are not merely living, but also life. For the archetypes which exist spiritually in the wisdom of God, and through which things were made by the Word, are life, just as the chest is in some sense living, insofar as it has an intellectual existence in the mind of the artisan."[7] For Thomas, these divine archetypes are, we could say, the particular thoughts of God—all conceived in and with the eternal Word— by which God will "think" all the creatures into their historical existence; "hence the creature in God is the creating essence" of God.[8] Thomas emphasizes that this conceiving of all things in God is one with the Father's eternal begetting of the Word: "Since God by understanding Himself understands all other things . . . [T]he Word conceived in God by His understanding of Himself must also be the Word of all things."[9]

Thomas draws a crucial conclusion from all this: because by God's "knowledge He produces things in being," and because this divine self-knowledge is none other than the Word, "therefore the Word of God must for all things which are made be the perfect existing intelligibility."[10] This means not only that there is a reason *why* we can (sometimes at least!) make sense of things, why they have an inner "logic" and rationale apprehensible by created minds; but even more significantly, it also means that the truth of things originates in the divinely truthful self-knowing, in the perfect imaging and correspondence between the Father and the Son—a truthfulness that itself springs from the eternal yearning (to know) of the Holy Spirit and overflows in the joyful affirmation which is the communion of the Holy Spirit. Perhaps we could say that human discernment of truth, in the deepest sense, takes place as the Holy Spirit works within the believing community this event of the self-expression of the Father and infinite acceptance to be this Word by the Son through the power of the Holy Spirit—an event that reaches its historical embodiment in our world in the incarnation, passion, and resurrection of Jesus.

Few theologians have reflected more profoundly on this trinitarian and christological grounding of truth than Thomas's contemporary, Bonaventure (ca. 1217–1274). The Seraphic Doctor not only teaches of course that the trinitarian life is itself the ground of all creatures, but more specifically that the deep structure of all creatures is a kind of echo or vestige of the trinitarian rhythm of existence. For, he says, "every one exists by virtue of the efficient cause, is patterned after the exemplary cause, and ordained toward the final cause."[11] Tracing these creaturely causal patterns back to their trinitarian ground, we see that Bonaventure is ascribing the sheer gratuity of creaturely existence to the Father, the fact that creatures each express a unique form or identity to the Son, and the fact that creatures are inherently moving toward their proper fulfillment to the Holy Spirit.

But Bonaventure is interested in far more than just noting this deep truth-structure of creation. He also believes that there is a crucial link between coming to know the trinitarian structure of truth and sharing in its historical embodiment in the paschal mystery. Speaking of the primordial fecundity of God's self-knowing and loving, in which all the ideas of creatures-to-be are expressed, Bonaventure writes:

> For all the exemplar reasons are conceived from all eternity in the womb or uterus of eternal wisdom. . . . And as it conceived them from all eternity, so also it produced [them] or bore [them] in time, and later, gave birth [to them] by suffering in the flesh. And the intelligence is able to understand this and in so doing, it has attained the highest contemplation.[12]

From the womb of eternal Wisdom, says Bonaventure, there comes a birth of creatures into time; and yet the full and consummate moment of labor that gives birth to the truth of creatures is only achieved as Wisdom incarnate is present "suffering in the flesh"—clearly referring, I should think, to the crucifixion. Why does Bonaventure believe not only that the paschal mystery is central to the full birth of truth but also that "the intelligence is able to understand this"?

By likening the journey of truth to a birth process, Bonaventure is pointing to what he sees as the real meaning of the scholastic commonplace that truth involves the correspondence or adequacy of mind to the thing that would be known. Bonaventure is suggesting that there is a deep reason why the knower can pass over into union (deep "correspondence") with the would-be known: just as the sheer *existence* of all things is the expression in time of the Father's truthful self-knowing in the Son, so also the full *truth* of things comes to be known in the consummation of the Word's return to the Father in the unity of the Holy Spirit. And this return, in and through our world, is by way of the cross. Furthermore, says Bonaventure, this is the real basis of our own discernment of truth, namely, that we can by grace come to participate in the passion of the Son and so journey with him into the unfathomable mystery of the Father. In this way, in and with our knowing of all things with the Son, we journey with him into that fullest and consummate "adequation" of the Son to the will of the Father, wherein lies the truth of all reality. The analogy here is with the adequation or growing correspondence of the knowing mind to the object of knowledge. I am suggesting that the ultimate ground of this possibility within human understanding is none other than the eternal divine self-knowing accomplished as the Father fully expresses the truth of God in the begetting of the Word and the Word perfectly corresponds or is adequate to this truth in the unity of the Holy Spirit.

I am *not,* however, saying that Bonaventure thinks the paschal mystery is a kind of handy visual aid for the some universally human logical process of knowing truth (i.e., the adequation between the intellect and the thing known); I am rather suggesting just the reverse! For Bonaventure, I believe, our human logical process of truth-seeking is the abstract reflection within human intellectual life of the immeasurably glorious, vivacious, and veracious journey of truth that is the trinitarian life of God. This is, I think, a reasonable conclusion to draw, for example, from the Seraphic Doctor's *Journey of the Mind to God.* In this brief but intensely argued work, Bonaventure sculpts all the vastness of his visionary systematic theology into a seven chapter theological and mystical itinerary—with the seventh chapter marking, as is most apt, the mind's passing over into the sabbath of divine joy. Throughout this work, Bonaventure has described a journey of the mind that begins by searching the depth of the meaning of the creatures and discovers that the desire for their truth leads the mind onward toward the divine mystery from which they spring.

Precisely because the truth of all creatures radiates from God's archetypal knowing and loving of them in the Word and Spirit, any authentic human knowing of the creatures can only be drawn into that infinite knowing and loving which is God's life. But this journey into the mystical (or hidden-in-God) truth of all things will only be undertaken by someone who is truly aroused to desire such truth, "and no one desires it except he who is pene-trated to the marrow by the fire of the Holy Spirit."[13] So the very divine yearning that, as it were, drives the Father to know in the Son and the Son to be this perfectly truthful Word, this same Spirit must animate human dis-cernment. The Holy Spirit must inflame and carry one into God, thus induc-ing within human knowing a participation in the divine knowing, in which one "knows" now only as one is known in the mutual knowing of the divine Persons. This is perhaps only conceivable in human terms via the mystical language, and here Bonaventure speaks of being consumed and transformed in fire—the very image of the ritual knowing communicated in the liturgy of burnt offerings in the Temple:

> God Himself is this fire, and His furnace is in Jerusalem; and it is Christ who enkindles it in the white flame of His most burning Pas-sion. This fire he alone truly perceives who says: My soul chooses hanging, and my bones, death. He who loves this death can see God, for it is absolutely true that Man shall not see me and live. Let us, then, die and enter into this darkness. Let us silence all our cares, our desires, and our imaginings. With Christ crucified, let us pass out of this world to the Father.[14]

For Bonaventure, Christ, who is the perfect offering—of the Father to the world and of the world to the Father—accomplishes in this liturgy of his dying and rising the consummation of the journey of truth. For he bears within himself, the Temple of his Body, the truth of all the creatures; and allowing their broken and distorted forms to be enkindled and consumed in the fire of his passion, he passes over into their fullness and truth in the Father. The truth of all creatures is an eschatological truth for now; the world waits for its revelation. It does, however, radiate from this eschato-logical future into our time; and the sign it makes here, the presence it has now, is the presence of the crucified and risen Jesus. He is the appearing in our present world of the truth of all things as they have passed from men-dacity to reality, from death to life. In the bitter economy of lies, Christ, who is the truth of all things, appears as alienated and accursed by God; the res-urrection reveals the truth of all things as vindicated and beloved of God.

Let me try stating all this slightly differently: all the authors we have been considering agree that the source and origin of all truth lies in the divine self-knowledge. We *could* say simply that God is truth and any other forms of truth derive from God, but by itself this would miss the absolutely crucial trinitarian point that all our authors have been making. And this is that truth springs precisely from the *relationship* of the Father and Son, that what is true is the perfect *likeness* and expression of the Father which the Word is and freely chooses to be. Or as the Letter to the Hebrews says regarding the Son, "He is the reflection of God's glory and the exact imprint of God's very being" (Hebrews 1:3). Moreover, all our writers agree that it is in this infinitely truthful relationship between the Father and the Word that God knows all the creatures-to-be (as eternal divine ideas). This would mean that the intelligibility and truth of every creature is discoverable most consummately as, in some way, it becomes translucent to the light of this trinitarian relationship.

Illumination: The Mystical Initiation of Communion with God

In the previous section, I argued a case for the intelligibility and truth of the world as the radiance within all things of the trinitarian knowing and loving of God from which all things come. I also suggested that the events of Jesus' life, death, and resurrection are not simply the earthly, historical manifestation of the trinitarian life but a constitutive moment in the journey of creation into its fullest truthfulness. Now I want to move a little further into a consideration of the implications of this intelligible cosmos for human knowers. Might not the Word and Spirit, who accomplish the truth of all things in

"Let us silence all our cares, our desires, and our imaginings. With Christ crucified, let us pass out of this world to the Father."

the incarnation and passion, also be at work unceasingly and mystically within the creatures, inducing the initial stirrings of that communion that is consummated in the resurrection of Christ and at Pentecost? The key to our thinking about this is an analogy between the Passion and Pentecost on one hand and, on the other hand, an event taking place in the noetic realm—an event usually called illumination.[15]

Let me offer a highly provisional version of the analogy just to get started. In the last section I argued that the eternal truth of all things exists *within* the knowing of the Father in the Son and the rejoicing of the Holy Spirit in this divine communion. Based on that, here are some theses leading to the basic analogy I want to draw:

1. Truth (including the truth of all creatures) lies in the correspondence of the Father and Son (as I hope I showed in the preceding section of this chapter).
2. The created consummation of this truth for all creatures is hindered by the distortions of sin, in which the creation is subjected to fallacious and corrupted self-understandings, thus preventing it from reaching its fullest truth as conceived by God.

3. The alienation of the creatures from their truth in the Father is overcome through the historical missions of the Word and Spirit.
4. Creatures endowed with freedom and intelligence are given the opportunity to participate in this redemption of creaturely truth through
obedience to Christ in the power of the Spirit.
5. *Illumination* is an event in the sphere of intelligence, judgment, and
wisdom that takes place in noetic analogy to the salvation-historical
work of the Word and Spirit. In other words, the same Word and Spirit
who bring to birth all truth within the mind of God and who "reconceive" and resurrect that truth within the brokenness of history are
also at work mystically (or hiddenly) throughout the creation—and
especially through creatures imbued with intellect—to foster this healing and reconciling discernment of the truth of things.

Perhaps I can make all this slightly clearer if I now take up an issue I had
to bracket earlier: if the eternal and perfect truthfulness of all creatures is
already present in the abundance of trinitarian life, then what use is there in
things becoming actually distinct from God as creatures in time and space?[16]
This question brings to light the crucial relational dimension within which
we are thinking about truth. God's goodness in conceiving all possible ways
in which creatures may be is not a bare, unitarian divine "substance"; rather,
we have been conceiving of that divine goodness and joy in the unfolding of
divine truth as *an event of freedom and love among the triune Persons*. This
means that the divine ideas of all creatures-to-be are imbued and made luminous, as Bonaventure saw, with a trinitarian deep structure: they are ordered
to a fullness and truth that can only come to fruition as a result of a free and
loving desire to be for another. The truth of all reality comes to expression
precisely within that free trinitarian giving space of the divine Persons one for
another. Therefore, the truth of the creatures, their consummation, entails
that they should have the possibility themselves of choosing freely to give
themselves in love to one another, each in its own terms.

To this end, God fosters and forwards their truth-faring journey from
archetypal existence in the divine mind into historical existence in finite
form. One might think, by analogy, of how a good author invests her characters with an authentic "life of their own," so that the more fully the
author thinks through her characters the more wholly and completely they
exist independently of her; by contrast, less fully developed characters all
feel unsatisfyingly alike, mere stick-figures or mouthpieces for different
aspects of the author herself. God's authoring of the creatures is so infinitely
perfect that they do indeed come to have a "life of their own." This is not
so they may each seek some spurious form of "autonomy" from each other
and from God (indeed, I would argue, this is exactly the self-destructive
counterfeit of the truth to which the creatures have been subjected—or so,

at least, I would interpret Genesis 3). Rather, God gives the creatures their historical existence so that they may have the space and opportunity (in direct analogy to the "space" the trinitarian Persons give to one another) to give themselves in love and freedom, that is, so that they may move toward communion with one another and thereby discover within their deep longing for knowing and communicating with one another their calling toward that infinite knowing and loving that is God's own life.

Moreover (as I will show in the next section of this chapter), within this truth-faring journey of the creatures, intelligent beings have a particular role in assisting all the other creatures by bringing to fruition their potential for communion. A preliminary example: by discerning in a batch of chemicals the potential for edible food, you can "realize" its capacity to become a meal, and indeed you can furthermore conceive the food (and indeed so offer it) as a shared meal, an act of friendship with others. Illumination makes possible this truth-realizing role that intelligent creatures can play for other creatures; in the example I've just given, human intelligence, illumined by the *divine intentions for things*, thinks chemicals into food and food into meal and meal into friendship.

Worth noting here is the fact that this transformation is not simply one of "freeing" creatures from their material form into a more spiritual and intellectual form as they come to exist within the minds of their knowers (this would indeed be subject to the usual suspicions about Neoplatonic ambivalence toward matter); rather, it is a process that does *include* a "realizing" of creatures within the minds of their knowers but precisely for the sake of reconceiving them (including their materiality) not simply as things but as occasions of deep communication and friendship. In other words the transposition is not so much from matter to intelligence as from isolation to communion. Fergus Kerr clarifies how this would work in the perspective of Aquinas:

> . . . knowledge is a product of a collaboration between the object known and the subject who knows: the knower enables the thing known to become intelligible, thus to enter the domain of meaning, while the thing's becoming intelligible activates the mind's capacities. Knowing is a new way of being on the knower's part; being known is a new way of being on the part of the object known. For Thomas, meaning is the mind's perfection, the coming to fulfilment of the human being's intellectual powers; simultaneously, it is the world's intelligibility being realized.[17]

My only supplement to this would be to invite us to push even beyond the noetic and cosmological implications right down to the trinitarian underpinning of the process. In other words, I am suggesting that this mutual realization of human being and world in noetic communion is possible precisely because both knower and knowable objects are themselves the creatures of an eternal trinitarian event of knowing and loving.

It is also worth noting that divine illumination presupposes a richness, mystery, and apophatic depth to all things. In a famous essay, the Thomist philosopher Josef Pieper remarks that the very createdness of things is in a curious way luminous with mystery; for the "designs, the archetypal patterns of things, dwell within the Divine Logos." Therefore, because all things partake so wholly in the expressive nature of the Word, "they are lucid and limpid to their very depths."[18] But by virtue of this very fact, all creatures also

> mirror an *infinite* light and can therefore not be wholly comprehended. It is not darkness or chaos which makes them unfathomable. If a man, therefore, in his philosophical inquiry, gropes after the essence of things, he finds himself, by the very act of approaching his object, in an unfathomable abyss, but it is an abyss of *light*. . . . Why is a finite spirit unable to acquire, in the last resort, such a comprehensive knowledge? The answer is: because the knowability of Being, which we are attempting to transform into knowledge, consists in its being creatively thought by the Creator.[19]

Pieper points to the paradox that the very ground of all creatures' intelligibility is also "an unfathomable abyss" of meaning, of trinitarian self-sharing communion. Illumination is the shimmering within the human mind of that ungraspable depth of meaning that all things have in virtue of their eternal expression in God. It might be helpful to think about this in more narrative terms, looking at the story of the first human's longing for companionship in Genesis 2:18-25. God gently brings each of the new creatures before the man "to see what he would call them; and whatever the man called each living creature, that was its name." Here we have the human role in the cosmos, bringing each creature into a fuller identity by thinking it, naming it, declaring its truth. And yet there is still something lacking. There is a depth in these creatures that mere classification and naming cannot speak; and furthermore this prototypical objectifying of all creatures also leaves the human feeling unfulfilled ("but for the man there was not found a helper as his partner"). So God, in a mystery of making space for another, opens the very being of the human and awakens him to another creature, but this time to another whom he cannot simply name but can only come to know in conversation and communion.

In the noetic event of illumination, God brings the creatures before the mind's eye by exposing to the mind the splendor of the divine ideas of all things. But as this happens the mind is newly awakened to an unfathomable depth, a depth which both enraptures and fulfills the mind, and also sets it free from a mere naming of the creatures as objects. In illumination the mind is awakened to discern the creatures as events of communion, and the mind is moved from mere language *about* the creatures to a recognition of the creatures as language. Illumination is the mystical presence of the trinitarian conversation of the divine Persons, hiddenly expressing itself in the conversation of the creatures.

We have a particularly choice expression of this view in Augustine's early treatise *On Free Will*. Speaking of moments when the mind seems to sense the mysterious presence of Wisdom clarifying its thoughts, he writes: "If it is given us to rejoice in these true and certain blessings as they glimmer for us even now on our still darkly shadowed way, perhaps this is what Scripture means when it describes how wisdom deals with the lovers who come to her."[20] This divine intimacy into which the mind is drawn glimmers within each discerning perception of reality, permitting a vision of its true beauty:

> Wherever you turn she [wisdom] speaks to you through certain traces of her operations. When you are falling away to external things she recalls you to return within by the very forms of external things. Whatever delights you in corporeal objects and entices you by appeal to the bodily senses, you may see is governed by number, and when you ask how that is so, you will return to your mind within, and know that you could neither approve nor disapprove things of sense unless you had within you, as it were, laws of beauty by which you judge all beautiful things which you perceive in the world.[21]

The form of things, their sign-fulness, says Augustine, beckons to the mind in virtue of their intrinsic intelligibility; the appeal of their sensible shapes resonates with a numerically articulable proportionality that delights the mind. So there is an intimacy between the wisdom glimmering in the creatures and the mind awakened to wisdom's intelligible beauty; and all this, says Augustine, is because the very pattern and order of eternal wisdom illuminates the mind like a principle of aesthetic judgment, enabling it to recognize the deeply beautiful truth of God's eternal art in the splendor of the creatures. Bonaventure would make a similar point by saying that just as "the sun by shining brings forth a variety and number of colors, so out of this Word there comes forth a variety of things."[22] In other words, just as the sun shining in the world lights up the colors and forms of things for our eye, so the Word (in whom all creatures are eternally known and created) shining in the mind lights up the intelligible beauty and truth of whatever the mind is considering.

This sense of God's mystical presence in the noetic realm had long been a feature of Christian teaching. As we saw in chapter 2 above, from Origen through Evagrius and Maximus and virtually throughout the patristic era, the second step in the Christian contemplative life (after growth in virtue) was to practice contemplation of the inner principles (*logoi*) in the creatures as a way of preparing for contemplation of their divine source. A leading Maximus scholar summarizes this perspective: "On account of the presence of the Logos in all things, holding their *logoi* together, the world is pregnant with divine reality, and knowledge of it—through the rational quality of man, his own *logos*—is itself a kind of communion with God, a participation in divine things through the aims and purposes that are recognized in creation."[23] Notice especially the links here between knowledge of truth and communion with God. Christian teaching about divine illumination, I want to suggest, can be understood as a further development of this common patristic teaching about contemplation of the *logoi*. But illumination theory clarifies two important points: first, that the ideas or principles of things are not somehow extraneous to God but events in the divine life; and second, that any Christian reflection on how humanity knows truth will be most fruitfully elucidated via the doctrine of the Trinity.

> *For Maximus, illumination is really another word for the free, gracious, and mystical companionship of Christ with creaturely minds.*

There always remains, as well, a significantly eschatological quality inherent in illumination theory. For it attends to a divinely awakened desire to know the true, a desire that cannot be fully satisfied in the present world. Origen draws an analogy with our desire to discover the underlying principles of a beautiful piece of craftwork:

> Much more, and beyond all comparison, does the mind burn with unspeakable longing to learn the design of those things which we perceive to have been made by God. This longing, this love has, we believe, undoubtedly been implanted in us by God; and as the eye naturally demands light and vision and our body by its nature desires food and drink, so our mind cherishes a natural and appropriate longing to know God's truth and to learn the causes of things.[24]

Origen is sure that God would not have implanted such a desire for truth if it could not be fulfilled, and it is because the fuller knowledge of God's handiwork (in the life to come) tantalizes us so in the present that we persevere and thirst for knowledge quite beyond the merely technical or utilitarian.

> When we were on earth we saw animals or trees and we perceived the differences among them and also the very great diversity among then.

But when we saw these things we did not understand the reasons for them; but this alone was suggested to us by the very diversity of what we saw, that we should search out and inquire for what reason all these were created diverse and arranged in such variety; and if we have cherished on earth a zeal and love for this kind of knowledge, there will be given to us after death an acquaintance with and understanding of that reason.[25]

Origen senses that the mind feeding upon whatever truth it *can* discern becomes increasingly sensitive of a yet deeper truth, a deeper rationale, that it cannot grasp but which is the condition for the possibility of what it does understand.

Along with Origen, Maximus emphasizes the integrity of the moral and noetic dimensions of such growth in understanding. The eschatological form of illumination, says Origen, will only be satisfying "*if* we have cherished on earth a zeal and love for this kind of knowledge." And Maximus even more clearly grounds illumination in the kinds of spiritual discernment we explored in earlier chapters; for him, the reason the evil spirits are concerned to captivate the mind by falsity and illusion is precisely that otherwise the mind will keep increasing company with the good. Indeed, for Maximus, there is a strong sense that the good spirits and the beneficent impulses that heal and guide human thought in a more discerning direction are in fact the *truths* of reality for which the mind so hungers. Goodness is really what is truthful and the truth is really what is good to the mind, consoling and purifying it:

When the mind is completely freed from the passions, it journeys straight ahead to the contemplation of created things and makes its way to the knowledge of the Holy Trinity. When the mind is pure and takes on ideas of things it is moved to a spiritual contemplation. But when it has become impure by carelessness, it imagines mere ideas of other things, so that receiving human ideas it turns back to shameful and evil thoughts. . . . The one who has had success with the virtues and has become rich in knowledge as at last discerning things by their nature does and considers everything according to right reason and is in no way misled. . . . Just as the sun in rising and lighting up the world manifests both itself and the things which it lights up, so the sun of justice [Christ the *Logos*] in rising on a pure mind manifests both itself and the principles (*logoi*) which have been and will be brought to existence by it.[26]

It would not, I think, be stretching the point to say that for Maximus illumination is really another word for the free, gracious, and mystical companionship of Christ with creaturely minds. In this mystical presence, Christ shares with the mind a sense of the truth of things as they exist in his eternal begetting from the Father.

Now let me conclude this section by clarifying why I think illumination theory is best understood within a theology of creation (rather than in more narrowly epistemological terms). We have an important glimpse of the full cosmological and indeed doxological significance and functioning of illumination in Augustine's *Literal Meaning of Genesis*. This was the bishop of Hippo's fourth major exposition of creation (completed in 415); and, along with *The Trinity* and *The City of God,* the *Literal Meaning of Genesis* is usually accounted as one of the three "major works of the mature mind of St. Augustine."[27] As he reflects on the significance of light in the creation, Augustine interprets it, in the first instance, as the radiance of the divine expressivity and productivity as it comes to be reflected in the creatures.

Light, we could say, is the "look," the shining appearance, of the divine self-giving as it comes to visibility in the production of creaturely existence. The divine giving of existence includes, of course, creatures that are simply the object of it, such as sea and dry land (though even such non-intellectual creatures reflect the light of divine giving as signs). But, very importantly for Augustine, there are other creatures whose role is not simply to reflect the light of divine giving in a passive way (as objects) but who are themselves *capable of receiving it appreciatively and offering a creaturely response of praise*. This is because such creatures, having intelligence, are capable of perceiving to varying degrees something of the divine intention and rationale, the eternal divine procession of the Word from the Father; and they are capable also of a free response of joyful praise which to varying degrees participates in the eternal yearning joy of the Holy Spirit. In this sense, intelligent creatures have a very special way of sharing in the creative activity of God.

One could imagine an explanatory analogy for Augustine's views here by thinking of the coming into performance of a play. There are some elements in the playwright's conception that come into being in the play as limited expressions of the whole: a telephone, a child's toy, a broken vase, for example, may be full of import in the drama, yet they are nonetheless props whose meaning will only be unfolded as they are taken up into the action of the players. Only in such a way can they fulfill their intention or truth as that springs from the mind of the playwright. By contrast, the actors (unless they are very bad at their job) are themselves capable of discerning the idea and rationale of the play. This sense of the author's purpose illumines their understanding of all the elements of the play, helping them to discern not only their own roles but the roles or truth of other elements whose full significance may not in fact be acted out until late in the play.

In a similar way, Augustine envisions God as unfolding the drama of creation by involving, in a delighted sharing and wondering praise, those creatures who can play a role in bringing the truth of other creatures into fullness. Indeed Augustine sees the pattern of darkness and light in the Genesis account as a continuing reflection of this creative unfolding; it marks the transition from dark and inkling knowing of things to an illuminated appreciation of things as their truth radiates from the Word into creaturely minds capable of sharing that rationale, fostering it, and bearing it back again to the Creator in praise. In Augustine's view, the paradigm case of such an illuminated appreciation and praiseful nurture of the creation is the company of intelligent spirits called angels. Each of these spiritual intelligences, at the moment of its own creation, passes from the darkness of unformed non-existence into light and so turns to reflect in intelligence and praise the "Light that is God, in the contemplation of which it is formed."[28] God continues to unfold the creation and involves the company of angels in each step, so that the repeated transitions from darkness to light signal the recurring delight of the angels:

> Evening of the first day, therefore, is the knowledge spiritual beings have of themselves, inasmuch as they know they are not God. The morning following the evening . . . is the conversion of spiritual beings, by which they direct to the praise of their Creator the gift of their creation, and receive from the Word of God a knowledge of the creature next made, namely the firmament. . . . Then there is the evening of the light, when created intellects know the firmament itself, not in the Word of God as before, but in its own nature.[29]

And then the process repeats itself in the production of the creatures through the sixth "day." In this way, Augustine envisions the whole symphony of creation as unfolding through the recurring theme of angelic sharing in knowledge of the divine plan and bringing, through its intelligent sharing, each phase of the creation into a state of praise or communion with its source.

Augustine then goes on to clarify the nature of this angelic participation in truth (which he says humanity will share fully only in the life to come).

> The holy angels, whose equals we shall be after the resurrection, if to the end we hold to Christ our Way, always behold the face of God and rejoice in his Word, the only-begotten Son, equal to the Father; and in them first of all wisdom was created. They, therefore, without any doubt know all creation . . . and they have this knowledge first in the Word of God Himself, in whom are the eternal reasons of all things made in time, existing in Him through whom all things have been

created. And then they have this knowledge in creation itself, as they look down upon it and refer it to the praise of Him in whose immutable truth they behold, as in the source of all creation, the reasons by which creatures have been made.[30]

For Augustine, the periodicity and rhythm of what will become time itself, the marking of each day by evening and morning, is a *noetic* event; it is the rhythm of creation structured, we might say, almost as liturgical time: a receiving of reality from God, a working out of its material possibilities, and an offering back of the creation to God now conceived and consecrated for praise. Explaining the meaning of "day," Augustine writes:

> That day, which God has made, recurs in connection with His works not by a material passage of time but by spiritual knowledge, when the blessed company of angels contemplate from the beginning in the Word of God the divine decree to create. And thus the work is first produced in their knowledge. . . . After that they know the creature itself in itself, and this is revealed to us where it is said that there was evening. Finally, they refer this knowledge of the creature to the praise of eternal Truth, where they had beheld the form of the work to be produced, and this is the meaning of the statement that it was morning.[31]

In Augustine's view, this rhythm of angelic discernment marks the phases of creaturely duration, and it is always ordered toward praise: "the knowledge angels have does not remain fixed in a creature without their immediately referring it to the praise and love of Him in whom they know not the fact, but the reason, of its creation."[32]

While knowledge of the "fact" of things as they are in themselves corresponds to ordinary human knowing, illumination for Augustine is a provisional human sharing in a higher glimpse (as the angels regularly enjoy) of the eternal "reason" for things. All this should make it abundantly clear that Augustine, who is the great progenitor of Western illumination theory, emphasizes the cosmological context of divine illumination. Whenever human beings are so companioned by the divine Wisdom as to touch, however briefly, the eternal reason of the creatures as expressed in the Word, such acts of knowing are really moments in the shining forth and appreciation of God's creativity, and they are ordered toward the transposition of all creatures into perfect praise. For Augustine this illuminated knowing usually takes the form of a wiser judgment and approbation, a discerning of the real truth of things in virtue of a sense and taste for their eternal reason in the divine Word.

This is not to say that divine illumination simply takes the place of the usual process of experiencing the creatures through the senses and reasoning about them. Bonaventure, for example, clearly argues that illumination is neither a divine infusion that substitutes for ordinary human knowing nor a general influence that merely grounds all "natural" cognitive activity whatsoever; rather, he holds, "there is a third interpretation, a middle position. . . . For certain knowledge, the eternal reason is necessarily involved as the regulative and motivating principle, but certainly not as the sole principle nor in its full clarity."[33] Perhaps we could clarify what Bonaventure means here by the phrase "regulative and motivating principle" if we consider an analogy: if a close friend who is a superb gardener takes you on a visit to the local botanical gardens, her knowledge of things will be a "regulative and motivating principle" for your own perception and understanding; her friendship with you will mediate to you a way of seeing things that is illuminated by her own knowledge. That is, you will not possess her knowledge or see her ideas directly, for they will be the light *by which* you see more deeply into the beauty and reality of the gardens. In this sense her knowledge will be regulative in that it provides a fundamental grammar or structure for seeing and making sense of things by placing them within an overall sense of design. And your friend's genuine joy and delight in the artistry of the gardens motivates within you an echoing sense of pleasure, which in turn inspires a deeper desire to see more fully and understand more completely what you see. As my analogy may have suggested, I think we could ascribe Bonaventure's "regulative" dimension of illumination to the mission of the Word and the "motivating" dimension to the mission of the Holy Spirit.

Divine illumination, we could say, highlights the cosmological and even the soteriological dimensions of every act of knowing. In fact, it might help us move beyond a peculiarly modern, individualized epistemology if we put the emphasis the other way round: divine illumination theory highlights the noetic dimension intrinsic to *God's* creative and salvific activity. It points to the spiritual encounter within which knowing takes place. Both Augustine and Bonaventure speak eloquently of illumination in terms of believers' companionship with Christ, befriending creaturely minds with truth. Christ as the interior teacher, says Bonaventure, "shines forth by means of His most clear species [intelligible forms] upon the obscure species of our understanding. And in this manner, these obscure species, mixed with the darkness of images, are lit up in such a way that the intellect understands."[34] Christ, in whom the truth of all creatures dwells as spoken by the Father, teaches the mind to discern the reality of creatures by imbuing the mind with an intuition of the full truth of creatures *as intended by God* and by opening the mind to that yearning desire (the outpouring of the Holy Spirit) for the creatures to come to their fullness as events of divine communion. So illumination means that creaturely knowledge is brought into the light of the eternal reasons of things, thus preventing it from shrinking and fading into a manipulable form of knowledge (easily suborned by fantasy and ego); divine illumination thus also means that the creature being known by an illuminated intellect is borne up toward its consummate truth as an event of praise and communion (and is therefore freed from becoming a mere object of the knower).

The Mind's Role in the Journey of Truth:
Thinking by Thanking

Now we turn at last to the particular vocation of intelligent creatures, especially the human sort, in the divine sharing of truth. Augustine, Bonaventure, and Thomas Aquinas agree that all human capacity to think and make judgments is given by God (God is the light by means of which the mind "sees" as the eyes see by the light of the sun, and so on).[35] But, in their different ways, they all also emphasize the particular vocation of human knowers, who *unite the material creation with the intelligible in every act of understanding*. As Thomas puts it in very clear fashion at *Summa Theologiae* 1.84.5:

> When, therefore, the question is asked: Does the human soul know all things in the eternal types [i.e., God's "ideas" of all things]? we must reply that one thing is said to be known in another in two ways. First, as in an object itself known. . . . In this way the soul, in the present state of life, cannot see all things in the eternal types; but the blessed who see God, and all things in Him, thus know all things in the eternal types. Secondly, one thing is said to be known in another as in a principle of knowledge: thus we might say that we see in the sun what we see by the [light shining from the] sun. And thus we must needs say that the human soul knows all things in the eternal types, since by participation of these types we know all things. For the intellectual light itself which is in us, is nothing else than a participated likeness of the uncreated light in which are contained the eternal types. . . . But since besides the intellectual light which is in us, intelligible species, which are derived from things, are required in order for us to have knowledge of material things; therefore this same knowledge is not due merely to a participation of the eternal types.

Thomas's nuanced treatment here underlines two points: first, it is in virtue of the ceaseless outpouring of the divine ideas in the trinitarian processions that there *is* any power of knowing whatsoever, within which a creaturely mind is called to participate; and second, while the blessed in the life to come enjoy this vision of all reality directly in God's knowing and loving of it, human creatures who are still wayfaring in the present life have a particular function to serve. For the human knower in this world is both called toward pure intelligence and also capable of appreciating the material stuff in which God has chosen to express some of this intelligence. Human knowers, as Thomas says, may be open to the "intellectual light," but unless there is some *thing* in the mind's eye (the mental image or "intelligible species"), the intellectual light will do no good. It would be like a shaft of light in a room, a light one only notices as it illuminates objects that come into it.

So human knowers have this function of gazing at an actual, particular, material rose, for example, and the rose passes into the mind's thoughts by stimulating and awakening and organizing the mind's activity to create an intelligible presence of the rose in the knower. Doubtless this may be analyzed in terms of previous experiences of roses, and the underlying neuronal patterning, and so on. But obviously, as Thomas and many others have pointed out, the rose as present in the mind cannot be the physical or material rose as such, or the brain is going to have a painfully thorny encounter; the material rose, we could say, speaks a word to the human mind, awakening it into a mental image of the rose.[36] But as the mind thinks this rose, it sees the rose as more than mere color and form stimulation; it is able to see it *as a rose* because the knower is part of a world in which such plants grow, and various cultures have prized and spoken of them, given them as signs of love, and so forth.

We could say this is the historical-cultural "light" that illuminates the mind to see the beautiful color and shape as "rose" with all that this may have come to signify. The theory of divine illumination, as we have seen, would go on to say in analogous fashion that there is yet a *more* intense and radiant "light" able to illuminate even more significance to the rose if—and this is a crucial if—the would-be knower is open to this deepest truth of rose not only in terms of its truth within human communities but in terms of its truth as an event within the divine communion itself. The fact is, say Augustine, Bonaventure, and Thomas, that human beings *can* choose only to know things in the dimmer, thinner way, just enough to make use of things. And while that may be sufficient for some purposes, it is not all there is to things nor is it sufficient for God's purposes. Why? Because it does not suffice to realize the full truth of knowable creatures, and it does not suffice to realize the beatitude of creatures who can know.

Thomas and Bonaventure both accept Augustine's view that the mind opens to greater illumination as it moves from simply knowing creatures to contemplating them, from knowledge as *scientia* (analytical certainty) to knowledge as *sapientia* (wisdom resting in the divine ideas of things).[37] But Augustine is not simply adopting the Aristotelian distinction (from book VI of the *Nicomachean Ethics*) between knowledge and wisdom; he is inspecting its moral undertones. And he suspects (as we saw in chapter 8) that the mind has a tendency, when it settles for purely analytical or technical knowledge, to know things concupiscently and slightingly, and to slide into partiality and bias.

This narrowness of view, prompting anxiety, self-preoccupation, and resentment of others, is precisely what, in Augustine's view, the church's common faith works to undo. By giving the human mind something temporal and graspable, it satisfies the tendencies of animal sense for something tangible, but because the common faith holds within it the inexhaustible mystery of God's incarnate life, it conducts the mind out of its fear and isolation and into the trusting delight of a shared presence to God. Augustine's life of faith "aims at obtaining those inner and higher things that are not possessed privately but in common by all who love them, possessed in a chaste embrace without any limitations or envy."[38] And what are such "higher things" that can be enjoyed even as they open up into inexhaustible mystery? The truth of creatures as they are released from small-minded knowing and borne up through praise and thanks into the divine archetypes. Such an illuminated and discerning form of thought would not only conduct the knower toward the beatific vision which is its true end but foster the journey of the creatures toward their own consummate forms of truthful being—precisely because it is a knowing of things, as Augustine says, "in a chaste embrace without any limitations or envy," a knowing opened up to the infinitely shared joy of their intended life in God.

Perhaps what all this is getting at is the idea that human being is a creature which can realize (in the fullest sense of the word) sheer existence as an act of personal freedom, potentially as an act of communion. Humanity's possibility and vocation would thus include bearing other creatures up into a state of sharable, communicable existence by knowing them not as private objects but as elements in a common language, a common life. In this sense, humanity's vocation is to intensify and realize the *relationality* intrinsic to creaturely existence in virtue of its creation from the self-sharing of divine Persons. Humanity can do this insofar as it is capable of discerning the inherent sign-fullness, the *logikos*-quality, of the creatures and then offering the creaturely "words" in a conversation of praise and thanksgiving. In Catherine of Siena's *Dialogue,* God says that the other creatures have been ordered to the service of humanity precisely so that humanity can serve the creatures by bringing them to God: "You who have the gift of reason were made not for yourselves but for me, to serve me with all your heart and all your love. So when you are drawn to me, everything is drawn with you, because everything was made for you."[39]

Similarly, Catherine's Dominican forebear Thomas Aquinas distinguishes (see *ST* 1.73.1) a first perfection of things (the wholeness of their essence) from their final perfection, which is the end for which they exist: "Now the final perfection, which is the end of the whole universe, is the perfect beatitude of the Saints at the consummation of the world." And for Thomas this final perfection is planned by God so as to include all the creatures as they are lifted up into *communal* praise by the intelligent creatures. One way of thinking about this for Thomas is to contrast the isolated individuality of a thing as it exists materially with the more communal communicability (or sociality) of a thing as it exists intelligibly (in the minds of those who know it). The former state is less than ultimately perfect, says Thomas, because each thing existing in material individuality is only "a part of the perfection of the entire universe, which arises from the sum total of the perfections of all individual things."[40]

But as we have seen, there is a remedy for this: things can exist intelligibly in those who know them, and indeed intellectual creatures can hold together a vast variety of creatures in the unity of knowing. Or as Bonaventure puts it, before the Fall, human being "had the knowledge of created things and through their significance, was carried up to God, to praise, worship, and love Him. This is what creatures are for, *and this is how they are led back to God.*"[41] (After the Fall, Bonaventure adds, Scripture is necessary to illuminate the symbolic reality of the creatures.) The crucial point here is that things "are led back to God" precisely through the discerning of the human mind, perceiving and praising in the creatures the intelligible self-sharing of the trinitarian life. The intelligible existence of creatures as they are known and cherished, received as divine gifts, complements their material existence and makes it possible for them to enter into a state of communion.

I believe I can best bring out the full integrity and comprehensiveness of this perspective by returning to a figure I introduced in the first chapter, the remarkable theologian Thomas Traherne (ca. 1637–1674). More amply than almost any other thinker in the Early Modern period, Traherne rediscovers and elucidates for a new era not only the trinitarian resonance of the creatures as events of divine self-sharing communication, but also the human vocation to participate in the truth-faring journey of the creatures into their consummate reality.[42]

Sometimes the young cleric and poet imagines what the world must have looked like to the innocent eyes of Adam and Eve in Eden. He delights at the very thought of the freshness and splendor that would meet them on every side; and in order to bring home to himself and his readers the power of such a vision, he recalls its vestigial form: that is, the innocent eye of his own childhood perception of the world: "Those pure and virgin apprehensions I had from the womb, and that divine light wherewith I was born are the best unto this day, wherein I can see the Universe. . . . Verily they seem the greatest gifts his wisdom could bestow, for without them all other gifts had been dead and vain."[43] Ignorant of his poverty and of the world's many miseries, Traherne describes his early vision of the world as charged with a divine glory and radiant with a sense of God's love for him. The purity and innocence of this early perception led him to intuit that God had made all things as cherishable gifts and wonders for each person, and indeed that every creature, and especially every human being, was given to every other as a sign of God's love. In perhaps his most famous passage he evokes something of this experience:

> The corn was orient and immortal wheat, which never should be reaped, nor was ever sown. I thought it had stood from everlasting to everlasting. The dust and stones of the street were as precious as gold; the gates were at first the end of the world. The green trees when I saw them first through one of the gates transported and ravished me, their sweetness and unusual beauty made my heart leap, and almost mad with ecstasy, they were such strange and wonderful things. The Men! O what venerable and reverend creatures did the aged seem! Immortal Cherubims! And young men glittering and sparkling Angels, and maids strange seraphic pieces of life and beauty! Boys and girls tumbling in the street, and playing, were moving jewels. I knew not that they were born or should die; but all things abided eternally as they were in their proper places. Eternity was manifest in the Light of the Day, and something infinite behind everything appeared: which talked with my expectation and moved my desire. The city seemed to stand in Eden, or to be built in Heaven. (III.3)

It would be easy to appreciate and then pass by this naively childlike rapture, but Traherne's account is resonant with the illumination theory we have been considering. He senses in all things the beauty and bounty of their divine source and seems to recognize in all of them the calling of the divine Creator to fellowship. We will see more clearly later that for Traherne this involves not a relinquishing or *abandoning* of all things in favor of God, but rather the marvelous freedom to embrace all things as themselves, each and every one uniquely, opportunities for communion with the divine Giver of all things.

We could even say that this contemplative form of discernment is a kind of foreshadowing of the beatific vision. It is a partial glimpsing in this life of that state of perfect communion which is the life of heaven, when all acts of sharing, interchange, conversation, and love will be directly and immediately events of the divine life, moments in the eternal knowing and loving that is the life of the Trinity. In Traherne's view, we are all created with an immense desire for this state of perfect and unhindered communion, precisely because God created all things as an act of love and in order to share that love which is God's life. Therefore, says Traherne, our vision, our understanding of reality is to be brought to that fullness of discernment that permits us to rejoice unlimitedly in the joy of others, their perfect sharing in the same felicity that animates our own lives. To see this, to be a part of that giving and receiving of joy one to another, will be heaven itself. As he writes in the *Ethicks*:

> The very sight of other mens Souls, shining in the Acts of their Understanding throughout all Eternity, and extending themselves in the Beams of Love through all Immensity, and thereby transformed (every one of them) into a Sphear of Light comprehending the Heavens, every Angel and every Spirit being a Temple of GODS Omnipresence and Perfection; this alone will be a ravishing Spectacle to that Goodness, which delights to see innumerable Possessors of the Same Kingdome. . . . The Saints on Earth apprehend [the joys of the blessed] in part, and believe them, desire and endeavour after them; they wait with Expectation for the whole, and by certain degrees, as it were in a Glass, enjoy the Image and Reflection of them: As many as they comprehend, they actually delight in: for their love is awakened, and extended to the goodness of all they understand, which it feeds upon by meditation, and turnes into Nourishment, for the Benefit of their Souls, which are made more Great, and Strong, and Vigorous by their Fruitions. But without Love, it is easie to see, that no Goodness can be at all enjoyed.[44]

"Eternity was manifest in the Light of the Day, and something infinite behind everything appeared."

The heart of this unending felicity is a mysterious mutuality: the joy each soul delights in is precisely the happiness it is able to give to others; its glory is the radiance streaming from each other's face. In Traherne's view, heaven is so constituted by divine Wisdom that it exists as every soul lives by "enjoying all, and adding to each others fruition."[45]

Traherne begins his *Ethicks* with a glimpse of this heavenly goal because he believes the most humane form of life is ceaselessly moving toward that divine communion, opening more and more of every thought and deed to the illumination of that end for which all things were created. Doing this, he believes, leads to two integrally related effects: we begin to permit the true rationale and natural orientation of all things to shine through and by doing so take our share in that life of mutual rejoicing. The saints, says Traherne just above, catch a partial glimpse of this and are even now nourished by it and feed upon it by meditation. We might say that Traherne joins Thomas and the other writers we have considered in this chapter by permitting a beatific light to illumine the present, ordering all things toward their end by bathing them even now in the light of God's intentions. But of course Traherne knows that the world looks at itself quite differently, and it is to his analysis of that less generous eye we must now turn.

The early light of his childhood, says Traherne, was eclipsed "by the customs and manners of men, which like contrary winds blew it out: by an innumerable company of other objects, rude, vulgar, and worthless things" (*Centuries* III.7). Whereas Traherne felt himself born with the intuition that the heavens and earth were filled with God's glory and given to him as a living treasure, the mean and grasping smallness of his daily life in childhood seemed almost unconsciously to quench his sense of the greater goodness all around him "and at last all the celestial great and stable treasures to which I was born, [were] as wholly forgotten, as if they had never been" (ibid.). It was as if the small desires of those around him taught his own heart to desire after the same manner, and so to become oblivious to the far greater gifts poured out on every side. The poisonous paradox of this new way of seeing reality was that (as Augustine feared) it taught Traherne to desire more and more, to want his own, to possess something separately for himself, but all the while he learned to prize such things, his grasp tightened on an ever smaller and meaner possession: "So I began among my play-fellows to prize a drum, a fine coat, a penny, a gilded book, &c., who before had never dreamed of any such wealth. Goodly objects to drown all the knowledge of Heaven and Earth! As for the Heavens and the Sun and the Stars they disappeared, and were no more to me than the bare walls" (*Centuries* III.10). It is worth noting that Traherne describes this process as not simply misperceiving the divine gifts of the creation, but as actually growing oblivious to them, unable any longer to discern the presence of so generous a giver in gifts that were too prodigiously abundant to be recognized.

Traherne confirms the strange degenerative impact this deflection of desire had upon his mind. Speaking about the desperate quest to keep up with fashion and other people's wealth, attire, and possessions, he comments:

> You would not think how these barbarous inventions spoil your knowledge. They put grubs and worms into men's heads that are enemies to all pure and true apprehensions, and eat out all their happiness. They make it impossible for them, in whom they reign, to believe there is any excellency in the Works of God, or to taste any sweetness in the nobility of Nature, or to prize any common, though never so great a blessing. They alienate men from the Life of God, and at last make them to live without God in the World. (*Centuries* III.13)

There is a vital link in Traherne between our ability to perceive the truth and reality of life and our ability to receive life gratuitously. We cannot really perceive things as they *are* unless we learn to perceive them in the light of the infinite generosity that pours them out to us and us to them. Perhaps a mean desire leads to this inability to perceive the good creation precisely because creation only *exists* fully and completely as the flowing mutual gift of the trinitarian Persons, the delight of the mutual giving and receiving of heaven. Unless the very principles of God's life—the profligate extravagance and infinite self-sharing—have become present in our minds, we do not in fact know how to think about things at all. The world therefore becomes, as Traherne puts it, merely "bare walls," a barren backdrop imperceptible to those whose hearts are set on reality only as it can be possessed for one-self rather than as a means of communion.

I think Traherne is suggesting something like this when he describes his state as being like a "prodigal son feeding upon husks with swine"; his devotion to small possessions and "worthless vanities" has led him to live "among dreams and shadows" (*Centuries* III.14). The unmistakable note of unreality and illusion should alert us to the falling away of the mind from truth. The more the young Traherne pursues the little pleasures instead of the greater gifts of God, the more he feels himself straying into private ego-istic fantasies, stranded in an alien land of "dreams and shadows." His diag-nosis of this strange exile into half-life is telling: "I had utterly forgotten all goodness, bounty, comfort, and glory: which things are the very brightness of the glory of God: for the lack of which therefore He was unknown" (ibid.). These qualities of goodness, bounty, and so on are the "brightness of the glory of God," that is, they are the look, the shining appearance of the divine generosity at the heart of all things; and when the mind has become closed to these principles, it can no longer perceive either the pres-ence of the Giver or the truth of the gifts themselves.

Traherne sees the world as grasping more and more contentiously after less and less. Because humanity has transferred its desire from the vast and endless treasures of God's giving to the small and artificial treasures of its own manufacture, humanity tumbles into an ever shrinking supply of life:

> for having refused those [riches] which God made and taken to them-
> selves treasures of their own, they invented scarce and rare, insufficient,
> hard to be gotten, little, movable and useless treasures. Yet as violently
> pursued them as if they were the most necessary and excellent things in
> the whole world. And though they are all mad, yet having made a com-
> bination they seem wise; and it is a hard matter to persuade them either
> to Truth or Reason. There seemeth to be no way, but theirs. . . . By this
> means, they have let in broils and dissatisfactions into the world, and
> are ready to eat and devour one another: particular and feeble interests,

false proprieties, insatiable longings, fraud, emulation, murmuring and dissension being everywhere seen; theft and pride and danger, and cousenage, envy and contention drowning the peace and beauty of nature, as waters cover the sea. (*Centuries* I.33)

Traherne probes most insightfully here into the systemically functioning illusion that has a hold over the human mind. Because, as he says, "they are all mad" and all follow the same path, there is hardly any voice declaring a different view of the world that they cannot drown out or mock.

Perhaps Traherne's most characteristic insight is the unusual solution he moves toward. He does not propose a rigorous course of self-denial to remake everyone into less of a possessive individualist; rather, Traherne feels himself groping most naturally after the *true* bounty and goodness he had longed for all along and found, unaccountably, to be lacking in his first pursuit of it. He noticed an occasional awakening, as if from a peculiar enchantment: "Sometimes in the midst of these dreams, I should come a little to myself, so far as to feel I wanted something . . . to long after an unknown happiness, to grieve that the World was so empty" (*Centuries* III.15). What he finds himself drawn toward is not a greater self-abnegation but a growing reception of God's bounty, not the extinguishing of his natural desire but the enlarging of it immeasurably. Again, what marks this new growth is a new apprehension of the divine generosity as the "highest reason in all things'" (*Centuries* III.18); this renewed discovery of the inner principle or rationale for everything goes hand in hand with a new understanding of them as gifts poured out freely to him by God and of their own respective truth and reality. All things begin to emerge from the half-light and shadows of his own projections and fantasies of them, and begin to stand in the clear light of God's givingness. I think we have here a fine depiction of the moral and spiritual development that coincides with divine illumination.

Traherne explores this important difference between, on the one hand, seeing everything in a narrow way as instrumental to our own purposes, as something we must either possess or control, and, on the other hand, seeing everything with a more understanding eye, that is, seeing its causes and purposes, seeing it as a beautiful feature of a vast mosaic. This is very similar to Augustine's distinction between seeing the world as a series of things and seeing it as a series of signs, each of which in its own way points to the Creator. This more contemplative vision of things does not in the least disallow our actual enjoyment and indeed use of them for our physical needs, but it does entice us into a far deeper kind of enjoyment of them for their value as signs, sacraments, messages to us from God. In this way, everything has a double availability for us, as meeting our present needs and as drawing us more and more into that heavenly communion that is the real goal of existence.

But, as Traherne points out, this ability of the world to become sacramental, to be the elements of our communion with God, depends upon our willingness to *see* the world as God does, as a gift intended to draw us into friendship, to see the world in the light of God's intentions and goals for it. Traherne makes this contrast with a splendid matter-of-factness by comparing the views of the world held by pigs and by angels:

> The services of things and their excellencies are spiritual: being objects not of the eye, but of the mind: and you more spiritual by how much you esteem them. Pigs eat acorns, but neither consider the sun that gave them life, nor the influences of the heavens by which they were nourished, nor the very root of the tree from whence they came. This being the work of Angels, who in a wide and clear light see even the sea that gave them moisture: And feed upon that acorn spiritually while they know the ends for which it was created, and feast upon all these as upon a World of Joys within it: while to the ignorant swine that eat the shell, it is an empty husk of no taste nor delightful savour. (*Centuries* I.26)

What Traherne is so eager to unveil before his readers is precisely the *greater* bounty available to them by understanding everything in this more contemplative way—that by feeding not only the body's hunger for food but the mind's keenness for truth and the spirit's yearning for communion, the greater goodness deep down within all things becomes all the more available.

When you perceive all things with a grasping and envious eye, says Traherne, you can only see a tiny fragment of their truth and goodness and meaning. But when your mind begins to think about all things in terms of God's gracious design in giving them to you, then a new light is present in your understanding, and it illuminates your mind to see into the depths of things. In one of his most beautiful passages, Traherne formulates nearly the whole of his message in one paragraph:

> You never enjoy the world aright, till you see how a sand exhibiteth the wisdom and power of God: And prize in everything the service which they do you, by manifesting His glory and goodness to your Soul, far more than the visible beauty on their surface, or the material services they can do your body. Wine by its moisture quencheth my thirst, whether I consider it or no: but to see flowing from His love who gave it unto man, quencheth the thirst even of the Holy Angels. To consider it is to drink it spiritually. To rejoice in its diffusion is to be of a public mind. And to take pleasure in all the benefits it doth to all is Heavenly, for so they do in Heaven. To do so, is to be divine and good, and to imitate our Infinite and Eternal Father. (*Centuries* I.27)

Because God has created all things with a purposive intent, that is, to draw the universe into communion with God, all things are (as we saw earlier in this chapter) marked and configured to be intelligible, readable, to other minds capable of grasping purpose and intention. And because that is so, says Traherne, we can not only drink wine with our bodies, but we can drink it spiritually, which in his view is precisely to "consider it," to receive it into our minds and spirits, not, obviously, as a liquid physical substance somehow distilled into the brain but as an intelligible sign, an idea the mind can feed upon, a sacrament of God's love. In so doing, of course, humanity is also fostering in things their consummate truth.

When this happens, says Traherne, we are changed. Because we are beginning to see things as God does, to think about things by means of God's thoughts of them, by means of the original intention or idea of them that God has—because, in other words, God's thinking is beginning to illuminate our thinking, we are also beginning to rejoice in all things in a new way. We no longer see them merely as potential personal possessions but as all the more wonderful precisely because, without diminishing our enjoyment of them in the least, we see that they are poured out for *all*. We "rejoice" in each thing all the more because we rejoice "in its diffusion"; and as this begins to happen we become, ourselves, a little more giving, a little more sharing, a little more animated by the heavenly life, which is entirely a life poured out and given away. To do so is "to imitate our Infinite and Eternal Father," who holds nothing back but pours out everything to the Beloved Son, who likewise does not grasp after his equality with God but empties himself again.

When Traherne discusses the creative activity of God, he encloses it all within the ordering beauty of God's wisdom. In other words, he understands all God's creation to be an ordered expression of God's goodness, to reflect the divine plan in a "logical" manner—much, for example, as a conversation overheard by another person would sound like ordered speech, have recognizable meanings and nuances that another person would also be able to understand and perhaps take part in. God's wisdom in the ordering of creation, says Traherne, is like that; it constantly brings "Light out of Darkness, and Good out of Evil" in such a manner that other beings capable of intelligence should be able to perceive in creation a definite meaning, truth, and intention. And, indeed, Traherne believes that God's design includes an important role for intelligent beings: "Nor would His love endure, but that I also should have a wisdom, whereby I could draw order out of confusion" (*Centuries* III.31). The human and angelic beholders of this divine order are integral features of the universe, for they are, in an image of the divine mind, capable of holding all things together in a whole, of perceiving their interrelationship and beauty. God has created this ordered wholeness by making all his Kingdome one Intire Object, and every Thing in it a Part of that Whole, Relating to all the innumerable Parts, receiving a Beauty from all, & communicating a Beauty to all, even to all objects throughout all Eternity. While every one among millions of Spectators, is endued with an Endless Understanding to see all, and enjoy all in its Relations, Beauties, and Services.[46]

We note here how much significance Traherne accords to the one-in-a-million creature who is capable of understanding the divine harmony and enjoying it. Why is this so important?

Because, says Traherne, the very quintessence of all that the harmonious order of creation reveals is the loving divine *goodness* that has so generously and freely chosen to create such a universe. This divine freedom and generosity pulses within every existent thing as its secret ground and life. And Traherne, following a long tradition in Christian Neoplatonism, holds that it is the very nature of such a freely given goodness to diffuse itself to the widest possible extent:

> It is infinite Wisdome to become infinitely Good and Delightful to others, and for that cause to be infinite in Bounty. For what is infinitely Good is infinitely *Glorious*. And therefore it is, that GOD needing Nothing in himself, gives all Things to others, Gives them in enjoying them, enjoys in Giving them, while his Goodness delights in the Felicity of others, and in being the Felicity of others. For by making them Great and Blessed he magnifieth himself; and by replenishing them increaseth his Treasures.[47]

Several vital points bear working out in this passage, so let me try to articulate Traherne's logic in slightly more pedestrian fashion. First, wisdom always chooses the best, and this would be goodness itself. And, as we have seen, it is the very part of goodness to be unstintingly bountiful. God, by definition, needs nothing at all, need not have created a universe at all; so the fact that creation exists at all is a sign of God's sheer loving gratuity in freely choosing to give existence to what was not and need not be existing. Once we realize that everything is sheer gift, we begin to notice the radiance and glory of the universe, shining with the divine life that gives it being. Now, since God is Goodness itself, it is joy for God to be good to others, to pour the divine life out in a way that rejoices all. And when one in a million of these creatures has the wit to notice this divine glory and rejoice in it, even to seek to imitate it by giving self away in love for others, this is above all a delight for God, for now at last the very image of God is shining forth within creation and the pattern of heavenly life is shown forth upon earth.

What calamity and grievous tragedy then, in Traherne's view, when the creatures, especially those made to reflect the image of God, grow dull and sullen, anxiously oblivious to the divine goodness poured out on every side. It would indeed be like a slide back into chaos, as the joyful giving and receiving that is the very structure of all existence becomes frozen and atrophies into grudging envy and possessive strife. The very freedom and loving generosity by which God called the universe into being must be woven again back into the fabric of the whole. And this, according to Traherne, is what the Incarnation and Passion of the Word accomplishes. In Jesus, we see in historically visible form this same eternal act of self-outpouring love by which God created all and longs to give all. Traherne connects his readers with Christ's self-giving in two ways: first, he straightforwardly argues, "Is not he an object of infinite Love for whom our Saviour died?" (*Centuries* II.34), so the infinite worth of every human being is proved by the price God willingly pays for our reconciliation. Second, Traherne asks us to trace the action of the cross up into its eternal ground in the inner-trinitarian self-sharing life of God: "He through the Eternal Spirit, offered up Himself a sacrifice to God for us. His Eternal Spirit from everlasting offered up itself . . . and He offered up Himself through the Eternal Spirit in time when He was slain upon the Cross" (*Centuries* II.37). So Traherne understands the life of Christ as recreating our capacity to discern the loving heart of God: first by showing us that love on the cross, and second by drawing us up into that loving relationship which is the trinitarian life of God.

In Traherne's view, humankind needs to practice envisioning this eternal divine outpouring in order to recover a truthful vision of the *creaturely* realm. It is no accident, therefore, that he immediately follows his portrayal of God's love at work in the death of Christ with an extended series of reflections (*Centuries* II.39-70) that begins with the eternal loving of the Trinity and reaches out into the midst of creaturely life to discover that same pattern of self-giving love that is the life of heaven. In a manner similar to the writers we have considered earlier in the chapter, Traherne traces this analogy of love between earthly and heavenly life. He sees its basis in the eternal loving of the Father for the Son and says that the Father's love for all creation is in fact eternally included within that loving and begetting of the Person of the Son: "this Person did God by loving us, beget, that He might be the means of all our glory" (II.43). And when this Son comes to dwell within us by the power of the Holy Spirit (II.45), our own capacity to see and love God are recreated: the Son, writes Traherne, "is the means by which the Father loveth, acteth, createth, redeemeth, governeth, and perfecteth all things. And the means also by which we see and love the Father: our strength and our eternity" (II.44). The Son's own capacity to know and love the Father becomes present by the Holy Spirit within us, and this makes possible our own new discernment of all reality; for animated by the same Love with which the Father and the Son know and love each other, we are imbued with their own understanding of all things.

This brings us to the idea of accomplishing the truth through praise, of thinking by thanking. For Traherne suggests that when the mind, imbued with trinitarian principles of understanding, begins to prize all creatures as they should be, then the mind in fact helps to accomplish the ultimate truth of all creatures by lifting them up into communion with God. Traherne places, as we have seen, a great weight on the shift in human knowing that redemption makes possible. His concern is not so much what we see "as with what eyes we beheld them, with what affections we esteemed them" (*Centuries* III.68). Believers grow new eyes and a new heart through Christ, and so come to discover that "all objects are in God Eternal: which we by perfecting our faculties are made to enjoy" (ibid.). We have to remember here that for Traherne all things were created as signs of God's love and as gifts to rejoice the recipients and the giver too. So the fulfillment of each thing can only be as it is esteemed as a gift from God, received and delighted in; otherwise it is simply a mute object without meaning. "What are the cattle upon a thousand hills," asks Traherne, "but carcasses, without creatures that can rejoice in God and enjoy them" (*Centuries* III.82). When believers learn to know things according to God's idea of them and to rejoice in the gift of them and to praise God for that gift, they are lifting up those existing things into the flowing of giving and receiving, praise and delight, that is the life of God. In other words, knowing the truth of reality by praising God for it actually transmutes each creature into its highest form of existence; it becomes an event of eternal joy:

> Praises are the breathings of interior love, the marks and symptoms of a happy life, overflowing gratitude, returning benefits, an oblation of the soul, and the heart ascending upon the wings of divine affection to the Throne of God. God is a Spirit and cannot feed upon carcasses: but He can be delighted with thanksgivings, and is infinitely pleased with the emanations of our joy. (*Centuries* III.82)

It is the special vocation of creatures with intelligence, who can choose to love freely, to recognize the gift of God's love in all creation, to receive it and delight in it, and so to rejoice the divine Giver who adores the happiness of all his creatures. Only the mind can reach out to so many things, holding them all together in the imagination, esteeming them, and praising God for them. And in so doing, the creatures gifted with intelligence fulfill themselves as well as all those things they know with appreciation. As Traherne writes: "The idea of Heaven and Earth in the Soul of Man is more precious with God than the things themselves and more excellent in nature" (*Centuries* II.90).

Perhaps it is a little hard for us to imagine quite what Traherne, along with Augustine, Maximus, Bonaventure, and Aquinas, has in mind with all this. We are so very used to thinking of things purely in their merely physical form. Our most successful way of thinking in the modern era has been, indeed, to think about things reductively, to break them down to their chemical structures or their subatomic events and so derive great powers from them, harnessing them to our needs. Traherne was writing at the very dawn of this era in modern science, and in many ways he would rejoice that we have so far penetrated into the deeper level of gifts that God pours out to us in all the creatures. But I think Traherne would also remind us that humanity will never understand the world aright so long as we limit ourselves to a merely reductive reading of things:

> The world within you [i.e., as intelligible, as thought] is an offering returned, which is infinitely more acceptable to God Almighty, since it came from Him, that it might return unto Him. Wherein the mystery is great. For God hath made you able to create worlds in your own mind which are more precious to Him than those which He created; and to give and offer up the world unto Him, which is very delightful in flowing from Him, but much more in returning to Him. (*Centuries* II.90)

By lifting up all things in the act of praise, the mind is able to translate them, so to speak, back into their native tongue, which is the language of pure giving and receiving. In so doing, believers receive these things as gifts, know the deepest truth of them, and delight God who created them to be enjoyed. Things are no longer things, but moments of relationship, events in the life of heaven begun on earth. Translated into praise, the world "is a valley of vision, wherein you see the Blessed Sight of all men's praises ascending, and of all God's blessings coming down upon them" (*Centuries* II.94). Such events in the life of truth have become translucent to the divine knowing and loving from which all truth springs.

Admittedly this beatific conception of truth is painfully eschatological; for the present it is purely a matter of hope. Nonetheless, I think theology might legitimately claim that this is the direction in which knowing is headed. Herbert McCabe remarks regarding the relationship in Aquinas of human understanding to the beatific vision:

> It is an important theme of Question 12 [of the Prima Pars] that when, in beatitude, a man understands the essence of God, the mind is not realized by a form which is a likeness of God, but by God himself. God will not simply be an object of our minds, but the actual life by which our minds are what they will have become.[48]

Or as the same author puts it in respect of the social dimensions of knowing all things in God:

Christ is, indeed, to be found in the present but precisely as what is rejected by the present world, in the poor and despised and oppressed, he is to be found in those who *unmask* the present world, those in whom the meaninglessness and inhumanity and contradictions of our society are exposed. Christ will only be, so to say, at home in the world, in the kingdom of the future: it will then be possible to express the exchange of love which is God directly with our bodily lives, simply as our human existence, in the language of what will then be the present. Until then the exchange of love, the Holy Spirit, between men is expressed in the language of the future: and this is what the sacraments are.[49]

In these two passages the crucial points for our purposes are the same: that the ultimate state of knowing is one in which God is the primal knowing subject in whose act we participate, and that this divine act by which God is God, knows and loves God, is an exchange of love which can only take place in human terms by means of the loving interactions of communal life. The truth of it far exceeds the capacity of any individual.

The Communal Life of Truth

The most obvious theological term for this communal life-ordered-to-God (at least in the present world) is church. If the church lives as the sacrament of this deep communion that Jesus makes possible among and between the members, then perhaps we can search for clues there to the communal realization of truth. How does God bring God's truth to expression in the church's common life? How does God voice the divine self-understanding in the patterns and rhythms of church? As I suggested earlier in this chapter, we might consider the resurrection as a means by which God draws the world, through the church's life, into a new participation in truth. Rowan Williams reflects:

The community of the Spirit is the place where the context and meaning of the human world is identified concretely as Jesus with his Father and his Spirit. It is not . . . that there is no meaningful life beyond the community; but here it is named, and in becoming identifiable becomes more readily communicable. Christian faith and the life of the Church offers humanity a language in which to speak of its ground and its aspiration.[50]

It seems important here that this "language" in which the world can come to understand its truth is a language of mutual self-sharing. That is, it's a creative practice of life that allows reality to become translucent, illuminated by the light from which it springs: the absolute self-sharing of the trinitarian life.

It is that practice of letting loose into the world the infinity of divine life that takes what is world and holds it out now marked with a sign, and this makes the world communicable, conversable, knowable. Jesus draws the disciples, a part of the world, into a new network of relations and practices that pour out his life. In doing this, Jesus is allowing the world to think again in a new way, not so much in terms of ideas as mental objects, but precisely by means of the practices that structure its life—a sign of the way that God knows and loves Godself not as a series of truths but by the eternal *relational patterns* of the trinitarian life. I am arguing, then, that the church is engaged in a profoundly noetic act when it takes world and makes signs with it by offering it and naming it as a means of divine self-sharing.

Perhaps an analogy would help here: think of the play in a poem between, on one hand, the meaning of particular *words,* and, on the other hand, the overall *structure* of meter, rhythm, and rhyme in which the particular words subsist. It is true that we can partially know the poem by knowing the definition of individual words, but there is another kind of knowing that takes place as we begin to sense the relations between the words, the patterns in which the words are flowing. We could say that this structural sensibility comes to inhabit our knowing minds, and it is undoubtedly noetically laden, not so much as a knowledge of objects "out there" but as a way of thinking and sensing that permits us to apprehend the objects (the particular words) in a whole new horizon of significance.

My hunch is that churchly knowing is more like that background structural sensibility, a sense of the relations and patterns by means of which the meaning of anything can come to expression. But of course in the case of the church these patterns are patterns, among others, of prayer, sacramental life, forgiveness, repentance, and communion. The church's life has very definite rhythms and structures, to be sure, but, on this reading, these practices are not meant to function as barricades that cut off the world; on the contrary, they are, precisely in all their particularity, the framework of signs within which the world should be able to commune with itself in love and peace, to recognize and enact its true calling toward God's universal desire for communion with all. Perhaps we could think of this liturgical knowing as a more overtly communal form of the divine illumination we examined earlier; "objects" of the world are taken and offered within a context that permits their full truth as divine gifts to become radically available.

Whatever kind of knowing takes place in the act of being church, it is going to be a knowing that is eventful, that happens, that takes place in practice and activity, and yet for all that is a real form of knowledge. Furthermore, because it is a knowing that is intrinsically a communal activity, it must in some sense be an intrinsically sharable reality that we are coming to know—not a reality that is accidentally sharable, but rather a reality so fundamentally constituted by its intrinsic sharability that it cannot be known other than by participating in sharable life: love comes to mind. The church exists, on this view, as the activity wherein this love enacts unashamedly in public the hidden pattern of its presence in all the world. In what ways might it be true to say, then, that the church exists (or is called to exist) as the place where the distorted patterns of the world's life are reconfigured according to Jesus' relationship with the Father? Or, to put it another way, how might the church make Eucharist of the world if its activity is sanctified and made fruitful by the Holy Spirit?

Few Christian writers have explored this theme of ecclesial noetics more creatively than Maximus the Confessor.[51] He consistently reinterprets the Alexandrian metaphysics of contemplation by the redemptive work of Christ, and he analyzes the church's life as the very means whereby the world is able to know itself truly again, reconciled in Christ. In *The Church's Mystagogy,* Maximus envisages the church as a community of formation. Maximus is especially instructive in this regard for he focuses our attention on the church as sign-making and sign-reading (actions of inherently noetic significance), and suggests that this is constitutive of the church's life: the church is church precisely insofar as it enacts authentically the sign of God's reconciling love.

> *My hunch is that churchly knowing is more like that background structural sensibility, a sense of the relations and patterns by means of which the meaning of anything can come to expression.*

What is the scene in which this churchly noesis is set? Throughout his works, Maximus (drawing on Gregory of Nyssa) suggests that the wonderful variety and differentiated quality of the creation, so multisplendored and evocative of divine glory, has been unable to grow up into its full potential. Its differences, because of a terrible failure in human will, have hardened into painful divisions, rivalries, and mutual recriminations. The problem, argues Maximus, is that "the human person is not moved naturally, as it was fashioned to do, around the unmoved, that is its own beginning (I mean God), but contrary to nature is voluntarily moved in ignorance around those things that are beneath it."[52] This desire to possess the created order by itself instead of enjoying all things in union with God has had the effect of weakening the human being, addicting the will to objects instead of setting it free for the whole. And because humanity "has abused the natural power of uniting what is divided," it is no longer able even to see or desire the whole, the unity, of things.[53]

Yet Maximus suggests further that the very Word who echoes throughout all the particularities of the created order reaches across the differences-become-divisions and draws all things to unity in himself. In the *Mystagogy* Maximus presents the church as nothing less than the ongoing communal event of Christ's reconciling activity. Adopting the genre of a mystical interpretation of the liturgy, Maximus portrays the inherently eucharistic quality of ecclesial existence: a gathering of the diverse and alienated world into a communal act of adoration and participation in the trinitarian self-offering and self-sharing. Maximus himself is at pains to show that what he has in mind is precisely *not* a vicious conformism in which individual differences are dismissed; for him, the whole point of ecclesial life is the nurturing of a way of understanding that permits each creaturely mind to grow into its own particular fullness by rediscovering its joyful kinship with all other creatures in Christ. And this kinship requires a relationality and diversity that are neither homogenized nor hardened into division. So we might say that it is this communal expansion of mind, this opening up to the recognition of the whole creation knit together through God in Christ, that is the characteristic action of ecclesial life.

This is not the place to give an exposition of the *Mystagogy* in its entirety, so let me simply draw attention to some especially thought-provoking points.[54] The first five chapters of the *Mystagogy* illustrate a prying open of the mind to the divine universality. Maximus regularly contrasts the way things appear in the world we have made with the new way we come to understand things as a result of the ecclesial patterning of our lives:

> On the basis of this surface appearance of things there has developed a perpetual war of these things with each other to the mutual destruction of all since everything is destroying each other and being destroyed in each other, and the only result is that they are unstable and perish and are never able to meet each other in a tranquil and secure situation. (204)

In the world, we see things only in terms of rivalry and mutual antagonism, but the Body of Christ exists in order to build up a new communal structure for the world's life, a patterning that reflects the mode of divine *self-sharing* life and therefore allows every creature "to meet each other in a tranquil and secure situation."

How does Maximus think this comes about? He argues that "the holy Church bears the imprint and image (*eikon*) of God since it has the same activity (*energeia*) as he does by imitation and figure" (186). The particular divine activity Maximus has in mind is importantly trinitarian; that is, it is a unifying power of freedom and love that permits true otherness to exist and fosters true unity without effacing difference. Near the end of the *Mystagogy*, Maximus shows how this trinitarian pattern of life has in fact been the deep structure gradually incarnating itself more radiantly in the church's life and understanding.[55] So the church becomes the place where God's unifying activity throughout the world becomes once again visible in the world. God is seen making each creature "converge in each other by the singular force of their relationship to him" (186), and this relationship of each creature to the other *by virtue of their mutual relationship to God* releases them from the lethally rivalrous relationships of each creature directly with others:

> This reality [their new relationship to each other through relationship to God] abolishes and dims all their particular relations considered according to each one's nature, but not by dissolving or destroying them or putting an end to their existence. Rather it does so by transcending them and revealing them, as the whole reveals its parts. (186).

Here Maximus's special use of an important trinitarian terminological distinction becomes extremely helpful. This is the distinction between nature (or essence), on the one hand, and a particular *mode* of existence or personal identity on the other. The world has set up conditions which distort each creature, forcing it to live out a stunted personal identity that can barely move beyond the conditions of its nature because it has been taught to see every other creature as a destructive threat to its own existence. And, says Maximus in the passage just quoted, God's activity is precisely to *release* the creatures from "their particular relations considered according to each one's nature." The creatures are going to discover God bringing about relationships among them based not on the necessarily self-preserving instincts of *nature* but based on the development of *persons* whose identities are given in God. The mutually antagonistic constraints of nature are superceded by the new economy of divine abundance, self-sharing relationality, in which the creatures can come out of themselves in love for God and discover themselves and each other through the gift of freedom and love. This sets up a divine pattern of life subverting the world's structures, a heavenly pattern in which a completely new mode of relation and personal identity can come to birth in the matrix of the divine unifying power. In other words, the relationships of all creatures to themselves and to each other are now grounded no longer on their own biological necessities and divisions but on God's own unifying life.

And this, says Maximus, is exactly what the church exists to make possible, "working for us the same effects as God":

> For numerous and of almost infinite number are the men, women, and children who are distinct from one another and vastly different by birth and appearance, by nationality and language, by customs and age, by opinions and skills, by manners and habits, by pursuits and studies, and still again by reputation, fortune, characteristics, and connections: All are born into the Church and through it are reborn and

recreated in the Spirit. To all in equal measure it gives and bestows one divine form and designation, to be Christ's and to carry his name. . . . The purpose of this is so that the creations and products of the one God be in no way strangers and enemies to one another by having no reason or center for which they might show each other any friendly or peaceful sentiment or identity, and not run the risk of having their being separated from God to dissolve into nonbeing. Thus, as has been said, the holy Church of God is an image of God because it realizes the same union of the faithful with God. As different as they are by language, places, and customs, they are made one by it through faith. (187-88)

The church's pattern of life is meant to be iconic of God's relational unity. The church's activity, articulated in visible symbolic form liturgically, becomes a communal event of contemplation in which the unity of all creatures in Christ begins to appear as the very heart of the world's true life. In Maximus's view this would make possible a new relationship among all creatures in which they see each other no longer as enemies but friends, no longer threatened by the mutual necessity of self-making.

Maximus reaches a climax in his description of the church's transforming life by illuminating the analogies between church and human person. Just as an individual is brought to a new freedom and relational personhood by contemplating the reconciling embrace of God in Christ, so the church reaches out to a new ecstatic wholeness beyond the mere sum of its parts. The church understands and sees into divisions in a way that is able to overcome alienation and recover genuine and fruitful difference. But since this new understanding of difference is not a merely mental operation for the church, but a painful yet joyful communal activity of repentance and reconciliation, the knowledge that the church gains of the divine reality is not merely notional.

As the church suffers through its work of bearing about in its body the healing and reconciling wounds of Christ, allowing the Spirit to knit all things together in him, the church is actually coming to know in itself, in the patterns of its own existence (symbolically enacted in the liturgy), the very principles or *logoi* that are the true meanings of each creature, the true shining forth of the divine loving which they are. As this happens, Maximus suggests, the church is functioning like a soul that has at last become unified and "centered on itself and on God," and in such a case it exists more personally, more fully actualized than ever, "because its head is crowned by the first and only unique Word and God" (194). The Incarnate Word's reconciling pattern of life, his identity, his personhood, has become the personal identity of this corporate reality, the church. This is a crucial moment, says Maximus:

It is in him as the Creator and Maker of beings that all the principles (*logoi*) of things both are and subsist as one in an incomprehensible simplicity. Gazing with a simple understanding on him who is not outside it [the soul/church]but thoroughly in the whole of reality, it will itself understand the principles of beings and the causes why it was distracted by divisive pursuits before being espoused to the Word of God. (194-95)

This is the church's knowing which is at the same time the church's life, holding all things together in contemplation and oblation through the One by whom and through whom they were made.

This in Maximus's judgment is a form of understanding that sets each creature free to be itself at last because it is no longer seen only partially, possessively, according to "divisive pursuits," as he puts it; instead every creature is seen and newly named and claimed, blessed and offered, in the church's life as it truly *is*, a particular sign of God's self-giving life. The church's mind is "made up," consummated, at the altar: "All of these things it gathers together for the mystery accomplished on the divine altar" (195). There the church brings all its encounters with every creature, and prays for them and itself, holding the world open to that transfiguring participation in God's life which reveals the truth of all things as God's holy gifts.

The church is actually coming to know in itself, in the patterns of its own existence, the very principles or logoi *that are the true meanings of each creature.*

From their first encounter with the crucified and risen Jesus, believers have been drawn into a worshiping community where truth has given itself to be known in the creation of a new life together. Spiritual discernment has arisen naturally and most necessarily for such a common life, because it reflects the pressure of a living truth—refusing partiality and bias, pushing beyond individual understanding, opening the discerning community to the creative, self-sharing life from which all truth springs. Discerning truth could never be a lonely form of life. The truth humanity hungers for seems far too large a feast for solitary diners. It requires a sharing far too joyful for any but the truly wise. For they alone discern the depth of thanks most justly due so great a giver. Knowing the giver in each gift, they are themselves set free from small desires and awake to God's desire in every thing; they discern its truth in praise.

Notes

Notes to Chapter One

1. John Bunyan, *The Pilgrim's Progress*, ed. N. H. Keeble, Oxford World Classics (Oxford: Oxford University Press, 1998), 98.

2. Ibid., 100.

3. Romans 1:20. All biblical citations are from the New Revised Standard Version of The Holy Bible (Division of Christian Education of the National Council of Churches, 1989) and will be noted parenthetically in the text.

4. For a mild and benign example of this, obviously growing slightly puzzled at the lack of traction provided by the standard neoscholastic categorizations, see Paschal Boland, *The Concept of Discretio Spirituum in John Gerson's "De Probatione Spirituum" and "De Distinctione Verarum Visionum A Falsis"* (Washington, D.C.: Catholic University of America Press, 1959). The author carefully sets forth the leading definitions and categorizations of such eminent figures as R. Garrigou-Lagrange and J. De Guibert in his second chapter, but as he analyzes the actual texts of Gerson, the distinctions seem to shed less light than one might have hoped. For a perceptive early critique of such an approach, see the article of Sister Augusta M. Raabe, "Discernment of Spirits in the Prologue to the Rule of Benedict," *American Benedictine Review* 23 (1972): 397-423.

5. Bunyan, *Pilgrim's Progress*, 131.

6. The literature on the so-called signs-source and its theological elaboration in John is enormous. For an older but still helpfully comprehensive analysis, see R. Schnackenburg, *The Gospel According to St. John*, vol. 1, *Introduction and Commentary on Chapters 1–4*, trans. Kevin Smith (London: Burns & Oates, 1980).

7. More complete bibliography for Traherne will be given in chapter 9, but a very fine introduction can be found in *Thomas Traherne: Poetry and Prose*, selected and introduced by Denise Inge (London: SPCK, 2002). I am gratefully indebted to Dr. Inge for her advice about Traherne and also to Canon A. M. Allchin for many encouraging and insight-bestowing conversations.

8. Thomas Traherne, *Centuries* (Oxford: Clarendon Press, 1960; reprint, Oxford: A. R. Mowbray, 1985), 28-29. The *Centuries* are in five books and numbered entries; the passage just quoted is from I.58-60. References will hereafter be given by book and numbered entry parenthetically in the text.

9. Jacques Guillet, in the biblical section of the article on "Discernement des Esprits" in the *Dictionnaire de Spiritualité*, vol. 111, cols. 1222-91; quoted in the English translation: Jacques Guillet, Gustave Bardy, Francois Vandenbroucke, Joseph Pegon, Henri Martin, *Discernment of Spirits*, trans. Innocentia Richards (Collegeville, Minn.: Liturgical Press, 1970), 17-18. See also Martin McNamara,

"Discernment Criteria in Israel: True and False Prophets" in *Discernment of the Spirit and of Spirits,* ed. Casiano Floristan and Christian Duquoc (New York: Seabury, 1979), 3-13.

10. For an insightful commentary, see Ellen F. Davis, *Proverbs, Ecclesiastes, and the Song of Songs,* Westminster Bible Companion (Louisville, Ky.: Westminster John Knox, 2000).

11. Surveying the theme of wisdom in the gospels, Stephen C. Barton comments with respect to Matthew (but perhaps *mutatis mutandis* of John): "divine wisdom is the fruit of being in a filial relationship with God, a relationship characterised on the human side by specific moral-religious qualities such as humility, obedience and trust. It is the fruit, in other words, of a way of life and a pattern of faithfulness" (Stephen C. Barton, "Gospel Wisdom" in Stephen C. Barton, ed., *Where Shall Wisdom be Found? Wisdom in the Bible, the Church and the Contemporary World* [Edinburgh: T&T Clark, 1999], 96. In the same volume see also James D. G. Dunn, "Jesus: Teacher of Wisdom or Wisdom Incarnate?" pp. 75-92).

Notes to Chapter Two

1. Joseph T. Lienhard, S.J., "On 'Discernment of Spirits' in the Early Church," *Theological Studies* 41/3 (September 1980): 505-29, here pp. 528-29.

2. Ibid. Lienhard concludes his study with the helpful summary: "the term 'discernment of spirits' was in use as long as the spirits were understood to be personal; in this period, too, discernment of spirits was looked upon as a charism given only to some, not to all. Once attention was turned to the working of the psyche, particularly by Evagrius Ponticus, the phrase was shortened and discernment became a virtue or technique needed by every ascetic to prevent him from falling victim to excess or bad judgment" (529).

3. Ibid.

4. Ibid.

5. For a good, brief introduction to Origen's life and works, see the very fine introductory chapters (1-4) to Joseph Trigg's translation and study of important texts in Joseph W. Trigg, *Origen,* Early Church Fathers (London and New York: Routledge, 1998). On visiting the martyrs in prison, see p. 14.

6. Origen, *On First Principles,* 3.1.3, trans. G. W. Butterworth (London: SPCK, 1936; reprint, Gloucester, Mass.: Peter Smith, 1973), 159-60.

7. Ibid., 1.6.1, p. 52.

8. Idem, "An Exhortation to Martyrdom," XVIII, in *Origen: An Exhortation to Martyrdom, Prayer, First Principles: Book IV, Prologue to the Commentary on the Song of Songs, Homily XXVII on Numbers,* trans. Rowan A. Greer (Mahwah, N.J.: Paulist Press, 1979), 53.

9. Ibid., 53-54.

10. Idem, *On First Principles,* 1.6.2-3, pp. 55-56.

11. Ibid., 2.11.3, p. 149.

12. Idem, "On Prayer," 13.4 in *Origen,* trans. R. Greer, 107.

13. Ibid., 13.3, p. 106.

14. Idem, "Exhortation to Martyrdom," XXVII, in *Origen,* trans. R. Greer, 59.

15. Idem, *On First Principles,* 2.11.4, p. 149.

16. Ibid., pp. 149-50.

17. Idem., *The Song of Songs: Commentary and Homilies,* trans. R. P. Lawson, Ancient Christian Writers (New York: Newman Press, 1956), 43-44.

18. Ibid., 45.

19. Ibid., 29.

20. Douglas Burton-Christie, *The Word in the Desert: Scripture and the Quest for Holiness in Early Christian Monasticism* (New York and Oxford: Oxford University Press, 1993), 261. See the bibliography in this fine work for both primary and secondary sources.

21. Athanasius, *The Life of St. Antony*, §5, trans. H. Ellershaw, in *Select Writings and Letters of Athanasius, Bishop of Alexandria,* ed. Archibald Robinson, Nicene and Post-Nicene Fathers 4 (reprint ed.; Grand Rapids, Mich.: Eerdmans, 1980), 197.

22. Ibid., §14, p. 200: when those who came out to see Antony wrench off the door of his cell, "Antony, as from a shrine, came forth initiated in the mysteries and filled with the Spirit of God. . . . Through him the Lord healed the bodily ailments of many present, and cleansed others from evil spirits. And he gave grace to Antony in speaking, so that he consoled many that were sorrowful, and set those at variance at one, exhorting all to prefer the love Christ before all that is in the world."

23. Ibid., §22, p. 202.

24. *The Sayings of the Desert Fathers: The Alphabetical Collection,* [Anthony 8], trans. Benedicta Ward (Kalamazoo, Mich.: Cistercian Publications, 1975; rev. ed., 1984), 3.

25. Ibid., Eulogius the Priest 1, pp. 60-61.

26. Ibid., Syncletica 15, p. 233.

27. Ibid., Poemen the Shepherd 35, p. 172.

28. Ibid., John the Dwarf 7, pp. 86-87.

29. Ibid., Nicon 1, p. 156.

30. See the splendid new study by Columba Stewart, *Cassian the Monk* (New York and Oxford: Oxford University Press, 1998); and also the still-valuable work of Owen Chadwick, *John Cassian: A Study in Primitive Monasticism,* 2nd ed. (Cambridge: Cambridge University Press, 1968).

31. John Cassian, *The Conferences,* 2.1.4, trans. Boniface Ramsey, O.P., Ancient Christian Writers (New York: Paulist Press, 1997), 84. References will hereafter be given in the text by book number, chapter, and paragraph.

32. Lienhard, "On 'Discernment of Spirits' in the Early Church," pp. 517-21, makes a similar point, though I sense more than he does a stronger continuing link between differentiation of spirits and the developing emphasis on discretion as a virtue. See also the section on Cassian in F. Dingjan, O.S.B., *Discretio: Les origines patristique et monastiques de la doctrine sur la prudence chez saint Thomas d'Aquin* (Assen: Van Gorcum, 1967), pp. 14-77.

33. For a helpful outline, see the fine introduction by Kallistos Ware in John Climacus, *The Ladder of Divine Ascent,* trans. Colm Luibheid and Norman Russell, Classics of Western Spirituality (New York: Paulist Press, 1982), 12-13. References to the *Ladder* will be given parenthetically by page number of this translation.

34. D. Bogdanović quoted by Ware in the introduction to *Ladder,* trans. Luibheid and Russell, 18.

Notes to Chapter Three

1. For excellent studies of the *Rule* and of Gregory, see chaps.1 and 2 of Bernard McGinn, *The Growth of Mysticism,* vol. 2 of *The Presence of God: A History of Western Christian Mysticism* (New York: Crossroad, 1994).

2. The literature on Bernard is vast; for an excellent starting point and bibliography, see chap. 5 in McGinn, *The Growth of Mysticism.* For Richard of St. Victor,

see the essay by Grover A. Zinn, "The Regular Canons," chap. 9, part IV in *Christian Spirituality I: Origins to the Twelfth Century,* ed. Bernard McGinn, John Meyendorff, and Jean Leclercq (New York: Crossroad, 1987).

3. Bernard of Clairvaux, *On the Song of Songs* 2.23.8, trans. Kilian Walsh, Cistercian Fathers Series (Kalamazoo, Mich.: Cistercian Publications, 1976), 32.

4. Idem, *On the Song of Songs* 3.49.5, trans Kilian Walsh and Irene M. Edmonds, Cistercian Fathers Series (Kalamazoo, Mich.: Cistercian Publications, 1979), 25.

5. Ibid.

6. Idem, *The Parables and the Sentences,* trans. Michael Casey and Francis R. Switek, Cistercian Fathers Series (Kalamazoo, Mich.: Cistercian Publications, 2000), 19-20.

7. Ibid., 20.

8. Ibid., 21.

9. Richard of St. Victor, *The Twelve Patriarchs,* xxix, in *The Twelve Patriarchs, The Mystical Ark, Book Three of the Trinity,* trans. Grover A. Zinn (New York: Paulist Press, 1979), 82. Hereafter citations will be given parenthetically by chapter number.

10. See the very fine introduction by Suzanne Noffke, O.P., to her translation of *The Dialogue,* Classics of Western Spirituality (New York: Paulist Press, 1980). All citations from this text will be cited parenthetically by chapter number. See also the informative doctoral dissertation of Diana Villegas, "A Comparison of Catherine of Siena's and Ignatius of Loyola's Teaching on Discernment" (Ph.D., Fordham University, 1986).

11. Catherine of Siena, *The Letters of Catherine of Siena,* trans. Suzanne Noffke, O.P., vols. 1 and 2 (Tempe, Ariz.: Arizona Center for Medieval and Renaissance Studies, 2000 and 2001), 1.120. All further citations will be given parenthetically by volume and page number in this edition.

12. Suzanne Noffke, trans., *Letters of Catherine of Siena,* 2.507, n. 3.

13. See also the illuminating views of Diana L. Villegas, "Discernment in Catherine of Siena," *Theological Studies* 58 (1997): 19-38, and Sandra M. Schneiders, "Spiritual Discernment in *The Dialogue of Saint Catherine of Siena,*" *Horizons* 9/1 (1982): 47-59.

14. Quotations from *Distinguishing True from False Revelations* will be drawn from Jean Gerson, *Jean Gerson: Early Works,* trans. Brian Patrick McGuire, Classics of Western Spirituality (New York: Paulist Press, 1998) and will be cited by page number in McGuire's edition. Quotations from *Testing the Spirits* will be drawn from the translation of that work given by Paschal Boland, O.S.B., *The Concept of Discretio Spirituum in John Gerson's "De Probatione Spirituum" and "De Distinctione Verarum Visionem A Falsis"* (Washington, D.C.: Catholic University of America Press, 1959) and will be cited by the paragraph numbers given in Boland.

15. *Gerson,* trans. McGuire, 350. Cited parenthetically hereafter.

16. For an illuminating discussion of the dream/sleep arguments in Descartes, see Stephen Menn, *Descartes and Augustine* (Cambridge: Cambridge University Press, 1998), 228ff. Menn also cites the background uses of this dream argument in Plato, *Theaetetus* 158d-e, and Aristotle, *Metaphysics* 4.5 1010b3-11. One could also point to Augustine, *The Trinity* 11.2.

17. For a useful compendium of sources, see *Saint Ignatius of Loyola: Personal Writers,* trans. Joseph A. Munitiz and Philip Endean (London: Penguin Books, 1996). For a definitive annotated translation of the *Spiritual Exercises,* see *The Spiritual Exercises of Saint Ignatius,* trans. George E. Ganss (Chicago: Loyola University Press, 1992). For comprehensive commentary, see the two volumes by Jules J. Toner, *A Commentary on St. Ignatius' Rules for the Discernment of Spirits* (St.

Louis, Mo.: Institute of Jesuit Sources, 1982), and *Discerning God's Will: Ignatius of Loyola's Teaching on Christian Decision Making* (St. Louis, Mo.: Institute of Jesuit Sources, 1991). For good scholarly bibliographies, see the works of Munitiz and Endean, Ganss, and Toner listed above. An insightful theological and historical analysis is given in Hugo Rahner, *Ignatius the Theologian*, trans. Michael Berry (San Francisco: Ignatius Press, 1990), chap. 4. More pastoral in orientation: William A. Barry, *Paying Attention to God: Discernment in Prayer* (Notre Dame, Ind.: Ave Maria Press, 1990); John J. English, *Spiritual Freedom*, 2nd ed. (Chicago: Loyola University Press, 1995); Thomas H. Green, *Weeds among the Wheat: Discernment Where Prayer and Action Meet* (Notre Dame, Ind.: Ave Maria Press, 1984); David Lonsdale, *Listening to the Music of the Spirit: The Art of Discernment* (Notre Dame, Ind.: Ave Maria Press, 1993); Pierre Wolff, *Discernment: The Art of Choosing Well* (Liguori, Mo.: Liguori Publications, 1993).

18. See Ganss, *Spiritual Exercises*, Appendix II, "Toward the Deeper Study of the Foundation," pp. 208ff. This initial deepening sense of the fundamental truth of one's relationship with God is understood by most commentators to be the prime goal of the section [23] of the *Exercises* headed "Principle and Foundation." Ganss, in the section just noted, provides a good sense of the developing interpretation and presentation of this.

19. H. Rahner, *Ignatius the Theologian*, 146; see also p. 154: "the human existence of God is the measure by which to judge the genuineness of any movements in the soul."

20. Toner, *Discerning God's Will*, 95.

21. All quotations from the *Spiritual Exercises* will be cited parenthetically by section number and are taken from Ganss, *The Spiritual Exercises of Saint Ignatius*.

22. Ganss, *Spiritual Exercises*, p. 195 n. 156.

23. Toner, *Commentary on St. Ignatius' Rule for Discernment*, 91: "Unless there is a split in the personality between understanding and affective appetite on one side and affective sensibility on the other, we have to grant that really believing what a Christian believes will necessarily issue in some sort of spiritual consolation, a feeling of spiritual peace and joy rooted in living faith. On the other hand, we have to grant the fact of spiritual desolation in Christians who believe and hope intensely and love generously. [This is explained by the fact that] acts of faith, hope, and charity vary not only in the breadth of conscious life which they dominate and integrate in relation to God. Recall that spiritual peace as a condition of spiritual life is constituted by such integration and, therefore, can also be of greater or less extent."

24. See Toner, *Discerning God's Will*, 37.

25. Ibid., 99.

26. Further on these developments in America, see James Turner, *Without God, Without Creed: The Origins of Unbelief in America* (Baltimore and London: Johns Hopkins University Press, 1985).

27. Michael Davies has recently argued persuasively for a revision of the traditional Calvinist reading of Bunyan in favor of a more moderate covenant theology in which the crux of the matter is faith in Christ's redeeming work, and therefore discernment is applied to the verity of one's faith rather than to the more dreadful question of one's eternal status. See Michael Davies, *Graceful Reading: Theology and Narrative in the Works of John Bunyan* (Oxford: Oxford University Press, 2003).

28. John Bunyan, *The Pilgrim's Progress*, ed. N. H. Keeble. Oxford World's Classics (Oxford: Oxford University Press, 1998), 62. Hereafter page references from this edition will be given parenthetically.

29. Idem, *Grace Abounding to the Chief of Sinners* in *Grace Abounding with*

Other Spiritual Autobiographies, ed. John Stachniewski and Anita Pacheco, Oxford World's Classics (Oxford: Oxford University Press, 1998), 32-33.

30. Further, see the excellent works of Stephen R. Holmes, *God of Grace and God of Glory: An Account of the Theology of Jonathan Edwards* (Edinburgh: T&T Clark, 2000), especially chap. 5; Robert W. Jenson, *America's Theologian: A Recommendation of Jonathan Edwards* (New York and Oxford: Oxford University Press, 1988), especially chaps. 6 and 7; and most recently, Amy Plantinga Pauw, *The Supreme Harmony of All: The Trinitarian Theology of Jonathan Edwards* (Grand Rapids, Mich., and Cambridge: Wm. B. Eerdmans, 2002), especially chap. 5.

31. Jonathan Edwards, *A Treatise Concerning Religious Affections,* ed. John E. Smith, The Works of Jonathan Edwards 2 (New Haven: Yale University Press, 1959), 86. All references to this edition will be given hereafter by page number parenthetically.

32. Jenson, *America's Theologian,* 83.

Notes to Chapter Four

1. Anselm Stolz, *The Doctrine of Spiritual Perfection,* trans. Aidan Williams (1938; new ed., New York: Crossroad Publishing, 2001), 115-25, 130-31.

2. Origen, *On First Principles,* 4.1.7, trans. G. W. Butterworth (London: SPCK, 1936; reprint, Gloucester, Mass.: Peter Smith, 1973), 267.

3. Idem, *The Song of Songs: Commentary and Homilies,* trans. R. P. Lawson, Ancient Christian Writers (New York: Newman Press, 1956), 263.

4. John Cassian, *The Conferences,* I.XVI, trans. Boniface Ramsey, O.P., Ancient Christian Writers (New York: Paulist Press, 1997), 56.

5. Ibid., XVII.1. Origen comments similarly at *First Principles* 3.13, and Evagrius at *Praktikos* 6.

6. Ibid.

7. Evagrius Ponticus, *The Praktikos and Chapters on Prayer,* trans. John Eudes Bamberger, Cistercian Studies Series 4 (Kalamazoo, Mich.: Cistercian Publications, 1981); *Praktikos,* Introductory Letter, p. 14.

8. Idem, *Chapters on Prayer* §50, p. 63.

9. Ibid., §51.

10. Idem, *Praktikos* §90, pp. 38-39.

11. Ibid., §83, p. 37.

12. Diadochus of Photiki, *On Spiritual Knowledge and Discrimination* §1, in *The Philokalia,* vol. 1, trans. G. E. H. Palmer, Philip Sherrard, Kallistos Ware (London: Faber and Faber, 1983 paper ed.), 153. This text will be cited parenthetically hereafter by paragraph number.

13. Catherine of Siena, *The Dialogue* §51, trans. Suzanne Noffke, Classics of Western Spirituality (New York: Paulist Press, 1980), 103. Hereafter citations will be given parenthetically by paragraph number.

14. Idem, *The Letters of Catherine of Siena,* trans. Suzanne Noffke, O.P., vol. 1 (Tempe, Ariz.: Arizona Center for Medieval and Renaissance Studies, 2000), 266.

15. Ibid.

16. Ibid., 267.

17. Ibid., 266.

18. This threefold distinction of origin can be found in Origen, *First Principles* 3.2.4, and in Cassian, *Conferences* 1.19.

19. Origen, *On First Principles* 3.2.4, p. 217.

20. Ibid., 3.2.6, p. 220.

21. Ibid., 3.3.4, p. 227.

22. Athanasius, *The Life of St. Antony* §§23-25, trans. H. Ellershaw, in *Select Writings and Letters of Athanasius, Bishop of Alexandria,* ed. Archibald Robinson, Nicene and Post-Nicene Fathers 4 (reprint ed.; Grand Rapids, Mich.: Eerdmans, 1980), 202.

23. Ibid., §35, p. 205.

24. Ibid., §36, p. 206.

25. Ibid.

26. Diadochus, *Spiritual Knowledge* §33, p. 262.

27. Catherine of Siena, *The Dialogue* §106, trans. Noffke, p. 199.

28. Ibid.

29. Ibid., 199-200.

30. Ibid., §71, p. 134.

31. Jules J. Toner, *A Commentary on St. Ignatius' Rules for the Discernment of Spirits* (St. Louis, Mo.: The Institute of Jesuit Sources, 1982), 80-81.

32. Ignatius of Loyola, *The Spiritual Exercises of Saint Ignatius* 313, trans. George E. Ganss (Chicago: Loyola University Press, 1992), 121. This text will be cited parenthetically by section number.

33. Ganss, trans., in Ignatius of Loyola, *Spiritual Exercises,* nn. 146 and 152, pp. 192, 194.

34. Origen, *On First Principles,* 3.3.4, p. 227.

35. Ibid., 3.3.2, p. 224.

36. Ibid., 3.3.6, p. 229.

37. Athanasius, *The Life of St. Antony* §35, p. 205.

38. The treatment of the eight vices in John Cassian can be found in *Conferences* V. While it follows the same pattern as Evagrius, I don't find it quite as penetrating psychologically. For a brief account of the differences between Evagrius's list and the "seven deadly sins" as they emerged in the West, see Tomáš Špidlík, *The Spirituality of the Christian East: A Systematic Handbook,* trans. Anthony P. Gythiel (Kalamazoo, Mich.: Cistercian Publications, 1986), 248ff.

39. Evagrius Ponticus, *The Praktikos* §14, trans. John Eudes Bamberger, Cistercian Studies Series 4 (Kalamazoo, Mich.: Cistercian Publications, 1981), 20. Hereafter this text will be cited parenthetically by paragraph number.

40. Idem, *Chapters on Prayer* §61, trans. Bamberger, p. 65.

41. For a useful survey of the image of counterfeit coins and shrewd money-changers in the history of discernment leading up to Ignatius of Loyola see Hugo Rahner, *Ignatius the Theologian,* trans. Michael Berry (San Francisco: Ignatius Press, 1990), pp. 171-80.

42. Jean Gerson, *On Distinguishing True from False Revelations* in *Jean Gerson: Early Works,* trans. Brian Patrick McGuire, Classics of Western Spirituality (New York: Paulist Press, 1998), 338.

43. Ibid., 357.

44. Cassian, *Conferences* 1.20.2, 4; 1.21.2.

45. Gerson, *Distinguishing True from False Revelations,* 348-49.

46. Cassian, *Conferences,* 1.20.4.

47. Ibid., 1.20.6-7.

48. Gerson, *Distinguishing True from False Revelations,* 354.

49. Toner, *Commentary on St. Ignatius' Rules for the Discernment of Spirits,* 70.

50. Michael J. McClymond, *Encounters with God: An Approach to the Theology of Jonathan Edwards* (New York and Oxford: Oxford University Press, 1998), 26.

51. Robert W. Jenson, *America's Theologian: A Recommendation of Jonathan Edwards* (New York and Oxford: Oxford University Press, 1988), 80.

52. Jonathan Edwards, *A Treatise Concerning Religious Affections*, ed. John E. Smith. The Works of Jonathan Edwards 2 (New Haven: Yale University Press, 1959), 206. This work will by cited parenthetically by page number.

53. Luke Timothy Johnson, *Scripture and Discernment: Decision Making in the Church* (Nashville, Tenn.: Abingdon Press, 1996), 119.

54. Ibid., 132.

55. *Lives of the Desert Fathers (History of the Monks of Egypt)*, trans. Norman Russell (Kalamazoo, Mich.: Cistercian Publications, 1981), 144-45.

56. Ibid., 145.

57. Evagrius, *Chapters on Prayer* §122, p. 75.

58. Origen, *On First Principles* 3.2.2, p. 214.

59. Ibid.

60. John Climacus, *The Ladder of Divine Ascent*, trans. Colm Luibheid and Norman Russell, Classics of Western Spirituality (New York: Paulist Press, 1982), 246.

61. Ibid., 253.

62. Toner, *Commentary on St. Ignatius' Rules for the Discernment of Spirits*, 224.

63. Ibid.

64. Origen, *On First Principles* 3.3.2, p. 224.

65. Ibid., 3.3.3, p. 225.

66. Idem, *Homily XXVII on Numbers* in *Origen: An Exhortation to Martyrdom, First Principles: Book IV, Prologue to the Commentary on the Song of Songs, Homily XXVII on Numbers,* trans. Rowan A. Greer (Mahwah, N.J.: Paulist Press, 1979), 257.

67. Toner, *Commentary*, 225.

68. Athanasius, *The Life of St. Antony* §25, trans. H. Ellershaw, in *Select Writings and Letters of Athanasius, Bishop of Alexandria*, ed. Archibald Robinson, Nicene and Post-Nicene Fathers 4 (reprint ed.; Grand Rapids, Mich.: Eerdmans, 1980), 203.

69. *Lives of the Desert Fathers*, trans. Russell, 56-57.

70. Ibid., 57.

71. Bernard of Clairvaux, *The Parables and The Sentences*, trans. Michael Casey and Francis R. Swietek (Kalamazoo, Mich.: Cistercian Publications, 2000), 33.

72. Ibid.

73. Catherine of Siena, *The Letters of Catherine of Siena*, trans. Noffke, 2.574.

74. Jonathan Edwards, *Personal Narrative* in *A Jonathan Edwards Reader*, ed. John E. Smith, Harry S. Stout, Kenneth P. Minkema (New Haven: Yale University Press, 1995), 285.

Notes to Chapter Five

1. Another version of this chapter was written as part of the Faith and Reason colloquium of the Center for Theological Inquiry, Princeton, N.J. I am gratefully indebted to the Center and to my colleagues in the colloquium for making this chapter possible.

2. Evagrius Pontikus, *The Centuries*, 4.36. Quoted in Olivier Clément, *The Roots of Christian Mysticism* (New York: New City Press, 1995), 131.

3. Maximus the Confessor, *Chapters on Knowledge*, 2.83 in *Maximus Confessor: Selected Writings*, trans. George C. Berthold (New York: Paulist Press, 1985), 165.

4. Joseph of Panephysis 7. *The Sayings of the Desert Fathers: The Alphabetical*

Collection, trans. Benedicta Ward (rev. ed.; Kalamazoo, Mich.: Cistercian Studies, 1984), 103. This is a translation of the Greek Alphabetical Series of the *Apothegmata Patrum,* PG 65.72-440.

5. The literature on the potential identities of the various factional parties in the Corinthian congregation is quite extensive. For a good introduction and survey to the range of critical views see the massive new commentary, Anthony C. Thiselton, *The First Epistle to the Corinthians: A Commentary on the Greek Text* (Grand Rapids, Mich.: Eerdmans, 2000).

6. Cf. Richard B. Gaffin, Jr., "Some Epistemological Reflections on 1 Cor 2:6-16," *Westminster Theological Journal* 57 (1995): 103-24. Though tending in this direction, Gaffin qualifies his attack on reason at 117ff.

7. Martyn shows how Paul adopts the *psychikos-pneumatikos* distinction of the spiritual elites in Corinth precisely so as to undo it from within and transfer its cognitive discernment function from criteria of human spiritual progress and ascent to the criterion of God's descent in Christ, especially in the crucifixion. J. Louis Martyn, "Epistemology at the Turn of the Ages," chap. 6 in his collection, *Theological Issues in the Letters of Paul* (Edinburgh: T. & T. Clark, 1997), see esp. 98ff.

8. Diadochus of Photiki, *On Spiritual Knowledge and Discrimination,* §11 in *The Philokalia,* vol. 1, trans. G. E. H. Palmer, Philip Sherrard, Kallistos Ware (London: Faber and Faber, 1983, paper ed.), 255. The best introduction is by Édouard des Places, S.J., in the introduction to his edition: Diadoque de Photicé, *Oeuvres Spirituelles,* Sources Chrétiennes 5 (Paris: Editions du Cerf, 1955).

9. Ibid.

10. Robin Scroggs, "New Being: Renewed Mind: New Perception," in *The Texts and the Times: New Testament Essays for Today* (Minneapolis: Fortress, 1993), 177.

11. See Paul W. Gooch, *Partial Knowledge: Philosophical Studies in Paul* (Notre Dame, Ind.: University of Notre Dame Press, 1987); Dale B. Martin, *The Corinthian Body* (New Haven: Yale University Press, 1995); Raymond Pickett, *The Cross in Corinth: The Social Significance of the Death of Jesus* (Sheffield: Sheffield Academic Press, 1997); Stephen M. Pogoloff, *Logos and Sophia: The Rhetorical Situation of 1 Corinthians* (Atlanta: Scholars Press, 1992); Stanley K. Stowers, "Paul on the Use and Abuse of Reason," in *Greeks, Romans, and Christians: Essays in Honor of Abraham J. Malherbe,* ed. David L. Balch et al. (Minneapolis: Fortress, 1990).

12. Pickett, *Cross in Corinth,* 37.

13. Stowers, "Paul on the Use and Abuse of Reason," 261.

14. Pogoloff, *Logos and Sophia;* see esp. chap. 5, "Rhetoric and Status."

15. Gooch, *Partial Knowledge,* 26. As the author goes on to say rather nicely: such boasters have in Paul's view "succumbed to the primal temptation to become as God without really being able to bring it off" (ibid.).

16. Ibid., 42.

17. Quoted by Evagrius Ponticus in *The Praktikos,* §99. *The Praktikos and Chapters on Prayer,* trans. John Eudes Bamberger, Cistercian Studies Series 4 (Kalamazoo, Mich.: Cistercian Publications, 1981), 41.

18. Further on the problems of anger, judgment, and wisdom, see the very fine study of Graham Gould, *The Desert Fathers on Monastic Community* (Oxford: Clarendon, 1993).

19. Very helpful surveys of Evagrius's life and thought may be found in Andrew Louth, *The Origins of the Christian Mystical Tradition* (Oxford: Oxford University Press, 1981), 100-113; and also in Bernard McGinn, *The Foundations of Mysticism,* vol. 1 of *The Presence of God: A History of Western Christian Mysticism* (New York: Crossroad, 1991), 144-57.

20. Evagrius, *Praktikos* §6, p. 17.

21. Ibid., §7, p. 17.

22. Ibid., §10, pp. 17-18.

23. Ibid., §§12, 13, pp. 18-19.

24. Greek Anonymous Series, *Apothegmata Patrum*, N 13. Quoted in Gould, *Desert Fathers on Monastic Community*, 126.

25. Alexandra R. Brown, *The Cross and Human Transformation: Paul's Apocalyptic Word in 1 Corinthians* (Minneapolis: Fortress, 1995), 138. On the *psychikos-pneumatikos* distinction, see also n. 6 above.

26. James Alison, *Raising Abel: The Recovery of the Eschatological Imagination* (New York: Crossroad, 1996), 181-82. See also the same author's excellent work, *The Joy of Being Wrong: Original Sin Through Easter Eyes* (New York: Crossroad, 1998). I am gratefully indebted to Alison throughout.

27. Diadochus, *On Spiritual Knowledge*, §71, p. 277.

28. Ibid., §68.

29. Origen, *Song of Songs Commentary*, 43-4.

30. Diadochus, *Spiritual Knowledge* §58, p. 270.

31. J. Louis Martyn, "Epistemology at the Turn of the Ages," 109.

32. Pickett, *Cross in Corinth*, 155-56.

33. Ibid., 157.

34. Anthony the Great 9, *Sayings of the Desert Fathers*, trans. Ward, p. 3.

35. Poemen 116, ibid., p. 184.

36. Poemen 92, ibid., pp. 179-80.

37. An anonymous saying from one of the Latin collections, in *The Wisdom of the Desert: Sayings from the Desert Fathers of the Fourth Century*, trans. Thomas Merton (New York: New Directions, 1970), 59.

38. Picket, *Cross in Corinth*, 61.

39. Marcus N. A. Bockmuehl, *Revelation and Mystery in Ancient Judaism and Pauline Christianity* (Tübingen: J. C. B. Mohr, 1990), 161.

40. Robert Jewett, *Paul's Anthropological Terms: A Study of their Use in Conflict Settings* (Leiden: Brill, 1971), 378.

41. Diadochus, *On Spiritual Knowledge* §92, p. 290.

42. Ibid., §19, p. 258.

43. Ibid., §1, p. 253.

44. Ibid., §14, p. 256.

45. Ibid., §15, pp. 256-57.

46. Luke Timothy Johnson, *Scripture and Discernment: Decision Making in the Church* (Nashville: Abingdon Press, 1996), 115-16.

47. Brown, *Cross and Human Transformation*, 139-48, esp. 146.

48. Diadochus, *On Spiritual Knowledge* §67, p. 275: "The gift which enflames our heart and moves it to the love His goodness more than any other is theology. It is the early offspring of God's grace and bestows on the soul the greatest gifts. First of all, it leads us gladly to disregard all love of this life, since in the place of perishable desires we possess inexpressible riches, the oracles of God. Then it embraces our intellect with the light of a transforming fire, and so makes it a partner of the angels in their liturgy . . . it nourishes the intellect with divine truth in the radiance of inexpressible light."

49. James Alison, *Joy of Being Wrong*, 189.

50. Ibid., 191.

Notes to Chapter Six

1. This chapter originated in a Lilly-funded research project on vocation at Loyola University Chicago. I am gratefully indebted both to the grantor and to my fellow participants at Loyola for their many contributions to this essay.

2. For good introductory reflections on this idea, see, e.g., Noel Dermot O'Donoghue, *Heaven in Ordinarie: Prayer as Transcendence* (Edinburgh: T & T Clark, 1979), chap. 3; and Rowan Williams, *A Ray of Darkness: Sermons and Reflections* (Cambridge: Cowley Publications, 1995), 147-59.

3. Williams, *Ray of Darkness*, 150.

4. Ibid.

5. Barbara J. Shapiro, *Probability and Certainty in Seventeenth-Century England: A Study of the Relationships between Natural Science, Religion, History, Law, and Literature* (Princeton, N.J.: Princeton University Press, 1983), 227.

6. See especially *Leviathan*, part 1, chap. 2, "Of Imagination"; chap. 3, "Of the Consequence or Train of Imagination"; and chap. 4, "Of Speech."

7. John Tillotson, "The Necessity of Repentance and Faith," in *Works*, 8.233; quoted in Shapiro, *Probability and Certainty*, 255.

8. John Bunyan, *The Pilgrim's Progress*, ed. N. H. Keeble, Oxford World's Classics (Oxford: Oxford University Press, 1984), 4; all references to *Pilgrim's Progress* are from this edition and will hereafter be noted parenthetically.

9. *Leviathan*, 1, chap. 2, ed. Edwin Curley (Indianapolis: Hackett, 1994), 8.

10. Fuming over the threat posed to civic control by traditional Christian teaching about grace, Hobbes writes: "they say that faith, and wisdom, and other virtues are sometimes poured into a man, sometimes blown into him from Heaven . . . and a great many other things that serve to lessen the dependence of subjects on the sovereign power of their country. For who will endeavour to obey the laws, if he expect obedience to be poured or blown into him?" (*Leviathan*, 4, chap. 46, p. 460).

11. Roger Pooley, "Spiritual Experience and Spiritual Autobiography: Some Contexts for Grace Abounding," *The Baptist Quarterly* 32 (October 1988): 393-402, 396.

12. Further on Bunyan's development of an allegorical rationality, see the fine essay by Barbara A. Johnson, "Falling into Allegory: The 'Apology' to The *Pilgrim's Progress* and Bunyan's Scriptural Methodology," in *Bunyan in Our Time*, ed. Robert G. Collmer (Kent, Oh.: Kent State University Press, 1989), 113-37.

13. John Wilkins, quoted in Isabel Rivers, "Grace, Holiness, and the Pursuit of Happiness: Bunyan and Restoration Latitudinarianism," in *John Bunyan: Conventicle and Parnassus, Tercentenary Essays*, ed. N. H. Keeble (Oxford: Clarendon Press, 1988), 53.

14. U. Milo Kaufman, *The Pilgrim's Progress and Traditions in Puritan Meditation* (New Haven: Yale University Press, 1966), 201; see also more recently, Kaufman, "Spiritual Discerning: Bunyan and the Mysteries of the Divine Will," in *John Bunyan*, ed. Keeble, 171-87.

15. John Bunyan, *Grace Abounding*, ed. John Stachniewski with Anita Pacheco (Oxford: Oxford University Press, 1998), 4-5.

Notes to Chapter Seven

1. Further on these themes, see Mark McIntosh, *Mystical Theology: The Integrity of Spirituality and Theology*, Challenges in Contemporary Theology (Oxford: Blackwell Publishers, 1998); and idem, *Mysteries of Faith*, The New Church Teaching (Boston: Cowley Publications, 2000).

2. An initial draft of this chapter was first offered as part of a consultation on "Apophasis and Incarnation" at the University of Birmingham, U.K. A slightly different version of the chapter appears in the papers from that consultation as McIntosh, "The Formation of Mind: Trinity and Understanding in Newman," in *Silence and the Word: Negative Theology and the Incarnation,* ed. Oliver Davies and Denys Turner (Cambridge: Cambridge University Press, 2002), 136-58. I am gratefully indebted to my colleagues at the consultation and to the publishers.

3. Quoted by Louis Dupré, *Passage to Modernity: An Essay in the Hermeneutics of Nature and Culture* (New Haven and London: Yale University Press, 1993), 83-84.

4. For wide-ranging but complementary studies of this early modern anxiety about mystery, see Michael J. Buckley, *At the Origins of Modern Atheism* (New Haven and London: Yale University Press, 1987); Stephen Toulmin, *Cosmopolis: The Hidden Agenda of Modernity* (New York: Free Press, 1990); William C. Placher, *The Domestication of Transcendence: How Modern Thinking about God Went Wrong* (Louisville, Ky.: Westminster John Knox Press, 1996).

5. George Berkeley, *Alciphron, or the Minute Philosopher,* Dialogue 7.8, ed. David Berman (London and New York: Routledge, 1993), 130. Cf. also 7.14, pp. 139-40: "Thus much, upon the whole, may be said of all signs: that they do not always suggest ideas signified to the mind: that when they suggest ideas, they are not general abstract ideas: that they have other uses besides barely standing for and exhibiting ideas, such as raising proper emotions, producing certain dispositions or habits of mind, and directing our actions in pursuit of that happiness, which is the ultimate end and design, the primary spring and motive, that sets rational agents at work: that signs may imply or suggest the relations of things; which relations, habitudes or proportions, as they cannot be by us understood but by the help of signs, so being thereby expressed and confuted, they direct and enable us to act with regard to things."

6. Ibid. A little later, a somewhat "enlightened" Alciphron replies: "It seems, Euphranor, and you would persuade me into an opinion, that there is nothing so singularly absurd as we are apt to think in the belief of mysteries; and that a man need not renounce his reason to maintain his religion. But, if this were true, how comes it to pass that, in proportion as men abound in knowledge, they dwindle in faith?" (7.11, p. 136).

7. For a somewhat picturesque account see, John Redwood, *Reason, Ridicule and Religion: The Age of the Enlightenment in England 1660–1750* (London: Thames and Hudson, 1976), especially chap. 7, "The Persons of the Trinity." On the particular example of the trinitarian argument that developed between John Locke and Bishop Edward Stillingfleet, see Richard H. Popkin, "The Philosophy of Bishop Stillingfleet," *Journal of the History of Philosophy* 9 (1971): 303-19; William S. Babcock, "A Changing of the Christian God: The Doctrine of the Trinity in the Seventeenth Century," *Interpretation* 45 (1991): 133-46.

8. David Hume, *Dialogues Concerning Natural Religion,* part X, ed. Richard H. Popkin (Indianapolis and Cambridge: Hackett Publishing Company, 1980), 64.

9. Gregory of Nazianzus, *The Theological Orations* 2.29, trans. Charles Gordon Browne and James Edward Swallow, in *Christology of the Later Fathers,* ed. Edward Rochie Hardie (Philadelphia: Westminster Press, 157).

10. Consider Locke's complaint that the very first principles of trinitarian thought were impossible to make sense of; I am supposed, Locke complains, "to find two individuals, without any difference: but that, I find, is too subtle and sublime for my weak capacity" (quoted in Babcock, "A Changing of the Christian God," p. 145; see n. 5 above).

11. John Coulson, *Newman and the Common Tradition: A Study in the Language of Church and Society* (Oxford: Clarendon Press, Oxford University Press, 1970), 4.

12. John Henry Newman, Sermon XV.38, "The Theory of Developments in Religious Doctrine," *Fifteen Sermons Preached before the University of Oxford*, 3rd ed. (Notre Dame, Ind.: University of Notre Dame Press, 1997), 344-45.

13. Idem, "Christ Hidden from the World," *Parochial and Plain Sermons*, IV.16 (San Francisco: Ignatius Press, 1987), 883.

14. Idem, "The Tamworth Reading Room," *Essays and Sketches*, vol. 2 (Westport, Conn.: Greenwood Press, 1970), 208-10.

15. Idem, *The Idea of a University Defined and Illustrated*, ed. Martin J. Svaglic (Notre Dame, Ind.: University of Notre Dame Press, 1982); see especially University Teaching, Discourse II, "Theology as a Branch of Knowledge."

16. Idem, *University Sermons*, "Wisdom as Contrasted with Faith and with Bigotry," 306.

17. Ibid., 306, 307.

18. Idem, *The Idea of a University*, University Teaching, Discourse VIII, "Knowledge Viewed in Relation to Religion," 146.

19. Idem, *An Essay in Aid of a Grammar of Assent* (Notre Dame, Ind.: University of Notre Dame Press, 1979), 137-38.

20. Ibid. Newman is quoting Locke, *An Essay Concerning Human Understanding*, book IV, chaps. xvi, "Of the Degrees of Assent," and xix, "Of Enthusiasm."

21. Ibid., 139.

22. Idem, *Idea of a University*, 28-29.

23. Ibid., 29.

24. Idem, *University Sermons*, "The Nature of Faith in Relation to Reason," 214.

25. See *University Sermons* XII, "Love the Safeguard of Faith against Superstition," and XIV, "Wisdom as Contrasted with Faith and with Bigotry."

26. Sir Joshua Reynolds, *Discourses on Painting and the Fine Arts*, 1768; quoted in *The Philosophical Notebook of John Henry Newman*, vol. 1, *General Introduction to the Study of Newman's Philosophy*, ed. Edward Sillem (New York: Humanities Press, 1969), 208-9.

27. Ibid., 209.

28. Newman, *Parochial and Plain Sermons*, IV.15, pp. 871-72.

29. Ibid., 872.

30. For a classic study of this theme in Newman, see Charles Frederick Harrold, "Newman and the Alexandrian Platonists," *Modern Philology* 37/3 (February 1940): 279-91.

31. Hans Urs von Balthasar, *Presence and Thought: Essay on the Religious Philosophy of Gregory of Nyssa*, trans. Mark Sebanc (San Francisco: Ignatius Press, 1995), e.g., 98-99.

32. Newman, *Apologia Pro Vita Sua*, ed. Martin J. Svaglic (Oxford: Oxford University Press, 1967), 37.

33. Newman, *Parochial and Plain Sermons*, IV.11, p. 835.

34. Ibid., V.1, p. 956.

35. Ibid., 957.

36. Ibid., III.16, p. 620.

37. Idem, *Grammar of Assent*, chap. 9.1, p. 275.

38. Ibid., 276.

39. Idem, *Parochial and Plain Sermons*, V.10, p. 1034.

40. Ibid., 1038.

41. Ibid., 1039.

42. For three thoughtful and concise discussions of Newman's epistemology (among very many), see Joseph Dunne, *Back to the Rough Ground: Practical Judgment and the Lure of Technique* (Notre Dame, Ind.: University of Notre Dame Press, 1997), chap. 1; Andrew Louth, *Discerning the Mystery: An Essay on the Nature of Theology* (Oxford: Oxford University Press, 1983), chap. 6; Mary Katherine Tillman, "Economies of Reason: Newman and the Phronesis Tradition," in *Discourse and Context: An Interdisciplinary Study of John Henry Newman*, ed. Gerard Magill (Carbondale, Ill.: Southern Illinois University Press, 1993).

43. Newman, *University Sermons*, "The Theory of Developments in Religious Doctrine," 334.

44. Idem, *Grammar*, 5.1, p. 105

45. Ibid., 106.

46. Ibid.

47. Ibid., 106-7.

48. Idem, *University Sermons*, 80.

49. Ibid., 86-87.

50. Idem, *Discourses Addressed to Mixed Congregations* (London: Burns & Oates, 1881), Discourse XV, "The Infinitude of the Divine Attributes," 313.

51. Ibid., 314.

52. Idem, *Parochial and Plain Sermons*, III.12, p. 581.

53. Ibid., 586-87.

54. Idem, *Discourses to Mixed Congregations*, XV, 309.

55. Ibid., 310-11.

Notes to Chapter Eight

1. Bernard Lonergan, "Finality, Love, and Marriage," in *Collection*, ed. F. E. Crowe (New York: Herder and Herder, 1967), 25-26.

2. Augustine, *The Trinity*, 12.3.14, trans. Edmund Hill (Brooklyn, N.Y.: New City Press, 1991), 330.

3. Ibid., 12.3.17, p. 332.

4. Francis Bacon, *New Atlantis*, in *Oxford Authors: Francis Bacon*, ed. Brian Vickers (Oxford and New York: Oxford University Press, 1996), all quotations from this edition are on pp. 482-86.

5. Ibid.

6. For a useful survey of this basic framework as it unfolds in many spiritual writers see Tomáš Špidlík, *The Spirituality of the Christian East: A Systematic Handbook*, trans. Anthony P. Gythiel (Kalamazoo, Mich.: Cistercian Publications, 1986), chap. 13, "Contemplation."

7. Iris Murdoch, *Henry and Cato* (Harmondsworth: Penguin Books, 1977), 173-74. Hereafter references will be given parenthetically in the text, e.g., *HC* 173-74.

8. Origen of Alexandria, *The Song of Songs: Commentary and Homilies*, trans. R. P. Lawson, Ancient Christian Writers 26 (New York: Newman Press, n.d.), 22.

9. Iris Murdoch, *The Green Knight* (New York: Penguin Books, 1995), 221. Hereafter references will be given parenthetically in the text, e.g., *GK* 221.

10. Origen, *Song of Songs*, 22. The full passage from Hebrews 5:11-14 in the New Revised Standard Version reads: "About this [the mystery of Christ] we have much to say that is hard to explain, since you have become dull in understanding. For teachers, you need someone to teach you again the basic elements of the oracles of God. You need milk, not solid food; for everyone who lives on milk, being still an infant, is unskilled in the word of righteousness. But solid food is for the mature, for those whose faculties have been trained by practice to distinguish good from evil."

11. Iris Murdoch, *Metaphysics as a Guide to Morals* (New York: Penguin Books, 1993), 341. Hereafter references given parenthetically, e.g., *MGM* 341.

12. Iris Murdoch, *The Sovereignty of Good* (London: Routledge, 1991), 67. Hereafter cited in the text as *SG*.

13. *The World of the Desert Fathers,* trans. Columba Stewart (Kalamazoo, Mich.: Cistercian Publications, 1986), 35.

14. Iris Murdoch, *The Bell* (Harmondsworth: Penguin Books, 1962), 190. Hereafter references given in text parenthetically, e.g., *B* 190.

15. Cf. e.g., *Existentialists and Mystics: Writings on Philosophy and Literature* (New York: Penguin Books, 1999), 28, 255f. Hereafter cited as *EM*.

16. Origen, *Song of Songs,* 29-30.

17. Simone Weil, in Murdoch, "Knowing the Void," in *Existentialists and Mystics.* See that work and *Metaphysics as a Guide to Morals* for references to Weil throughout.

18. Simone Weil, *Intimations of Christianity among the Greeks* (London and New York: Routledge, 1998), 90.

19. Ibid.

20. Ibid.

21. Simone Weil, "The Love of God and Affliction," in *Waiting for God,* trans. Emma Craufurd (New York: HarperCollins, 1973; reprint, Perennial Classics ed., 2001), 78. Hereafter noted as "LGA" and page number parenthetically.

22. Idem, *Intimations of Christianity,* 101.

23. Idem, "Forms of the Implicit Love of God," in *Waiting for God,* 100. Hereafter noted parenthetically as "FLG."

24. Idem, *Intimations of Christianity,* 104.

25. Idem, *Gravity and Grace,* trans. Emma Craufurd (London and New York: Routledge, reprint ed. 1992), 28.

26. Ibid., 30.

Notes to Chapter Nine

1. Karl Barth, *Church Dogmatics,* vol. IV/2, *The Doctrine of Reconciliation,* trans. G. W. Bromiley (Edinburgh: T. & T. Clark, 1958), 38-39.

2. St. Augustine, *The Lectures or Tractates on the Gospel according to St. John,* Tractate 1.17, trans. J. Gibbs and J. Innes, in *A Select Library of the Nicene and Post-Nicene Fathers of the Christian Church,* vol. 7 (Edinburgh: T & T Clark, reprint ed., 1986), 12.

3. Ibid., Tractate 1.16, p. 12.

4. Origen, *On First Principles,* 1.2-3, trans. G. W. Butterworth (London: SPCK, 1936; reprint, Gloucester, Mass.: Peter Smith, 1973), 16.

5. Ibid., 1.3-4, pp. 16-17.

6. Maximus the Confessor, *Chapters on Knowledge,* 1.42ff. and 2.10-11, in *Maximus Confessor: Selected Writings,* trans. George C. Berthold (New York: Paulist Press, 1985), 136, 149-50.

7. Thomas Aquinas, *Commentary on the Gospel of St. John,* Lecture 2.91, trans. James A. Weisheipl and Fabian R. Larcher, Aquinas Scripture 4 (Albany, N.Y.: Magi Books, 1980), 56.

8. Ibid.

9. Thomas Aquinas, *Summa Contra Gentiles, Book Four: Salvation* 13.6, trans. Charles J. O'Neil (Notre Dame, Ind.: University of Notre Dame Press, 1975), 94.

10. Ibid. See also Thomas's answer to the question, Whether God is Truth?:

"Truth is found in the intellect according as it apprehends a thing as it is; and in things according as they have being conformable to an intellect [i.e., that they are intelligible]. This is to the greatest degree found in God. For His being is not only conformed to His intellect, but it is the very act of His intellect; and His act of understanding [the eternal begetting of the Word] is the measure and cause of every other being and of every other intellect, and He Himself is His own existence and act of understanding. Whence it follows not only that truth is in Him, but that He is truth itself, and the sovereign and first truth" (*Summa Theologiae* 1.16.5, trans. Fathers of the English Dominican Province (1911; reprint ed. Westminster, Md.: Christian Classics, 1981), 1.92.

11. Bonaventure, *The Breviloquium*, 2.1.4, *The Works of Bonaventure*, vol. 2, trans. José de Vinck (Paterson, N.J.: St. Anthony Guild Press, 1963), 71.

12. Idem, *Collations on the Six Days*, 20.5, *The Works of Bonaventure*, vol. 5, trans. José de Vinck (Paterson, N.J.: St. Anthony Guild Press, 1970), 302.

13. Idem, *The Journey of the Mind to God*, 7.4, trans. Philotheus Boehner (Indianapolis: Hackett Publishing, 1993), 38.

14. Ibid., 7.6, p. 39.

15. The literature on the history of the illumination theory of knowledge is fairly extensive and not without a degree of controversy between various schools of interpretation (the rancor of thirteenth-century University of Paris debates seems to have a long historical afterlife in this subject). For a very particular but undoubtedly influential treatment, see the analysis of Etienne Gilson in his two great volumes: *The Christian Philosophy of Saint Augustine*, trans. L. E. M. Lynch (London: Victor Gollancz, 1961); and *The Philosophy of St. Bonaventure*, trans. Illtyd Trethowan and Frank J. Sheed (Paterson, N.J.: St. Anthony Guild Press, 1965). For temperate and insightful discussions of illumination in Augustine, see Richard Acworth, S.J., "God and Human Knowledge in St Augustine," *The Downside Review* 75 (January 1957): 207-21; and Ronald H. Nash, *The Light of the Mind: St. Augustine's Theory of Knowledge* (Lexington, Ky.: University Press of Kentucky, 1969), both of which, while aging, provide a good sense of the debates over the years. On Bonaventure, see the massively learned and thorough John Francis Quinn, *The Historical Constitution of St. Bonaventure's Philosophy* (Toronto: Pontifical Institute of Medieval Studies, 1973); especially on illumination theory and contrasts with Aquinas, see pp. 443-663. For a very clear, recent survey see Robert Pasnau, "Divine Illumination," *Stanford Encyclopedia of Philosophy*, http://plato.standford.edu/entries/illumination, 1999. In this and several other works (e.g., Pasnau, ed., *The Cambridge Translation of Medieval Philosophical Texts*, vol. 3, *Mind and Knowledge* [Cambridge: Cambridge University Press, 2002]), Pasnau, while eminently fair, takes a lugubrious view of the viability of illumination. In no way do I dispute his facts, but I note his own more recently nuanced position in his work *Thomas Aquinas on Human Nature* (Cambridge: Cambridge University Press, 2002), especially pp. 302ff. My own small contribution to the debate would, I suppose, be this: while illumination may falter philosophically as it is pulled into late medieval philosophical epistemology (Scotus was a particular opponent), that is probably due to the fact that it was never a purely "philosophical" doctrine (in our modern usage) in first place, and particularly not a narrowly epistemological one. It is best understood not simply as a now antiquated account of the human cognitional process but as way of thinking about the mystical interaction between the divine and the creaturely within the cosmic event of divine truth-expression (i.e., the production of the universe within the Father's speaking of the Word).

16. For a good survey of the issues, see Norris Clarke, "The Problem of the Reality and Multiplicity of Divine Ideas in Christian Neoplatonism," in *Neoplatonism*

and Christian Thought, ed. Dominic J. O'Meara (Albany, N.Y.: State University of New York Press, 1982), 109-27.

17. Fergus Kerr, *After Aquinas: Versions of Thomism* (Oxford: Blackwell Publishing, 2002), 30.

18. Josef Pieper, *The Silence of St. Thomas,* trans. John Murray and Daniel O'Connor (1957; reprint ed., South Bend, Ind.: St. Augustine's Press, 1999), 96. For further excellent insight on the themes of knowledge and truth in Thomas, see John I. Jenkins, *Knowledge and Faith in Thomas Aquinas* (Cambridge: Cambridge University Press, 1997).

19. Ibid., 96-97.

20. Augustine, *On Free Will,* 2.16.41, in *Augustine: Earlier Writings,* trans. John H. S. Burleigh, Library of Christian Classics (Philadelphia: Westminster Press, 1953), 161.

21. Ibid.

22. Bonaventure, *Collations on the Six Days,* 3.9, pp. 46-7.

23. Lars Thunberg, *Man and the Cosmos: The Vision of St Maximus the Confessor* (Crestwood, N.Y.: St. Vladimir's Seminary Press, 1985), 127.

24. Origen, *On First Principles* 2.11.4, pp. 149-50.

25. Ibid., 2.11.6, p. 152.

26. Maximus the Confessor, *The Four Hundred Chapters on Love* 1.86-95, in *Maximus Confessor: Selected Writings,* trans. George C. Berthold (New York: Paulist Press, 1985), 45.

27. John Hammond Taylor, "Introduction" to Taylor's translation of Augustine, *The Literal Meaning of Genesis (De Genesi ad litteram),* 2 vols., Ancient Christian Writers (New York: Paulist Press, 1982), 1.4.

28. Augustine, *Literal Meaning of Genesis,* 4.22, vol. 1, p. 130.

29. Ibid.

30. Ibid., 4.24, vol. 1, p. 132.

31. Ibid., 4.26, vol. 1, p. 134.

32. Ibid., 4.24, vol. 1, p. 132.

33. Bonaventure, *Disputed Questions on the Knowledge of Christ,* Question 4, conclusion, trans. Zachary Hayes, Works of Saint Bonaventure 4 (Saint Bonaventure, N.Y.: Franciscan Institute, 1992), 134.

34. Idem, *Collations on the Six Days,* 12.5, p. 175.

35. See also, e.g., Augustine, *Literal Meaning of Genesis,* 12.31, vol. 2, p. 222, or Bonaventure, *Journey of the Mind to God,* 3.3.

36. For a useful recent presentation of the viability of this form of realism, see the fine essay by John Haldane, "Mind-World Identity Theory and the Anti-Realist Challenge," chap. 1 in *Reality, Representation, and Projection,* ed. John Haldane and Cripin Wright (New York: Oxford University Press, 1993).

37. See Bonaventure, *Disputed Questions on the Knowledge of Christ,* Question 4, reply 2, p. 137 and Thomas, *Summa Theologiae* 1.79.9.

38. Ibid., 12.3.15, p. 330.

39. Catherine of Siena, *The Dialogue,* trans. Suzanne Noffke, Classics of Western Spirituality (New York: Paulist Press, 1980), 65-66.

40. Thomas Aquinas, *Truth,* Question 2.2, trans. Robert W. Mulligan (1954; reprint ed., Indianapolis: Hackett Publishing Company, 1994), 1.61. For intriguing considerations of this theme in Thomas, see Oliva Blanchette, *The Perfection of the Universe according to Aquinas: A Teleological Cosmology* (University Park, Pa.: Pennsylvania State University Press, 1992); and John Milbank and Catherine Pickstock, *Truth in Aquinas,* Radical Orthodoxy (London: Routledge, 2001).

41. Bonaventure, *Collations on the Six Days,* 13.12, p. 190. My emphasis.

42. Because of the remarkable series of Traherne manuscript discoveries in the last few years (many of which are not yet available in print, let alone in critical editions), it seems more likely than ever that Traherne will emerge as one of the great theologians of the seventeenth century. For orientation in Traherne, see the introduction by Denise Inge to her edition, *Thomas Traherne: Poetry and Prose* (London: SPCK, 2002); A. M. Allchin, Anne Ridler, and Julia Smith, *Profitable Wonders: Aspects of Thomas Traherne* (Wilton, Conn.: Morehouse Publishing, 1989); Carol L. Marks, "Thomas Traherne and Cambridge Platonism," *Publications of the Modern Language Association of America* 81 (December 1966): 521-34; and Louis L. Martz, *The Paradise Within: Studies in Vaughan, Traherne, and Milton* (New Haven: Yale University Press, 1964). For an intriguing next step, see A. Leigh Deneef, *Traherne in Dialogue: Heidegger, Lacan, and Derrida* (Durham, N.C., and London: Duke University Press, 1988).

43. Traherne, *Centuries* (Oxford: Clarendon Press, 1960; reprint, Oxford: A. R. Mowbray, 1985), III.1. All references will be given parenthetically and include the *Century* in roman numeral followed by the section in arabic.

44. Thomas Traherne, *Christian Ethicks,* eds., Carol L. Marks and George R. Guffey (Ithaca, N.Y.: Cornell University Press, 1968), 55-56.

45. Ibid.

46. Ibid., 69.

47. Ibid.

48. Herbert McCabe, Appendix 1, "Knowledge," in *St. Thomas Aquinas, Summa Theologiae,* 1a. 12-13. Volume 3, *Knowing and Naming God,* trans. Herbert McCabe (London: Eyre & Spottiswoode, 1964), 100.

49. Idem, *God Matters* (London: Geoffrey Chapman, 1987), 175.

50. Rowan Williams, *Resurrection: Interpreting the Easter Gospel* (New York: Pilgrim Press, 1984), 71.

51. On the particular advances made by Maximus, see John D. Zizioulas, *Being as Communion: Studies in Personhood and the Church* (Crestwood, N.Y.: St. Vladimir's Seminary Press, 1985), 93-98.

52. Maximus the Confessor, *Difficulty* 41, 1308CD, in *Maximus the Confessor,* introductions and translations by Andrew Louth, Early Church Fathers (London: Routledge, 1996), 158.

53. Ibid.

54. For a truly luminous and comprehensive reading of Maximus's ecclesiology, see Alain Riou, *Le Monde et l'Eglise selon Maxime le Confesseur* (Paris: Beauchesne, 1973).

55. *Mystagogy,* chapter 23: the church/soul is led by the Word into "the knowledge of theology made manifest after its journey through all things, granting it an understanding equal to the angels as far as this is possible for it. He will teach it with such wisdom that that it will comprehend the one God, one nature and three Persons. . . . The same unity and trinity has a unity without composition or confusion and a distinction without separation or division" (205). And as always it is crucial to remember that such a knowledge is granted to the church only in and through the transforming patterns of its own life in imitation of God, indeed the knowledge and the life are the same. The analogy here on the level of the individual would be the saint, whose wisdom about God is not separable from her own vocation and participation in God's life.

Selected Bibliography

Primary Sources

Aquinas, Thomas. *Commentary on the Gospel of St. John*. Translated by James A. Weisheipl and Fabian R. Larcher. Aquinas Scripture series 4. Albany, N.Y.: Magi Books, 1980.

———. *Summa Contra Gentiles*. Book Four: Salvation. Translated by Charles J. O'Neil. Notre Dame, Ind.: University of Notre Dame Press, 1975.

———. *Summa Theologiae*. Translated by the Fathers of the English Dominican Province. 1911. Reprint, Westminster, Md.: Christian Classics, 1981.

———. *Truth*. Translated by Robert W. Mulligan. Vol. 1. 1954. Reprint, Indianapolis, Ind.: Hackett Publishing Company, 1994.

Athanasius. *The Life of St. Antony*. Translated by H. Ellershaw. In *Select Writings and Letters of Athanasius, Bishop of Alexandria*, ed. Archibald Robinson. Vol. iv, Nicene and Post-Nicene Fathers. Grand Rapids, Mich.: Eerdmans, 1980.

Augustine. *The Lectures or Tractates on the Gospel according to St. John*. Translated by J. Gibbs and J. Innes. Vol. vii, A Select Library of the Nicene and Post-Nicene Fathers of the Christian Church. Edinburgh: T & T Clark, 1986.

———. *The Literal Meaning of Genesis* (De Genesi ad litteram). Translated by John Hammond Taylor. 2 vols, Ancient Christian Writers. New York: Paulist Press, 1982.

———. *The Trinity*. Translated by Edmund Hill. Brooklyn: New City Press, 1991.

Bacon, Francis. *New Atlantis*. In *Oxford Authors: Francis Bacon*, ed. Brian Vickers. Oxford and New York: Oxford University Press, 1996.

Barth, Karl. *Church Dogmatics*. Vol. IV/2, *The Doctrine of Reconciliation*. Translated by G. W. Bromiley. Edinburgh: T. & T. Clark, 1958.

Berkeley, George. *Alciphron, or the Minute Philosopher*. Edited by David Berman. London and New York: Routledge, 1993.

Bernard of Clairvaux. *On the Song of Songs* II. Translated by Kilian Walsh. *On the Song of Songs* III. Translated by Kilian Walsh and Irene M. Edmonds. Cistercian Fathers. Kalamazoo, Mich.: Cistercian Publications, 1976 and 1979.

———. *The Parables and The Sentences*. Translated by Michael Casey and Francis R. Swietek. Kalamazoo, Mich.: Cistercian Publications, 2000.

Bonaventure. *The Breviloquium*. Translated by José de Vinck. Vol. 2, *Works of Bonaventure*. Paterson, N.J.: St. Anthony Guild Press, 1963.

———. Collations on the Six Days. Translated by José de Vinck. Vol. 5, *Works of Bonaventure*. Paterson, N.J.: St. Anthony Guild Press, 1970.

———. *Disputed Questions on the Knowledge of Christ*. Translated by Zachary

Hayes. Vol. 4, *Works of Saint Bonaventure*. Saint Bonaventure, N.Y.: The Franciscan Institute, 1992.

———. *The Journey of the Mind to God*. Translated by Philotheus Boehner. Indianapolis: Hackett Publishing, 1993.

Bunyan, John. *Grace Abounding to the Chief of Sinners*. In *Grace Abounding with other Spiritual Autobiographies*. Edited by John Stachniewski and Anita Pacheco. Oxford World's Classics. Oxford: Oxford University Press, 1998.

———. *The Pilgrim's Progress*. Edited by N. H. Keeble. Oxford World Classics. Oxford: Oxford University Press, 1998.

Cassian, John. *The Conferences*. Translated by Boniface Ramsey, O.P. Ancient Christian Writers. New York: Paulist Press, 1997.

Catherine of Siena. *The Dialogue*. Translated by Suzanne Noffke. Classics of Western Spirituality. New York: Paulist Press, 1980.

———. *The Letters of Catherine of Siena*. Translated by Suzanne Noffke, O.P. Volumes I and II. Tempe, Ariz.: Arizona Center for Medieval and Renaissance Studies, 2000 and 2001.

Climacus, John. *The Ladder of Divine Ascent*. Translated by Colm Luibheid and Norman Russell. Classics of Western Spirituality. New York: Paulist Press, 1982.

Diadochus of Photiki. *On Spiritual Knowledge and Discrimination*. Vol. 1, *The Philokalia*. Translated by G. E. H. Palmer, Philip Sherrard, Kallistos Ware. London: Faber and Faber, 1983.

Edwards, Jonathan. *Personal Narrative*. In *A Jonathan Edwards Reader*. Edited by John E. Smith, Harry S. Stout, Kenneth P. Minkema. New Haven: Yale University Press, 1995.

———. *A Treatise Concerning Religious Affections*. Edited by John E. Smith. Vol. 2, *The Works of Jonathan Edwards*. New Haven: Yale University Press, 1959.

Evagrius Ponticus. The *Praktikos and Chapters on Prayer*. Translated by John Eudes Bamberger. Cistercian Studies 4. Kalamazoo, Mich.: Cistercian Publications, 1981.

Gerson, Jean. *On Distinguishing True from False Revelations*. In *Jean Gerson: Early Works*. Translated by Brian Patrick McGuire. Classics of Western Spirituality. New York: Paulist Press, 1998.

———. *On Testing the Spirits*. In *The Concept of Discretio Spirituum in John Gerson's "De Probatione Spirituum" and "De Distinctione Verarum Visionem A Falsis"* by Paschal Boland, O.S.B. Washington, D.C.: Catholic University of America Press, 1959.

Gregory of Nazianzus. *The Theological Orations*. Translated by Charles Gordon Browne and James Edward Swallow. In *Christology of the Later Fathers*, ed. Edward Rochie Hardie Philadelphia: Westminster Press, 1977.

Hobbes, Thomas. *Leviathan*. Edited by Edwin Curley. Indianapolis: Hackett, 1994.

Hume, David. *Dialogues Concerning Natural Religion*. Edited by Richard H. Popkin. Indianapolis and Cambridge: Hackett Publishing Company, 1980.

Ignatius of Loyola. *Saint Ignatius of Loyola: Personal Writings*. Translated by Joseph A. Munitiz and Philip Endean. London: Penguin Books, 1996.

———. *The Spiritual Exercises of Saint Ignatius*. Translated by George E. Ganss. Chicago: Loyola University Press, 1992.

Lives of the Desert Fathers (History of the Monks of Egypt). Translated by Norman Russell. Kalamazoo, Mich.: Cistercian Publications, 1981.

Maximus the Confessor. *The Four Hundred Chapters on Love and Chapters on*

Knowledge. In *Maximus Confessor: Selected Writings*. Translated by George C. Berthold. Classics of Western Spirituality. New York: Paulist Press, 1985.

———. *Maximus the Confessor*. Introduced and translated by Andrew Louth. The Early Church Fathers. London: Routledge, 1996.

Murdoch, Iris. *The Bell*. Harmondsworth: Penguin Books, 1962.

———. *Existentialists and Mystics: Writings on Philosophy and Literature*. New York: Penguin Books, 1999.

———. *The Green Knight*. New York: Penguin Books, 1995.

———. *Henry and Cato*. Harmondsworth: Penguin Books, 1977.

———. *Metaphysics as a Guide to Morals*. New York: Penguin Books, 1993.

———. *The Sovereignty of Good*. London: Routledge, 1991.

Newman, John Henry. *Apologia Pro Vita Sua*. Edited by Martin J. Svaglic. Oxford: Oxford University Press, 1967.

———. *An Essay in Aid of a Grammar of Assent*. Notre Dame, Ind.: University of Notre Dame Press, 1979.

———. *Discourses Addressed to Mixed Congregations*. London: Burns & Oates, 1881.

———. *Fifteen Sermons Preached before the University of Oxford*, 3d ed. Notre Dame, Ind.: University of Notre Dame Press, 1997.

———. *The Idea of a University Defined and Illustrated*, Edited by Martin J. Svaglic. Notre Dame, Ind.: University of Notre Dame Press, 1982.

———. Parochial and Plain Sermons. San Francisco: Ignatius Press, 1987.

———. "The Tamworth Reading Room," Vol. II, *Essays and Sketches*. Westport, Conn.: Greenwood Press, 1970.

Origen. *On First Principles*. Translated by G. W. Butterworth. London: SPCK, 1936. Reprint, Gloucester, Mass.: Peter Smith, 1973.

———. *Origen: An Exhortation to Martyrdom, First Principles: Book IV, Prologue to the Commentary on the Song of Songs, Homily XXVII on Numbers*. Translated by Rowan A. Greer. Classics of Western Spirituality. Mahwah, N.J.: Paulist Press, 1979.

———. *The Song of Songs: Commentary and Homilies*. Translated by R. P. Lawson. Ancient Christian Writers. New York: Newman Press, 1956.

Richard of St. Victor. *The Twelve Patriarchs*. In *The Twelve Patriarchs, The Mystical Ark, Book Three of the Trinity*. Translated by Grover A. Zinn. Classics of Western Spirituality. New York: Paulist Press, 1979.

The Sayings of the Desert Fathers: The Alphabetical Collection. Translated by Benedicta Ward. Kalamazoo, Mich.: Cistercian Publications, 1975; rev. ed., 1984.

Traherne, Thomas. *Centuries*. Oxford: The Clarendon Press, 1960. Reprint, Oxford: A. R. Mowbray, 1985.

———. *Christian Ethicks*. Edited by Carol L. Marks and George R. Guffey. Ithaca, N.Y.: Cornell University Press, 1968.

———. *Thomas Traherne: Poetry and Prose*. Selected and introduced by Denise Inge. London: SPCK, 2002.

Weil, Simone. "Forms of the Implicit Love of God". In *Waiting for God*. Translated by Emma Craufurd. New York: HarperCollins, 1973. Reprint, Perennial Classics ed., 2001.

———. *Gravity and Grace*, reprint ed. Translated by Emma Craufurd. London and New York: Routledge, 1992.

―――. *Intimations of Christianity among the Greeks*. London and New York: Routledge, 1998.

―――. "The Love of God and Affliction." In *Waiting for God*. Translated by Emma Craufurd. New York: HarperCollins, 1973. Reprint, Perennial Classics ed., 2001.

The World of the Desert Fathers. Translated by Columba Stewart. Kalamazoo, Mich.: Cistercian Publications, 1986.

Secondary Sources

Acworth, Richard, S.J. "God and Human Knowledge in St Augustine." *The Downside Review* 75 (January 1957): 207-221.

Alison, James. *Raising Abel: The Recovery of the Eschatological Imagination*. New York: Crossroad Herder, 1996.

―――. *The Joy of Being Wrong: Original Sin Through Easter Eyes*. New York: Crossroad Herder, 1998.

Allchin, A. M., Anne Ridler, and Julia Smith. *Profitable Wonders: Aspects of Thomas Traherne*. Wilton, Conn.: Morehouse Publishing, 1989.

Babcock, William S. "A Changing of the Christian God: The Doctrine of the Trinity in the Seventeenth Century." *Interpretation* 45 (1991): 133-46.

Balthasar, Hans Urs von. *Presence and Thought: Essay on the Religious Philosophy of Gregory of Nyssa*. Translated by Mark Sebanc. San Francisco: Ignatius Press, 1995.

Barry, William A. *Paying Attention to God: Discernment in Prayer*. Notre Dame, Ind.: Ave Maria Press, 1990.

Barton, Stephen C. "Gospel Wisdom." *In Where Shall Wisdom be Found? Wisdom in the Bible, the Church and the Contemporary World*. Edited by Stephen C. Barton. Edinburgh: T& T Clark, 1999.

Blanchette, Oliva. *The Perfection of the Universe according to Aquinas: A Teleological Cosmology*. University Park, Pa.: Pennsylvania State University Press, 1992.

Bockmuehl, Marcus N. A. *Revelation and Mystery in Ancient Judaism and Pauline Christianity*. Tübingen: J. C. B. Mohr, 1990.

Boland, Paschal. *The Concept of Discretio Spirituum in John Gerson's "De Probatione Spirituum" and "De Distinctione Verarum Visionum A Falsis"*. Washington, D.C.: Catholic University of America Press, 1959.

Brown, Alexandra R. *The Cross and Human Transformation: Paul's Apocalyptic Word in 1 Corinthians*. Minneapolis: Fortress, 1995.

Buckley, Michael J. *At the Origins of Modern Atheism*. New Haven and London: Yale University Press, 1987.

Chadwick, Owen. *John Cassian: A Study in Primitive Monasticism*. Cambridge: Cambridge University Press, 2nd ed., 1968.

Clarke, Norris. "The Problem of the Reality and Multiplicity of Divine Ideas in Christian Neoplatonism." In *Neoplatonism and Christian Thought*, ed. Dominic J. O'Meara. Albany, N.Y.: State University of New York Press, 1982, 109-27.

Clément, Olivier. *The Roots of Christian Mysticism*. New York: New City Press, 1995.

Coulson, John. *Newman and the Common Tradition: A Study in the Language of*

Church and Society. Oxford: At the Clarendon Press, Oxford University Press, 1970.

Davies, Michael. *Graceful Reading: Theology and Narrative in the Works of John Bunyan*. Oxford: Oxford University Press, 2003.

Davies, Oliver and Denys Turner, eds. *Silence and the Word: Negative Theology and the Incarnation*. Cambridge: Cambridge University Press, 2002.

Davis, Ellen F. *Proverbs, Ecclesiastes, and the Song of Songs*. Westminster Bible Companion. Louisville, Ky.: Westminster John Knox, 2000.

Deneef, A. Leigh. *Traherne in Dialogue: Heidegger, Lacan, and Derrida*. Durham and London: Duke University Press, 1988.

Dingjan, F., O.S.B. *Discretio: Les origines patristique et monastiques de la doctrine sur la prudence chez saint Thomas d'Aquin*. Assen: Van Gorcum, 1967.

Dunne, Joseph. *Back to the Rough Ground: Practical Judgment and the Lure of Technique*. Notre Dame, Ind.: University of Notre Dame Press, 1997.

Dupré, Louis. *Passage to Modernity: An Essay in the Hermeneutics of Nature and Culture*. New Haven and London: Yale University Press, 1993.

English, John J. *Spiritual Freedom*, 2d ed. Chicago: Loyola University Press, 1995.

Floristan, Casiano, and Christian Duquoc, eds., *Discernment of the Spirit and of Spirits*. New York: Seabury, 1979.

Gaffin, Richard B., Jr., "Some Epistemological Reflections on 1 Cor 2:6-16." Westminster Theological Journal 57 (1995): 103-24.

Gilson, Etienne. *The Christian Philosophy of Saint Augustine*. Translated by L. E. M. Lynch. London: Victor Gollancz, 1961.

———. *The Philosophy of St. Bonaventure*. Translated by Illtyd Trethowan and Frank J. Sheed. Paterson, N.J.: St. Anthony Guild Press, 1965.

Gooch, Paul W. *Partial Knowledge: Philosophical Studies in Paul*. Notre Dame, Ind.: University of Notre Dame Press, 1987.

Gould, Graham. *The Desert Fathers on Monastic Community*. Oxford: Clarendon, 1993.

Green, Thomas H. *Weeds among the Wheat: Discernment Where Prayer and Action Meet*. Notre Dame, Ind.: Ave Maria Press, 1984.

Guillet, Jacques. "Discernement des Esprits." Vol. 111, *Dictionnaire de Spiritualité*, cols. 1222-1291.

Haldane, John. "Mind-World Identity Theory and the Anti-Realist Challenge." In *Reality, Representation, and Projection*, ed. John Haldane and Cripin Wright. New York: Oxford University Press, 1993.

Harrold, Charles Frederick. "Newman and the Alexandrian Platonists." *Modern Philology* 37/3 (February 1940): 279-91.

Holmes, Stephen R. *God of Grace and God of Glory: An Account of the Theology of Jonathan Edwards*. Edinburgh: T & T Clark, 2000.

Inge, Denise, ed. *Thomas Traherne: Poetry and Prose*. London: SPCK, 2002.

Jenkins, John I. *Knowledge and Faith in Thomas Aquinas*. Cambridge: Cambridge University Press, 1997.

Jenson, Robert W. *America's Theologian: A Recommendation of Jonathan Edwards*. New York and Oxford: Oxford University Press, 1988.

Jewett, Robert. *Paul's Anthropological Terms: A Study of their Use in Conflict Settings*. Leiden: E. J. Brill, 1971.

Johnson, Barbara A. "Falling into Allegory: The 'Apology' to *The Pilgrim's Progress* and Bunyan's Scriptural Methodology." In *Bunyan in Our Time*, ed. Robert G. Collmer. Kent, Oh.: Kent State University Press, 1989.

Johnson, Luke Timothy. *Scripture and Discernment: Decision Making in the Church*. Nashville, Tenn.: Abingdon Press, 1996.

Kaufman, U. Milo. *The Pilgrim's Progress and Traditions in Puritan Meditation*. New Haven: Yale University Press, 1966.

———, "Spiritual Discerning: Bunyan and the Mysteries of the Divine Will." In *John Bunyan*. ed. Keeble, N. H.

Keeble, N. H., ed. *John Bunyan: Conventicle and Parnassus, Tercentenary Essays*. Oxford: Clarendon Press, 1988.

Kerr, Fergus. *After Aquinas: Versions of Thomism*. Oxford: Blackwell Publishing, 2002.

Lienhard, Joseph T., S. J. "On 'Discernment of Spirits' in the Early Church." *Theological Studies* 41/3 (September 1980): 505-29.

Lonergan, Bernard. "Finality, Love, and Marriage."In *Collection*, ed. F. E. Crowe. New York: Herder and Herder, 1967.

Lonsdale, David. *Listening to the Music of the Spirit: The Art of Discernment*. Notre Dame, Ind.: Ave Maria Press, 1993.

Louth, Andrew. *The Origins of the Christian Mystical Tradition*. Oxford: Oxford University Press, 1981.

———. *Discerning the Mystery: An Essay on the Nature of Theology*. Oxford: Oxford University Press, 1983.

Marks, Carol L. "Thomas Traherne and Cambridge Platonism." *Publications of the Modern Language Association of America* LXXXI (December 1966): 521-34.

Martin, Dale B. *The Corinthian Body*. New Haven: Yale University Press, 1995.

Martz, Louis L. *The Paradise Within: Studies in Vaughan, Traherne, and Milton*. New Haven: Yale University Press, 1964.

Martyn, J. Louis. *Theological Issues in the Letters of Paul*. Edinburgh: T. & T. Clark, 1997.

McCabe, Herbert. God Matters. London: Geoffrey Chapman, 1987.

———. "Knowledge." in St. Thomas Aquinas, *Summa Theologiae*, 1a, 12-13. Vol. 3, Knowing and Naming God, trans. Herbert McCabe. London: Eyrie & Spottiswoode, 1964.

McClymond, Michael J. *Encounters with God: An Approach to the Theology of Jonathan Edwards*. New York/Oxford: Oxford University Press, 1998.

McGinn, Bernard. *The Foundations of Mysticism*. Vol. 1, *The Presence of God: A History of Western Christian Mysticism*. New York: Crossroad, 1991.

McIntosh, Mark. *Mystical Theology: The Integrity of Spirituality and Theology*. Challenges in Contemporary Theology. Oxford: Blackwell Publishers, 1998.

———. *Mysteries of Faith*. The New Church Teaching Series. Boston: Cowley Publications, 2000.

McNamara, Martin. "Discernment Criteria in Israel: True and False Prophets." In *Discernment of the Spirit and of Spirits*, ed. Casiano Floristan and Christian Duquoc. New York: Seabury, 1979.

Milbank, John, and Catherine Pickstock. *Truth in Aquinas*. Radical Orthodoxy. London: Routledge, 2001.

Nash, Ronald H. *The Light of the Mind: St. Augustine's Theory of Knowledge*. Lexington, Ky.: The University Press of Kentucky, 1969.

O'Donoghue, Noel Dermot. *Heaven in Ordinarie: Prayer as Transcendence*. Edinburgh: T & T Clark, 1979.

Pasnau, Robert. "Divine Illumination." *Stanford Encyclopedia of Philosophy*. http://plato.stanford.edu/entries/illumination, 1999.

———, ed. *The Cambridge Translation of Medieval Philosophical Texts*. Vol. 3, *Mind and Knowledge*. Cambridge: Cambridge University Press, 2002.

———. *Thomas Aquinas on Human Nature*. Cambridge: Cambridge University Press, 2002.

Pauw, Amy Plantinga. *The Supreme Harmony of All: The Trinitarian Theology of Jonathan Edwards*. Grand Rapids and Cambridge: Eerdmans, 2002.

Pickett, Raymond. *The Cross in Corinth: The Social Significance of the Death of Jesus*. Sheffield: Sheffield Academic Press, 1997.

Pieper, Josef. *The Silence of St. Thomas*, reprint ed. Translated by John Murray and Daniel O'Connor. South Bend, Ind.: St. Augustine's Press, 1999.

Places, Édouard des, S.J., Introduction and ed. *Diadoque de Photicé, Oeuvres Spirituelles*. Sources Chrétiennes 5 (Paris: Editions du Cerf, 1955).

Placher, William C. *The Domestication of Transcendence: How Modern Thinking about God Went Wrong*. Louisville, Ky.: Westminster John Knox Press, 1996.

Pogoloff, Stephen M. *Logos and Sophia: The Rhetorical Situation of 1 Corinthians*. Atlanta: Scholar's Press, 1992.

Pooley, Roger. "Spiritual Experience and Spiritual Autobiography: Some Contexts for Grace Abounding." *The Baptist Quarterly* 32 (October 1988): 393-402.

Popkin, Richard H. "The Philosophy of Bishop Stillingfleet." *Journal of the History of Philosophy* 9 (1971): 303-19.

Quinn, John Francis. *The Historical Constitution of St. Bonaventure's Philosophy*. Toronto: Pontifical Institute of Medieval Studies, 1973.

Raabe, Sister Augusta M. "Discernment of Spirits in the Prologue to the Rule of Benedict." *American Benedictine Review* 23 (1972): 397-423.

Rahner, Hugo. *Ignatius the Theologian*. Translated by Michael Berry. San Francisco: Ignatius Press, 1990.

Redwood, John. *Reason, Ridicule and Religion: The Age of the Enlightenment in England 1660–1750*. London: Thames and Hudson, 1976.

Riou, Alain. *Le Monde et l'Eglise selon Maxime le Confesseur*. Paris: Beauchesne, 1973.

Rivers, Isabel. "Grace, Holiness, and the Pursuit of Happiness: Bunyan and Restoration Latitudinarianism." *In John Bunyan*, ed. N. H. Keeble. Oxford: Clarendon Press, 1988.

Schneiders, Sandra M. "Spiritual Discernment in The Dialogue of Saint Catherine of Siena." *Horizons* 9/1 (1982): 47-59.

Scroggs, Robin. "New Being: Renewed Mind: New Perception." In *The Texts and the Times: New Testament Essays for Today*. Minneapolis: Fortress, 1993.

Shapiro, Barbara J. *Probability and Certainty in Seventeenth-Century England: A Study of the Relationships between Natural Science, Religion, History, Law, and Literature*. Princeton: Princeton University Press, 1983.

Sillem, Edward, ed. *The Philosophical Notebook of John Henry Newman*, vol. 1, *General Introduction to the Study of Newman's Philosophy*. New York: Humanities Press, 1969.

Špidlík, Tomáš. *The Spirituality of the Christian East: A Systematic Handbook*. Translated by Anthony P. Gythiel. Kalamazoo, Mich.: Cistercian Publications, 1986.

Stowers, Stanley K. "Paul on the Use and Abuse of Reason." In *Greeks, Romans, and Christians: Essays in Honor of Abraham J. Malherbe*, ed. David L. Balch et al. Minneapolis: Fortress, 1990.

Stewart, Columba. *Cassian the Monk*. New York and Oxford: Oxford University Press, 1998.

Thiselton, Anthony C. *The First Epistle to the Corinthians: A Commentary on the Greek Text*. Grand Rapids, Mich.: Eerdmans, 2000.

Thunberg, Lars. *Man and the Cosmos: The Vision of St Maximus the Confessor*. Crestwood, N.Y.: St Vladimir's Seminary Press, 1985.

Tillman, Mary Katherine. "Economies of Reason: Newman and the Phronesis Tradition." In *Discourse and Context: An Interdisciplinary Study of John Henry Newman*, ed. Gerard Magill. Carbondale, Ill.: Southern Illinois University Press, 1993.

Toner, Jules J. *A Commentary on St. Ignatius' Rules for the Discernment of Spirits*. St. Louis: The Institute of Jesuit Sources, 1982.

————. *Discerning God's Will: Ignatius of Loyola's Teaching on Christian Decision Making*. St. Louis, Mo.: The Institute of Jesuit Sources, 1991.

Toulmin, Stephen. *Cosmopolis: The Hidden Agenda of Modernity*. New York: Free Press, 1990.

Trigg, Joseph W. *Origen*. The Early Church Fathers. London and New York: Routledge, 1998.

Turner, James. *Without God, Without Creed: The Origins of Unbelief in America*. Baltimore and London: Johns Hopkins University Press, 1985.

Villegas, Diana. *A Comparison of Catherine of Siena's and Ignatius of Loyola's Teaching on Discernment*. New York: Fordham University, 1986.

Villegas, Diana L. "Discernment in Catherine of Siena." *Theological Studies* 58 (1997): 19-38.

Williams, Rowan. *A Ray of Darkness: Sermons and Reflections*. Cambridge: Cowley Publications, 1995.

————. *Resurrection: Interpreting the Easter Gospel*. New York: Pilgrim Press, 1984.

Wolff, Pierre. *Discernment: The Art of Choosing Well*. Liguori, Mo.: Liguori Publications, 1993.

Zinn, Grover A. "The Regular Canons." In *Christian Spirituality I: Origins to the Twelfth Century*, ed. Bernard McGinn, John Meyendorff, and Jean Leclercq. Vol. 16, *World Spirituality: An Encyclopedic History of the Religious Quest*. New York: Crossroad, 1987.

Zizioulas, John D. *Being as Communion: Studies in Personhood and the Church*. Crestwood, N.Y.: St. Vladimir's Seminary Press, 1985.

Questions for Reflection
and Study

Chapter One

1. Of the five "moments" of discernment, the middle three have frequent expressions (or at least parallels) in everyday life. Taking advantage of this background familiarity may help you to think preliminarily about these ideas. For example, think of an occasion when you became aware of motivations for your actions that you hadn't previously noticed.
   a. What was this like?
   b. What people, in your experience, have a great deal of practical judgment and how have they acquired it?
   c. When you have a sense of goal or purpose that appeals to you, what difference does that seem to make to the way you perceive things?
2. This chapter argues that reality in some sense reflects or echoes characteristics of God as its creator. Assume, for the sake of argument at least, that reality is in fact the continuous effect of a divine creator.
   a. Would it then be reasonable to think that it does reflect its source? In what ways?
   b. What would the alternatives be?
3. It has often been thought that some dimensions of reality are only fully perceptible by persons attuned to that particular dimension of reality. Consider the logic of this view by trying it out for a range of objects of knowledge. For example, knowing the sum of 2 + 2 does *not* seem to require much particular training or capacity in the knower. What about knowing the full reality of a combustion engine, a painting, a person?

Chapter Two

1. According to Origen, what is the link between discerning the influences shaping one's life and discerning the cosmic dimensions or implications of one's decisions?

2. In the view of the desert elders and of John Cassian, what are the chief criteria for discerning a truthful and healthy form of life?

Chapter Three

1. Bernard of Clairvaux sees discretion as the voice of moderation steering one between excessive zeal and deficient devotion.
   a. How does this view differ from that of Richard of St. Victor?
   b. How do the narrative structures they both employ assist in clarifying the role of discretion?
2. Why precisely does Catherine of Siena find self-love to be such a hindrance to clear discernment?
3. What parallels, if any, do you see in the views of Jean Gerson and Ignatius of Loyola?
4. If the human self is in some sense a nearly ungraspable puzzle for Bunyan and Edwards, what then can they propose to ground its deliberations? In other words, how would you know if you were thinking rightly or only deceiving yourself?

Chapter Four

1. Compare the role of charity in Diadochus and in Catherine. Which thinker seems to interpret love's role more directly within a trinitarian conception?
2. In the section on distinguishing between spirits or influences, the chapter groups various approaches under affective, noetic, and relational categories. Choose one or more of the thinkers discussed, and explain how these categories are related to each other in the view of that thinker.
3. Consider the various analyses of the problem of deception. Is there any common view regarding what makes human beings so susceptible?

Chapter Five

1. According to Paul the Apostle, how does the crucifixion of Christ both reveal and work to undo distortion in human knowing?
2. Explain the link between divine generosity and truthful human perception, according to the thinkers examined in this chapter.

Chapter Six

1. How are creation, calling, and human freedom related?
2. Consider the characters one meets in *Pilgrim's Progress*. Which ones seem most important in discerning the truth of one's life, and why?

Chapter Seven

1. Consider a range of academic and practical divisions of knowledge.
   a. What counts as "successful" knowing in each of them?
   b. When is an encounter with mystery a failure in knowing, and when is it vital?
2. What role in human knowing does Newman think is played by an awareness of God?
3. Why does a recovering sense of God as Trinity make any difference to human attitudes regarding truth?

Chapter Eight

1. What are the characteristics of a reductionistic view of reality as compared with a teleological understanding?
2. According to Iris Murdoch, what relation is there between deep and truthful perception of reality and the moral or spiritual character of the knower?
3. How in the view of Simone Weil could the laws of nature be both completely autonomous and also expressions of the divine?

Chapter Nine

1. According to Origen, Augustine, and Thomas Aquinas:
   a. What is the relation between the divine ideas or design and the creaturely existence of things?
   b. How does this explain the possibility of intelligibility or logic in the universe?
2. How does Bonaventure understand the Trinity to be at work in the world's intelligibility?
3. Illumination theory proposes that the "light" by which the mind discerns the truth of reality is in fact the presence of God. Draw on one of the figures discussed in the section on illumination theory to say how illumination might be related to prayer, on one hand, and analytical rationality on the other.
4. How does Thomas Traherne understand the vocation of intelligent creatures?
5. In the view of Maximus the Confessor, what does life in community add to intelligence and understanding?

Index of Subjects